Eva Brems, Christophe Van der Beken (Eds.)

Federalism and the Protection of Human Rights in Ethiopia

Recht und Politik in Afrika
Law and Politics in Africa

herausgegeben von/edited by

Heinrich Scholler
(Universität München)

Band/Volume 8

LIT

Federalism and the Protection of Human Rights in Ethiopia

edited by

Eva Brems and Christophe Van der Beken

LIT

Bibliographic information published by the Deutsche Nationalbibliothek
The Deutsche Nationalbibliothek lists this publication in the Deutsche Nationalbibliografie; detailed bibliographic data are available in the Internet at http://dnb.d-nb.de.

ISBN 978-3-03735-940-2 (Schweiz)
ISBN 978-3-8258-1128-0 (Deutschland)

A catalogue record for this book is available from the British Library

Dufourstr. 31
CH-8008 Zürich
Tel. +41 (0) 44-251 75 05
Fax +41 (0) 44-251 75 06
e-Mail: zuerich@lit-verlag.ch
http://www.lit-verlag.ch

LIT VERLAG Dr. W. Hopf
Berlin 2008
Verlagskontakt:
Fresnostr. 2
D-48159 Münster
Tel. +49 (0) 2 51/620 32 - 22
Fax +49 (0) 2 51/922 60 99
e-Mail: lit@lit-verlag.de
http://www.lit-verlag.de

Auslieferung:
Deutschland/Schweiz: LIT Verlag Fresnostr. 2, D-48159 Münster
Tel. +49 (0) 2 51/620 32 - 22, Fax +49 (0) 2 51/922 60 99, e-Mail: vertrieb@lit-verlag.de

Österreich: Medienlogistik Pichler-ÖBZ GmbH & Co KG
IZ-NÖ, Süd, Straße 1, Objekt 34, A-2355 Wiener Neudorf
Tel. +43 (0) 2236/63 535-290, +43 (0) 2236/63 535 - 243, mlo@medien-logistik.at

Distributed in the UK by: Global Book Marketing, 99B Wallis Rd, London, E9 5LN
Phone: +44 (0) 20 8533 5800 – Fax: +44 (0) 1600 775 663
http://www.centralbooks.co.uk/html

Distributed in North America by:

Transaction Publishers
New Brunswick (U.S.A.) and London (U.K.)

Transaction Publishers
Rutgers University
35 Berrue Circle
Piscataway, NJ 08854

Phone: +1 (732) 445 - 2280
Fax: + 1 (732) 445 - 3138
for orders (U. S. only):
toll free (888) 999 - 6778
e-mail:
orders@transactionspub.com

Proceedings of the Contact forum "Ethiopian Federalism and the Protection of Human Rights" (12-13 July 2006), supported by the Royal Flemish Academy of Belgium for Science and the Arts.

TABLE OF CONTENTS

1. Introduction

Eva Brems and Christophe Van der Beken

1. BACKGROUND

Since the beginning of the colonisation of Africa by the European powers at the end of the 19th century, Ethiopia has held a special position on the African continent. In the 1870s and 80s, the Ethiopian empire succeeded in withstanding colonial expansionism; a successful resistance crowned with the victory of the Ethiopian army over the Italians at Adua in 1896. The loss of the Italian army generated a lot of consternation, throughout Europe, and was an important factor in the conservation of Ethiopian sovereignty. Ethiopia would remain free of colonial predominance, except for a short period of Italian occupation. From a human rights perspective however, Ethiopia's sovereignty did not create a better situation for its citizens than that in the African colonies. Up to 1974 Ethiopia was an autocratically controlled empire where most of the inhabitants put up a daily struggle for survival and were denied elementary economic and social rights. In addition, most population groups in ethnically diverse Ethiopia were not able to develop their cultural identity nor to participate in state administration, which was in the hands of an ethnic elite. This situation did not improve at all under the military regime that took over power in the autumn of 1974. The military regime, which after a few years became completely dominated by Mengistu Haile Mariam, installed a communist dictatorship that violated the rights of Ethiopian citizens in an inconceivable manner. Ethnic discrimination continued as well, although the regime showed some attention to this problem, at least rhetorically. Various resistance movements increasingly responded to the brutal repression of the soldiers. In the end, it was a coalition of ethnically organised movements, the EPRDF (Ethiopian Peoples' Revolutionary Democratic Front), which came to play a dominant role in the struggle against the military regime. In the spring of 1991, the EPRDF, supported by other ethnically and regionally organised movements, brought about the final demise of the Mengistu regime. Under the guidance of the EPRDF, the new power holders declared their intention to pursue a radical break with both the imperial and the Mengistu regimes. A national conference, organised at the beginning of July 1991 in Addis Ababa, established a transitional administration and adopted a Transitional Period Charter, a constitution for the transitional period that would be concluded with the coming into force of a new constitution. Already the first provisions of the Transitional Period Charter indicated how the new rulers wanted to concretise the break with the past. Article 1 of the Charter emphasised the individual human rights, as included in the Universal Declaration of Human Rights, but particularly surprising were the provisions of Article 2 that granted extensive group specific rights to the "nations, nationalities and peoples" or ethnic groups of Ethiopia. All ethnic groups of Ethiopia (more than 80) were, under the denominator of the right to self-determination, provided with extensive rights to protect their culture, language, history – hence their ethnic identity – as well as the right to territorial autonomy and the right to participation in the central government. Should they be prevented from exercising these rights, Article 2 of the Charter even granted them the right to secede. Again Ethiopia takes a special position on the African continent. It is one of the few African countries granting such group-specific rights to its ethnic groups. That the new rulers were serious about the implementation of 'ethnic' rights was confirmed in January 1992 when the Ethiopian territory was administratively divided into 14 ethnically organised regions. The significant focus on human rights of the Transitional Period Charter and the resulting ethnic recomposition of Ethiopian territory were confirmed in the constitution that was approved by a Constituent Assembly on 8 December 1994.

This constitution, which has been in force since August 1995, includes a good number of provisions concerning the protection of universal rights and thus develops the fundamental option from Article 1 of the Transitional Period Charter. However, the most striking provisions of the constitution are once again those that grant far-reaching rights to all nations, nationalities and peoples of Ethiopia. The relevant provisions from Article 2 of the Transitional Period Charter were included in Article 39 of the constitution. The right to secession was given an even broader interpretation compared to the Charter. The constitutional drafter did consider the protection of fundamental rights and freedoms not only as an objective, but also as an instrument in a nation and state building strategy. The drafters of the constitution, dominated by ethnic organisations, judged that the ethnic discrimination of the imperial and military era risked being a cause of permanent dispute and conflict within the Ethiopian state. In their eyes the stability – and survival – of the Ethiopian state could only be guaranteed by the creation of a new national identity based on the recognition of and respect for the ethnic diversity of the Ethiopian population. In this perspective it was decided to reform the Ethiopian state into a federation of nine ethnically based regional states. Because of their ethnic basis, the regional states are conceived as the framework within which the ethnic groups exercise their rights. In their regional states, the ethnic groups exercise their language rights and cultural rights and, because of the important powers granted to the regional states by the federal constitution, they can pursue locally driven policies in different fields. At the same time, the federal constitution gives the ethnic groups the possibility to defend their interests vis-à-vis the federal government. The federal constitution contains the fundamental provisions for the organisation of the federal legislative, executive and judicial institutions. The constitution provides for a two-chamber federal parliament of which the second chamber, the House of the Federation, is composed of representatives of the diverse ethnic groups. As a matter of fact, it is the House of the Federation that through its constitutional review power insures that the federal government respects the constitutionally protected rights of ethnic groups/regional states. In the same manner, the House of the Federation protects the constitutionally guaranteed rights of Ethiopian citizens against unconstitutional government action. It needs to be stressed that the fundamental rights and freedoms of Ethiopian ethnic groups and citizens are not only determined by the federal constitution. The federal constitution allocates constitutional autonomy to the regions, i.e. the power to enact their own constitutions. All Ethiopian regional states have exercised this power so that the constitutional framework in Ethiopia is composed of one federal constitution and nine regional constitutions. These regional constitutions contain extensive lists of universal human rights and they also grant specific rights to ethnic groups. As mentioned in different contributions in this book, the population of the nine Ethiopian regional states is also characterised by ethnic diversity. Hence, there is no overlap between ethnic and administrative/regional borders – that would have been difficult to conceive anyway with only nine regional states and more than 80 ethnic groups. Some ethnic groups have their 'own' state, but most groups are a minority in a state dominated by a particular group or live together in multi-ethnic regional states. Moreover, the members of a dominant group living outside 'their' region can also be considered as belonging to a minority. Therefore, the protection of the rights of ethnic groups – a fundamental political and constitutional objective – requires more than the establishment of nine regional states. It also requires the regional states to develop constitutional mechanisms that allow ethnic minorities inside their territories to exercise their right to self-determination (as a complex concept). Indeed, constitutional autonomy of the regional states does not only imply the power to adopt human rights catalogues, but also to determine the form of the regional legislative, executive and judicial institutions. This way, several regional constitutions provide ethnic groups with the possibility to establish their own sub-regional territorial administrations, they provide for a second chamber of the regional parliament within which ethnic groups are represented and for the right of ethnic groups to be represented in the regional institution for constitutional interpretation/review. Indeed, in order to enforce the universal and group specific rights guaranteed in the regional constitutions, the regional constitutions also provide for regional institutions of constitutional review.

Federalism has thus resulted in a partitioning of powers amongst the federal and regional level. When exercising their respective powers both the federal and regional governments have to protect and fulfil human rights. The above has indicated that in the Ethiopian federal structure universal and group specific rights are guaranteed in the federal constitution as well as in the regional constitutions. Moreover, the federal and regional constitutions provide for administrative and institutional mechanisms to effectively realise and enforce those rights. But what is the impact of this novel constitutional construction upon the effective protection of human rights in Ethiopia?

This link between federalism and human rights formed the central topic of an expert seminar that was organised in July 2006 both in Brussels and in Mekelle, Tigray, Ethiopia. This seminar was the formal conclusion of the joint research between the law faculties of the University of Ghent and Mekelle, carried out within the framework of a three-year cooperation project. Since it was the intention to present the research to and to discuss it with the wider academic community, several external experts on Ethiopia also participated in the seminar. This book contains a selection of papers that were presented at the seminar. The topic of the seminar, the link between federalism and human rights, is the central theme of the book and acts as the context against which the different individual contributions must be situated.

2. OVERVIEW

In the first instance, the book explores Ethiopian federalism from a constitutional angle. Although the constitutional bases of a decentralised state structure were established during the transitional period (1991 – 1995), Ethiopian federalism as such exists only since the entry into force of the federal constitution in August 1995. Ethiopian 'ethnic federalism' has since generated substantial interest in the literature. However, the constitutional aspects of federalism remain generally under-explored. Nevertheless, thorough knowledge of and insight into these aspects are essential for an evaluation of Ethiopian federalism and for proposals to strengthen its human rights protecting capacity. While the importance of the social climate for the effectiveness of constitutional provisions should not be denied, neither should the social impact of constitutional provisions be underestimated.

Assefa Fiseha starts his paper by outlining the historical and political context of the introduction of federalism in Ethiopia. During the reign of Emperor Menelik at the end of the 19th century and the beginning of the 20th century, attempts were made to centralise state power, which was traditionally exercised in a decentralised way. These reforms were continued during the reign of Emperor Haile Selassie (1930 – 1974) who effectively managed to concentrate state power in the central government, entirely controlled by the emperor. A centralised exercise of power also characterised the military regime. The centralised exercise of power did not take into account the ethnic diversity of the Ethiopian population. Strong centralisation and ethnic discrimination did not result in the desired stability, but gave rise to the development of regional and ethnic rebel movements and, as indicated above, it is one of these rebel movements – the EPRDF – that overthrew the military regime. The EPRDF considers the rights of ethnic groups as central and views banning ethnic discrimination as a necessary condition for the stability of the Ethiopian state. This stance ultimately resulted in the introduction of federalism in the constitution. After having discussed the historical and political framework of Ethiopian federalism, Assefa continues his contribution with a discussion of some of its particular features. What immediately catches the eye when reading the constitution is the emphasis on the rights of "nations, nationalities and peoples" or ethnic groups. Article 8 states that "*All sovereign power resides in the Nations, Nationalities and Peoples of Ethiopia.*" Hence, it is not surprising that Article 39 grants these nations, nationalities and peoples of Ethiopia the right to self-determination, including the right to secession. Articles 46 and 47 provide for the establishment of nine ethnically organised regional states: the states of Tigray, Amhara, Oromia, Somali, Benishangul/Gumuz, the Southern Nations, Nationalities and Peoples, Gambella and Harar. Because of this, a number of large ethnic groups such as the Tigrayans, Oromo and Amhara have their 'own' region within which they can exercise the various aspects of their right to self-determination. However, the large number of ethnic groups indicates that most groups do not have their own region. However, for these groups as well, the constitution provides for the creation of their *own* state as a mechanism to exercise their ethnic rights. Article 47(2) stipulates that the ethnic groups within the nine already existing states (these are the groups which do not have their own region yet) also have the right to establish their own regional state. Constitutionally, therefore, the emphasis lies very strongly on diversity, on the rights of ethnic groups, but on the other hand there is very little attention to what unites them. The constitution fails to integrate what it unites, what is not favourable for the stability of the state. For Assefa it is thus clear that institutional arrangements have to be developed that give effect to power sharing schemes between the various actors at federal, regional and local levels. An important observation is also that, in spite of the constitutional construction of symmetrical federalism in practice there is political asymmetry where the states are in a different position with respect to each other and with respect to the federal government. Some regional states (in particular the so-called peripheral states Afar, Somali, Benishangul-Gumuz and Gambella) are unable to exercise their regional autonomy necessitating a larger influence of the federal government in regional matters. Above, it was already pointed out that in Ethiopia there is no perfect overlap between regional and ethnic borders. Several ethnic groups inhabit all Ethiopian regional states, including those established for one particular group. This raises interesting questions about the possibility for these non-dominant groups to exercise their ethnic rights - a question that is also dealt with in the contributions of Asnake Kefale and Christophe Van der Beken. Assefa also indicates - and this is related to his observation about the lack of power sharing mechanisms - that the second chamber of the federal parliament, the House of the Federation, hardly plays a role in the legislative process. Federal law does not need the consent of the House of the Federation to become law. The major emphasis on the rights of ethnic groups - of which the grant of a right to secession is the ultimate consequence - as well as the absence of power sharing mechanisms, supports the theory that "*The Ethiopian federation, unlike other federations, is based on a unity-diversity combination in which the latter slightly prevails over the former.*" But at the same time Assefa rightly points out that the dominance of the regional states at the federal level is compensated for by the role of the ruling party. The EPRDF, which has dominated the Ethiopian political scene since 1991, controls both the federal government as well as all regional governments. The author concludes his paper with a case study that shows very clearly the impact of Ethiopian federalism on human rights, i.e. the study of the position of ethnic groups in Benishangul-Gumuz, one of the nine regional states of the Ethiopian federation. The position of the ethnic groups and their mutual relationship comprises two aspects. Firstly, there is the position of and the relationship between the endogenous groups of the regional state. Benishangul – Gumuz is a regional state that was not established for one specific group, but for five groups of which two make almost half of the regional population: the Berta and Gumuz. For these traditionally marginalised groups the creation of the Benishangul-Gumuz region has opened large perspectives for access to state power, but at the same time it has led to new conflicts between the Berta and Gumuz over control of the region. Beside the ethnic groups for whom the regional state was established, and that are indicated by the constitution of Benishangul-Gumuz as "endogenous groups", there is also a large presence of Amhara and Oromo in the regional state. The implicit designation of the latter groups as non-endogenous indicates a hierarchy in the relation between endogenous and non-endogenous groups. The political, social and economic implications of this hierarchy are extensively discussed in the contribution of Asnake Kefale. Moreover, Christophe Van der Beken points out that this reality (the dichotomy between endogenous and non-endogenous groups) is reflected and supported by the provisions of the regional constitution. At the same time, the Ethiopian constitutional construction provides for mechanisms to protect the rights of non-endogenous groups. In a conflict between endogenous and non-endogenous groups in Benishangul-Gumuz, the House of the Federation, by means of its power to interpret the constitution, was able to find a balance between the universal rights of the non-endogenous citizens and the group specific rights of the endogenous groups.

That the constitutional allocation of powers between the federal government and the regional governments is not always unequivocal and leaves room for interpretation is illustrated in the papers of Amha Tesfay and Tecle Hagos.

In his contribution, *Amha Tesfay* studies the allocation of powers between the federal and regional courts and specifically the cassation power of the federal Supreme Court. The author describes the Ethiopian judicial organisation and states that the Ethiopian constitution has provided for a parallel judicial structure of courts at the federal and regional level. The federal Supreme Court exercises the highest judicial authority. Concerning the federal judicial structure, the constitution furthermore stipulates that the House of Peoples' Representatives – the first chamber of the federal parliament – may establish federal High Courts and First Instance Courts. Awaiting such a decision, the powers of the federal High Courts and First Instance Courts are delegated to the regional courts (respectively the regional Supreme and High Courts). The regional judicial structure also comprises three levels with a Supreme Court, High Courts and First Instance Courts. Concerning the allocation of the cassation power, *prima facie* there doesn't seem to be a problem since Article 80(1) and (2) of the federal constitution assign the federal and regional Supreme Courts *"the highest and final judicial power"* over federal and state matters respectively. However, the difficulty results from Article 80(3) that gives the federal Supreme Court the cassation power over "any final court" decision. This seems to imply that the federal Supreme Court has cassation power over final decisions of state Supreme Courts. Amha Tesfay states that this poses no problem if the application of the cassation power of the federal Supreme Court is limited to matters that are tried by the state courts in their delegated powers. In that case, the exercise of cassation power by the federal Supreme Court cannot be taken as an encroachment on state court powers. However, the controversial issue is whether or not the interpretation of the terms "any court decision" can extend to final court decisions on originally state matters. If we follow this interpretation, which is based on a literal reading of the concerned constitutional provisions, this will lead, as Amha Tesfay rightly points out, to cassation over cassation. The author considers the practice of cassation over cassation, which is confirmed by the jurisdiction of the federal Supreme Court, an unacceptable violation of regional states' autonomy. It goes against the spirit of the constitution that has distributed judicial powers, including cassation, over the parallel structure of federal and regional courts.

The difficult demarcation of the federal and the regional powers for civil and commercial matters is discussed by *Tecle Hagos*. The basic rule for the allocation of powers between the federal and the regional governments can be found in Article 52(1) of the federal constitution: "*All powers not given expressly to the federal government alone, or concurrently to the federal government and the states are reserved to the states*." Article 55, listing the powers of the House of Peoples' Representatives (HoPR), stipulates *inter alia* that the HoPR is competent for interstate commerce and foreign trade and that it shall enact a commercial code. The same article stipulates that the HoPR shall enact civil laws that the House of the Federation deems necessary to establish and sustain one economic community. Commercial matters thus belong to the competence of the federal government and the regional states are in principle competent for civil matters, unless the House of the Federation considers a federal legislative action to be necessary. However, Tecle Hagos points out that this allocation of competences poses several interpretation problems. Firstly, demarcating commercial and civil matters is a complex matter and secondly it is not at all clear which criteria will be used by the House of the Federation to refer civil matters to the federal level. By way of possible starting points the author suggests the example of other federations, such as Australia. Another element that can impact negatively upon the power of the regional states in civil matters is the competence of the HoPR to ratify international agreements. By ratifying international agreements in the field of civil matters that, in principle, belong to the powers of the regional states, the federal government can considerably limit the autonomy of the regional states. This risk is reinforced by the fact that the House of the Federation – the representative institution of the regional states at the federal level – plays no role in the ratification of international agreements. Finally, the exercise by the federal Supreme Court of cassation power over cassation decisions of the regional Supreme Courts on regional matters impacts negatively upon the power of the regional states for civil matters. It allows the federal Supreme Court to give a binding interpretation of regional laws.

In his paper, *Getahun Kassa* discusses the mechanisms of constitutional control in the Ethiopian constitutional construction. The Ethiopian federal constitution and the regional constitutions provide for the protection of many fundamental rights and freedoms. To enforce these human rights, the respective constitutions also provide for mechanisms of constitutional control. At the federal level, the constitutional control power has been granted to the second chamber of Parliament: the House of the Federation. In the exercise of this power the House of the Federation is assisted by the Council of Constitutional Inquiry. The Council of Constitutional Inquiry is not a constitutional court, but an advisory body to the House of the Federation. It is the House of the Federation that has been granted the ultimate authority for the interpretation of the constitution. After having explained the federal mechanism of constitutional control, the author discusses several decisions of the Council of Constitutional Inquiry and the House of the Federation about which until recently only fragmentary information was available. Particularly interesting is also the attention paid to the mechanisms of constitutional control at the regional state level. While research on Ethiopian federal constitutional law is limited, it is almost non-existent on the constitutional law of the regions. Nonetheless, constitutional autonomy for the regions is a characteristic of Ethiopian federalism and all nine regional states have effectively adopted their own constitution. In these constitutions, the regional states determine the regional state institutions among which the regional institutions for constitutional control. The allocation of competences between the federal and the regional institutions for constitutional control is for the time being unclear. The similarities between several provisions of the federal and regional constitutions (e.g. the provisions on human rights) imply the possibility that the same case is submitted to both the regional and federal institutions. However, Getahun adds that in some regional states no institutions for constitutional control have been established yet. In the conclusion the author pleads for strengthening the functioning of the Council of Constitutional Inquiry and for a better publicity of the decisions of the House of the Federation.

The most remarkable, and most contested, Article of the federal constitution is undoubtedly Article 39. As already noted, this Article grants a right to self-determination to all nations, nationalities and peoples of Ethiopia and as such it forms the basis for the federal construction. However, at the same time Article 39 provides for the possibility of dissolving the federal construction by granting, as a component of the right to self-determination, the right to secession to the nations, nationalities and peoples. Hence, all nations, nationalities and peoples of Ethiopia have a right to secede from the Ethiopian federation. But is a right to secession an inevitable consequence of a right to self-determination and what is the attitude towards secession in international law and international practice, in the African regional context and in individual states? These questions are dealt with in the contribution of *Stefaan Smis* who offers the necessary information and a frame of reference for the evaluation of the right to secession in the Ethiopian constitution. Stefaan Smis argues that the international community does not exclude secession, but that it is subject to certain conditions; secession is only acceptable as an *ultimum remedium* or as a solution of last resort when all other options to live together in one state entity have failed. In Africa the attitude towards secession is even more restrictive than at the international level, which is *inter alia* caused by the principle of intangibility of borders, as they existed at the time of independence. In individual states, the inclusion of a right to secede in the constitution is certainly exceptional, but not unseen. The author gives the example of the 1936 and 1977 constitutions of the USSR. The 1977 constitution, in its Article 72, stipulated, "*each Union Republic shall retain the right freely to secede from the USSR.*" However, neither of those constitutions provided for mechanisms to effectively realise the right to secession. The Ethiopian constitution on the other hand, does provide for such a mechanism. Beside these historic examples, there is also a secession provision in the present constitution of Uzbekistan. Although the constitutional grant of a right to secession is not a unique Ethiopian construction, the grant of such a wide right to self-determination is, particularly in the African context, an exceptional fact. Stefaan Smis mentions the tough discussions on the constitutional inclusion of this right in the Constituent Assembly. Opponents argued that Article 39 would lead to a reinforcement of ethnic identifications, to national fragmentation and ultimately to the demise of the state. Proponents on the other hand thought that the inclusion of such a right would result in a larger attention to the interests of ethnic groups and hence in a stronger unity of the state. Even today, there is no consensus on the issue, as described by Assefa Fiseha. Stefaan Smis points out the following paradox: "*on the one hand if no federal solution would have been adopted with such a broad right to self-determination, not so many sub-nationalities or centrifugal forces would today claim self-determination or threaten with separation. On the other hand, the recognition of the right to self-determination was probably the only way to hold the country together."*

The implications of the introduction of ethnic federalism for the position of ethnic groups in Ethiopia are discussed in the paper of *Christophe Van der Beken.* As mentioned already, none of the nine regional states of the Ethiopian federation is ethnically homogeneous. Some ethnic groups have their 'own' region, but most groups are a minority in a regional state dominated by a particular group or live together in multi-ethnic regional states. Christophe Van der Beken considers these groups minorities compared with the ethnic groups that have their own region. But he also considers members of dominant groups who live outside their 'own' region, such as Oromo who live in the Amhara region, minorities. In the paper it is examined whether the regional constitutions, following the example of the federal constitution, have also developed mechanisms for the protection of the ethnic rights of these minorities. The author studies the constitutions of four regional states: Amhara, Oromia, Benishangul-Gumuz and the state of the Southern Nations, Nationalities and Peoples (the Southern state). He notes that all these constitutions (except for the constitution of Oromia) include administrative and institutional mechanisms for the realisation of the rights of ethnic minorities. These mechanisms are clearly inspired by the federal constitutional mechanisms and comprise two categories: the creation of a separate territorial entity and the guaranteed representation of ethnic minorities in the regional state institutions. However, the author notes that the protection of ethnic rights by the regional constitutions does not extend to all minorities, but only to the so-called 'endogenous' minorities, minorities that are endogenous in the concerned regional state. The regional constitutions do not include specific protection mechanisms for the non-endogenous or – as they are called by the author – exogenous minorities. Concretely, this means that for instance the Amhara are considered non-endogenous in the Oromia region so that the Oromia constitution contains no specific mechanisms. The political, economic and social implications of this distinction between endogenous and non-endogenous groups are shown in the paper of Asnake Kefale.

In the subsequent articles, the emphasis shifts from the constitutional mechanisms to the protection of fundamental rights.

Eva Brems examines current human rights issues in Ethiopia through the eyes of the international human rights protection mechanisms. The monitoring of compliance with the major United Nations human rights treaties is done by committees of experts. States report to the relevant treaty committees and on this basis the latter formulate 'concluding observations'. The author examines the 'concluding observations' concerning Ethiopia of the committees to which Ethiopia has submitted recent reports. These concern the implementation of the Convention on the Elimination of All Forms of Discrimination against

Women and of the Convention on the Rights of the Child. Thus, a snapshot of Ethiopia's cooperation with international human rights monitoring bodies is combined with an overview of some of the huge challenges confronting Ethiopia in the field of human rights protection.

Several of these challenges are further developed in other papers: the gender issue, the impact of traditional rules and practices, the responsibility of the regional states to respect and realise human rights in their policies, and the position of ethnic minorities.

This last topic, the position of ethnic minorities, is the central issue in the paper of *Asnake Kefale.* More specifically, Asnake discusses the impact of the introduction of ethnic federalism upon the relative position and the mutual relationship between the different ethnic groups in the Benishangul-Gumuz region. It was already mentioned above that the constitution of Benishangul-Gumuz designates particular ethnic groups as endogenous: the Berta, the Gumuz, the Shinasha, the Mao and the Komo. Separately, none of these groups forms a majority in the regional state, but together the Berta and Gumuz make up almost half of the regional population. An important characteristic of the regional population is furthermore the large presence of non-endogenous groups such as Amhara and Oromo. Asnake Kefale starts with an overview of the regional political developments shortly before and after EPRDF took power. After that, he proceeds with a study of the conflictual relationship between several ethnic groups in the state. This conflictual relationship comprises two aspects: on the one hand, the relationship between the endogenous Berta and Gumuz and on the other hand the conflict between endogenous and non-endogenous groups. The conflict between Berta and Gumuz was essentially a struggle for political dominance in the region. This conflict is a clear consequence of the unprecedented possibilities for regional political power that the introduction of ethnic federalism has created for previously marginalised population groups. At the same time, the creation of ethnic based regional states has led to a distinction within the states between endogenous and non-endogenous groups. As a matter of fact, this is implicitly confirmed by the constitution of Benishangul-Gumuz that designates five ethnic groups as endogenous. The endogenous groups are considered 'owner nationalities' and this has negative implications for the political, economic and social position of the non-endogenous groups.

That the rights of Ethiopian citizens are not only determined by state sources of law, but also by non-state traditional rules and institutions is illustrated in the paper of *Mengistu Hailu, Getahun Kassa* and *Mulubrhan Balehegn*. They study the traditional mechanisms of conflict resolution in Aba'ala *Woreda* (district) in the Afar region. A traditional institution that plays a central role in conflict resolution in the study area is the *ADDA*: a council of clan leaders and elders who are known for their skill in conflict resolution. The decisions of the

ADDA, which especially aim at the realisation of social reconciliation, are characterised by a large legitimacy, and hence effectiveness, among the Afar population. Besides the informal mechanisms, the Afar region also has state institutions such as the police, prosecutor and the regular courts. In their fieldwork the authors have noticed that these formal institutions are at the most considered complementary to the traditional institutions and that it is the latter institutions that play the central role in resolving conflicts. Another interesting feature is the presence of Sharia courts in the study area. The authors note that these courts play an important role in conflict resolution since they are considered by the Moslem Afar as being part of their intergenerational tradition. Hence, in the study area there are traditional, Sharia as well as state institutions of conflict resolution, which inevitably give rise to overlaps, e.g. with regard to punishment. However, social primacy is attached to the traditional mechanisms as a result of which a dispute is settled only after going through the traditional procedures. Traditional institutions are used to settle intra-Afar conflicts, but the authors note that traditional mechanisms for inter-ethnic conflicts also exist.

The starting point for the study of *Wray Witten* is that federalism has offered Ethiopian regional states the possibility to develop locally driven policies that respect and realise the constitutionally guaranteed human rights. In addition to the problem of ethnic discrimination, the land issue was an important source of resistance against the imperial regime. The imperial regime had an exploitative land system that victimized numerous, particularly southern, peasants and in the course of the 1960s far-reaching land reforms were demanded. The military regime, inspired by Marxism-Leninism, decided to nationalise all land in 1975. Today, the federal constitution also stipulates in its Article 40(3) "*The right to ownership of rural and urban land, as well as of all natural resources, is exclusively vested in the State and in the peoples of Ethiopia.*" But in Article 40(4) the constitution grants a right to rural land: *"Ethiopian peasants have right to obtain land without payment and the protection against eviction from their possession."* In his contribution Wray Witten discusses the present state of affairs in the field of protection of land rights in Ethiopia with a special attention to the Tigray region. Tigray is important in this context, because the region was the first in the post-*Derg* era in which systematic reforms with a view to a better protection of land rights were undertaken and because it stimulated land reforms in other regional states. The paper demonstrates however that different Ethiopian regional states have different policies adapted to their respective contexts. In Tigray, for instance, there is a very unfavourable ratio of population to land. There is not enough land to insure the constitutional right to land and this has resulted in specific measures. Wray Witten systematically studies the different components of the land protection mechanism in Tigray (land identification, allocation of rights, preservation of evidence, registration, protection of rights, etc.) and he assesses their respective qualities and flaws. What is notable is the large role played by local institutions, such as the village Social Courts, in the protection of land rights. In his conclusion the author emphasises the importance of efforts to strengthen the capacity of the national institutions of human rights protection. According to him, national institutions play a primordial role in the protection of land rights and other human rights: "*there are, in the end, only the existing domestic institutions and organizations to turn to for protection of human rights.*"

Hassen Mohammed studies the state of affairs in the field of press freedom in Ethiopia. He uses Article 10 of the ECHR (European Convention on Human Rights) concerning freedom of expression as a point of reference. The author motivates the relevance of the European Convention with a reference to Article 13(2) of the Ethiopian constitution: "*The fundamental rights and freedoms specified in this chapter* (among which freedom of expression) *shall be interpreted conforming to the principles of ...International Covenants on Human Rights.*" International human rights treaties, such as the ICCPR (International Covenant of Civil and Political Rights), contain provisions on freedom of expression that are similar to the provisions of the European Convention. Hence, the interpretation of Article 10 is relevant to the similar provisions of the ICCPR and the Ethiopian constitution. Hassen Mohammed's paper comprises three parts: in the first part the author discusses the main principles of the jurisprudence of the European Court of Human Rights on Article 10 in which the European Court has clarified which limitations to the freedom of expression and, in particular, to press freedom, are permitted. In the second part the author examines press freedom in Ethiopia. The central research question is whether the present limitations of press freedom in Ethiopia originate in the legislation related to the press. In order to find an answer, the author analyses the relevant provisions of the press law, the Civil Code and the Criminal Code. In the third part Hassen Mohammed concludes that the Ethiopian legal provisions concerning the press, in light of the jurisprudence of the European Court, are not compatible with press freedom as protected in the Ethiopian constitution and that remedial legislative action is therefore required.

The gender issue is central to the contribution of *Tigist Gossaye Melka* who examines affirmative action policy in Ethiopia. Before proceeding with the study of the Ethiopian case, the author discusses the position of affirmative action (aka positive discrimination) in international law. Article 4 of the CEDAW stipulates that "*temporary special measures aimed at accelerating de facto equality between men and women shall not be considered discrimination*" – thus allowing for affirmative action. However, these special measures have to be temporary and must be discontinued when a *de facto* equality between men and women has been realised. The author notes that affirmative action (such as the adoption of quotas) has been particularly effective in increasing the political participation of women (e.g. Burundi, Rwanda). In Ethiopia, Article 35(3) of the constitution grants women the right to "affirmative measures". The objective of these measures, according to the same Article, is "*to enable them* (women) *to compete and participate on the basis of equality with men in political, social and economic life as well as in public and private institutions.*" Affirmative action measures have especially been taken in the field of education, which has effectively led to a larger participation of female students in higher education. The author regrets however the lack of assessment of the policy. As far as political participation of women is concerned, measures have been taken only very recently. The number of female members of the federal parliament after the 2005 election is considerably larger compared to the situation after the previous elections of 2000. This increase is caused by the fact that the EPRDF ensured that 30% of its candidates for the election were women. But, as noted by the author, this is the commitment of a political party and not a commitment of the Ethiopian state. As a matter of fact, in the highest positions of the executive, women remain seriously underrepresented. In her conclusion, the author formulates a number of recommendations that should lead to a more sustainable improvement of the position of women in Ethiopia.

The book concludes with a description by *Getaneh Agegn* of the objectives, the construction and the development of the 'Ethiopian Legal Information Website', an Internet site that has been created within the framework of the cooperation project between the universities of Ghent and Mekelle.

2. Fundamental Features of the Ethiopian Federal System and its Implications for the Enforcement of Human Rights

Assefa Fiseha•

1. INTRODUCTION

Since 1995 Ethiopia has embarked on a multicultural federal system with a view to addressing the age-old concentration of power and resources at the centre and to accommodate the diverse ethno-linguistic and religious groups. This essay explains the essential/peculiar features of the Ethiopian federal system and the implications for the unity diversity combination that is assumed to exist in every federation and the central issues that multicultural federations like Ethiopia face while ensuring self-rule to the different groups. Chief among such challenges is the issue of the treatment of minorities in the constituent units which this paper considers in some detail taking the case of the Benishangul-Gumuz regional state. Given the constitution's emphasis on the rights of nationalities, the institutionalization of power sharing schemes at various levels and the protection of minorities within the constituent units will remain two of the major gaps of the federal system in tying together the ethno-linguistic groups.

1.1. Historical Background

Leaving out some exceptions,[1] Ethiopia existed for the most part of its long and independent history, principally under a monarchy with its Orthodox Christian religion that served as a pillar of unity and a political system established on a balance of forces between centripetal and regional forces. The plurality of kings, with the *Niguse Negast* (king of kings) above them signified some kind of federal or confederal government structure. The throne represented the symbol of unity and regional forces exercised decentralized power. The *Niguse Negast de facto*[2] dealt with national matters while the kings exer-

• LL.B Addis Ababa University, LL.M University of Amsterdam, Ph.D. University of Utrecht, currently Assistant Professor at the Institute of Federalism and Legal Studies, Ethiopian Civil Service College. E-mail: assefafish@yahoo.com

[1] The exceptions include Yodit/Gudit's attack on the Christian empire in the 10th century; the campaign of Imam Ahmed (1527-1543) and the Age of Princes (*Zemene Mesafint* 1769-1855). The power at the centre had to subject itself almost completely to regional forces.

[2] The Ethiopian state, in its loose sense begins with Axum. The Axumite state lasted from the first century AD to approximately 1150. It became a Christian state at about 335 AD making it the third

cised powers over matters of local interest. There is no doubt that this presents in the words of Livingston, a typical "federal society".[3] These are essential features of what we understand today as the federal principle. Suffice it to emphasize here that before the emergence of the modern federal system in the United States in 1787, its features were never as clearly articulated as they are today. The more amorphous confederate form was predominant.[4]

The beginning of the 20th century marked the first serious attempt to curb the autonomy of the regional forces. It was reported in 1906 that Emperor Menelik II (1889-1913) could at any time take away the authority of the highest *rases* (heads) without giving any reasons for his action. But this is far from the measures taken by Haile Selassie. According to Levine, Menelik did not decisively undercut the authority of the great provincial lords and towards the end of his reign the provincial *rases* became largely independent. It is true that the power of Jimma Aba Jifar II survived for instance until 1932.[5]

The coming to power of Emperor Haile Selassie in 1930 and the subsequent issuance of the 1931 Constitution, the first *written* constitution in the history of the country, marks a new epoch. It heralded the end of the role of the duality that existed for centuries. Provincialism and/or the autonomous kingdoms, the traditional check against the power of the king of kings, were completely absorbed into the centralized administration.[6] Haile Selassie in conformity with his policy of centralization refused to confer the title of king, thereby disappointing expectations at the time of his coronation. This is particularly clear from the nature of the two houses established under the 1931 Constitution. The

---

political entity in history, after Armenia (301 AD) and the Roman Empire (312 AD). With its written script *Geez*, its number (*Kutur*), its own calendar and Christian religion, everything that defined the Ethiopian state until 1974 was the result of Axumite invention and innovation. Teshale Tibebu, *The Making of Modern Ethiopia 1896-1974* XXI-XXVII (Lawrenceville, New Jersey: The Red Sea Press Inc. 1995); see also Haggai Erlich, *The Cross and the River: Ethiopia, Egypt and the Nile* 15 (Boulder: Lynne Rienner Publishers, 2002); D. Levine, *Greater Ethiopia: The Evolution of a Multiethnic Society* 90-110, 2nd ed. (Chicago: The University of Chicago Press, 2000) hereinafter referred as *Greater Ethiopia*.

3 W. Livingston, A Note on the Nature of Federalism, 67 (1) *Political Science Quarterly* 81-95 (March, 1952). By that he meant a territorially grouped diversity and the notion of diversity is used here in its widest sense as it may be reflected in many forms ranging from differences in religion, ethnic identity, language, historical background, previous experience as semi-autonomous units and perhaps differences in social and political institutions. All of these or some or even one of them may be a cause for demanding self-rule.

4 Confederations are loose forms of alliances between states and there is a very weak central government that is mainly dependent on the will of the delegates from the constituent states. It as such does not have any direct authority over the citizen. K. C. Wheare, *Federal Government* 1-30, 4th ed. (London: Oxford University Press, 1963).

5 D. Levine, *Wax and Gold: Tradition and Innovation in Ethiopian Culture* 177-185 (Chicago: The University of Chicago Press, 1965). This does not, however, fully describe the impact of his reign as far as several of the southern and south-western kingdoms are concerned.

6 M. Perham, *The Government of Ethiopia* 262 (London: Faber & Faber Limited, 1963).

emperor made sure that all potential contenders for power were members of these chambers that in effect had only an advisory role.

Apart from the introduction of the modern army after dissolving the private armies of the regional notables, Haile Selassie's measure of direct individual taxation without the involvement of the intermediary notables, which in a way centralized the taxation system, hit hard the economic base of those regional notables. Their right to collect tax was taken over by the centre.[7]

Nor did the 1974 Revolution, which gave a mortal blow to the old monarchy, bring any change in the move towards more centralization of power. As far as regional autonomy and accommodation of the diverse groups into the political process are concerned, except for the change of ideology from Solomonic genealogy to Socialism, the centralist character of the state remained intact and was even strengthened to a degree that far exceeded the imperial regime.[8]

The process of centralization, modernization, nation building or by whatever name it was conducted, was not without consequences. Firstly, the incorporation of the South, the Southwest and the Eastern sides from their previously autonomous position to complete absorption meant that the notion of the state, its institutions and culture were imposed on the incorporated kingdoms. Secondly, it brought about all sorts of diversities in terms of religion, language, tradition and culture. However, as the state failed to accommodate this diversity, the religious, lingual, cultural as well as political and economic dominance gave birth to the 'question of nationalities'.[9] Thirdly, the state became extremely centralized at the expense of regional rulers. The political marginalization of the bulk of the community led to civil wars the causes of which fundamentally differed from earlier ones. This time resistance not only called

---

[7] Gebru Tareke, *Ethiopia: Power and Protest: Peasant Revolts in the Twentieth Century* 80-83 (Cambridge: Cambridge University Press, 1991). The transition was certainly not smooth. Most of the peasant rebellions were meant to stop this process of centralization.

[8] Many contend that the Revolution was not in the real sense a revolution in terms of the impact on political power and the change in the structure of the state. True, there were some sweeping measures taken like the nationalization of land that gave a relief to the tenants living in the south, but the core of the issue, that is political power and the marginalization of the large majority of the people, was almost kept as it was. See J. Young, Ethnicity and Power in Ethiopia, 23(70) *Review of African Political Economy* 534 (1996); see also I. Strecker, "Glories and Agonies of the Ethiopian Past" review article at http://ntama.uni-mainz.de/~aau/glories.html as visited on 2/11/01.

[9] The meaning of this notion is far from clear. Young university students in the 1960s and 1970s influenced by Marxism-Leninism and frustrated by the age old Monarchy argued in favour of liberating oppressed nationalities from an oppressor group but as later events indicate, it meant different things to different groups. For the Ethiopian Peoples Revolutionary Party (EPRP) and All Ethiopia Socialist Party (MEISON), it meant respect for diversity but to be implemented from a class perspective. For the now ruling party, Ethiopia is nothing but the outcome of the free will of the nationalities rather than abstract individuals and the nationalities have not only a right to self-rule but also a right to self-determination, secession included. For details, see J. Young, *Peasant Revolution in Ethiopia: The Tigray People's Liberation Front, 1975-1991* (Cambridge: Cambridge University Press, 1997).

for state reform but even at times challenged the state itself.[10] Several studies have indicated that conflict in traditional Ethiopia was mainly an instrument for asserting some level of regional autonomy and not for upsetting the whole system, nor was it for separation.[11] "God cannot be blamed, the King can not be accused" was the main tenet. The opposition mainly looked for adjustment and restoration of violated rights like better administration, lower taxes, respect for local autonomy and reduction of corruption. By and large the legitimacy of the monarch and its ideological roots were not attacked. In the 1960s, however, things started to change. The new forms of resistance changed significantly in terms of leadership, social composition, motivation and ideological orientations.[12]

1.2. Explaining the Crisis

With the emergence of centralized administration towards the end of the 19th century and that was prevalent for most of the 20th century, however, Ethiopia faced a serious state crisis.

Attempts at explaining the cause of the state crisis have not only been less satisfactory but are also found to be diverse. While the instrumentalists[13] focused on the concentration of political and economic resources at the centre and emphasized the proliferation of ethnicity as an erroneous comprehension of political and economic deprivation, the ruling party, a product of the 1960s Ethiopian Student Movement, focused on the 'operation of nationalities' as a main cause and the economic and political marginalization as a consequence rather than a cause. Needless to say both approaches have their own limitations.

The former while focusing on objective factors and some implied assumptions (ethnicity is an erroneous comprehension of political and economic deprivation and the idea that ethnic identity is fluid and perhaps an elite creation) does not address the issue that at the heart of the debate is the identity of the state and the values behind its institutions. The Ethiopian state that emerged as a

---

[10] C. Clapham, Constitutions and Governance in Ethiopian Political History, in: *Constitutionalism: Reflections and Recommendations, Symposium on the Making of the New Ethiopian Constitution* 30-31 (Addis Ababa: Inter Africa Group, 1993).

[11] See Gebru, *supra* note 7, 199, 203; Mesfin Wolde-Mariam, *The Horn of Africa: Conflict and Poverty* 140-141 (Addis Ababa: Commercial Printing Press, 1999).

[12] Clapham, *supra* note 10, 29.

[13] Such thinkers are called instrumentalists because they view religious and ethnic groups as a means to achieve some political and economic goal and having no relevance thereafter. Included in this category are J. Markakis, *Resource Conflict in the Horn of Africa* (London: Sage Publications, 1998); C. Clapham, Ethnicity and the National Question in Ethiopia, in: P. Woodward and M. Forsyth (eds.) *Conflict and Peace in the Horn of Africa: Federalism and its Alternatives* 30-35 (Aldershot: Dartmouth, 1994); J. Abbink, New Configurations of Ethiopian Ethnicity: The Challenge of the South, 50(1) *Northeast African Studies* 60 (1998).

result of the centralizing trend was qualitatively different from historic Ethiopia not only in terms of its territorial size but also in terms of ethno-linguistic composition and religious diversity. The majority of the ethno-linguistic groups incorporated were told in no ambiguous terms to assimilate into this state. Rather than attempting to forge a state from the newly introduced diversity, the regime imposed a narrowly defined imperial state, whose cultural, social, political and religious foundation and its institutions failed to reflect the existing diversity on the ground. One needs to note how other multicultural societies[14] like India and Switzerland faced this reality.[15] The identity of the state and its institutions thus take centre stage in the debate between those who defined it and those who were considered its subjects.

We should also note that in Ethiopia while there are close to eighty nationalities/ethnic groups, depending on how one may prefer to call them, none of them taken alone at federal level constitute a majority.[16] In other words, the challenging issue once again is how to constitute a legitimate government from all the ethno-linguistic groups that do not squarely fit the usual notion of national majorities versus national minorities.[17] The nation state as is commonly understood has its own assumptions, which are not suitable for multicultural societies.

It is frequently mentioned in academic discourse, however limited it may be, as well as among some political party leaders that the model subscribed to (at least in the Ethiopian context) is the 'ethnic free' United States style of federal system.[18] It is not surprising that this is better known than other more relevant multicultural federal systems like India and Switzerland. Ironically, America

---

[14] The terms "multi-ethnic" or "multicultural" are used here to signify the fact that many states today contain a plurality of distinct ethno-linguistic and religious groups. Multiculturalism acknowledges, recognizes and at times promotes diversity against cultural unification and homogenization. See N. Topperwein, *Nation-State and Normative Diversity* 35 (Helbing & Lichtenhahn, PIFF, 2001).

[15] The situation in Ethiopia stands in sharp contrast with the experience of India and Switzerland, similarly multicultural states. While the same process of expansion by Napoleon brought new diversities in Switzerland in the 19th century, the diverse groups were from the outset accommodated into the political process. Similarly, India pursued a policy of pluralism and political integration while recognizing the existence of diverse groups in the polity. Although there was a strong push by Hindu nationalists to impose their language on others, the leaders rightly recognized that it would not be effective in a multicultural setting and thus in the 1960s, Indian provinces set up by the British had to be reorganized on a linguistic basis. See W. Linder, *Swiss Democracy: Possible Solutions to Conflict in Multicultural Societies* (New York: St. Martin's Press, 1994); Harihar, Bhattacharyya, *India as a Multicultural Federation: Asian Values, Democracy and Decentralization in Comparison with Swiss Federalism* (Bale: Helbing and Lichtenhahn, PIFF, 2001).

[16] See *Central Statistical Authority: The 1994 Population and Housing Census of Ethiopia v. II Analytical Report* (Addis Ababa, 1999).

[17] Attempts at explaining how nation states may cope with minorities often focus on the usual notion of national majorities versus national minorities but some multicultural societies do not even have national majorities to begin with and this makes the analysis less helpful. See for instance W. Kymlicka, *Multicultural Citizenship* (Oxford: Clarendon Press, 1995).

[18] See for instance Bahru Zewde, What did we Dream? What did we Achieve? And where are we Heading? At http://eeaecon.org/miscellaneous/vision2020/bahruv2020.htm as visited on 18/05/2004.

despite its geographical distance is so close to Ethiopia and Ethiopians. The CNN.com effect is so close and so powerful in this 'global world'. It is also a hard fact that the United States' federal system, the great invention of the famous Philadelphia convention of 1787, has influenced many federal systems, young and old. Yet having carefully studied multicultural federal systems, as distinct from what are commonly referred to as nation state federal systems (like the United States and Germany that assume a homogeneous society and the individual as a pioneer political actor), the Ethiopian system has more in common with the former than the latter. They provide us with alternative scenarios on crucial issues of accommodation of diversity both at federal and state level, issues that the federal system in Ethiopia is trying to address at the moment.

For those who insist that the United States' federal system is an 'ethnic free' federal system, however attractive that may appear to be, let me state a hard fact from the outset. For those who are familiar with the arguments articulated on *The Federalist Papers* (particularly No. 2) it is unmistakably stated that it is a federal system founded on the Anglo-Saxon tradition with English as its language. In the last decade or so many have studied and exposed this myth. The so-called 'civil-nation state',[19] the only alternative that liberal democracy pretends to prescribe is itself founded on some exclusionist elements. In the end it is the majority culture, language and religion that becomes the national culture, language or religion. It is the assumption in this short essay that for multicultural states this is the wrong solution. Multicultural countries like Ethiopia, lacking a dominant majority both in terms of number and political hold, cannot afford to impose one ethnic group's culture, language or religion on others. Those who attempted it, like Ethiopia, have paid rather dearly, while those who ventured on a different course of political action, like India and Switzerland, are doing well, at least, so far.

It is exactly this aspect of the nation state that makes it troublesome for multicultural societies like Ethiopia and more so when there is no clear national majority at federal level. It is not surprising then that the legitimacy of the government, its institutions and the values upon which it is established remain one of the sources of tension and at times the cause of its terminal crisis.

Nation states have at one time or another resorted to different forms of repression to claims of minorities ranging from genocide, forced assimilation, 'citizen equal' to some kind of cultural and linguistic recognition. Depending on the strength of the claims, identity and history of minorities however, a decentralized or federal system of government appears to be the genuine solution if

[19] For an elaborate discussion on the distinction between the ethnic versus civic nation state and its limits in dealing with the issue of multicultural societies see M. Seymour, J. Couture, K. Nielsen, Introduction: Questioning the Ethnic/Civic Dichotomy, in: M. Seymour, J. Couture, K. Nielsen (eds.), *Rethinking Nationalism* 2-3 (Calgary: University of Calgary Press, 1998).

the state is to survive by accommodating diverse groups while maintaining unity and avoiding fragmentation.[20]

After the collapse of the Cold War and at a time when globalization is penetrating traditional nation-state territories, differences arising from ethnic and religious backgrounds within states, have become a serious cause of violence.[21] According to some studies there are 5,000 to 8,000 ethno cultural groups in the existing 195 or so states. Of these, one-tenth of them are estimated to have interest for self-rule and some form of autonomy.[22] What is worse, such conflicts are becoming much more common than interstate violence and are often difficult to stop. Compared to traditional interstate wars, contemporary conflicts have not only changed dimension but have also become common among peoples.[23] Although many states considered to be sovereign today are multicultural, the issue of integrating different ethnic and cultural groups as well as the questions of accommodating religious and other minorities within the boundaries of existing states has remained one of the main challenges in the contemporary world.[24]

Earlier on it was argued that ethnicity or group affiliation would be weakened with the modernization of societies.[25] However, this appears to be only half true because the success of modernization in weakening group identity depends on its ability in eliminating or minimizing group exclusion. "*As far as there are losers and winners and the basis of winning or losing is attached to group identity, modernity has no positive role in reducing ethnic conflicts.*"[26]

---

[20] See C. Young, Case Studies in Cultural Diversity and Public Policy: Comparative Reflections, in: C. Young (ed.), *Accommodation of Cultural Diversity* 1-18 (New York: St. Martin's Press, 1999); also by the same author, The Dialectics of Cultural Pluralism: Concept and Reality, in: C. Young (ed.), *The Rising Tide of Cultural Pluralism: The Nation-State at Bay*? 1-29 (Madison: University of Wisconsin Press, 1993).

[21] While there are something like 190 or so sovereign states, the number of ethno-linguistic groups far exceed the number of existing states. There is a mismatch between ethnic groups and the internal boundary of existing states and this is more acute in Africa where boundaries were hastily and artificially drawn during the scramble for the continent. I. Duchacek, Antagonistic Cooperation: Territorial and Ethnic Communities, *Publius: The Journal of Federalism* (Fall, 1977), hereinafter called Antagonistic Cooperation.

[22] See for instance Dimitrios Karmis and Wayne Norman, The Revival of Federalism in Normative Political Theory, in: Dimitrios Karmis and Wayne Norman (eds.), *Theories of Federalism: A Reader* 13 (New York: Palgrave Macmillan, 2005).

[23] Since 1945 ethnic violence has played a major role in about half of all wars, caused an estimated 12 million refugees and resulted in at least 11 million deaths and because contemporary wars are between people rather than states, civilian casualties have increased tremendously. It is estimated that some three quarters of today's war casualties are civilians. N. Bermoe, A New Look at Federalism: The Import of Institutions, 13(2) *Journal of Democracy* 96 (April 2002).

[24] W. Linder, *supra* note 15, XVI.

[25] See for instance M. Esman, Political and Psychological Factors in Ethnic Conflicts, in: J. V. Montville (ed.), *Conflict and Peacemaking in Multiethnic Societies* 53-64 (Lexington: Lexington Books, 1990).

[26] Mengistu Arefaine, *Federalism and Accommodation of Diversity: With Special Reference to Divided Societies* 53 (Bale: Helbing and Lichtenhahn, 2004).

Furthermore, post Cold War developments as well as empirical evidence from multicultural societies indicate that "*identity does not necessarily vanish from the face of the political discourse even if political and economic situations are favourably accommodative, let alone when it is a state target of destruction under the guise of "nation- building.*"[27] Thus, while the instrumentalists have a point by hammering out the economic and political factors, they often fail to consider the identity factor as a cause of tension in multicultural societies.

On the other hand, the ruling party, the Ethiopian Peoples' Revolutionary Democratic Front (EPRDF) has for long advocated that it is the oppression of nationalities that is at the heart of the crisis and the political and economic marginalization is a consequence rather than a cause. It has thus championed the right of the nationalities to self-determination up to and including secession as a decisive remedy for the resolution of Ethiopia's long-standing problem of the 'nationality question'. With that in view, the ruling party, as a main architect of the transitional and the 1995 Constitution, stipulated a distinct clause that placed sovereignty on the "nationalities, nations and people" and consequently reorganized the constituent states in a manner that ensures self-rule to at least the major nationalities and even permits them to secede after going through some procedures.[28] Yet, this in itself fails to underscore the point that in the end, political and economic factors are crucial factors behind every conflict. Thus an approach that combines the accommodation of diversity with genuine sharing of power and resources among the diverse groups will better explain the success or failure of the state in multicultural societies in general and in Ethiopia in particular.

Thus the change of government in 1991 by regionally based forces and the subsequent state reform based on federalism and explicit acknowledgement of diversity is an attempt to decentralize power and to accommodate diversity.[29]

---

[27] Are not India and Switzerland living examples? If Haile Selassie's and *Derg*'s policy of forced assimilation were effective, by now we would have seen individual citizens with no group affiliation. On the contrary however the group affiliation in Ethiopia rather was reinforced in reaction to the repression from the state.

[28] See Articles 8, 39, 46, 47 of the 1995 Ethiopian Constitution. The present federal constitution was adopted on 8 December 1994 but came into force on 21 August 1995. See Articles 2 and 3, The Constitution of the Federal Democratic Republic of Ethiopia, Proclamation No. 1/1995, A Proclamation to Pronounce the Coming into Effect of the Constitution of the Federal Democratic Republic of Ethiopia, hereinafter referred to as the Ethiopian Constitution. All articles referred to below are from this text, unless stated otherwise.

[29] Certainly there are some critical limitations on the new federal system and there is no attempt to discuss them here. For some of the views see Assefa Fiseha, *Federations and the Accommodation of Diversity in Ethiopia: A Comparative Study* (Nijmegen: Wolf Legal Publishers, 2005) Chapter 5; Maimire Mennasemay, Federalism, Ethnicity and the Transition to Democracy, 21 *Horn of Africa*, Special Issue on Federation in the Horn 88-115 (2003); Alemante G. Selassie, Ethnic federalism: Its Promise and Pitfalls, 28 *Yale Journal of International Law* 51 (2003).

2. FEDERAL FEATURES

Comparing the Ethiopian federation with the basic features of a federal system it exhibits major similarities. Federal political systems combine self-rule for some purposes and shared rule for other purposes or combine unity with diversity.[30] Often there is the federal government and the states between which power is divided, the pact enshrined in a written constitution which is supreme and rigid and each exercising direct authority over the people. Commonly, it is understood that unity is achieved through the exercise of power by the federal government in relation to the polity as a whole while diversity represents the exercise of power by the constituent states over a portion of the population, generally territorially identified. As the division of power is never neatly done, the constitution is interpreted and enforced by a court or tribunals. Besides, institutions that accommodate the interest of the constituent units (mainly but not exclusively through the second chamber) and intergovernmental relations remain vital.[31] Yet despite such general features, the balance of power that exists between the forces of unity and diversity in every federal system is never as clear as we would want it to be. It is often assumed to have some shape or another but as federal history and the Ethiopian case reveal, the balance might tilt at one time towards unity and at another time towards diversity.

Since 21 August 1995 Ethiopia has constitutionally been a multiethnic federation. Ethiopia introduced the federal system against the background of a widely held sceptical view about federalism both at home[32] and in Africa at large. Despite the continent's pluralistic nature and federalism's promise to accommodate diversity, the overriding aim almost everywhere in Africa, except in Nigeria and except the new developments in South Africa and the Sudan, has been the pursuit of political unity and territorial integrity giving no political expression to diversity.[33] Seen in this context, the post-1991 Ethiopian experiment stands as an exception.

---

[30] D. Elazar, *Exploring Federalism* 5-12 (Tuscaloosa, AL: University of Alabama Press, 1987); R.Watts, *Comparing Federal Systems* 1-13, 2nd ed. (Montreal & Kingston: Mc Gill-Queen's University, 1999).

[31] These features are incorporated in several clauses of the Ethiopian Constitution. See Articles 1, 9, 50, 51, 62, 83, 84, 104 and 105.

[32] Although there was a major consensus about the need for a federal system, there was serious disagreement about the basis for reorganizing the constituent units. See for details Assefa Fiseha, *supra* note 29, Chapters 1 and 5.

[33] Even though there is a widely held view that federalism provides midway options for those who want to maintain the territorial integrity of existing states and for those who claim regional autonomy and that federalism enables the forging of unity out of diversity, until recently, Nigeria was the only country in the continent that claimed to be federal. In many other African countries federalism is viewed as a means for disintegrating the state. Nigeria is an exception but it certainly is not a happy case, as for most of its time, the federal system has been under military dictators, which is contrary to the spirit of negotiation, the idea of federalism as a covenant and the division of power in federalism.

The federal system intends to decentralize power and resources and resolve the 'nationalities question' by accommodating the country's various ethno-linguistic groups. The federal system operates within a parliamentary form of government.[34] At federal level there are two Federal Houses: the House of Peoples' Representatives (HoPR) and the House of the Federation (HoF).[35] The former is composed of members elected by the people for a term of five years in a direct and fair election and contains 547 members, 20 of which are allocated to minorities. The members of the House are believed to be representatives of the Ethiopian people as a whole and not of a specific group.[36] Although on appearance one may get the impression that the two-chamber parliament is responsible for policy making at federal level, it is only the HoPR that has the sole power of legislation in all matters assigned to the federal government. The same House is the highest authority in the federal government.[37]

The HoF is a representative organ whose members are representatives of each nation and nationality and its main task is constitutional interpretation and determination of revenue derived from joint federal and state tax and subsidies that the federal government grants to the states.[38] It was meant to be a counter majoritarian institution to balance against the HoPR but it could hardly serve that role primarily because it is barely involved in law making and secondly because in its composition it by and large replicates the HoPR.[39]

In line with other parliamentary federal systems,[40] there is a fusion of legislative and executive powers in a popularly elected lower house. Authority is divided between the federal government and the states but within each level, power is concentrated in the parliamentary fusion of legislature and the executive.[41] Although a discussion of the details of the competence of each level of government is beyond the scope of this short essay, one could broadly state that except in the area of foreign affairs and policy making at federal level, the regional governments in Ethiopia, at least formally speaking, do have wide powers.[42]

---

[34] Article 45 of the Ethiopian federal constitution.

[35] Article 53.

[36] Article 54.

[37] Article 50(3).

[38] Articles 61 and 62.

[39] For more on this point see Assefa Fiseha, Federations and Second Chambers, XXXIX (3) *Indian Journal of Politics* 87-128 (2005).

[40] R.Watts, *supra* note 30, 85-86.

[41] By contrast, in presidential federal systems there is separation of legislative and executive powers. It is directed at limiting possible abuse of power at the centre and the separation of powers is a further extension of the principle of dispersion of power. Power is not only divided between the federal and state governments but within each level of government. This, therefore, has the advantage of checks and balances among the institutions.

[42] For a detailed treatment of the division of legislative and executive power between the federal and state governments see Assefa Fiseha, Theory versus Practice in the Implementation of Ethiopia's

The federal executive consists of the ceremonial president and a powerful Prime Minister along with his cabinet. The federal President, who is the head of state, is nominated by the HoPR from among its members but approved in a joint session of the two Houses by a two-thirds-majority vote for a term of six years. The powers of the President are nominal and symbolic. The President opens a joint session of both Houses every September, signs a draft law before its promulgation and receives credentials of foreign ambassadors.[43]

The most powerful federal executive figure remains the Prime Minister along with the Council of Ministers. The political party or coalition of political parties that has the greatest number of seats in the HoPR is entitled to form the executive and lead it. The Prime Minister is elected from among members of the HoPR and in this sense is not necessarily the party leader. The Prime Minister is the chief executive, the chairman of the Council of Ministers and the commander in chief of the national armed forces. The Prime Minister submits candidacies for ministers and commissioners as well as for the highest judicial posts to the HoPR for approval. The PM also follows up and ensures the implementation of laws, policies, directives and other decisions adopted by the HoPR, leads the Council of Ministers and exercises overall supervision of the implementation of foreign policy and policies, regulations, directives and decisions adopted by the Council of Ministers.[44]

3. SOME DISTINCT FEATURES OF THE FEDERAL SYSTEM

3.1. The Explicit Recognition of Nations/Nationalities as Building Bricks of the Federation and its Implications

As indicated in the introductory section, as the ruling party was an architect of the 1995 Constitution and the champion of the 'Nationality question', the right of nationalities became not only the basic principle of political organization but also constituted the foundation for restructuring the unitary and centrist state in the process of setting up the federal system. While the authors of the constitution argue that one way to resolve ethnic tension is to redraw the state boundaries along language criteria and that territories should meet the interests of people, not *vice versa*, others stipulate the return to the pre-1991 epoch of provincialism as a basis of dividing political power or at least suggest the American style of territorial federalism.[45] Thus, the choices seem to be limited

---

Ethnic Federalism, in: D. Turton (ed.), *Ethnic Federalism: The Ethiopian Experience in Comparative Perspective* 131-164 (Oxford: James Currey, 2006).

[43] Articles 70 and 71.

[44] Articles 72, 73 and 74.

[45] For a brief summary of the position of the different parties on federalism see Merera Gudina, Contradictory Interpretations of Ethiopian History: The Need for a New Consensus, in: D. Turton (ed.), *Ethnic Federalism: The Ethiopian Experience in Comparative Perspective* 119-130 (Oxford: James

between the ethnic versus the American territorial federal system but as indicated elsewhere,[46] there are some midway options.

One feature one notices throughout the constitution is the utmost importance given to the ethno-linguistic groups within the Ethiopian polity. Unlike many constitutions, the Preamble of the Ethiopian Constitution does not commence with the traditional constitutional formula of "we the people", but with "We the Nations, Nationalities, and Peoples of Ethiopia" and somewhat vaguely the constitution grants ethno-linguistic groups a kind of 'confederate' position, in the federation. Dealing with the fundamental principles of the constitution, Chapter Two declares, "*All sovereign power resides in the Nations, Nationalities and Peoples of Ethiopia.*"[47] The same constitution grants the nations, nationalities and peoples the right to self-determination. It insists that there must be some congruence between the nation, nationality and territory they inhabit.

A consequence of this is the fact that the constitution organizes the constituent states on "*the basis of settlement patterns, language, identity and consent of the people concerned.*"[48] While this provision does not in so many words state that they are organized along ethnic lines, most analysts and practice so far make it clear that the key factor in delineating the states seems to have focused mainly on the criteria of language.[49] Accordingly, the constitution enumerates nine member states of the federation.[50] The constitution employs the term "state" but in common usage they are called regional governments (*kilil*), a name carried over from the transitional period (1991-1994). They are the states of: Tigray, Afar, Amhara, Oromia, Somalia, Benishangul/Gumuz, the State of the Southern Nations, Nationalities and Peoples (SNNPRS), the Gambella Peoples and the Harari people. The notion of granting to the nations/nationalities their own 'mother' states as enshrined in the constitution entitles every nation/nationality (that is those who have not yet been granted a state) the right to establish their own state[51] at any time. This is an expression

---

Currey, 2006). Of late, right wing and multinational opposition parties have merged and formed the Coalition for Unity and Democracy (CUD), and its election manifesto seems to be critical, if not opposing any federal arrangement. See also CUD goes for Constitutional Reform as Election Platform at http://www.ethiopianreporter.com/displayenglish.php?id=2104 as visited on 12 April 2005; also Daniel Kindie, Problems and Prospects for a Horn of Africa Confederation/Federation, 21 *Horn of Africa Journal* 1-19 (2003); Bahru Zewde, *supra* note 18.

[46] See Assefa Fiseha, Federalism in Ethiopia in Particular and in Multicultural Societies in General, *Recht in Afrika* 1-31 (2006).

[47] Article 8.

[48] Article 46 (2).

[49] P. Brietzke, Ethiopia's Leap in the Dark: Federalism and Self-Determination in the New Constitution, 39 (1) *Journal of African Law* 19-20 (1995); Fasil Nahum, *Constitution for a Nation of Nations: The Ethiopian Prospect* 51-52 (Lawrenceville, NJ: The Red Sea Press, 1997).

[50] Article 47 (1).

[51] Article 47(2). The constitution, under Article 47(3), provides strict procedures to be followed in such process. The required procedures among others include: the approval by a two-thirds majority of the members of the council of the nations, nationality and people concerned, presumably at local government level, and the approval by a majority vote of the nation/nationality or people in a refer-

of the idea that the right to self-determination and the right to self-rule can best be realized through the creation of states whose borders coincide with the nations/nationalities. The federal system, therefore, takes the territorial principle seriously.[52] Theoretically, therefore, every nation/nationality can have its own state and hence we can imagine no less than eighty states. It is important to point out that seven out of the nine constituent states (the only exceptions are the SNNPRS and Gambella) are named after the major nationalities that 'dominate'[53] the respective states. Addis Ababa[54] and Dire Dawa[55] are specially administered autonomous city-states directly accountable to the federal government and do not fall within the territory of any of the constituent states. Their position is, therefore, less autonomous compared to the constituent states.

Many multicultural federal systems like India and Switzerland provide in one way or another for recognition and accommodation to groups. But the most striking feature of the Ethiopian federal system, compared to many others, is the "*explicitness, at constitutional level, of its affirmation of the national self-determination and the logical consistency with which it attempts to institution-*

---

endum organized by the State Council. Interestingly enough, the constitution is silent about the role of the federal government in the whole process except one vaguely stipulated provision. According to Article 62(6): "*The House of Federation shall strive to find solutions to disputes or misunderstandings that may arise between the states*." The role of the state beyond organizing a referendum is also far from clear. For other experiences see the Swiss Constitution Article 53(3), T. Fleiner, Legal Instruments and Procedures to Prevent and Solve Ethnic conflicts: Experience of the Swiss Constitution, in: L. Basta and T. Fleiner (eds.), *Federalism and Multiethnic States: The Case of Switzerland* 127 (Fribourg: Publications de l'Institut du Fédéralisme, 2000).

[52] This seems to be the logic behind Articles 46 and 47.

[53] This is a rather fluid expression and is elaborated more in the section dealing with the treatment of minorities.

[54] Addis Ababa is the capital city of the federal government and has the right to self-government but it is responsible to the federal government (Article 49 of the Ethiopian federal constitution). It used to be one of the fourteen regional governments during the transition period (1991-1994) but not under the new constitution. Economic stagnation, unemployment, sanitation issues were crucial factors that challenged the Addis Ababa local government for the last decade. There were also discussions among the African leaders to move the African Union capital elsewhere. A decision by the Oromia regional government to move its capital from Addis Ababa to Nazreth/Adama was also a serious issue among the Oromo elites. In 2002 the Prime Minister dissolved the Addis Ababa government and substituted it by an unelected party coalition from among ruling party members and in a year's time or so the new leadership under the popular Mayor Arkebe Ukbay was able to introduce major changes within the civil service but his team lost in the May 2005 election and as CUD, the winner for the municipality council, failed to take its seat as of May 2006, Addis Ababa remained under a caretaker administration. See Guykervella, Broad Support for Mayor's Overhaul of Addis Ababa at
http://www.citymayors.com/mayors/addis_mayor.html as visited on 8 April 2005.

[55] Dire Dawa is also administered directly by the federal government. There have been issues of disagreement over the town between the Oromia and Somali regional states and since 1995, it has been under the supervision of the federal government. It has special geo-political significance particularly after the war between Ethiopia and Eritrea broke out in 1998. The only railway that connects Ethiopia with Djibouti passes through Dire Dawa.

alize that principle."[56] Not only are nations and nationalities granted the right to form their own states but they are also guaranteed the right to walk away from the federal pact after going through some strict procedures. Interestingly, it is the state and the constitution itself that encourages any group to think of itself as a nation/nationality and promotes it as a candidate for statehood. The granting of 'mother' states to some of the major nationalities is a logical consequence of this. In principle there is no constitutional asymmetry among the states, although there is some level of political asymmetry.[57]

3.2. Viable Federal Units?

There is another peculiar feature related to the explicit recognition of the nationalities as building bricks of the federation. In many other multicultural federations, the federal outcome arose in response to a particular sort of problem, namely the problem of competing nationalisms within a single state. It evolved out of piecemeal democratic negotiations and in response to particular nationally mobilized groups.[58] To borrow Richard Simeon's phrase there is bound to exist "diversity of diversities"[59] both within the global context and within each respective federation. The strength of the claims of these diverse groups is therefore expected to be different requiring flexibility in the design of the constitutional solution. The Ethiopian approach is revolutionary in its straightforward grant of self-determination and self-rule to all nations and nationalities. Certainly, there were dozens of ethno-nationalist movements claiming some form of regional autonomy and even at times secession.[60] However, it is also true that not all groups within the Ethiopian state were mobilized and if mobilized, they were not necessarily mobilized on a nationalist basis. The point is that federal autonomy has been accorded to groups that had not in fact been politically mobilized.

This is not without implications. Because the groups have not mobilized for it and because some of them failed to articulate regional interests as political entities, not as anthropological units, some of the constituent units have not yet

---

[56] W. Kymlicka, Emerging Western Models of Multination Federalism: Are They Relevant for Africa?, in: D. Turton (ed.) *Ethnic Federalism: The Ethiopian Experience in Comparative Perspective* 54-55 (Oxford: James Currey, 2006).

[57] Article 47(4); federal practice suggests that because of the system of intergovernmental relations via the Ministry of Federal Affairs, the fiscal competence of the states and the court structure (in some states dual and in others delegated) some level of political asymmetry is inherent in the federal system. See Assefa Fiseha, *supra* note 29, Chapter 7 for details.

[58] Kymlicka, *supra* note 56, 55. By this he meant the nation-state with a dominant national ethos trying to impose its values on national minorities and the latter trying to resist such imposition and federalism being instituted to guarantee self-rule to such national minorities.

[59] R. Simeon, Managing Conflicts of Diversity, in: *Unity in Diversity: Learning from Each Other Conference Reader* of the 4th International Conference on Federalism Nov. 2007, New Delhi, 104.

[60] Many of the nationalist parties that claim to represent the Oromo, Somali, Afar and principally the EPRDF are clear examples.

been able to evolve into viable entities as expected, even after a decade of federal experience. Certainly, there are many contributory factors to their crisis.[61] It must be noted that the federal system was introduced after the fall of the most centralized regime that neglected the bulk of the ethno-linguistic groups. Thus, from their inception most of the constituent states lacked skilled manpower and resources to man the newly established local institutions. There were only a few hundred experts, for example, in Afar, Somali, Gambella and Benishangul-Gumuz in 1995/1996 and the situation remained the same until the Ethiopian Civil Service College took the responsibility of training civil servants for these regions with a view to breaking the historic marginalization from political power and resources. Historic marginalization also meant that there was little or no infrastructure in the less integrated regions, making self-rule difficult. Less integration in historic Ethiopia also implies that the inhabitants of lowland regional states, in relative terms, being mostly pastoralists lacked the tradition of indigenous settled administration and a disciplined ruling party capable of articulating regional interest. These and other factors facilitated governmental and party interference from the centre. The low level of political development in these regions means that the ruling party plays a greater role in local administration than in other constituent states.

Thus, close observation of the performance of some of the states also suggests that they have not yet been able to articulate distinct regional interests and that they have not yet developed into a viable political unit that can compete with the federal government in intergovernmental relations. In short, some do not seem to have acquired the status of nation/nationality, which the constitution seems to generously grant them.[62] In such circumstances, it may be wise to rethink the federal system again and set up an asymmetric federal system. In a

---

[61] The point made by Maimire, "the constitution establishes regions on the basis of sociological diversity and out of which no political community can be driven," (*supra* note 29, 93), seems to be partly true, but is indiscriminate. Nations/nationalities in the sense they are understood in the west are much more than ethnic groups with a possible candidacy for statehood and so many of them claim that right in Ethiopia. So not all of them could be dubbed as ethnic groups. Some of the constituent states under discussion include Afar, Somali and Gambella. The two-tier nature of the federal system (those with relatively better experience in self-rule versus marginalized ones) has been made clear in a number of studies. See for instance J. Young, Along Ethiopia's Western Frontier: Gambella and Benishangul in Transition, 37(2) *The Journal of Modern African Studies* 321-346 (1999); J. Abbink as well remarked that in the constituent states under discussion, there have been dismal failures. See his article Ethnicity and Constitutionalism in contemporary Ethiopia, 41 *Journal of African Law* 173(1997); also Dereje Feyissa, The Experience of Gambella Regional State, in: D. Turton (ed.), *Ethnic Federalism: The Ethiopian Experience in Comparative Perspective* 208-230 (Oxford: James Currey, 2006).

[62] There appears to be a problem of distinguishing politically between ethnic groups in situations in which national consciousness has not yet evolved. In some of these constituent units their inability to create a regional interest worth constituting a federal unit is clear. There have been several reports indicating that different groups in a state fight over local power and resources by capturing different offices of the regional government, which in effect result in a state government fragmented into pieces. See, for instance, an interesting article about the crisis in Gambella by Dereje Feyissa, *supra* note 61.

way this is not an earth-shattering discovery. The federal system in practice is asymmetric in many respects. For instance, as far as intergovernmental relations is concerned, the constitutional principle "*Member states* ...[of the Federation]... *shall have equal rights and powers*"[63] is compromised to a considerable extent in relation to some of the member states. The fiscal competence of the states, the court structure, their representation in the second chamber, the political implications of Articles 46 and 47 (constituent states for some and not for all) are clear evidence of an already existing political asymmetry. Comparative studies also point to the fact that it is possible to increase from the norm the federal authority and correspondingly reduce the competence of some of the states in particular circumstances.[64] This could be done in a transitory phase and at such time that the constituent states demonstrate some level of institutional competence to rule their own affairs.

3.3. Shared Rule

There is another consequence of the emphasis on the territorial principle (Articles 46 and 47). In as much as a federal system is about self-rule it is also about shared rule. The balance between the two has always been subject to debate but their importance is beyond doubt. The grant of 'mother states' may be important in terms of concrete recognition of diversity,[65] but the recognition and promotion of diversity as can be observed from the Swiss federal experience does not stop there. What is important is the *political expression of diversity*. Several studies have indicated that diversity as such is not in itself a threat to integration[66] but it becomes a fertile ground for federal instability if the political system is not able to give it political expression. The federal arrangement by territorializing the state concretizes self-rule and as some critics indicate, "fragments" the state. With a view to ensuring the right to self-rule to the nationalities, the constitution either grants 'mother states' to the nationalities or does ensure them at least a local government at zone or *woreda* level. Thus it takes the right to self-rule seriously. Yet there is an important aspect that is missing. It fundamentally fails to integrate what it 'fragments'. The emphasis

---

[63] Article 47(4).

[64] Apart from this option, federal experience indicates two other options of asymmetry: increase from the norm the jurisdiction of particular member states (increase the regional competence of some states as in Jammu and Kashmir, the only Indian state that has its own constitution) and secondly while maintaining the constitutional symmetry it is possible to include provisions that permit in certain cases to "opt in" or "opt out" of some of the norms, for instance by delegation. See for more R. Watts, *supra* note 30, 63-68; Balveer Arora, Adapting Federalism to India: Multilevel and Asymmetrical Innovations, in: Balveer Arora and Douglas Verney (eds.), *Multiple Identities in a Single State: Indian Federalism in Comparative Perspective* 71-104 (Delhi: Konark Publishers Pvt. Ltd., 1995).

[65] Another area where diversity has been given political expression is the language policy.

[66] D. Elazar, *supra* note 30, 66; Akhtar Majeed, Conflict Management in Federal Plural Societies: Some Lessons from India, in: *First National Conference on Federalism, Conflict and Peace Building*, 132-141 (Addis Ababa: United Printers Plc., 2004).

on self-rule should be complemented by proportional representation in elections,[67] in the civil service, in the executive and the judiciary. One might state that there is Article 39(3), which provides for the equitable representation of the states at federal and state level as well as the composition of the ruling party (that is a coalition of parties from different nationalities) that looks like a typical feature of Lijphart's model of consociational ethnic accommodation, namely the principle of power sharing among ethnic leaders at federal level. Yet this has at least some limitations.

First and foremost, the practice so far indicates that Article 39(3) is limited to executive power sharing and does not include legislative power sharing at federal level. Secondly, the decade of federal experience points out that being part of the coalition within the ruling party is conditional upon subscribing to the ruling party's membership and its ideology. So many political parties that more or less share the ideology of the ruling party are forced to operate autonomously because they are not encouraged to form a coalition as the ruling party insists that such parties subscribe to its conditions. To a large degree, this goes a long way in explaining some of the troubles in the Southern Nations, Nationalities and Peoples and Oromia regions.

Thirdly, it has already been pointed out that the role of the nations/nationalities in the central decision-making process, a crucial element of sharing power at the centre, is almost insignificant.

In the area of fiscal transfers too, the role of the smaller nationalities is becoming less significant and the House of the Federation that is supposed to be their guardian is evolving along the interests of the more populous states and nationalities. The fact that its composition is more or less similar to the lower house is creating a problem in the decision-making process. The most populated states are pushing the House to increase the weight of population size in the allocation of shared revenue and grants. The less populated states are consistently becoming the losers and it seems that it is hardly possible to reverse this trend. As a result, while the House of the Federation might have been envisaged as the most legitimate body to decide on fiscal transfers, it is becoming less relevant to the less populated states. It is for this reason that one might be tempted to conclude, as far as the less populated nationalities are concerned, that the federal principle is not taken seriously. In this regard, the much-politicized right of nationalities has not been translated into political realities. These are crucial factors of integration that focus on shared rule and that counter balance the emphasis on self-rule. Thus while ensuring self-rule to the nationalities is a step in the right direction, this measure needs to be com-

[67] For a more detailed account of how a country's electoral system contributes to the stability or instability of a country see Maimire, *supra* note 29, 107-110.

plemented by institutional arrangements that give effect to power sharing schemes to the various actors at federal, regional and local levels.

3.4. Congruence between the Nationalities and the Territories?

However, the presentation of the federal system as granting 'mother states' to nationalities could be misleading. Despite the attempt to grant a mother state to some of the dominant nationalities, the process has not resulted in homogeneous states. In this sense, to adopt the words of Duchachek, Ethiopia like other multicultural federations is characterized by "partial ethno-territorial federalism"[68] or, in the words of Hoekema, by "indirect consociationalism".[69] In the ideal (non-existent) case of perfect "integral ethno-territorial federalism" there will be a perfect coincidence of all intra-federal and national boundaries. However, in the case of partial ethno-national federalism one can observe a federation in which only major nationalities have and administer their own autonomous units. That certainly is the case in India with many hundred ethno-national groups but with only twenty-eight states and the same holds true for Nigeria. The Ethiopian federation as well submits to this reality despite the promise to elevate every group to a nation/nationality. While the states of Amhara, Oromia, Tigray, Afar and Somalia have clear dominant nationality groups, the other states are clearly multicultural. Benishangul/Gumuz has Berta, Mao-Komo, Shinasha and Gumuz nationalities. Gambella has Nuer, Anuak and Mejenger, and Harari has an enormous number of Oromo, Amhara and Gurage. The Southern Nations, Nationalities and Peoples region has more than fifty-six "nationalities".[70] The federally administered cities of Addis Ababa, Dire Dawa and many other cities found within the states like Awassa, Nazreth/Adama, Shashemene, to mention a few are particularly heterogeneous as they are inhabited by economic migrants. Even the states with dominant nationalities have not escaped their own multi-ethnicity. The state of Tigray, which many consider to be homogeneous, has Amhara, Oromo, Kunama and Saho minorities within its borders. The state of Amhara has a number of Agaw, Oromo and Argoba peoples in addition to the dominant Amhara.

---

[68] Duchachek, *supra* note 21, 17-18.

[69] A. Hoekema, Aspects of Legal Pluralism in the Federal Set up of the Ethiopian State, 24(2) *Ethiopian Journal of Development Research* 2-3 (October 2002). The boundaries and composition of autonomous entities are determined in such a way that as a matter of social fact, some of the nationalities will have a majority in the government, in the executive and the judiciary and embark on a political and legal course of their own. But certainly almost all of them are multicultural.

[70] The term nationalities has to be applied carefully here. It seems that in the case of the SNNPRS, Gambella and Benishangul-Gumuz states in practice they are not treated as nations/nationalities. The most multicultural states are treated with some level of scepticism from the centre. If one has to interpret the federal practice, the meaning appears like this: for the moment you are not nations/nationalities but should you one day become so then you have the constitutional right to form your own states.

Oromia hosts close to three million Amhara and a number of ethnic groups belonging to the Southern Nations, Nationalities and Peoples region.

The Southern Nations, Nationalities and Peoples region is peculiar in some respects.[71] One can make two conflicting hypotheses.

On the one hand, it is possible to state that the territorial approach is less feasible there taking into account the many ethno-linguistic groups. Certainly, there has been a move along that line in recent years. It has become the region in which the EPRDF has experimented with party reform for the first time. The SEPDF (South Ethiopian Peoples Democratic Front), the ruling party in the region and also a member of the EPRDF, was originally a coalition of some twenty ethnic fronts operating in the South. It has now been transformed into one party (movement), SEPDM, in 2002.[72] Along with it, following the post 2001 state constitutional reform, more emphasis was put on the *woreda* as regards the allocation of budget. It is reported that this was done in order to reduce claims for more and more local government as fuelled by the budget allocation formula. By creating more and more subunits, the ethnic groups rightly or wrongly thought that they would share more and more of the national budget. It is no surprise then that the Prime Minister in his 1994 E.C. (July 2000) report to parliament declared "*they ought to have used their budget as Maresha*" (ploughshares), implying to finance specific plans bringing returns "*but they used it instead as Genfo*" (porridge). According to sources, the move was triggered by two reasons, being the sudden expansion of parochial ethnic sentiments often manipulated by local elites and the aggravation of this tendency by the budget allocation formula. If new sub-state units were created, they were entitled to run their own budget and so everyone wanted to have one. This led to further restructuring in the region from nine to thirteen zones

[71] It is estimated that the fifty-six nationalities amount to thirteen million people (17% of the total population) of which the Sidama are 1.8 million, Gurage (Silte included, 1.6 million), Wolayita 1.2 million. In this region, unlike the case in Amhara, Oromia, Afar, Somali and Tigray there is no single numerically dominant group. Several political parties have emerged in the post-1991 period, notably being the SEPDF and the SEPDC, the latter an opposition coalition founded in March 1992. Both parties claim to represent the interests of the south: mainly the right to self-determination and regional autonomy of the nationalities (the former including secession). Compared with the Somali and some factions within Oromia, the SNNPRS has always shown willingness to be part of the larger Ethiopian state in a genuine federal setup. For more on the SNNPRS, see J. Abbink, New Configurations of Ethiopian Ethnicity: The Challenge of the South, 5(1) *Northeast African Studies* 59-81 (1998); S. Vaughan, Response to Ethnic Federalism in Ethiopia's Southern Region, in: D. Turton (ed.) *Ethnic Federalism: The Ethiopian Experience in Comparative Perspective* 181-207 (Oxford: James Currey, 2006).

[72] What the transformation from a front to a movement implies is far from clear. However, some hint that SEPDF, which was a front of some twenty ethnic groups, was dependant on the fronts in decision-making. Important decisions were made by the twenty parties at zone level and then implemented by the SEPDF. This led to a weak regional state and strong zones. After the reform, major decisions have been made by the movement and not by the twenty parties. The role of the fronts accordingly has diminished. Interview, Speaker of the second chamber in the SNNPRS Ato Tekle Didu, Awasa, 3 March 2005.

and eight Special *Woreda.*[73] Compared to the relative peace in regions like Tigray and Amhara, dominated by one nationality and relatively able to articulate regional interest in their relations with the federal government, some have suggested an asymmetric federal system, that is, a greater role of the federal government in the Southern Nations, Nationalities and Peoples (SNNPRS), Afar, Gambella and Benishangul-Gumuz states.[74]

However, this argument is not without limitations and this brings us to the second hypothesis. The most frequent and deadly conflicts ever since the introduction of the federal system in 1995 have been in the same states: SNNPRS, Gambella and Benishangul-Gumuz.[75] It is true that there are many factors that brought about the conflicts but one certainly is the failure to design adequate mechanisms for dealing with the complex reality of the multi-ethnic population living in each of the respective states. These are the states in which the grant of 'mother states' has not fully been materialized because of an alleged lack of a dominant nationality or because of constituting too many small ethnic groups. Relative peace has been restored in some of them, for instance, in SNNPRS after the Wolayita, Silte and Kaffa-Sheka were granted local governments. If this argument is convincing then it makes a strong case for further restructuring of the regional governments, along with the general view that nationalities should be granted their own 'mother states' even within multiethnic regional states. The fact that there have been frequent conflicts in the SNNPRS (as well as in other regions with a similar multi-ethnic population composition like Gambella and Benishangul-Gumuz) compared to other states (in which the EPRDF insisted that the boundaries of the constituent states should match the boundaries of the nationalities, thereby creating more homogeneous states resulting in relative peace) seems to suggest that the multi-ethnic states should also be structured along similar lines. The south has been relatively more stable and peaceful after the series of regional state restructurings than, for instance, four years ago. But this brings with it the issue of where to begin and end the reorganization of the subunits within the regions. There are still claims for more zones and *woreda* in several parts of the SNNPRS and the creation of a new state as a member of the federation cannot be ruled out either.

---

[73] Interview with Assefa Kessito, Lecturer and who is actively involved with political developments in the SNNPS, November 2002; see also *Zemen Magazine* Hidar 1995, *Ye Debub Ye Politica Tikusat* : 8-11; *Human Rights Watch World Report* (2003): Africa: Ethiopia http://www.hrw.org/wr2k3.africa5.html as visited on 15 June 2003.

[74] However unsubstantiated by empirical evidence it may be, there also appears to be a political consensus for a federal option for treatment of the regions on a case-by-case basis. This was, for instance, one of the kernels of a recent seminar on Ethiopian federalism held in Addis Ababa. The papers of the seminar have recently been published in book form. See D. Turton (ed.), *Ethnic Federalism: The Ethiopian Experience in Comparative Perspective* (Oxford: James Currey, 2006).

[75] For a detailed account of the conflicts see Assefa Fiseha, *supra* note 29, Chapter 5.

Both are tentative arguments and not much can be said about this very dynamic region. One rather promising point about the SNNPRS, given its size and incorporation into mainstream Ethiopian politics, is the potential role that it can play in stabilizing the federal game. The SNNPRS being composed of relatively smaller nationalities that benefit more from interdependence and some form of self-rule than from a unitary system and independence, has a major role to play in bringing equilibrium to the two potential threats to the Ethiopian federation: centralism (as reflected in the 20th century) and secession (as many political elites seem to be aspiring for).

3.5. Unicameral Legislature/Adjudication of Disputes

The 1995 Ethiopian Constitution provides for a two-house federal parliament: the House of Peoples' Representatives (HoPR) and the House of the Federation (HoF). But this is to some extent misleading because the second/upper chamber (HoF) is not part of the law making process at federal level. In other words, federal law does not need the consent of the HoF to become a law. It is the lower house (House of Peoples' Representatives) that has exclusive power as far as law making at federal level is concerned.[76] Federal practice elsewhere suggests that a genuine federation should not only guarantee autonomy to the states but should also incorporate the states in the central decision-making process.[77] Nevertheless the Ethiopian federal system departs from this trend and grants the HoF among other things the power to interpret the constitution, to resolve disputes among the regions, and to decide on intergovernmental subsidies and joint taxes.[78]

The policy choice of the framers to vest the power to interpret the constitution and to review the constitutionality of laws in the HoF, and not in the judiciary, has something to do with the reputation of the judiciary and with ideological matters. Firstly, the framers of the constitution thought that interpretation of the constitution is not purely a legal/technical matter that should be left to the judiciary. The framers of the constitution felt that the constitution is the political contract among the nationalities and only a house that is composed of representatives from the nationalities should be vested with the task of determining the scope and meaning of the text of the constitution. Thus the power of the HoF is firmly tied with the idea that the constitution provides an overriding place for the right of nationalities. Secondly, in historic Ethiopia, adjudication of cases formed part and parcel of public administration. Indeed, adjudication of cases was considered to be the principal function of the executive. For ex-

[76] See Articles 51, 55 and 54(3).
[77] D. Elazar, *supra* note 30, 12.
[78] For more on the role of second chambers in federations and the role of the HoF in adjudication of disputes see Assefa Fiseha, Federalism and the Adjudication of Constitutional Issues: The Ethiopian Experience, 52 (1) *Netherlands International Law Review* 1-31 (2005).

ample, when Emperor Menelik took the historic decision to appoint ministers in 1908, the Minister of Justice was also the Chief Justice.[79] The attempt to separate the judiciary from the executive was not that easy either. In 1942, a long and tiring process of negotiation led to a partial victory as far as the judiciary was concerned. The highest benches, that is the High Court and the Supreme Imperial Court, but only them, were able to be relatively free from the influence of provincial administrators. In all other respects, until 1992, the court structure reflected the traditional practice of combining judicial and executive functions in the person of the local chiefs and provincial governors. At the apex of the court structure one found until 1974, the emperor, dispensing justice in the *Zufan Chilot* (Crown Court).[80] This blend of judicial and executive functions in the latter was not without its implications. The crisis of the Ethiopian state for the most part of the 20th century had its effect on the judiciary as well. Indeed it is difficult to see the judiciary in isolation from the whole political system under which it operates. First and foremost the judiciary had never had an autonomous existence of its own as an institution. It was subject to all kinds of pressures from the other branches. Thus external pressure on the judiciary has deep roots and is not without some hangovers in the new federal judiciary. Administrators at state level even today think that it is natural to order the judge. Second, the judiciary has never survived a political regime change. It was no surprise to see every new regime setting up its own version of the judiciary that suited its mission. The judiciary was never designed to be an institution as a third branch of the government in the real sense. This has left an impression on the ordinary citizen to the effect that change in government will entail another round of appointments and dismissals of judges. Thus in 1991 when EPRDF came to power and started the new federal system, the prestige and reputation of the judiciary was at its ebb, associated with all forms of nepotism, corruption and worst of all, an arm of the most despotic regime on earth, well known for executing life without any semblance of due process of law. Thus both the historical context and the ideological factor contributed to the shift of reviewing constitutional issues from the regular judiciary to the HoF.

3.6. Federal Supremacy and Implications for the Unity-Diversity Rationale behind Federations

At the centre of the federal idea is the constitutionally guaranteed division of political power between the federal and state governments. Accordingly, the

---

[79] Aberra Jembere, *An Introduction to the Legal History of Ethiopia 1434-1974* pp. 219, 227, 240 (Hamburg: LIT Verlag, 2000).

[80] Under the unitary systems, the judiciary was contained within the executive branch. The federal Supreme Court was separated from the Ministry of Justice in 1992. It suffers from a severe shortage of qualified legal and judicial personnel to operate its many layers of courts.

two kinds of government are more or less autonomous in respect of the powers vested in them. However, this does not tell the whole story of the relationship between the federal government and the states. However neatly demarcated the division of power may be, the existence of an overlap between the two orders of government is unavoidable. Besides, powers granted to one or the other of the two governments are not necessarily exercised exclusively by one level of government. Power may be shared in concurrent fashion. Furthermore, in federations like the United States, it is common to see the introduction of a new brand of powers to the federal government other than those expressly granted. The doctrine of implied powers is a case in point. The scope of national power has remained ever expanding. As a result, the line between federal and state powers becomes somewhat blurred.[81]

In such cases of overlap of power between the federal and state governments, the need for a coherent principle that governs potential conflicts between the two authorities remains of crucial importance in federations. Many federations have as a result introduced in their federal constitutions provisions that in one way or another declare the supremacy of federal law over state law.[82] In other words, regional states may regulate a certain field but only insofar as such a regulation is consistent with, or permissible under, the policy of the federal government. In those fields where both federal and state government may sometimes be active, the decision of federal authorities made within the legitimate exercise of powers, prevails over contrary decisions of state authorities.[83] Of course, we know for sure that the supremacy principle operates within the context of the overall federal system. Respecting the authority of the states remains one of the cardinal principles upon which federations are based. Otherwise the federal government could quite simply undo the whole of federalism by passing legislation that infringes on state powers.[84]
The Ethiopian Constitution, however, does not have a similar provision. It may be argued here that the absence of a provision on supremacy of federal law over state law is not after all a serious flaw, so long as the system remains a federation as one can assume the principle as inherent in any federation. However, this has to be seen in light of the overall position of the states under the 1995 Constitution and viewed from that angle, the lacunae appears to add one more point to the observation that the system is, at least formally speaking,

[81] Robert Carr, *The Supreme Court and Judicial Review* 85 (New York: Rinehart & co, INC., 1942).
[82] See for instance, United States Constitution Article VI; Swiss Constitution Article 49 and German Basic Law Article 31 that respectively state: "the laws of the United States which are made in pursuance of the constitution shall be the supreme law of the land, anything in the laws of the states to the contrary notwithstanding"; "federal law takes precedence over contrary cantonal law" and "federal law takes precedence over state law".
[83] R. Carr, *supra* note 81, 82.
[84] L.F.M. Besselink, The Protection of Human Rights in Federal Systems - The Case of Ethiopia, in: Baye Yimam, R. Pankhurst, D. Chapple, Yonas Admasu, A. Pankhurst and Birhanu Tefera (eds.), *Proceedings of the XIVth International Conference of Ethiopian Studies*, *Volume 3*, 1359-1387 (Addis Ababa: Institute of Ethiopian Studies, 2002).

more of a confederation than a federation. If one concedes that it is a confederation of states, such lacunae may be consistent with the overall constitutional design. Indeed, it appears that the Ethiopian federation, unlike other federations, is based on a unity-diversity combination in which the latter slightly prevails over the former. Otherwise the lack of the principle of federal supremacy in a federal context is not common in a federation and there are three main arguments in support of the inclusion of the federal supremacy clause.

The first argument stems from the unity-diversity combination and its impact on the federal structure. As we have noted already, the ethno-linguistic groups that the constitution considers to be its building bricks are declared "sovereign" and for the same reason the constitution places the legitimacy of the federal state upon them. Besides, each ethno-linguistic group has the right to form its own state, and the right to self-determination, secession included.[85]

If we analyze the lack of the clause that declares the federal law to be supreme in this context then it may be tempting to conclude that unlike many of the federations established from a balance between the forces of unity and diversity or as this author contends when the federal forces slightly prevail over the forces for diversity, the Ethiopian federation appears to have been established rather on the unity-diversity combination in which the forces of diversity slightly prevail over the forces of unity. One has to add another crucial indicator to the list of points indicated above. In the process of adopting the clause on self-determination, it was the radical view that urged for the inclusion of the right to self-determination, secession included, which was approved by an overwhelming majority. A perfect compromise would have resulted in adopting the moderate position. The moderate view proposed for the inclusion of the right to self-determination, short of secession, while the most conservative position insisted on "the one country, one people with undivided sovereignty".[86]

In such a design K. C. Wheare warned that the region may ensure a loyalty greater than that of the union and in time of conflict the union may fall apart.[87] Indeed, some argue that the present federation is in the hands of regional forces. There is a real concern as this may lead to a case where the loyalty to the states may prevail over the loyalty to the union.[88] So far this risk is moderated by the party harmony that existed for a decade or so at federal and state level. Although the two loyalties should be there as prerequisites for a federation, an imbalance in which the forces of diversity prevail as Watts notes "*unless accompanied by the institutional encouragement of common institu-*

---

[85] Articles 8, 46, 47 and 39.

[86]See *Ye Ethiopia Hige Mengist Gubae Kale Gubae Tiraz 3,* Addis Ababa, Hidar 8-13, 1987 E.C. (Minutes of the Constitutional Assembly volume 3 November 17-21, 1994): 1-59.

[87] K. C. Wheare, *supra* note 4, 50-51.

[88] Minasse Haile, The New Ethiopian Constitution: Its Impact upon Unity, Human Rights and Development, *Suffolk Transnational Law Review* 1-84 (Winter 1996).

tions that provide the glue to hold the federation together", could be disintegration in the making.[89] Note here how weak and insufficient the institutions for power sharing are in the Ethiopian context.[90] If one agrees with this proposition, then the design goes counter to the underlying principle of federalism. Although it combines unity and diversity, federalism *imposes a limit on both.* To quote Duchachek, "*federations result from a compromise between two territorial forces pulling in opposite directions: one toward national unity, which if excessive, could suppress diversity and eliminate state autonomy and the other toward diversity, which if excessive could dissolve the federal nation into its several constituent units.*"[91]

To come to the nexus between federal supremacy and the unity-diversity matrix in the established federations, one should note the fact that the explicit declaration of the supremacy of federal law over state law is something that reflects the outcome of the unity-diversity combination during the federal bargain. When federal constitutions state that federal law prevails over contrary state law, it is implied that the reasons for local diversity give way to the common goals of the federation. There is abundant literature making this point clear.[92] With the emergence of the social welfare state it even became a myth in the old federations. It is changed to a co-operative/coercive form.[93] Only confederal arrangements stipulate that the parties to a pact are equally supreme and retain the last word for themselves.

Secondly, not only is the unity-diversity combination in the Ethiopian context weighted towards the latter, the imbalance is further reinforced by the "sovereignty of nation/nationality". However, there does not seem to be room for sovereignty of nationalities in federations. Federations remain single political units with their core feature of autonomous existence of federal government and states. Of course we know for sure that states retain their sovereignty in confederations. They only give up a certain portion of their sovereignty in relation to, for instance, foreign relations and military power but even then the decision-making procedure is designed in such a way as to reflect state rights requiring unanimity or qualified majority. Otherwise any view of a federation which holds the co-equal position in the relationship between the federation and the states or that subordinates the federal government to the states (in our case to the nationalities), digresses from the federal principle. Indeed, this has

---

[89] Watts, *supra* note 30, 16-17.

[90] See Assefa Fiseha, *supra* note 29, Chapters 3 and 7.

[91] I. Duchachek, *Comparative Federalism: The Territorial Dimensions of Politics* 194 (New York: Holt, Renehart and Winston, 1970).

[92] Duchachek, *supra* note 91, 233; M. Burgess, Can Comparative Federalism Really be Comparative?, in: Lloyd Brown-John (ed.), *Centralizing and Decentralizing Trends in Federal States* 15 (Lanham: University Press of America, 1988); Nicolas Schmitt also states federalism is a form of government that allows minorities a large measure of autonomy but not the right to secede. N. Schmitt, *Federalism: The Swiss Experience* 119 (Pretoria: HSRC, 1996).

[93] See Assefa Fiseha, *supra* note 29, Chapter7.

been at the centre of the debate between the advocates of national sovereignty, on the one hand, and state rights - otherwise known as compact theory - on the other, within the United States federation in the 19th century. There was a dilemma as to whether the source of authority of the federation is the citizen or the states[94] but the post 1860s development proved that state sovereignty in a federal context is nothing more than respect for the autonomy of the states. Strictly speaking, a federation is the result of the cumulative consent of not only the states but of the citizens as well.

Like many other federal constitutions, the Ethiopian Constitution incorporates the fact that the individual citizen is the source of government authority. Article 50(3) clearly incorporates the idea that the citizen remains the source of authority both at federal and state level. We have already noted that all powers of the federal government are exercised by the lower house composed of representatives based on population size. King rightly argues that federations are based on a dual source of authority. "*Every federation accords each citizen in principle an equal entitlement to vote. First to elect members of the regional government and second to elect members of the national government. But in federations representation of the states is also in some manner entrenched.*"[95] It is only along this line that federations have to be understood.

From this perspective one can only be critical of the concept of sovereignty of nationalities incorporated under the Ethiopian Constitution. In federations there is no such thing as absolute state sovereignty. Let alone in the case of the Ethiopian federation where the states had no prior existence as constituent states, even where states were independent before the emergence of the federation, states give up a major portion of their sovereignty when they join the federation. To sum up, federations, as we know, impose limits on unity as well as on diversity. They operate within the general framework of the supremacy of the federal government. Even the supremacy of the federal government is limited in the sense that the terms of the federal bargain are contained in a constitution that is supreme and that guarantees the autonomy of the states. In this regard, the concept of nation/nationality or state sovereignty in the Ethiopian Constitution should be construed to have a limited scope only giving emphasis to the dominant position given to ethnicity. If this observation is true, then we can still see the system as federal and imply the principle of federal supremacy as inherent in federations.

The third proposition is based on the compact theory and this can be gathered from the 19th century United States and Swiss Confederations, the former re-

[94] For details see R. Davis, *The Federal Principle: a Journey through Time in Quest of Meaning* 113-114 (Berkeley: University of California Press, 1978); B. M. Sharma and L. P. Choudhry, *Federal Polity* 170 (London: Asia Publishing House, 1967).
[95] Preston King, Federation and Representation, in: M. Burgess and A. Gagnon (eds.), *Comparative Federalism and Federation* 98-100 (London: Harvester, 1993).

sulting from the vague position adopted by way of compromise between the authors of the Virginia and the New Jersey plan at Philadelphia in 1787.[96]

The gist of the argument is that contracting parties remain free to join or withdraw from such an association, if the other party violates the terms of the compact. This is further reinforced by the fact that federations are established, at least as far as the older ones are concerned, from previously sovereign states. The fact that they entered into the compact, it is argued, does not imply that they have surrendered their sovereignty. Accordingly, "*no state member of the federation can ever be obliged to act in a manner inconsistent with its own reading of the constitution which defines its relations with other members*."[97]

But the compact theory has some limitations. Primarily, not all federations have resulted from originally pre-existing sovereign states. Even when they result from such states, the terms of the federal bargain do not leave matters as they were before the establishment of the new federation. They assume entirely new obligations.[98] No doubt the new arrangement guarantees the states, as it should, the right to participate in the federal decision-making process, amendment included, but it does not leave them sovereign. Only in confederal arrangements can the states retain such sovereign position. It is an undeniable fact that they will submit to the union, which they have voluntarily created. After the union, a centre that did not previously exist, now, in fact, exists. The states have entered by giving up part of the sovereignty they might previously have had.

We have noted already that unlike confederations, federations are not based exclusively on the presumed existence of states. Both orders of government derive their authority from the individual citizen and there is a combined role for the principle of proportionality based on population size on the one hand and territorial representation on the other. As a result, states are not the sole sources for the compact.

Secondly, not all states (if there existed any sovereign ones) freely agree to enter or remain in the union. In both the US and Switzerland one clearly observes the impact of the forces of unity in shaping the federal process. In other federations like Germany, India and Nigeria we know very well the respective role of the allied forces, Union government and colonial forces. Thirdly, even

---

[96] B. M. Sharma and L. P. Choudhry, *Federal Polity* 170-173 (London: Asia Publishing House, 1967); in Switzerland this happened in 1847 when some cantons attempted to secede from the confederation. See T. Fleiner and L. Basta, Federalism, Federal States and Decentralization, in: L. Basta and T. Fleiner (eds.), *Federalism and Multiethnic States: The Case of Switzerland* 36 (Fribourg: Publications de l'Institut du Fédéralisme, 1996).

[97] John Calhoun's position as expounded by King: Preston King, *Federalism and Federation* 108 (London: Croom Helm, 1982).

[98] Id. 109.

where the federation results from such sovereign states, it has a unilateral character. In the case of 'coming together' federations, the centre is almost absent during the federal bargain and in the opposite process of 'holding together' federations, the states are absent in the bargain. Indeed, the states are creations of the federal constitution and in some cases even of the federal parliament.[99]

From the comparative studies, unless one subscribes to the assertions made in this section, one could deduce that the federal system in Ethiopia deviates in form from the common trend in other federations but not so much in practice as it operated under a dominant ruling party at federal and state level.

3.7. Some of the Contending Views on the Federal System

The federal system with its overriding features focusing on the right of nationalities and particular emphasis on self-rule has generated intense scholastic interest. Its sceptics underline the hegemonic aspiration of the TPLF (Tigray People's Liberation Front) to create a federal system under its tight control without genuine autonomy for the states[100] or at worst, because "*power remains in the hands of those ethnic groups, who occupy power because of their position in overthrowing the former regime*", the federal system is viewed as a "new form of dictatorship".[101] Along the same line, some others like Markakis describe it as a high-risk strategy and cast doubt on its workability: "*the empowerment of ethnicity is a bold attempt to resolve the conflict, it remains to be seen if it will succeed.*"[102]

Its critics consider the 'ethnic' federation as a sign of the first mark of disintegration.[103] Some analysts have warned that the dual loyalty requisite in federalism is not kept in balance. As a result, they contend that the whole arrangement is a treaty of alliances among near sovereign ethnic groups and concluded that since the adoption of ethnic based states, Ethiopia's federation is

---

[99] G. Parthasarathy for instance argues that unlike the United States, the Indian union was not constituted by an agreement between the states and therefore the states have no right to secede. Parthasarathy, Federalism and Constitutional Process in India, in: I Copland and J Rickard (eds.), *Federalism Comparative Perspectives from India and Australia* 284-285 (New Delhi: Manohari, 1999).

[100] That is the essence of Merera Gudina's thesis entitled *Ethiopia: Competing Ethnic Nationalisms and the Quest for Democracy, 1960-2002*, 119 (Maastricht: Shaker Publishing, 2003).

[101] C.E. Ehrlich, Ethnicity and Constitutional Reform: The Case of Ethiopia, *ILSA J. Int'l. and Comp. L.* 57 (1999).

[102] J. Young, *Ethnicity and Power*, *supra* note 8, 532; J. Markakis, *Resource Conflict in the Horn of Africa* 139 (London: SAGE Publications, 1998).

[103] Bekele for instance argues that unless something is done, the federal system will crumble once the ruling party is voted out of office. Bekele Haile-Selassie, *Ethiopia: A Precarious Ethno-Federal Constitutional Order* 7 (Doctoral dissertation University of Wisconsin Law School 2002) Unpublished.

virtually extinct.[104] Ethnicity, self-determination and secession coupled with the fact that the decision-making procedure in the unicameral federal legislature is based on majority of heads, the two larger ethnic groups, if they so wish can adopt any decision of their choice. Cohen also states that "*regionally based ethnicity may reinforce the demands of some ethnic groups for more and more states and finally for secession.*"[105] Brietzke too wrote that the ethnic federation gives ethnic groups too much power, placing the integrity of the federation at risk.[106] Overall, they underline the emphasis on the politics of difference and the subsequent threat of fragmentation.[107]

While the argument that in practice (as opposed to the formal powers in the text) the federal system was centralized as it operated under a dominant ruling party that is responsible for generating most of the policy documents and that relied heavily on its party machinery rather than on the formal institutions makes some sense, the argument that 'ethnic' federalism tends to sharpen and institutionalize previous differences and carries with it the danger of fragmentation, although valid to some extent, needs qualification.[108] It is a global problem that any multicultural federal system be it Ethiopia, India or any other country, carries with it two existential problems, however successful it may be. There is always the problem of integration in any country with minorities and more so in multicultural federations. There are bound to exist "two solitudes"[109] or "three nationalities with their backs to each other"[110] or the "hard and open ethnic identities".[111] Multicultural federations also attempt to contain the threat of secession but by the mere fact that they are multicultural they cannot avoid it altogether. After all, multicultural federations are potentially (in the worst case scenario) many nation-states in the making. It is not, therefore, endemic to Ethiopia nor is the ruling party to be blamed for institutional-

---

[104] Minasse Haile, *supra* note 88.

[105] J.M. Cohen, Ethnic Federalism in Ethiopia, 2(2) *Northeast African Studies* 168 (1995).

[106] P. Brietzke, *supra* note 49, 37.

[107] Some have dubbed it as suicidal, C. Ehrlich, Ethnicity and Constitutional Reform: The Case of Ethiopia, *ILSA J. Int'l. and Comp. L.* 62 (1999); others have called it "a recipe for disaster," Brietzke, *supra* note 49, 35; Minasse states that by placing sovereignty on the nations/nationalities rather than on the people the "*constitution can be said to have juridically extinguished Ethiopia as a sovereign entity and created nine sovereign states in its place on the same territory,*" *supra* note 88, 21-22.

[108] Kymlicka points out that these are existential problems in every multicultural federal state including in the west. *Supra* note 56.

[109] This is a reference made to Canada.

[110] This is a reference made to Switzerland.

[111] Maimire employs this notion in order to analyze the interethnic relations before and after the introduction of the federal system in Ethiopia. "Open ethnic identity", he claims, recognizes the "other" as different but not alien and not subject to double exclusion-identity and location, while "hard identity" makes identity and location inseparable leading from the "different" to double exclusion. This makes sense in the light of the present state crisis in Gambella, Oromia and Benishangul-Gumuz regional states where a significant number of people from different backgrounds are treated like "guest workers" for not being the "son of the soil". Dereje calls them "inconvenient minorities". Maimire, *supra* note 29, 98; Dereje, *supra* note 61, 215.

izing it. Thus whether the federal system will consolidate unity in diversity or fragment the different groups depends on several factors.[112]

One critic forwarded the idea that ethnicity or sociological diversity should be left to the private sphere. Another author noted, "*Disagreements about one's ethnic origin, an outcome of ethnic diversity is a private matter that should not have an effect on the way the common goods are defined and pursued.*"[113]However, this approach of separation of state and ethnicity is not only based on a wrong analogy but is also based on the wrong transplantation of American ideas into a multicultural federal system. Will Kymlicka rightly points out that the notion of the separation of state and ethnicity, a concept drawn from the principle of separation of church and state and used widely in many Western democracies as a basis to de-ethnicize the state, is an incorrect analogy. In the 16th century, many European states faced serious conflict between Catholics and Protestants over the question of which religion should rule the land. These conflicts were finally resolved by separating church and state and by guaranteeing each individual the freedom of religion. Many thought then that religious tolerance based on the separation of church and state provided a model for dealing with ethno-cultural differences as well. According to this view, ethnic identity, like religion, is something that people should be free to express in their private life, but it should not be the concern of the state.[114] In short, there should be a 'benign neglect' of ethnic and national differences. But as has been argued in the introductory section this does not work in multicultural societies like Ethiopia.[115] In the context of multicultural federations, the state might pretend to be neutral but deciding crucial matters like the language of instruction or the official language or drawing territories of constituent units for election or for self-rule are pretensions for imposing the will and choice of the majority on other nationalities.[116] Thus a pluralistic approach towards language is one mechanism for accommodating groups in such societies.

The supporters of the new federal system have hailed the process as an aspect of democratisation of state and society and as a "stroke of genius" that will

---

[112] Some of them include the commitment to the federal principle, tolerance and the accommodation of difference, strengthening the institutions of democracy as well as the prevalence of the rule of law and constitutionalism.

[113] Maimire, *supra* note 29, 94; Professor Mesfin has also devoted a small book to make this case. Mesfin Wolde-Mariam, *The Horn of Africa Conflict and Poverty*, (Addis Ababa: Commercial Printing press, 1999).

[114] W. Kymlicka, *supra* note 17, 6.

[115] Id. 110-111.

[116] The most frequently cited statement by John Jay (the co-author of *The Federalist No. 2)* "providence has been pleased to give this one connected country to one united people - a people descended from the same ancestors, speaking the same language, professing the same religion, attached to the same principles of government, very similar in their manner and customs…," for instance in the United States which pretends to be "ethnic free", clearly proves that the federal system is rather founded on an Anglo-Saxon culture, tradition, including the language, English.

reduce tension and conflict in the country and at its very best as a model for governing multi-ethnic states in Africa.

> Ethiopia is implementing a radical programme of decentralizing state power to ethnic-based regional units, which could be of interest to other countries in Africa faced with demands of ethnic communities for a greater role in the state. This apparent empowerment of ethnicity represents a complete reversal of the country's past practice consciously adopted, and is the joint product of the legacy of ethnic domination and marginalization in the Ethiopian state and secondly, it is a product of a long course that EPRDF followed in the conduct of a revolutionary struggle and not a leap in the dark as some tend to describe it. Throughout its struggle EPRDF consistently opined that its struggle is against ethnic domination and in the end to liberate nations, nationalities and peoples and confer to them the right to self-determination.[117]

By now it must be clear what the political implications were that started with the transition and got reinforced during the post 1995 political development. Nation/nationality became not only the basic principle of political organization but also constituted the foundation for restructuring the unitary and centrist state in the process of setting up the federal system. This was believed to bring a decisive remedy for Ethiopia's long-standing problem of the 'nationality question'.[118] This is in sharp contrast to the two previous regimes.[119] Leenco Lata, prominent figure from the OLF (Oromo Liberation Front), which was a partner in the transitional government, concurs with this view.

> It [the process of transition] was more than a regime change. Recasting it on a totally new basis became the only alternative for *its survival as an entity*. The recognition of the right to self-determination of the nationalities was conceptualized and the reconfiguration of the Ethiopian state was to bring about wide-ranging changes. The policy of Ethiopian identity, which was traditionally projected to coincide with Amhara identity, was to undergo fundamental changes. The previous policy of gradual homogenization through Amharization was to be abandoned. Instead of imposing a single Ethiopian identity, a mosaic was to be projected. Contrary to the previous practice of defining Ethiopian

[117] Young, *supra* note 8, 531-532; also Kinfe Abraham, *Ethiopia from Empire to Federation* 453-493 (London: EIIPD, 2001); Fasil Nahum, *supra* note 49, 51.

[118] For a detailed account of the context of the present federal system and this notion see Assefa, *supra* note 29, Chapter 1; also J. Young, *supra* note 9.

[119] E. Keller, Regime Change and Ethno-Regionalism in Ethiopia: The Case of the Oromo, in: Asafa Jalata (ed.), *Oromo Nationalism and the Ethiopian Discourse: The Search for Freedom and Democracy* 109-111 (Lawrenceville, NJ and Asmara: The Red Sea Press Inc., 1998).

> identity in a manner that excluded or failed to embrace the identities of the various nationalities a more inclusive image was to be projected. Much more importantly, it was intended that the reconfigured Ethiopian state would be the reflection of a composite of sovereignties of each of the component nationalities. Their entitlement to exercise such sovereignty was considered inalienable hence it was anticipated that this composite sovereignty of the new polity could be achieved only if these nations would decide to voluntarily give an element of this right for the good of each and all of the concerned peoples.[120]

Taken from the angle of the most marginalized areas, principally Afar, Somali, Gambella, Benishangul-Gumuz and even the Southern Nations, Nationalities and Peoples regional state and Oromia, the implementation of the federal system has created a new political space and institutional design to promote local empowerment. The post 1991 state restructuring based on federalism is one of the most visible political steps ever taken by the Ethiopian state to integrate historic minorities. Some of them have been promoted from obscure districts to a regional state. As one author rightly pointed out, the state has "delivered at the periphery".[121] One should note that except for the coming to power of Haile Selassie, Ethiopia had for the most part been under decentralized rather than centralized governments. The federal system, therefore, partly restores the *de facto* federal system, albeit in a different fashion. This contributed to regaining group pride and individual dignity and consequently feeling proud of being Ethiopian. At no other time has this been more vividly seen than during the Ethio-Eritrean war and in the May 2005 election. Significant numbers of the nationalities from these peripheral states were more than willing to voluntarily respond to the national call. In the case of Somali and Gambella it was even more than that. When they were told that the national quota was over, they officially petitioned to the federal government. In the May 2005 election when the ruling party lost all major support in major urban centres, it survived mainly because of the support from the ethnic-based constituent states as they showed their stake in federalism against CUD (Coalition for Unity and Democracy) that had been critical of collective rights.

Despite some critical limitations, the federal system, seen in the light of the fragile situation that the country had been in a decade ago, in the face of ardent national liberation movements like the OLF and some factions from the Ethiopian Somali, the commitment to national self-determination and establishment of the regional governments was probably the only measure that could ensure the survival of the Ethiopian state. Its contribution to relative peace is therefore

[120] Leenco Lata, The Making and Unmaking of Ethiopia's Transitional Charter, in: Asafa Jalata (ed.), *Oromo Nationalism and the Ethiopian Discourse: The Search for Freedom and Democracy* 51 (Lawrenceville, NJ and Asmara: The Red Sea Press Inc., 1998).

[121] Dereje, *supra* note 61.

beyond doubt.[122] By creating regional governments whose boundaries coincide with at least some of the major nationalities, the federal system is an attempt to serve as a conflict-regulating device as it creates more homogeneous states. In light of the degrading and inhuman situation the nationalities were in, the post 1991 federal system has also positively responded to the nationalities quest to preserve their own identity in the form of internal self-rule. The federal system expressly recognizes a 'pluri-national' and 'pluri-cultural' state. It has created distinct political and legal institutions at regional level. The federal system, at least in form, does permit all kinds of plurality and the parallel existence of formal and traditional institutions.[123]

However, despite the positive contributions of the new federal system discussed above, it also has its own shortcomings. Some of the limitations are inherent in the basic foundations of the federal system while others are failures resulting from inexperience and wrong perceptions of the federal system. Leaving out other limitations, for the purpose of this seminar, I will focus on the treatment of minorities at regional level focusing on the case study of the Benishangul-Gumuz region, but the challenges are more or less the same in other regions and thus the study has implications for other regions.

4. FEDERALISM AND THE TREATMENT OF MINORITIES IN THE REGIONS: THE BENISHANGUL GUMUZ CASE

4.1. The Notions of Ethnic Majority and Minority in Ethiopia

From the decade of federal experience, it can be observed that one major challenge the Ethiopian federal system is facing relates to the issue of local tyranny at constituent unit level. Traditionally, federal systems regulate relations between the federal government and the states. Despite recent developments in some federations on the status of local governments,[124] the tradition has been that local governments are at the discretion of regional states. In multicultural federations, this raises the thorny issue of the position of minorities within each respective regional state.

The notion of majority and minority in the Ethiopian federal context is indeed confusing. One possible approach to understand it is to figure out its meaning at federal and state levels. If majority is understood to be a numerical majority dominating a certain political process, then at federal level none of the nation-

[122] Medhane Tadesse and J.Young, TPLF: Reform or Decline?, 30(97) *Review of African Political Economy* 401 (2003).

[123] Hoekema states that the system allows for a system of legal pluralism that is the coexistence of not only formal laws but also Islamic law and customary law, for instance. Hoekema, *supra* note 69, 2-3.

[124] See Basic Law of Germany Article 28; Swiss Constitution Article 50.

alities taken alone constitute a majority. In principle the constitution appears to transform every nationality into a majority by granting a 'mother state' or local government but that applies only to some of the dominant ethnic groups. The Oromo constitute the largest ethnic group but they are by far less than fifty per cent of the total Ethiopian population. Perhaps the absence of such a numerical majority that dominates the political process at the centre can explain the persisting regime instability, the interethnic tension and rivalry for exclusive control of power.

At constituent unit level, two contradictory notions of majority and minority are emerging. In the states of Oromia, Amhara, Tigray, Afar and Somali, five out of the nine regional states, the ethnic groups to which the regional names refer dominate the political process in their respective states. Other ethnic groups in each of these regions are, therefore, minorities. However, these contextually defined majorities will become minorities in other regional states. Another dimension emerging in the city state of Harar and in Gambella and Benishangul-Gumuz states is that the numerical majority remains a political minority in terms of its influence in the regional political process. In the state of Harar, the Harari, constituting only 7% of the total population in the region play a key role compared to the other ethnic groups living in the region. In Gambella, despite some controversy over figures, the Nuer stand to be numerically greater than their rivals, the Anuak, but the latter, at least until 2003, have dominated the region's political process since 1991. The same holds true for the Benishangul-Gumuz state. While the Berta remain numerically larger than the Gumuz, the latter dominate the political process in the region. In these three cases, therefore, the notion of majority and minority seems to have been reversed from the ordinary understanding of the concepts.[125]

In this context, the danger is that the respective regional states and the dominant ethnic groups consider themselves 'owners' of the 'mother state'. Other citizens of different ethnic background or those who do not like to associate themselves with any ethnic group have practically no place, which certainly contradicts the constitutional provisions that stipulate the right to work and live in a place of one's choice. In this respect, frequent conflicts between the Oromo and minority Amhara living in Oromia region have led to loss of life and destruction of property at different times. The crisis in Gambella and the tension in Benishangul-Gumuz, and partly in Harar and Oromia, with respect

[125] Another notion of minority can be observed in relation to the composition of the House of Peoples' Representatives and the House of the Federation: out of 547 representatives in the HoPR 20 seats are allocated for special representation of minority groups. A single seat in the HoPR represents an electoral constituency with a population of roughly 100,000 and implicitly, minority refers to those groups whose population is less than 100,000. In the case of the HoF each nation, nationality and people has one representative for each one million of its population, but even those who constitute less than one million do have one representative. Hence an ethnic group that constitutes less than one million people could also be considered a minority.

to the individual citizen's right to live and work in a place of one's choice, is not because of constitutional form but because of failure to enforce constitutionally stipulated principles. The constitution is clear in stating that every Ethiopian has the right to engage freely in any economic activity and to pursue a livelihood of his/her choice anywhere within the national territory.[126] The constitution does impose an obligation on all branches of government at both levels to respect and enforce the fundamental rights and freedoms enshrined in it. Yet these provisions seem to have been overshadowed in practice by the emphasis on self-rule and collective rights. Nor are the necessary institutions for enforcing human rights well entrenched.[127]

Thus in the five regional states with dominant nationalities, the dominant nationalities constitute a majority in their respective states and any one other than them is a minority. In the three remaining constituent states, the situation is slightly different from that in the other regional states. What is distinct in these regional states is the fact that the tyranny arises from a minority against the majority. Particularly precarious cases have arisen in the last decade or so in Gambella and Benishangul-Gumuz regional states.[128]

4.2. The Tension between the Berta and Gumuz

The tension in Benishangul-Gumuz regional state has two aspects. There is tension between the Gumuz and Berta on the one hand and on the other hand tension has arisen between the indigenous ethnic groups (mainly Berta, Gumuz, Shinasha, Komo and Mao) and highlanders who moved to the region during the resettlement programme of the *Derg* in the 1980s. According to the 1994 census, out of the region's total population of 460,459 (see table below), the largest communities are the Muslim Berta constituting 26.7% and the mixed religion Gumuz constituting 23.4% of the regional population. Hence, together they constitute about half of the population of Benishangul/Gumuz. In addition there are smaller indigenous communities of Shinasha (32,000), Komo and Mao. Secondly, the region has Amhara, Oromo, Tigrayan and other nationalities approximately constituting 47% of the population in the region.

---

[126] Article 41.

[127] Some have warned that "*In interethnic relations, therefore, the convenient democratic game of numbers - majoritarian decision-making in the framework of a broad consensus - does not work since the unalterable power symmetry between permanent majority and permanent minorities impedes the formation of a consensual community.*" E. Keller and B. Thomas-Woolley, Majority Rule and Minority Rights: American Federalism and African Experience, 32(3) *Journal of Modern African Studies* 413 (1994). Laws establishing the institutions of Human Rights Commission and Ombudsman were enacted a long time ago but it took more than four years to set up the institutions. The judiciary has not yet been able to deal with human rights issues satisfactorily.

[128] From a population size of 131,000, the Harari constitute only 7%. However, key political issues in the region are decided by the Harari. The Oromo have some say but other ethnic groups can only vote and are not eligible for office.

Nationalities in the region	population size from a total population of the region 460,000	percentage	Representation in the 2000-2005 Regional Council (total seats: 80)
Berta	122,883	26.7%	28
Gumuz	107,495	23.4%	35
Shinasha	32,105		6
Mao	2,732		2
Komo	1,109		2
others (Amhara, Oromo, Agew, Tigrayans...)	194,135	47%	7

Source: 1994 Central Statistical Authority and Interview

As far as the indigenous groups are concerned, while the Muslim Berta are relatively larger in number than the Gumuz, the Gumuz seem to dominate the political dynamic in the region. In a manner similar to what happened in other parts of the country during the *Derg* and thereafter, dissidents in Benishangul-Gumuz who opposed the *Derg* but later could not resist its might, escaped to the Sudan. They were mainly dominated by the Berta, with a small representation from the Gumuz, and were able to establish with the assistance of the Sudanese, the Benishangul Peoples Liberation Movement (BPLM).[129]

During the transition, while the OLF had had some control over the region and had suppressed the BPLM, the defeat of the OLF left the BPLM in a dominant position in the region. BPLM support derived almost entirely from the Berta people and as a result other indigenous communities began to establish their own parties and to make demands. From its inception the BPLM has been based on an uneasy coalition of contending factions, in part due to competitions over access to the rewards of office, but also due to ideological factors related to the Sudanese government's influence to mobilize substantial numbers of Muslims based on religion.[130]

The relationship with the Sudanese National Islamic Front (NIF) of Sudan and Islamic influences led to a strong federal intervention in the region and to the 1996 *gimgema* (evaluation) in which the federal government dismissed the entire Berta dominated regional government. Since then the BPLM acquired a new leadership, became secular and renamed itself the Ethiopian Berta Democratic organization.[131] Top leaders have been kept in prison and the present chairman Yaregal Aysheshim (Gumuz) has held office since 1995. The shift in

[129] For more on the political development in this region see Young, *supra* note 61, 325.
[130] Id., 333.
[131] Id., 336.

power certainly was clear after the 1996 *gimgema* in which the Berta were blamed for allying with the NIF. Since then (until 2001), as can be observed from the table above, power seems to have shifted to the Gumuz. The Berta simply saw the post 1995 development as a shift of alliance by the federal government from the Berta to the Gumuz. They particularly requested the House of the Federation (HoF), the regional President and the Secretary to be from the Berta nationality and the number of zones and *woreda* to be redrawn taking into account the size of the population and the contribution in the struggle to overthrow the Military regime.

However, in mid-June 2002, the HoF had to deal with the tension between the two while at the same time it was adjudicating the case between the highlanders and the indigenous population. Towards the end of August of 2003, the HoF was able to reach a certain proposal acceptable to the contending parties representing the Berta and the Gumuz, which finally led to a proportional representation of all the groups in the regional government and the redrawing of zones/Special *Woreda* ensuring self-rule and fair allocation of resources to these units.[132]

4.3. The Tension between the Berta-Gumuz versus the "Highlanders"

The second aspect of the tension in this region is between the indigenous groups and the highlanders. Candidates from Amhara, Oromo and Tigray nationalities for the 2000 election for the regional council were prohibited on the basis that they were not able to speak any one of the five indigenous languages namely Berta, Gumuz, Shinasha, Komo and Mao. Particularly the Berta insisted that the candidates should not be allowed to run for office if none of them were versed in the Berta language. It accordingly petitioned the Election Board and the latter decided to bar the highlanders from running as candidates stating that they were not able to speak the Berta language. The Amhara, Oromo and Tigrayans, most of them transferred to the region during the *Derg's* resettlement programme and constituting some 47% of the population in the region, submitted a complaint to the House of the Federation (HoF) against the decision of the Electoral Board on *Yekatit* 10, 1992 E.C. (February 2000). The applicants argued that the decision of the Board violated their constitutional right to be elected granted to every citizen without any discrimination and asked the House to quash the decision as it contravened the supremacy clause of the federal constitution (Article 9).

The Council of Constitutional Inquiry (CCI) gave its opinion on *Sene* 29, 1992 (June 2000) to the HoF admitting that the application raised constitutional in-

[132] See the Memorandum of Understanding Between the leaders of Berta and Gumuz, Shinasha, Mao/Komo, end of August 2003 (unpublished in the archives of the HoF).

terpretation questions. The expert opinion constitutes a majority opinion and a dissenting one. The issues formulated were: as to whether the law[133] which sets the conditions for candidature, one of which is knowledge of the vernacular of the state, was in violation of the constitution or not and as to whether the decision of the Electoral Board based on such law was constitutional or not.[134] The majority, after considering the relevant law and the constitution,[135] rather briefly opined that because the proclamation stated knowledge of the local language as a condition for candidacy, it violated the constitutional provision on the right to take part in the conduct of public affairs as well as on the right to be elected. It stated that the proclamation discriminates against those who are not versed in one of the local vernaculars and concluded the proclamation violated the constitution. In a nutshell, the majority focused on the non-discrimination clause of the constitution (Article 25).[136] On the Board's decision, the majority opinion stated that it was based on this unconstitutional provision and because the law is referred to the HoF the viability of the decision hinges on the constitutionality or unconstitutionality of the proclamation referred to the HoF.

The minority view is more elaborate and is mainly based on the constitutional argument that the issue has to be seen in light of the letter and spirit of the whole constitutional text rather than in light of a single provision and a balance is needed between two or more competing constitutional values.[137] The minority acknowledged that there is an express clause on the right to elect and to be elected as well as the fact that the constitution does not allow discrimination on the basis of language. However, it articulated that in this case there was no

---

[133] The law in question is the Proclamation to make the Electoral Law of Ethiopia conform with the Constitution of the Federal Democratic Republic of Ethiopia Proc. No. 111/1995, *Negarit Gazeta* TGE, 54th year, No. 9 Addis Ababa, 23 February 1995.

[134] See the opinion of the CCI (unpublished).

[135] Article 38(1) of the federal constitution states "*every Ethiopian national, without any discrimination based on colour, race, nation, nationality, sex, language, religion, political or other opinion or other status has the following rights:*

a. To take part in the conduct of public affairs, directly and through freely chosen representatives,

b. On the attainment of 18 years of age to vote in accordance with law,

c. To vote and to be elected at periodic election to any office at any level of government."

While Article 38 of Proclamation 111/1995 stating the criteria on candidacy states: 1. Any person registered as an elector shall be eligible for candidature where he…

b. is versed in the vernacular of the national region of his intended candidature and the Amharic version states Y*e Miwedaderbetin Ye Biherawi Kilil Kuanka Ye Mi Yawik.*

[136] Although the majority of the CCI did not state it so, this approach of constitutional interpretation is what is commonly known in the United States constitutional discourse as clause bound textualism, which merely focuses on the parts without looking at the whole. See for example Murphy et al, *American Constitutional Interpretation* 387, 2nd ed. (Westbury, NY: Foundation Press, 1995).

[137] The position of the minority is also frequently employed in the United States constitutional discourse and is referred to as structural textualism that examines the relationship between the parts and the whole of the text in order to understand the constitution. See Murphy et al. cited above p. 387.

discrimination on the basis of language and considered the decision of the Board not in violation of the constitution. It stated that the proclamation does not discriminate on the basis of language. In much the same way as in the Oromia, Amhara or Tigray regional states, that is constituent states in which the regional official language is the language of the dominant nationality, anyone who is not versed in the regional government's official language cannot run for office as a candidate. By the same analogy, anyone who does not speak any of the local vernacular languages in Benishangul-Gumuz, whatever his or her nationality may be, cannot run for office and the minority view insisted that this cannot be considered a violation of the constitution on grounds of discrimination. The minority focused on the peculiarity of the Ethiopian federal system and its emphasis on the sovereignty of nationalities and the fact that language constitutes one essential attribute of identity.

The HoF considered both opinions but rendered a different decision, which was more in line with the opinion of the minority than with that of the majority.[138] It emphasized that there is no doubt that if the candidate is to speak for the people he/she claims to represent in parliament or to introduce his/her aims and programmes to the electorate, he/she is required to know the regional official language. By virtue of the proclamation, the candidate is required to know the official language of the *region* and to that extent the proclamation does not contradict the principles of the constitution. On the other hand, the House found the Board's interpretation of the proclamation to mean that a candidate should be versed in any of the indigenous languages, particularly the Berta language, one of the five languages spoken in the region that is not the official language of the regional state, unconstitutional and declared it null with prospective effect. Of interest in this regard is the fact that because of the multi-ethnic nature of the regional state and because Amharic is widely spoken by a large majority of the people in the region, the regional Council has adopted Amharic as the official language.[139]

---

[138] See decision of the HoF of *Megabit* 5, 1995 E.C. (March 2003) that in a nutshell upheld the law as constitutional but declared the decision of the Board as unconstitutional and hence of no effect with prospective effect. It articulated that Article 38 of the proclamation is not in violation of Article 38 of the constitution. It also underscored that whoever wants to run as a candidate is required to know the working language of the *regional state, and not one of the local vernaculars* (unpublished).

[139] See Article 6(1) Of Proc. No. 31/2002 of the Revised Constitution of the Benishangul-Gumuz Regional State. Nevertheless the decision of the HoF was not effectively implemented as the Benishangul Gumuz Peoples' Democratic Unity Front (mainly backed by the Berta) requested the HoF for reconsideration and the latter acknowledged that the implementation of the decision requires further restructuring of some *woreda* and this in itself needed recent population census. Thus, it has to wait until the new census result that was held in 2007 is released.

Comment

It is easier to start with the expert opinion of the CCI majority. They emphasized the constitutional provision of the right of the citizen to elect and to be elected and the principle of non-discrimination stipulated in the same text. According to the majority it does not matter whether the candidate who is elected in the regional council speaks or understands the local vernacular. The candidate has the right to be elected and cannot be prohibited because he/she does not speak the language. This opinion misses the fundamental virtue of not only the Ethiopian Constitution, which is apparently based on the free will of nationalities, but also of the values of federalism, i.e. unity in diversity. The nationalities are declared sovereign under the Ethiopian Constitution and constituent states are established to empower at least some of the major nationalities to have their own 'mother' states, the right to administer themselves, to use their own language and even to secede. In multicultural federations in as much as we need to have a politically and economically integrated society, we also have to respect and promote diversity. The crucial issue is to draw a balance between the two.

The minority opinion, even though it emphasized the importance of investigating the whole text and the fact that the nationalities are considered the building bricks of the federation, did not emphasize, in contrast with the decision of the HoF, that what is required under the proclamation is the candidate's knowledge of the working language of the regional state, and not of any of the local vernaculars. But in doing so the minority has touched upon one of the thorny issues in the federal system to which neither the majority nor the HoF was able to provide an answer. Could one really argue with a lot of emphasis that a candidate cannot run for office as long as she/he cannot understand even one of the local languages? Would it be possible to give an affirmative answer to this question under the constitution or should these multi-ethnic regions be subject to a different treatment: the endogenous groups of these regions do not have their own regional governments and because many ethnic groups are living there they had to adopt Amharic for communication and because of this highlanders are not required to know any of the local vernaculars. This raises the central issue of the dilemma in the federal system;[140] on the one hand declaring the equality of states and nationalities whereas on the other hand only some nationalities have their own constituent states. Those who do not have their own constituent states cannot impose the language requirement on candidates as is the case in other regional states, for example Amhara, Somali, Oromia and Tigray. This is a question that opens Pandora's Box.

---

[140] This dilemma is clear under Article 47, which recognizes only nine members of the federation, while in fact there are more than eighty ethnic groups and secondly there is the dilemma that we are noting in this section: ethnic versus multicultural federation.

There are two options here. One may be tempted to state that if in the states of Amhara, Oromia, Afar, Tigray and Somali knowing a local language is a requirement to run for public office, there is no reason to deny multi-ethnic regions the same right. It is not because the endogenous groups of these regions do not have their own constituent state that they should be subjected to different treatment. Otherwise a clear constitutional asymmetry is going to evolve between those nationalities that have their own 'mother states' and those that do not. Or should we simply reiterate that after all, the constitution has made that asymmetry clear by recognizing only nine constituent states with its own implications?[141]

A related argument can be deduced from the federal constitution. Given the position of the nationalities within the constitution, formally speaking, the Ethiopian state seems closer to a confederation than a federation. The constitution emphasizes the sovereignty of nationalities and grants nationalities the right to self-determination, secession included; there is no federal supremacy clause unlike in many other federal constitutions. It appears that the nationalities are considered as building bricks, as if they preceded the federation. All this taken together seems to indicate that at the time of the federal bargain, the forces of diversity prevailed over the forces of unity whereas in many working federations one finds a balance in which forces of unity slightly prevail over the forces of diversity. If this argument is pushed further then it may imply that the constitution has taken a position as far as the tension between collective versus individual rights is concerned, in favour of the former. If so, the decision of the Electoral Board, however absurd it may be in creating 'small islands' everywhere, forcing every citizen to find out where his 'mother state' is, could be justified.
This is, however, contrary to the political and economic integration envisaged by the federal constitution. In the Preamble it is stated "*We, the nations, nationalities and peoples of Ethiopia: strongly committed, to* building a political community *founded on the rule of law.... Convinced that to live* as one economic community *is necessary in order to create sustainable and mutually supportive conditions...have, therefore, adopted this Constitution through representatives we have duly elected for this purpose as an instrument that binds us in mutual commitment to fulfil the objectives and the principles set forth above.*" Thus, it is a clear political and economic integration that the federation envisages. It is good to note the emphasis given to the free movement of labour and capital across the country as a means to enhance this project in a re-

[141] His Excellency Dr. Gebreab, Minister of State at the Ministry of Federal Affairs, speaks of "minority states", in reference to these multi-ethnic states, particularly Harari, Gambella and Benishangul-Gumuz states, in which the numerical minority is permitted to dominate the local political process, as the consequence of the inherent feature of the federal system. Speech made at the First National Conference on Federalism, Conflict and Peace Building, Addis Ababa, 5-7 May 2003.

cent federal document.[142] Seen from this angle, the minority opinion is extreme.

Another argument against the minority opinion could be deduced from the constitution. The constitution has for one reason or another made a choice (Article 46). By outlining only nine member states, it seems to have defined what constitutes majority and minority nationalities. One can then conclude that the language test under Article 38 of the proclamation is only applicable to those states defined under Articles 46 and 47 and not to other states. Lastly, the position of the minority in the Council of Constitutional Inquiry'(CCI)s decision not only enhances majority-minority tension but goes even further and creates minority tyranny over majority in some of the constituent states. The CCI minority by adopting such a position closes its eyes to the rights of other Ethiopians who were forcefully resettled in the region during the *Derg* era and to the rights of economic migrants. Yet, the decision of the HoF skilfully escapes this thorny issue by focusing on the technical interpretation of the provisions of the proclamation without substantively addressing the concerns of the indigenous ethnic groups.

While the analysis is based on a single case, there are ample indications of this kind of tension and threat to minorities in several parts of the country. On several occasions (between 2005 and 2006) the author has observed a high sense of insecurity felt by minorities in Oromia (Jimma area) and SNNPRS, so much so that the minorities have started to remit the income they generate from their business to places of their ethnic origin. Further confusion to this delicate position of minorities arises from the constitutional clauses of some of the regions, issued after the decision of the HoF, that further relegate the status of minorities to second rate citizenship. For example, Article 34 of both the Revised Benishangul Gumuz Regional Constitution and that of Gambella, distinct from what is provided in other state constitutions, only ensure the right of minorities to work and live and do not provide for the right to elect and to be elected.[143] The practice combined with such constitutional anomaly simply indicates how difficult the position of the minorities is in some regions.

4.4. The Way Forward

From the discussion of the Benishangul-Gumuz case two conclusions seem to be inescapable. Firstly, there is obvious tension between a constitutional form implying multicultural federalism in which the forging of unity from diversity is the goal, and as some critics indicate an 'ethnic' federal system in operation. Ethnicity is a state of mind emanating from a feeling of separate identity,

[142] See *Be Ethiopia Ye Democrasiyawi Sirat Ginbata Gudayoch*, Ginbot 1994 E.C. (Addis Ababa, Ministry of Information): 32-35; 169, 180, 207, 214.

[143] The state constitutions of Amhara and Tigray for example ensure the right of minorities not only to work and live but also to elect and to be elected. See the respective constitutions Article 38.

which in turn is based on shared cultural markers (culture, language, religion, etc.), but more importantly on the myth of common descent. It is important to point out that the myth of common descent is an essential characteristic of an ethnic group but not of national groups that share a common language, religion, custom, history and tradition but not necessarily a common descent. The subjective belief in the myth of common descent is in short the essence of an ethnic group or ethnicity.[144] This is not without some implications when it is mobilized to attain certain goals. The myth of common descent serves as a basis for excluding people who share the culture but not common descent or in the opposite case to include people who share common descent but not culture.[145] If we uphold the ethnic notion briefly considered here, it appears that a large number of Ethiopians are by and large excluded from some aspects of the regional political process. The case is a living example of the ambiguities and tensions inherent in the federal system: not clear is which way the federal system is evolving.

Secondly, as long as federalism is viewed as a means of sharing power and resources among contenders and a means for accommodation of diversity and peaceful coexistence of diverse groups in multicultural federations, the case hints that there is failure on both counts. We observe not only the lack of consensus on power and resource sharing among the indigenous groups but also the exclusion of 47% of the region's population from the political process.

One possible solution is the setting up of two chambers at state level, one composed on the basis of the democratic principle (population size or one man, one vote) and another house for the protection of local minorities. Both houses should have law making powers and the second chamber could even be granted veto power on some crucial issues of prime importance to minorities.[146] Secondly, the federal executive, the federal and state judiciary and the institutions of Human Rights Commission and Ombudsman have to be well organized throughout the country if the bulk of human rights provisions enshrined in the constitution are to be enforced in a meaningful manner. This is perhaps the only way to guarantee interstate mobility of labour and capital. Besides, as in Benishangul-Gumuz and certainly other multiethnic regional states, genuine power and resource sharing among the contenders for power seems the only viable solution to bring stability to the regions. As already indicated, the approach so far has not been satisfactory to the major contenders for power in each of the respective regions. The federal government simply shifted its alliance from one group to another without trying to provide a solu-

---

[144] Chaim Gans, *The Limits of Nationalism* 10 (Cambridge: Cambridge University Press, 2003); James Kellas, *The Politics of Nationalism and Ethnicity* 51 (London: Macmillan, 1991).
[145] Chaim, *supra* note 144, 28.
[146] Indeed the Revised Constitution of the Benishangul-Gumuz Region, Articles 74-82, stipulate about the Nationality Council but this Council simply strengthens the position of the indigenous nationalities rather than the disenfranchised/excluded groups.

tion acceptable to all groups. Federalism's role in regulating conflicts in multicultural societies depends on whether the actors in the political process intend to use federalism to achieve those goals.

At national level, the rather exemplary and generous federal system is operating in relatively less favourable socio-economic and political conditions on the ground. As observed from the politics of the early 1970s and following the May 2005 election, two threats seem to be recurring. One is the lack of consensus on the federal option partly resulting from an incomplete process of transition and partly from an authoritarian, uncompromising and rigid political culture within the political elite. The second as already hinted at is the political culture. Both combined made the transition to democracy more challenging and protracted.

3. The Cassation Powers of the Federal Supreme Court of the Federal Democratic Republic of Ethiopia

Amha Tesfaye•

1. INTRODUCTION

The Constitution of the Federal Democratic Republic of Ethiopia (hereinafter referred to as the "FDRE Constitution")[1] has established federal courts and state courts. The FDRE Constitution apportions judicial powers between the federal courts and the state courts. Both have separate judicial powers and, as a matter of principle, one cannot interfere within the jurisdiction of the other. By the same token, neither is superior nor subordinate to the other.

The objective of this paper is to discuss the cassation powers of the federal Supreme Court of Ethiopia. To be more precise, special emphasis is given to issues that relate to the division of powers between the federal and state courts in relation to cassation. It also aims to provoke further discussions on the topic. As it is clearly stipulated in the federal constitution both the federal and state courts do have cassation powers on matters falling within their jurisdiction. However, identifying the limits of the cassation power of the federal Supreme Court is a very delicate constitutional issue that requires close scrutiny and understanding of the context of the constitution as a whole. The fact of the matter is that some of the constitutional provisions that deal with the relationship of the cassation power of the federal Supreme Court and the state Supreme Courts are either over generalized or vague. Indeed, they need interpretations and clarifications. Thus the topic in this paper is worthy of academic discussion.

2. OVERVIEW OF THE COURT STRUCTURE IN ETHIOPIA

The Constitution of the Federal Democratic Republic of Ethiopia has established a federal state and has divided state powers between the federal government and the member states of the federation. The FDRE Constitution has vested legislative, executive and judicial powers both in the federal govern-

---

• LLM Ghent University.

[1] The Constitution of the Federal Democratic Republic of Ethiopia was ratified by the Constitutional Assembly on 8 December 1994. The constitution has come into full force and effect as of 21 August 1995. The whole text of the constitution can be found in the Federal Negarit Gazeta, 1st year No.1.

ment and the member states.[2] As a result, judicial powers are given to the courts at the federal and state levels.[3]

As a matter of principle, federal and state powers, including judicial powers, are defined by the FDRE Constitution. The constitution expressly obliges the states to respect the powers of the federal government and *vice versa*.[4] In general, be it that this is not free from criticism, one can argue that the FDRE Constitution has established parallel courts as it is the case in ideal federalism. "*If the federal principle were to be strictly applied, one would expect a dual system to be established in a federation, with one set of courts to apply and interpret the law of the central government, and another to apply and interpret the laws of each state.*"[5] However, the mere fact that a country adopted a federal system does not in any way imply that it has a parallel court structure. For instance, in Germany, the Lander Courts are not parallel to the Federal Courts in the strict application of the term.[6]

The above mentioned constitutional principle and the related constitutional rules embodied in the FDRE Constitution, as well as the subsequent legislation reveal the horizontal division of judicial powers between the federal and state courts and the vertical or hierarchical division of powers within both the federal and state courts.

The FDRE Constitution establishes the federal Supreme Court. Besides, it empowers the federal House of Peoples' Representatives to establish, nationwide or in some parts of the country only, the federal High Court and First Instance Courts.[7] Article 78(2) of the FDRE Constitution states:

"*Supreme Federal judicial authority is vested in the Federal Supreme Court. The House of Peoples' Representatives may, by two-thirds majority vote, establish nationwide, or in some parts of the country only, the Federal High Court and First Instance Courts it deemed necessary. Unless decided in this manner, the jurisdictions of the Federal High Court and of the First Instance Courts are hereby delegated to the State Courts.*"

As a result, the federal House of Peoples' Representatives enacted Proclamation No.25/1996. The Proclamation establishes and determines the jurisdiction

---

[2] See, Chapter five of the FDRE Constitution, particularly Article 50. Art. 50(1) and (2) reads: "*1. The Federal democratic Republic of Ethiopia comprises the Federal Government and the State members.*
2. The Federal Government and the states shall have legislative, executive and judicial powers."

[3] Articles 50(7) and 79(1) of the Ethiopian Federal Constitution.

[4] Article 50(8) of the Ethiopian Federal Constitution.

[5] B.O. Nwabueze, *The Machinery of Justice in Nigeria* 82 (London: Butterworths, 1963).

[6] P.B. Kurland and R. Lerner, *The Founders' Constitution* (Chicago: the University of Chicago press, 1987).

[7] Article 78(2) of the Ethiopian Federal Constitution.

of the federal courts.[8] The FDRE Constitution further obliges the member states to establish a state Supreme Court, High Court and First Instance Courts.[9] All of the member states have already established their own courts in accordance with the federal constitution and the state constitutions. Having said this about the general structure of the Ethiopian courts, the next section discusses the meaning and nature of cassation. The extent of the cassation power of the federal Supreme Court, particularly whether it has cassation power over state matters or not, will be discussed in the later sections.

3. THE CONCEPT OF CASSATION

To begin with the origin and literal meaning of the word 'cassation', it originates from the Latin word 'cassare' and it refers to the judicial power to quash the force and validity of a final judgment.[10] The literal meaning of the word, however, tells us very little about the nature of this important legal instrument. Indeed, cassation is quite a crucial and indispensable procedural instrument mainly in civil law countries. The institution that administers cassation and the contents of cassation powers differ from one legal system to the other partly because of historical reasons and partly because of the difference in policy considerations employed by their respective legislature. Thus, to study each country's pertinent legislation is a prerequisite to fully understanding the nature of cassation in the given country. There are commonalities though.

Generally speaking, cassation is a system of review. At the same time, it is different from the other systems of review like appeal and revision. For instance, in France and Italy cassation courts have the power to quash final judgments of courts that have an error of law. Then, they do not determine the case by themselves; rather they refer the case for final determination to an appellate court other than that which rendered the quashed judgment. In Italy, for instance:

"*If the court finds that errors of law did exist in the trial and that these errors were prejudicial to the appellant, it quashes the judgment below. The case is then remanded to another court, usually at the same levels as the court that gave the quashed decision, for retrial in accordance with the principles announced in the court of cassation's opinion.*"[11]

On the other hand, different legal systems have their own institutions to determine cassation matters. The French 'Cour De Cassation', the Belgian 'Hof

---

[8] See the Federal Courts Proclamation No.25/1996, *Federal Negarit Gazeta*, 2nd year No.13.
[9] Article 78 (3) of the Ethiopian Federal Constitution.
[10] B. A. Garner, *Black's Law Dictionary*, 7th ed. (Saint Paul: West publishing co., 1999).
[11] A. Engelmann et al, *A History of Continental Civil Procedure* (Boston: Little, Brown and Company, 1927). See also J.H. Merryman and V. Vigoriti, When Courts Collide: Constitution and Cassation in Italy, 15(4) *The American Journal of Comparative Law* 669 (1966).

Van Cassatie', the Dutch 'Hoge Raad' can be cited as examples.[12] In Ethiopia, the federal and state Supreme Courts have cassation powers as it is stipulated in Article 80(3) of the FDRE Constitution. We do not have separate cassation courts in Ethiopia. Instead, the Supreme Courts have cassation divisions that are composed of the Supreme Court judges.

Since both the federal and state courts have cassation powers, one has to look at the basic laws of each level of court to see how the cassation courts are organized in a given court. For example, according to Federal Courts Proclamation No. 25/1996, Article 21(2)(c) cassation matters shall be heard by a division with not less than 5 judges of the Supreme Court.

As regards the objective of cassation powers, it is a procedural mechanism by which the court internally controls itself in order to guarantee the correct application and uniform interpretation of laws. For instance, in Italy, "*the fundamental purpose of the court of cassation as stated in Article 65 of the Ordinamento Givdizianio, the law that governs court organization in Italy, is to assure 'correct observance and uniform interpretation of the law'*."[13] Similarly, in France, "*the Cour De Cassation...was established to ensure the correct application of the legislation in force, and to preserve its uniformity.*"[14] Nowadays, the Cour de Cassation gives more emphasis to the uniform application of laws.[15]

In Ethiopia, cassation is different from the other forms of review like appeal. It is not only different though; there are also very stringent requirements for its application. According to the FDRE Constitution, first and foremost the Supreme Courts need to establish the existence of a 'basic error of law' in order to exercise cassation power.[16] Thus, it is employed in order to secure the uniformity of the basic laws only.

4. THE CASSATION JURISDICTION OF THE FEDERAL SUPREME COURT

Historically speaking, the concept of cassation is not introduced in Ethiopia for the first time by the FDRE Constitution. Nevertheless, the history of the cassation power that used to exist before the adoption of the FRDE Constitution

---

[12] See also S.M.F. Geeroms, Comparative Law and Legal Translation: Why the terms Cassation, Revision and Appeal should not be translated, 50 *The American Journal of Comparative Law* 204 (2002).

[13] J. H. Merryman and V. Vigoriti, When Courts Collide: Constitution and Cassation in Italy, 15(4) *The American Journal of Comparative Law* 669 (1966).

[14] Geeroms, *supra* note 12, 205.

[15] Id., 206.

[16] Article 80(3) of the Ethiopian Federal Constitution.

goes beyond the scope of this paper. The pertinent provisions in the FDRE Constitution and Federal Courts Proclamation No.25/1996 are the legal basis for the discussion of the cassation powers of the federal Supreme Court. On top of that, Article 80 of the FDRE Constitution is the linchpin to determine the extent of the cassation powers of the federal Supreme Court.

The FDRE Constitution vested the federal Supreme Court with the highest and final judicial power over federal matters.[17] Similarly, as it is stated in Article 80(3)(a), "*the Federal Supreme Court has a power of cassation over any final decision containing a basic error of law. Particulars shall be determined by law.*" Consequently, the federal House of Peoples' Representatives enacted the details in Federal Courts Proclamation No.25/1996. Accordingly, Article 10 reads:

"*Powers of cassation of the Federal Supreme Court:*
In cases where they contain fundamental error of law, the Federal Supreme Court, shall have the power of cassation over:

1) *final decisions of the Federal High Court rendered in its appellate jurisdiction;*
2) *final decisions of the regular division of the Federal Supreme Court;*
3) *final decisions of the Regional Supreme Court rendered as a regular division or in its appellate jurisdiction.*"[18]

The above-mentioned provisions raise some technical and legal questions, like what is the meaning of "error of law"? And which one is "basic" and which one is 'not basic'? Nevertheless, most of such issues go beyond the scope of this paper. The focus of this paper is to determine the extent of the scope of the cassation powers of the federal Supreme Court. Specifically, the discussion is focused on the issue whether the federal Supreme Court has cassation powers over originally state matters. Put differently, whether the state Supreme Courts have exclusive judicial jurisdiction over state matters is the core issue to be resolved.

The literal reading of the above mentioned provisions in the FDRE Constitution and Proclamation No.25/1996 apparently gives the impression that the federal Supreme Court is authorized to hear and determine state matters in its cassation jurisdiction, provided that the final judgment contains at least one basic error of law. However, the issue is far more complicated than it appears. The fact that the state courts are delegated to hear and determine federal matters and that the state Supreme Courts have cassation powers on state matters, are some of the points that contribute to the complication of the issue. Furthermore, the context that the FDRE Constitution apportions power between

[17] Article 80(1) of the Ethiopian Federal Constitution.
[18] Federal Courts Proclamation No.25/1996, Art.10.

the federal and state entities and the use of words/terms in Article 80 of the constitution by itself can be taken as other complicating factors. Although one can argue that the practice of courts does not have the power to abrogate laws in Ethiopia, undoubtedly the current practice of the federal Supreme Court has also a significant impact on the development of the national jurisprudence on the issue. Therefore, to decide whether the constitution recognizes cassation over cassation has far-reaching constitutional and procedural implications.

To begin with the constitution itself, there is no doubt that it empowers the federal Supreme Court and the state Supreme Courts with cassation jurisdiction on federal and state matters respectively.[19] When the constitution determined the judicial power of the federal Supreme Court, it vested the Court with the highest and final judicial power over federal matters. Similarly, it uses the same loaded words, i.e. highest and final, when it determines the judicial powers of the state Supreme Courts. Article 80(1) and (2) states:

"*1. The Federal Supreme Court shall have the highest and final judicial power over Federal matters.*
2. State Supreme Courts shall have the highest and final judicial power over state matters. They shall also exercise the jurisdiction of the Federal High court."

The constitution uses exactly the same words to describe the extent of the powers of the Supreme Courts on the different levels. Thus, it affirms the fact that one is neither superior nor subordinate to the other. That means that, as a matter of principle, the two levels of courts are parallel to each other. Moreover, it conveys the message that the federal courts are categorically excluded from interfering with purely state judicial matters.

However, the wording and spirit of the next Sub-Article, i.e. Sub-Article 3 of Article 80, raises the question as to whether the cassation power of the federal Supreme Court is an exception to this general principle or not. Sub-Article 3 reads:

"*Notwithstanding the Provisions of Sub-Article 1 and 2 of this Article;*
- *(a) The Federal Supreme Court has a power of cassation over any final court decision containing a basic error of law. Particulars shall be determined by law.*
- *(b) The state Supreme Court has power of cassation over any final court decision on state matters which contains a basic error of law. Particulars shall be determined by law.*"

[19] Article 80 of the Ethiopian Federal Constitution.

It has to be underlined that Sub-Article 3 is not only a special provision; it may also be taken as an exception to the general rule in Sub-Article 1. When the constitution determines the cassation power of the federal Supreme Court, it expressly gives the Court the cassation power over "any final court" decision. This seems to imply that it has also cassation power over final decisions of state Supreme Courts.

The FDRE Constitution, Articles 78(2) and 80(2) + (4), delegated state Supreme Courts and state High Courts the jurisdictions of the federal High Court and of the federal First Instance Courts respectively. Article 78(2) also empowers the federal House of Peoples' Representatives to establish nationwide, or in some parts of the country only, the federal High Courts and First-Instance Courts it deems necessary. So far, the House of Peoples' Representatives has established federal first-Instance Courts only in the cities of Addis Ababa and Dire Dawa, which do not have statehood status. Federal High Courts have recently been established in five of the nine regions (Gambella, Benishangul/Gumuz, Afar, Somali and the Southern region). This implies that in many cases the regional state courts are still exercising federal jurisdiction by delegation. As it is recorded in the minutes of the Constitutional Assembly, the reasons for the constitutional delegation were practical considerations about the financial expenses and lack of adequately trained manpower to maintain two separate levels of courts in a given state.

So taking the principle of delegation as a background, if the application of the cassation power of the federal Supreme Court is limited to matters that are tried by the state courts in their delegated powers, it is reasonable that the federal Supreme Court should have cassation power over them. This is because of the reason that the case originally belongs to the federal Courts. Let alone cassation, the federal Supreme Court is competent to hear appeals on delegated matters. According to Article 80(6) of the FDRE Constitution, decisions rendered by a state Supreme Court on federal matters are appealable to the federal Supreme Court. So, when the federal Supreme Court exercises cassation power in such cases, it cannot be taken as an encroachment on state court powers. Besides, the state courts are not authorized to have cassation power over federal matters that they tried by delegation; Article 80(3)(b) expressly authorizes them to have cassation power over state matters only. Therefore, this does not amount to cassation over cassation.

However, the controversial issue in this case is whether or not the interpretation of the terms "any court decision" can extend to final state court decisions on originally state matters. The literal understanding of the matter answers the question in the affirmative. However, this is misleading. That means it leads to cassation over cassation. This leads to the situation that, on the one hand, the state Supreme Courts have cassation power over final court decisions on state matters and that, on the other hand, the federal Supreme Court has cassation power over state matters that are already examined by the cassation power of the state Supreme Courts. Obviously, this opens the door to unnecessary redundancy and overlapping of powers. On top of that, it raises serious constitutional issues of division of powers and sovereignty.

Although it can be argued that the provisions in Sub-Article 3 are not only special provisions but exceptions to Sub-Articles 1 and 2 of Article 80 of the constitution, it is legitimate to ask whether such open-ended application of Sub-Article 3 can be tolerated to frustrate the very foundation of the principle in Sub-Articles 1 and 2. Moreover, the above conclusion departs from the general context of the division of powers employed in the constitution. Close scrutiny of the relevant principles in the FDRE Constitution implies that the constitution intends to clearly demarcate and protect the sovereignty of the states. That is the reason why the constitution recognizes dual courts with distinct powers.

Article 50(8) of the FDRE Constitution obliges the federal courts to respect the powers of the state courts. So, extending the application of Article 80(3)(a) to originally state matters, contradicts the principle incorporated in Article 50(8) and the spirit of the constitution. Had the constitution intended to recognize cassation over cassation, logically speaking it would not have used loaded words like "highest" and "final" when it determined the judicial powers of the state Supreme Courts. It is hard to imagine the fact that the FDRE Constitution uses such strong words while it does not mean them. It goes without saying that constitutions are general documents by their very nature and neither are they supposed to waste key words/terms nor use them without clear target. Since the words "highest" and "final" are key words in this case, they need to convey their intended meanings. Here, one should not be confused as to the difference of wordings of the constitution in Article 80 Sub-Articles 3(a) and (b). When it determines the cassation powers of the federal Supreme Court, the constitution uses the term "any court decision", while it uses the phrase "state matters" for determining the cassation powers of the state Supreme Courts. This might be the case partly because of the fact that state courts are exercising both original and delegated jurisdictions and partly because of poor drafting. Whatever the reason, in cases of apparent inconsistency, the principles embodied in the provisions have to be given a meaning that is in line with the contextual understanding of the whole text.

Setting aside the division of powers in the constitution or the use of words of the constitution for the time being, the objective of cassation by itself does not seem to warrant the existence of cassation over cassation. Cassation is a rare procedural mechanism employed to guarantee the correct and uniform application of laws. It is used as a last resort to check basic legal errors. Therefore, to let a given case be reviewed twice by cassation does not serve the purpose of cassation. There is no valid reason at all to have two levels of cassation for a case that has received a final decision after the application of all the regular procedures including appeals.

Federal Courts Proclamation No.25/1996 follows the constitution in adopting an over generalized statement in Article 10(3). It generally subjects "*final decisions of the Regional Supreme Courts rendered as a regular division or in its appellate jurisdiction*" to the cassation division of the federal Supreme Court. In other words, it repeated the same confusion created in the constitution. Furthermore, the current practice of the federal Supreme Court recognizes cassation over cassation in purely state matters. The federal Supreme Court is exercising cassation powers over final decisions of state courts that are already reviewed by cassation in the state Supreme Court. The writer of this paper, who is a former federal First Instance Court judge, has made personal observations of the practice of cassation over cassation. Moreover, a case between W/rit Menfesawit Amdemariam and Ato Mehari, et. al. in Civil Case No.149/88, can be cited as an example. In this case, a petition for the removal of a family arbitrator was lodged before a competent court in one of the states, and it was rejected both by the trial and appellate courts. The party, who was not satisfied by the decision of the appellate court, brought the matter before the cassation division of the state Supreme Court, and the latter rejected the case by upholding the decision of the appellate court. Finally, the same party brought the matter before the federal Supreme Court Cassation Division that rejected the case because of the absence of a basic error of law. In this case, the Cassation Division of the federal Supreme Court did not reject the case because of lack of jurisdiction; instead it examined the decision and determined that there was no error of law. So, technically, the court exercised cassation over cassation.

To make matters worse, the newly introduced amendment to the Federal Courts Proclamation No.25/1996 has complicated the matter further. The Federal Courts Proclamation reamendment Proclamation No.454/2005, Article 4 introduced the principle of precedent for the first time in the Ethiopian legal system. It reads:

"*Interpretation of a law by the Federal Supreme Court rendered by the cassation division with not less than five judges shall be binding on federal as well as regional councils at all levels. The cassation decision may however render a different legal interpretation some other time.*"[20]

Thus, according to its current practice, the federal Supreme Court interprets the laws in a way that enables it to encroach upon the powers of the state Supreme courts and it has the power to set precedent for all related future cases.

---

[20] Federal Courts Proclamation Reamendment Proclamation No.425/2005, Article 2 (4), *Federal Negarit Gazeta*, 11th year No.42.

This seriously hinders the state courts power to interpret and apply state laws and to exercise its power in originally state jurisdictions.

According to the relevant articles of the FDRE Constitution, the federal courts have exclusive power to interpret federal laws and to adjudicate federal matters save for the delegated powers. Even in the case of the delegated powers they can still exercise it once the federal House of Peoples' Representatives decides by a two-thirds majority. Likewise, the state courts have exclusive jurisdiction to interpret state laws and adjudicate in state matters. Hence, the current practice of the federal Supreme Court violates the jurisdiction of the state courts. It is hard to believe that the constitution intended to empower the federal Supreme Court to hear cassation on matters that originated as low as the First Instance or '*Woreda*' Courts of the states.

As stated earlier, the objective of cassation is to secure proper application and uniformity of laws. The federal Supreme Court is supposed to be the guardian of the federal laws, save for constitutional interpretation matters that are given to the House of the Federation. Thus, it is logical for the Court to secure the proper application and uniformity of federal laws. Based on the general guidelines in the FDRE Constitution, Federal Courts Proclamation No.25/1996, Article 3(1), expressly empowers the federal courts to adjudicate cases arising under the federal laws. Similarly, the federal Supreme Court can exercise cassation powers over federal matters in order to guarantee the proper application and uniformity of federal laws. In contrast, it does not have similar powers as to the state laws. Rather, the state Supreme Courts are supposed to be the guardians of the state laws. The FDRE Constitution empowers them to exercise state jurisdiction. The same constitution guarantees their supremacy on state matters and vests in them cassation powers over state matters. Therefore, there is no legitimate justification, apart from the over generalized terminology of the constitution and the subsequent law, for the federal Supreme Court to exercise cassation over cassation (in state matters).

5. CONCLUSION

The federal Supreme Court has cassation jurisdiction on final court decisions that have a basic error of law. The purpose of this mechanism is to quash decisions that are based on the wrong application or interpretation of federal laws. It is a last resort to rectify basic errors of law and it gives the Court the last chance to provide correct justice and to defend public interests. The cassation division of the federal Supreme Court is neither a trial nor appellate court. It only determines cases that have basic errors of law and refers them back to where they came from with instructions for the correction of the error.

The federal constitution obliges the states to respect the powers of the organs of federal government and *vice versa.* Consequently, the cassation power of the federal Supreme Court should fall only within the limits of the powers that are given to the federal government. Any other law or practice that frustrates the constitutional division of powers is of no effect because of the principle of the supremacy of the constitution.[21]

To accentuate the core point, the constitution apportions judicial powers, including cassation between the federal courts and the state courts. Accordingly, the federal Supreme Court has cassation powers only in federal matters. Likewise, the state Supreme Courts have cassation powers in state matters. On the other hand, the current practice of the federal Supreme Court to exercise cassation power in originally state matters goes beyond the limits of the jurisdiction of the federal courts. Though the practice of the federal Supreme Court is based on the direct application of Article 80(3)(a) of the FDRE Constitution, this particular provision should be interpreted in light of the whole context of the constitution and the principle of division of powers embodied in the constitution. In short, it should be interpreted in a manner that does not contradict the very foundation of the constitution and the related provisions in the constitution

---

[21] Article 9(1) of the Ethiopian Federal Constitution.

4. Federal and State Legislative Powers in Civil and Commercial Matters in Ethiopia: Striking the Balance and Maintaining it

Tecle Hagos Bahta[•]

1. INTRODUCTION

A famous analyst summed up the basic tenets of federalism in the following words:

"Federal government exists when the powers of government for a community are divided substantially according to the principle that there is a single independent authority for the whole area in respect of some matters and that there are independent regional authorities for other matters, each set of authorities being co-ordinate with and not subordinate to the others within its own prescribed sphere."[1]

This daunting task of allocating "some matters" to one authority and "other matters" to another is not done overnight. In the long process of so doing, the federal government and state governments must carefully tread on thin lines lest they should step on each other's toes. In this regard, the following allegory illustrates the situation briefly and succinctly:

"The problem which all federal nations have to solve is how to secure an efficient central government and preserve national unity, while allowing free scope for the diversities, and free play to the members of the federation. It is ...to keep the centrifugal and centripetal forces in equilibrium, so that neither the planet States shall fly off into space nor the sun of the Central government draw them into its consuming fires."[2]

But why is this so delicate and problematic? Douglas-Scott puts in more glaring terms that delineation of competences is still problematic for two reasons:[3]

• LLB Addis Ababa University, LLM Ghent University, Lecturer in Law, Mekelle University, Faculty of Law. E-mail: teclehi@fastmail.fm

[1] K.C. Wheare, *Federal Government* 35 (New York: Oxford University Press, 1947).

[2] D. McKay, *Designing Europe: Comparative Lessons from the Federal Experience* 127 (Oxford: Oxford University Press, 2001), citing Lord Bryce.

[3] S. Douglas-Scott, *Constitutional Law of the European Union* 172 (Harlow: Pearson Education, 2002).

"Federalism is by definition unfinished business because many issues cannot be foreseen at the time of the initial bargain...[and]... that catalogues of competences will always be subject to interpretation, opening the door to all sorts of court challenges."

This limited work does not attempt to delineate the federal-state power divide for all matters. Far from it, it rather tries to show the complex nature of demarcating the border line of federal and state legislative competences for civil and commercial matters in the Ethiopian federal system and tries to draw possible lessons pertaining to the subject matter from some of the long-established federal systems in the world, particularly the United States of America, the Australian Commonwealth and the evolving semi-federalism of the European Union (EU).

Space does not allow me here to depict the complete panoply of the Ethiopian federal structure and all its components. It is, however, proper to start by highlighting the general panoramic view of the main functionaries in Ethiopian federalism.

Ethiopia is comprised of nine federated states,[4] a self-governing federal capital city, Addis Ababa,[5] and a federal enclave city, Dire Dawa, whose status is not yet determined. The federated states are:[6]

a) The State of Tigray
b) The State of Afar
c) The State of Amhara
d) The State of Oromia
e) The State of Somalia
f) The State of Benishangul/Gumuz
g) The State of The Southern Nations, Nationalities and Peoples (SNNP)
h) The State of The Gambela Peoples, and
i) The State of The Harari People.

The federal government and the federated states have legislative, executive and judicial powers.[7] The House of Peoples' Representatives and the State Councils are the highest authorities of the federal government and the federated states respectively.[8]

Article 52(1) of the federal constitution states:

---

[4] Article 47(1) of the Constitution of the Federal Democratic Republic of Ethiopia, *Federal Negarit Gazeta*, Year 1, No. 1, AA, August 1995, (hereinafter "The Federal Constitution").
[5] Article 49(2) of the Federal Constitution.
[6] Article 47(1) of the Federal Constitution.
[7] Article 50(2) of the Federal Constitution.
[8] Article 50(3) of the Federal Constitution.

"All powers not given expressly to the Federal Government alone, or concurrently to the Federal Government and the States are reserved to the States."

To put it in simple terms for our purpose here, all powers exercisable in Ethiopia are reposed in:
(a) the federal government where the power is expressly vested in it;
(b) the federal government and the state governments where the power is expressly and concurrently vested in them, and,
(c) the state governments for all the residual powers.
Accordingly, the federal constitution establishes that "*the States shall respect the powers of the Federal Government. The Federal Government shall likewise respect the powers of the States.*"[9] The federal government's legislative power is listed under Article 55 of the federal constitution. For our purpose here, it is worthwhile mentioning that the House of Peoples' Representatives has the power to enact specific laws on:

"Article 55(2)...(b) Inter-State Commerce and Foreign Trade; ...(g) patents and copyrights; Article 55(3): It shall enact a labour code; (4) It shall enact a commercial code...(6) It shall enact civil laws which the House of the Federation deems necessary to establish and sustain one economic community...(12) It shall ratify international agreements concluded by the Executive."

One should also bear in mind that the federal government and the state governments have their respective legislative, executive and judicial bodies.

2. LEGISLATIVE COMPETENCES IN CIVIL AND COMMERCIAL MATTERS

In the main, whilst legislative power on inter-state commerce and foreign trade, and the enactment of a Commercial Code is vested in the federal government, civil matters are left to the states' legislative power unless and until the House of the Federation refers them to the federal government by virtue of Article 62(8) *cum* Article 55(6) of the federal constitution.

The crux of the matter is: where does a commercial activity end so it becomes non-commercial? Or, where does a civil activity end and become a commercial activity? To be specific, what is the place and scope of commercial law within the picture of the Ethiopian private laws? In this regard, resort should be made to the approach taken to deal with 'commercial matters' so far, albeit that it cannot be taken for granted that it applies to demarcate the commercial/civil divide for the purpose of allocating legislative powers between the two legislative bodies.

---

[9] Article 50(8) of the Federal Constitution.

The Commercial Code of Ethiopia of 1960[10] does not directly define what is 'commercial'. It, nevertheless, lists the commercial activities in Ethiopia. The Commercial Code's implied definition does not include all activities of an 'economic' nature. This becomes obvious when one reads Article 10 *cum* 211 of the Code which states that ordinary partnership (one of the six forms of business organizations in Ethiopia) can carry out activities of an "economic" nature but not the "commercial activities" enumerated under Article 5 of the Code. Furthermore, the list of "commercial activities", under Article 5 of the Code, is largely modified under the Federal Commercial Registration and Business Licensing Proclamation No. 67/1997.[11] This Proclamation maintains that:[12]

"'Commercial activities' means any activities carried on by a business person as defined under sub-Article (2) of this Article."

Article 2(2) of the Proclamation provides thus:

"'Business person' means any person who, professionally and for gain carries on any of those activities specified under Article 5 of the Commercial Code, or who dispenses services, or who carries on those commercial activities designated as such by regulations issued by the Government."

This no doubt widens the scope of "commercial activities" compared to what is envisaged under Article 5 of the Commercial Code. It should be mentioned, though, that not only is the scope not defined and as such left open, but it also seems bizarre to vest the power of designating what is 'commercial' in the federal government, i.e. the federal executive. In essence, the federal government can play a determinant role in the process of defining the scope of commercial activities in two ways. First, from the reading of the aforementioned provision, it seems clear that the power is vested in the federal government to do so. Secondly, as it is the body that initiates federal draft laws into the House of Peoples' Representatives, the federal government does, *prima facie*, exercise the screening process of what is and what is not a commercial matter.

Be that as it may, on what bases, then, can the federal government designate such commercial matters? To be sure, the definition of the word 'commercial' is fluid. Some states have adopted a narrow definition and others have a wider definition of it. It is suggested that the general approach, internationally, is to define 'commercial' as to encompass all types of trade or business transactions.

---

[10] The Commercial Code of Ethiopia of 1960, Proclamation No.166, *Negarit Gazeta* (extraordinary), Year 9, No.3.

[11] Federal Commercial Registration and Business Licensing Proclamation No. 67/2002, *Federal Negarit Gazeta*, Year 3, No.25, March 1997.

[12] *Ibid,* Article 2.

The following prototypes may be presented here to show that the word 'commercial' is not uniformly used: The UNICITRAL Model Law on International Commercial Arbitration provides that:[13]

"The term 'commercial' should be given a wide interpretation so as to cover matters arising from all relationships of a commercial nature, whether contractual or not. Relationships of a commercial nature include, but are not limited to, the following transactions: any trade transaction agreement; commercial representation or agency factoring; leasing construction; financing; banking; insurance; exploitation agreement or concession; joint venture and other forms of industrial or business cooperation; carriage of goods or passengers by air, sea, rail or road."

The Egyptian Arbitration Law of 1994, which is largely inspired by the UNICITRAL Model Law on International Commercial Arbitration, on the other hand, provides:[14]

"An arbitration is commercial within the scope of this Law when the dispute arises over a legal relationship of an economic nature, whether contractual or no-contractual. This comprises, for example, the supply of commodities or services, commercial agencies, construction and engineering or technical know-how contracts, the granting of industrial, touristic and other licenses, technology transfer, investment and development contracts, banking, insurance and transport operations, natural wealth, energy supply, laying of gas or oil pipelines, building of roads and tunnels, reclamation of agricultural land, protection of the environment and establishment of nuclear reactors."

The use of the word "commercial" by the UNICITRAL Model Law to describe the nature of the legal relationship covered by it is in the Egyptian Law replaced with the more expansive word "economic". It should also be noted that the items enumerated under both laws are not identical.
The Ethiopian approach of classifying commercial acts and civil acts seems to have been inspired by the French approach. The following words briefly explain how the classification is approached in France:[15]

"Some acts are considered commercial by virtue of their nature, i.e taking account of what is done and by whom (actes de commerce par nature); *certain*

[13] A. Redfern and M. Hunter, *Law and Practice of International Commercial Arbitration* 3-15, 3rd ed. (London: Sweet and Maxwell, 1999).
[14] Egyptian Arbitration Laws, Law No. 27 of 1994 promulgating the law concerning Arbitration in Civil and Commercial Matters, 21 April 1994, translated from the Arabic Official Text under the auspices of the "Association for Arab and African Arbitration" having its headquarters in Cairo, and revised under the supervision of Prof. Ahmed S. El Kosheri, published in the official Gazette No. 16, on 21 April 1994.
[15] Andrew Bell, in: J. Bell et al. (eds.), *Principles of French Law* 432 (New York: Oxford University Press, 1998).

acts are automatically deemed to be commercial because of the form of the act itself or of the organization involved: actes de commerce par la forme. *In addition, acts which would normally be regarded as civil (i.e., not commercial) will be categorized as commercial if they are done as an ancillary part of a commercial activity:* actes de commerce par accessoire."

Despite the strong traditional French insistence on commercial law being a distinct branch of the law, however, it still lacks a comprehensive set of rules; it is submitted that many of its aspects have no special text to govern them and, thus, one has to have recourse to the provisions of *droit civil.*[16] Thus, the apparent inextricable interplay between civil and commercial laws makes the efficacious delimitation of the matters a daunting task.

In Ethiopia, as the federal government is in a better position in terms of expertise and financial capabilities in initiating draft bills, it can be submitted that the "commercial code" clause in the federal constitution may be used for permitting a, as one scholar put it,[17] "creeping extension" of the federal legislative jurisdiction. This can be, to some extent, compared to the US Commerce Clause, Article 1 of the US Constitution.[18] The Commerce Clause gives Congress the power to regulate "commerce with foreign nations, among the several states, and with the Indian tribes". The US Supreme Court has long given a broad interpretation to the Commerce Clause.[19] It has been long held by the Supreme Court that Congress can regulate under its Commerce Clause power "*those activities having a substantial relation to interstate commerce…i.e., those activities that substantially affect interstate commerce*".[20] It is submitted that although the Commerce Clause "*seeks to regulate economic activity…it had been interpreted to admit legislation with no obvious economic impact"*.[21]

In a similar vein, Section 51(i) of the Australian Commonwealth Constitution of 1900 gives the power of regulating "Trade and Commerce with other countries, and among the States" to the Commonwealth government. In fact, a number of cases indicate that the High Court has permitted the Commonwealth Congress to regulate any intra-state activity that has any connection with interstate commerce.[22] Like the US Supreme Court, the High Court of Australia accepts that this power can be exercised to regulate intrastate activities provided they have a sufficient connection with interstate and overseas commerce.

---

[16] Id, 437.
[17] Douglas-Scott, *supra* note 3, 160.
[18] The US Constitution of 1787.
[19] Douglas-Scott, *supra* note 3, 167.
[20] NLRB v Jones and Laughlin Steel Corp 301 US 1 (1937).
[21] Douglas-Scott, *supra* note 3, 167.
[22] Airlines of NSW v NSW (No.2) (1965) 113 CLR 54; O'Sullivan v Noarlunga Meat Ltd (1954) 92 CLR 565.

The High Court is, however, a bit stricter in the sense that it requires a *substantive physical connection* rather than a mere economic connection as sufficient.[23]

Unlike the US Supreme Court and the Australian Commonwealth High Court, however, in the Ethiopian federal system, it is not the federal Supreme Court that has the power to check constitutional validity of legislative enactments. It is the House of the Federation[24] that has this power. The House of the Federation is empowered to determine the constitutional validity of any law "*where any Federal or State law is contested as being unconstitutional and such a dispute is submitted to it by any court or interested party…*"[25]

3. HOUSE OF THE FEDERATION'S POWER OF REFERRAL

Article 62(8) of the Ethiopian Federal Constitution establishes that the House of the Federation has the power to refer civil matters to the House of Peoples' Representatives for federal legislation. Article 62(8) provides thus:

"It (the House of the Federation) *shall determine civil matters which require the enactment of laws by the House of Peoples' Representatives."*

It is worth reiterating once again that except for the powers exclusively and concurrently given expressly to the federal government, all residual powers rest with the states. Thus, civil matters are vested in the states' legislative power. Whilst establishing the power referral, Article 62(8) fails to concomitantly set a defined criterion on the basis of which the House determines as to why the House of Peoples Representatives' enactment of the civil matter in question is required.

There are, however, a few constitutional provisions that help us grope in the darkness. First, by virtue of Article 55(6) of the federal constitution, the House of Peoples' Representatives is vested with the federal legislative power on civil matters that originally lie in the states' legislative power when and if the House of the Federation divests the states of their original legislative power and refers same to the House of Peoples' Representatives. This power referral is exercisable by the House of the Federation on the condition that the specific civil matter that is to be or is referred to the House of Peoples' Representatives

[23] G. Carney, Syllabus on Comparative Federalism: Australia and Europe (2005-6), Ghent University, School of Law, Master of Advanced Studies in European and Comparative Law, topic 5.
[24] Article 62 of the Ethiopian Federal Constitution enumerates the powers and responsibilities of the House of the Federation.
[25] Article 84(2) of the Federal Constitution.

for federal legislation must be such that "*it is* necessary *to* establish *and* sustain *one* economic community".[26] [Emphasis added]
Determining the perimeters and parameters of the decisive words such as "necessary", "to establish", "to sustain", etc. may prove to be essential at some time, but, indeed, the idea of "one economic community" is so amorphous that, I believe, its interpretation should not have been left to the mercy of the virtually unfettered discretionary power of the House of the Federation. What does "one economic community" mean? What does it take to establish and sustain it? How much of their current legislative power should the states bring to the altar as sacrificial lambs to establish and sustain one economic community.

The federal constitution does not attempt to define what the drafters had in mind by "one economic community". Nevertheless, as is clear from the fifth recital in the Preamble to the federal constitution, "The Nations, Nationalities and Peoples of Ethiopia" have made it clear that "*...to live as one economic community is necessary in order to create sustainable and mutually supportive conditions for ensuring respect for [our] rights and freedoms and for the collective promotion of [our] interests*." In other words, the creation of "one economic community" is believed to be an indispensable prerequisite for the prevalence of "sustainable and mutually supportive conditions". As to what these conditions are, we are yet left in limbo. However, not only must these conditions, in turn, be stepping-stones for "*ensuring respect for rights and freedoms*" but also for the "*collective promotion of the [shared] interests*".

The crux of the matter is, therefore: what legal framework or infrastructure is necessary so that one economic community can be established and sustained in Ethiopia? Or what extent of their individual legislative powers should the regional states give away to realise the common end of establishing and sustaining one economic community? In the absence of a guiding definition, perhaps the House of the Federation might find it a little too wide a discretionary power where it would play a major role in the continued refinement of the federal/state balance of legislative power. The balance, it may be said, could tip in favour of either the federal government or the states depending on the political make-up at any particular time in the House itself. In other words, the House of the Federation, being a body representing all the nations, nationalities and peoples of Ethiopia and being directly elected by them or by the State Councils, would normally have the proclivity to decide in favour of the states being given wider legislative powers. This situation may, however, be easily upset whenever a stronger political party (dominating both the House of Peoples' Representatives and the House of the Federation) is in power. It should, however, be borne in mind that the House of the Federation, at least in theory, would not plummet into a completely partisan political instrument as, one can

[26] Article 55(6) of the Federal Constitution.

safely say of, the Senate in the United States where Senators are called upon to act on the basis of their political dereliction rather than remaining faithful as being genuine representatives of the states.[27] The same trend is also witnessed in the Australian Commonwealth where the Senate is composed of personalities elected from the individual states but, somehow, the Senators align themselves to their political parties and apparently seem to act according to party lines rather than their constituencies.[28]

In Ethiopia, how the House of the Federation is going to evolve is difficult to tell at this juncture. Can we, however, draw some parallels with other countries so that we can ultimately have a common understanding of what the "one economic community" is all about? A very preliminary comparison to the European Economic Community might be of some help here. The comparison, however, by no means claims to be inclusive of institutional frameworks and political set-ups; it is rather limited to the specific issue at hand in an attempt to draw a lesson as to what "the one economic community" might be.
When the six European states[29] decided to create a European Economic Community in the EEC Rome Treaty, Article 2 of the Treaty had the following resonating words:

"The Community shall have as its task, by establishing a common market and progressively the economic policies of Member States, to promote throughout the Community a harmonious development of economic activities, a continuous and balanced expansion, an increase in stability, an accelerated raising of the standard of living and closer relations between the States belonging to it."

In this regard the Rome Treaty has provided all the necessary legal and institutional preconditions for the establishment and consolidation of the European Economic Community. Article 3 provides, *inter alia*, for any necessary harmonisation of Member States' laws to see to it that free movement of goods, services and factors of production is facilitated and that competition within the Economic Community is not distorted. This line of approaching the problem may help stamp out any potential intra-state trade barriers and distorted conditions of competition stemming from the disparities in the civil laws in the federated states. Nevertheless, it may turn out to be an unruly horse as virtually any state measure, single-handedly meted out, in the economic and social spheres may have some impact on the conditions of competition. This, in effect, would engender a situation in which the House of the Federation will have too wide a discretion to approximate the laws.

---

[27] Wheare, *supra* note 1, 16.
[28] Carney, *supra* note 23, at topic 5, p.4.
[29] Germany, France, Belgium, Luxembourg, the Netherlands and Italy.

In this regard, the Australian Commonwealth Constitution approached the problem differently. Section 51(xxxvii) of the Commonwealth Constitution empowers the Commonwealth to enact laws with respect to matters referred to the Commonwealth by the states, and permits other states to adopt those laws as Commonwealth laws. The reasons for the referrals have been in the main to provide consistency or to avoid conflicts or to effectively regulate a matter that was incapable of being effectively regulated by individual state and Territory enactments.[30] Thus, the power referrals coupled with Section 92 of the Commonwealth Constitution that "*...trade, commerce and intercourse among the States...shall be absolutely free*" has been "*designed to eliminate all border customs duties and other measures which restricted the free flow of interstate trade.*"[31]

Thus, in Ethiopia, the referral power, if properly utilised, may serve as an efficacious tool, as stated above, to avoid any trade distortions that may potentially surface owing to the disparities in the laws.

Nevertheless, its scope and nature, and whether power referrals are revocable at any time by the House of the Federation is yet left in limbo.

4. POWER OF THE HOUSE OF PEOPLES' REPRESENTATIVES TO RATIFY INTERNATIONAL AGREEMENTS

The federal government is empowered by the federal constitution, *inter alia*, to "*...formulate and implement foreign policy; ... negotiate and ratify international agreements.*"[32] Specifically, the House of Peoples' Representatives is given the power to ratify international agreements concluded by the federal executive body.[33]

Taking civil matters as our focus, this would mean that states will be incessantly ceding their legislative power if and when the federal government negotiates and ratifies international agreements pertaining to civil matters that squarely fall within the purview of the states' legislative powers. In effect, not only would this be tantamount to levying the agreements on the states despite their respective local preferences but also usurping the legislative power that would otherwise remain with them.

This has been witnessed in the Australian Commonwealth where such right of negotiating and ratifying has been tipping the balance of power in favour of

[30] Carney, *supra* note 23, at topic 8, p.9.

[31] G. Carney, The Re-Interpretation of Section 92: The Decline of Free Enterprise and the Rise of Free Trade, 3(2) *Bond Law Review* 150 (1991).

[32] Article 51(8) of the Federal Constitution.

[33] Article 55(12) of the Federal Constitution.

the Commonwealth government, notwithstanding the checking mechanisms in place.[34] While the number and range of treaties made in international law has grown greatly, the Commonwealth has succeeded in ratifying them despite there being areas that would not otherwise be within the Commonwealth power. This may seem paradoxical in the face of the fact that Australia is a dualist state in terms of international agreements and that treaties should pass as bills both through the House of Representatives and Senate, coupled with the fact that treaties are ratified through consultations between the Commonwealth and the states in a 'Treaties Council'. The Treaties Council was established in 1996 to play an advisory role in relation to treaties and other international instruments "of particular sensitivity and importance to the States and Territories".[35] This process of consultation begins as soon as the Commonwealth enters into discussions about joining a treaty and continues through international negotiation, signature, ratification and implementation.[36]

This institutional checking mechanism is yet absent in the Ethiopian federal system. Such an institution is particularly indispensable for the Ethiopian federal system in light of the fact that the House of the Federation, as it represents the states, has no say in the process of ratifying international agreements, unlike the Senate in Australia.

It should, thus, be noted that although reposing the power of ratifying international agreements in the House of Peoples' Representatives may be helpful in unifying the civil laws in Ethiopia, it may, nevertheless, be easily misapplied to wield, if not usurp, the legislative powers of the states. This is particularly important in the light of the fact that quite a number of civil matters are being harmonised in the international arena via two methods: namely, through private international laws or by directly unifying them. Mention can be made here of some of the civil law areas where an attempt is being made to solve inconsistencies, partially through private international laws or fully by unifying them:[37] The Hague Convention on the Law Applicable to Matrimonial Property Regimes (1978), The Hague Convention on the Law Applicable to Succession to the Estates of Deceased Persons (1989), The Hague Convention on the law Applicable to Product Liability (1973), The Hague Convention on the Law Applicable to Maintenance Obligations (1973), The Hague Convention on the Form of Wills, Convention on the law applicable to Trusts and on their recognition (1985), and so on.

---

[34] The Senate and the Treaties Council. The latter is comprised of the Prime Minister, the Premiers, and the Chief Ministers of the Australian Commonwealth Territories and the Northern Territory.

[35] Carney, *supra* note 23, at topic 8, p.19. The Treaties Council consults with the States and the Territories in relation to those treaties and instruments that have the potential to affect future policy decisions of the States and Territories or will need their participation for implementation.

[36] Ibid.

[37] M. Koppenol-Laforce, *International Contracts: Aspects of Jurisdiction, Arbitration and Private International Law* 124,127 and 128, 1st ed., (London: Sweet and Maxwell, 1996).

Whilst theoretically speaking, it is difficult to envisage inconsistencies of laws in civil matters currently as states are fully vested with it, the power to ratify international agreements relating to civil matters by the House of Peoples' Representatives will perhaps potentially render them to abound. Attempt has been made to settle in advance such inconsistencies if and when they occur. Article 6(2) of the Federal Courts Establishment Proclamation No. 25/ 1996 empowers federal courts to reject state laws that would have been otherwise applicable, whenever they are found to be "inconsistent with Federal laws and international treaties".[38] This provision is, however, tainted with two significant problems. First, by virtue of Article 9(4) of the federal constitution, "*All international agreements ratified by Ethiopia are an integral part of the law of the land.*" Thus, when and if the House of Peoples' Representatives ratifies an international agreement, it will be an integral part of the federal laws. This is further accentuated by the fact that all laws of the federal government are published in the Federal Negarit Gazeta and that judicial organs are expected to take judicial notice of only the laws published in the Federal Negarit Gazeta.[39] Thus, the courts are neither expected to apply international treaties not ratified by the House of Peoples' Representatives nor international treaties ratified by the House of Peoples' Representatives but not published in the Federal Negarit Gazeta. In other words, this means that a bilateral or multilateral agreement that Ethiopia ratifies does not automatically become Ethiopian law until it is, in addition to ratification, passed into the federal law and published in the Federal Negarit Gazeta. Hence the reference to "international treaties" in the legal provision is unfounded. Secondly, although as I have tried to explain above, there is no concurrency *sensu strictu* in the legislative power on civil matters between State Councils and the House of Peoples' Representatives, undoubtedly, as the House of Peoples' Representatives intensifies its power in this dimension, inconsistencies between the state laws and federal laws (i.e., domesticated international treaties) will resurface. In such instances, the House of the Federation will decide on the constitutional validity of the inconsistent laws.

5. THE FEDERAL SUPREME COURT'S POWER OF CASSATION[40] OVER STATE MATTERS

Article 79(1) of the federal constitution establishes that "*Judicial powers, both at Federal and State levels, are vested in the courts.*" The federal courts con-

[38] The Federal Courts Establishment Proclamation No. 25/1996, *Federal Negarit Gazeta*, Year 2, No.13, February 1996.
[39] Article 2 of the Federal Negarit Gazeta Establishment Proclamation No. 3/ 1995, *Federal Negarit Gazeta*, Year 1, No. 3, August 1995.
[40] For the meaning and background of the concept and practice of cassation in Ethiopia, see Muradu Abdo, I (1) *Mizan Law Review* 60-74 (June 2007). The writer also argues against the federal Supreme Court's power of cassation over state matters.

sist of the federal Supreme Court, High Courts and First Instance Courts. The states can also establish the state Supreme Court, High Court and First Instance Courts.[41] The states and the federal government may also give recognition to Religious and Customary Courts.[42] In line with this, the federal Supreme Court will have "*the highest and final judicial power over federal matters*" whilst the state Supreme Courts "*shall have the highest and final judicial power over state matters...*"[43] At this juncture, the following constitutional provision[44] is worth noting:

"*...The House of Peoples' Representatives may, by two-thirds majority vote, establish nation wide, or in some parts of the country only, the Federal High Court and First-Instance Courts it deems necessary.* Unless decided in this manner, *the jurisdictions of the Federal High Court and of the First-Instance Courts are hereby* delegated *to the State Courts.*" [Emphasis added]

From the reading of the provision, it is clear that the House of Peoples' Representatives has the right to set up federal High Court and First Instance Courts in all the states. However, until and unless it does so, the federal judicial powers are to be exercised by the state Supreme and High Courts respectively in the states where the federal courts are not established. Thus, state courts are, to a large extent, charged with federal matters in addition to state matters. In this regard, it stands to reason that the federal Supreme Court exercises some degree of control over the state courts in their function of interpreting the federal laws.

Nevertheless, the exercise of cassation power over cassation decisions seems, to say the least, of some oddity. The legal ground still remains dubious, too. The practice is pervasive, though. One would wonder if the constitutional provisions substantiate the prevailing practice. Thus, Article 80(1)-(3) is presented here *verbatim* in an attempt to see if the legal framework is such as to nurture the federal Supreme Court's cassation power over a cassation decision given by the Cassation Divisions of the states Supreme Courts. Thus, the provision provides:
"*(1): The Federal Supreme Court shall have the highest and final judicial power over Federal matters. (2): State Supreme Courts shall have the highest and final judicial power over State matters... (3): Notwithstanding the Provisions of sub-Articles 1 and 2 of this Article; (a): The Federal Supreme Court has a power of cassation over any final court decision containing a basic error of law... (b): The State Supreme Court has power of cassation over any final court decision on State matters which contains a basic error of law...*"

[41] Article 78(3) of the Federal Constitution.
[42] Article 78(5) of the Federal Constitution.
[43] Article 80(1) - (2) of the Federal Constitution.
[44] Article 78(2) of the Federal Constitution.

From a reading and re-reading of this constitutional provision between the lines, it may not be impossible to muster up the momentum to marshal the argument that the Cassation Division of the federal Supreme Court has the power to review cassation decisions given by state Supreme Courts on state matters. Moreover, the practice so far looms large in Ethiopia so much so that it appears to have been taken for granted both by the courts and the litigants. Nevertheless, it flies in the face of one of the basic tenets of federalism; i.e., in a federal set-up, each set of authorities must be "*…co-ordinate with and not subordinate to the others* within its own prescribed sphere".[45] [Emphasis mine]. This tenet seems to have been firmly entrenched in the United States Constitution that "*the United States Supreme Court cannot hear appeals on matters of State law and the highest court in each of the 50 States*" is the final decision-maker of the meaning of the law of that state.[46] It appears, to say the least, a bizarre situation for the federal Supreme Court to exercise a cassation power over a cassation decision by the state Supreme Court. Moreover, one would but wonder as to how the federal judge, being only accountable to the federal government, would interpret specific laws enacted by the State Council which laws necessarily take the particular socio-economic and cultural values and policies into consideration. To complicate matters, the cassation decision of the federal Supreme Court's Cassation Division is binding upon federal and state courts alike at all levels.[47] Whilst the constitutional provisions are silent as to the binding nature of the federal Supreme Court's Power of Cassation, the aforementioned proclamation blesses them with their being of a binding nature.

The fact that the federal Supreme Court's cassation decisions on federal matters are binding upon the federal and state courts is a welcome scenario as it might be an efficacious tool to see to it that federal laws are uniformly and consistently interpreted throughout the country, regardless of which state court is charged with the case. Nevertheless, the federal judges sitting at the cosmopolitan capital city to tell the state-appointed judges and their appointing sovereign State Councils as to how to interpret their own localised and socio-culturally-driven laws seems to manifest the strong centripetal pull often present in existing federal systems[48] or, perhaps, prolong 'the-centre-knows-it-all' dogma that has prevailed in Ethiopia during the previous unitary government systems.

---

[45] Wheare, *supra* note 1.

[46] M. Tilbury, G. Davis and B. Opeskin, *Conflict of Laws in Australia* 551 (New York: Oxford University Press, 2002). It is also worth mentioning that, strictly speaking, the concepts of "appeal" and "cassation" differ. In terms of exercising judicial power of the state matters by the federal courts, however, they can be paralleled.

[47] Article 2(1) of the Federal Courts Proclamation Re-amendment Proclamation No. 454/2005, *Federal Negarit Gazeta,* Year 11, No.42, June 2005.

[48] Douglas-Scott, *supra* note 3, 172.

At this juncture, it is worth noting the similarities and differences between Ethiopian and Australian federalism with regard to the issue at hand. Although the Australian Constitution heavily relied on the United States Constitution,[49] unlike its progenitor, it granted "...the right of appeal from state courts to the High Court in matters of state as well as federal jurisdiction." [50] Although one may need a further study as to whether the spirit of the aforementioned Ethiopian constitutional provision is taken from the Australian Commonwealth Constitution, the contextual set-up in the exercise of this power, however, presents a marked disparity. First, all the states in the Australian Federation consist of a homogeneous community, the reason for a federal system being that the six states were separately colonised by the United Kingdom. Thus, unlike the Ethiopian federal system, there was no question of cultural oppression or dominance by one against the other. The latter issue played a major role in the creation of the Ethiopian federal system. Secondly, for the six states in Australia, it was already in place that for certain matters, appeal lay to the Queen in Council from the highest courts of the six states[51] and, thus, the constitutional provision simply gave the blessing for its continuity. Thirdly, the legislative competence of the states is so diverse and wide in scope in Australia that the Commonwealth may, I believe, need some control on some specific matters, e.g. commercial matters. In Ethiopia, commercial matters are exclusively vested in the federal legislative remit. Civil matters are reserved for the states so that the community in each state may be able, without hindrance, to reflect and promote its own socio-cultural values and norms within the purview of the federal constitution. This was essential in the constitution-making process of the 1995 federal constitution of Ethiopia. Finally, whilst the Australian Commonwealth federal courts (other than the High Court) are entitled to exercise appellate jurisdiction over federal matters only, the express constitutional blessing, so to say, of the exercise of appellate jurisdiction in federal and state matters to the High Court, it is submitted, has made the Court "... a national rather than a purely federal institution".[52]

6. CONCLUSION

I have tried to show that the process of delineating legislative power competences on civil and commercial matters between the federal government and states in a federal system is far from being a one-time shopping experience; it is a continuous process of refinements which both the federal government and the states should carefully handle lest either of them should tamper with the other's power. In the Ethiopian federal system, there are particularly interest-

[49] Tilbury et al., *supra* note 46, 545.
[50] Ibid.
[51] Article 73 of the Australian Commonwealth Constitution.
[52] Tilbury et al., *supra* note 46, 546.

ing issues that potentially help strike a balance of power and maintain or disturb it.

In civil and commercial matters, the situation is a bit perplexing in the Ethiopian federal system in that whilst all commercial matters are given to the federal government for federal legislation, civil matters are left intact with the states with the proviso that the House of the Federation may refer them for federal legislation when it is deemed necessary for the "establishment and sustainability of one economic community". The question as to how we can distinguish between matters of commercial activity and civil activity is far from clear. Furthermore, what constitutes the "one economic community" envisaged by the drafters of the federal constitution is left for determination by the House of the Federation.

The House of Peoples' Representatives' power to ratify international agreements pertaining to civil matters that fall within the legislative remit of the states could greatly tilt the balance in favour of the federal government especially when and as it continues to be exercised shorn of any participation by the states in the process. Whether the federal Supreme Court has the power of cassation over the cassation decisions of the state Supreme Courts on state matters is still controversial. The practice is, however, pervasive. This may not be a welcome breath of fresh air for the states as it unnecessarily lets the federal Supreme Court tamper with their own local laws and imposes binding laws on them. This process, I believe, also unnecessarily prolongs litigation. I believe it is essential that the task of unifying civil laws, whenever it is necessary, be left for the House of the Federation to exercise it within the ambit of Article 62(8) of the federal constitution, i.e. under the head of power of the power referral.

5. Mechanisms of Constitutional Control: A Preliminary Observation of the Ethiopian System

Getahun Kassa•

1. INTRODUCTION

This paper seeks to provide an examination of the mechanisms of constitutional control as depicted in the present constitutional system of Ethiopia. In an attempt to do that, reference is made to the powers and functions of the House of the Federation (the final authority in the interpretation of the federal constitution), to the Council of Constitutional Inquiry and to the organs of the regional states that assume similar functions. It attempts to provide an overview and analysis of the background, legal basis and practices related to the powers and functions of the House and the Council and of the regional state organs with similar functions as of 1996; the time when this new approach was started to be practised at the federal state level. The exercise of constitutional control, as practised by many other countries, is mainly undertaken by the judiciary as an important aspect of its role of controlling against arbitrary exercise of governmental power. In the present constitutional system in Ethiopia, this role is mainly assumed by the second chamber of the federal parliament (the House of the Federation) with the Council of Constitutional Inquiry organised to assist it in the accomplishment of this task.

The aim of this paper is therefore to examine the following issues. How is this function of determination of constitutionality and constitutional interpretation being executed? Which organ or organs are charged with this task? What is or what should be the role of the federal and state organs in this process of constitutional adjudication? How do these organs interact? What is the delimitation of jurisdiction between federal and state organs with regard to such a competence?

In an attempt to deal with these issues, the paper draws on the already existing limited experience of constitutional adjudication as exercised by the Council of Constitutional Inquiry and The House of the Federation and on available local literature. With a view to provide a realistic account of the process, the author of this work has exerted his utmost effort to access the records of the Council of Constitutional Inquiry and the House of the Federation and attempted to review the cases addressed by the Council and the House. These

• Executive Director Ethiopian Human Rights Commission, former Dean and Lecturer, Mekelle University, Faculty of Law. E-mail: ateykg96@fastmail.fm

cases are reviewed with a view to providing the practical dimension of this process. For comparative analysis purposes, the paper has, in addition to the federal constitution, consulted the regional state constitutions of the states of Tigray, Afar, Amhara, Oromia, Benishangul-Gumuz, Southern Nations Nationalities and Peoples Regional State, Somali, Gambella and Harari and relevant subsequent legislation.

2. AN OVERVIEW

Prior to the promulgation of the 1931 constitution, Ethiopia had no tradition of having a written constitution to regulate such issues like mechanisms of constitutional control and checks and balances. The first formal document was the 1931 constitution, which was modelled after the Japanese Meiji constitution. However, long before 1931, Ethiopia had legal texts that determined the power relations in the royal dynasty or the relations of the government with the church and the role of the church in the governance system. More specifically, the old tradition of Ethiopian history refers to much older Ethiopian legal texts like the *Fitha Ngest,* which is considered by legal scholars as an important development in Ethiopian legal tradition. This was a legal instrument that dealt with important aspects of the relationship between government, church and nobility. Pertaining to the then system of governance, it was necessary to determine the relationship between these organs that had an essential role in the whole system of governance. A wider consensus revolves around the view that the growing interactions with the West, the emergence of Ethiopian scholars educated in Europe and the growing diplomatic relations during the reign of Emperor Haile Selassie were the major driving force that led to the promulgation of the first written constitution in 1931.

The 1931 constitution was considered by many as a step towards centralization and modernization of the system of governance in Ethiopia. Its peculiar feature was that more power or almost all powers of the state were bestowed on the emperor. This was reflected explicitly in the constitution itself:

"By virtue of his Imperial blood, as well as by the anointing which he has received, the person of the emperor is sacred, his dignity is inviolable and his power is indisputable. Consequently he is entitled to all the honours due to him in accordance with tradition and the present constitution."

A five-year colonial subjugation by the Italians ended in 1941 after a struggle for liberation. The involvement of the West in this struggle for liberation and its role in post-colonial Ethiopia gave rise to an increasing interest in modernising the Ethiopian legal system. As a result of this historical event and of other internal developments, a revised constitution was adopted in the Ethiopian legal system in 1955. This revision of the 1931 constitution implied a change in the organisation of the system of governance, limiting the power of the emperor to a certain extent and a relatively better recognition of rights and freedoms.

As a reaction to changes in the socio-political reality, written constitutions have subsequently been issued at different times. These were the 1974 draft constitution, issued by the emperor as a compromise to calm down the political turmoil (which merely ended up as a draft due to the deposition of the emperor before its adoption); the 1986 constitution which was promulgated during the military administration period; the 1991 charter which served as an interim constitution for the transitional period and the 1995 constitution of the Federal Democratic Republic of Ethiopia (FDRE). Furthermore, regional state constitutions were promulgated in 1995 and these were amended between 2001 and 2003.

The 1931 and 1955 constitutions, as pointed out by various authors and as some of the provisions of the constitutions themselves clearly imply, were more inclined to legitimise the all-embracing (executive, legislative and judicial) authority of the emperor. Compared to its predecessors, the 1995 constitution has some peculiar aspects. As often cited by various authors, the introduction of a federal form of governance and the assignment of the competence of determining constitutionality to the second chamber of the parliament are among the notable features the 1995 constitution came up with. The 1995 constitution protects fundamental rights and freedoms broadly recognized in a number of international human rights instruments. This necessitated putting appropriate mechanisms of constitutional control in place.

Obviously the issue of who shall interpret the constitution and whether the power of interpreting the constitution shall be assigned to the judiciary or to an organ other than the judiciary has been the subject of debate. Depending on the socio-political realities that have influenced the process of constitution-making, constitution drafters of different countries have opted for an approach that, they believe, suits their realities. It seems that the current political trend in Ethiopia has greatly influenced the development in this regard and led to the adoption of a unique mechanism. Though different views are evolving this time around with regards to the role and extent of engagement of the House of the Federation on issues of constitutional interpretation, the practice of according this power to the legislative arm of the state has prevailed over all other model options.

Since member states of the Ethiopian federation have the legislative power to issue their own constitution, the competence of constitutional adjudication is organised in two tiers, i.e. at the federal and state level. Article 62 of the federal constitution and Proclamation 251|2001 on the House of the Federation have entrusted this power to the House of the Federation. The House is thus empowered with the power to interpret the constitution and to determine the constitutionality of legislative or other acts The Council of Constitutional Inquiry, by virtue of Article 84 of the FDRE constitution and Proclamation 250|2001 on the Council of Constitutional Inquiry, has the power to investigate constitutional disputes and submit recommendations to the House of the Federation.

In a similar fashion, the regional state constitutions granted this power to the Council of Nationalities (in the Southern Nations, Nationalities and Peoples state) and to a Commission for Constitutional Interpretation in the states of Afar, Tigray, Amhara, Oromia, Harar, Benishangul-Gumuz, Gambella and Somali. All of the state constitutions envisaged the establishment, by the regional Council, of a constitutional organ (the Constitutional Inquiry Council) designed to assist the Commission for Constitutional Interpretation or the Council of Nationalities. In general, the present system of constitutional adjudication in Ethiopia at federal and state level includes the House of the Federation, the Council of Nationalities, the Commission for Constitutional Interpretation and the Council of Constitutional Inquiry.

3. THE HOUSE OF THE FEDERATION

With the advent of the 1995 constitution a new form of government has been introduced into the Ethiopian constitutional system. Besides the transformation of the country from a unitary into a federal system of governance, a two chamber parliamentary system has been established, formed through direct popular election and, in the case of the House of the Federation, through direct or indirect representation. The two chambers are the House of Peoples' Representatives and the House of the Federation. The House of the Federation, which represents Nations, Nationalities and Peoples (whereby each Nation or Nationality is represented by one representative and one additional representative for each one million of its population), is entrusted with powers that range from determining requests for the exercise of the right to self -determination to constitutional interpretation.

With the introduction of this unique arrangement of constitutional adjudication the judiciary in Ethiopia is left aside from having a direct power on constitutional interpretation. Dr. Fasil Nahum has stated this as:

"The Ethiopian Constitution, on the other hand, in a creative stroke provides for something quite different, emanating from and consistent with the overriding supremacy of the nations, nationalities and peoples whose sovereignty the

constitution expresses……… Thus the ultimate interpreter of the constitution is made, not the highest court of law, but the House of Federation."[1]

This power is accorded to the upper House of the parliament over and above its sensitive responsibilities of deciding on issues such as the request by nations, nationalities and peoples for the exercise of their self-determination rights up to secession. The task of constitutional adjudication and ruling on matters of constitutional interpretation is thus entrusted to the upper House of the parliament that is to be assisted by the Council of Constitutional Inquiry. With such an explicit recognition of the power of the upper House to be the ultimate authority on issues of such nature, the courts in Ethiopia are kept aside from dealing with those matters. This, however, doesn't seem to prevent them from applying the constitution in the day-to-day exercise of their duties and responsibilities.

Proclamation 251|2001, which was enacted to consolidate the House of the Federation of federal Ethiopia, has, among other things, attempted to elaborate on the functions of the House on matters of constitutional adjudication. With a view to ensuring the implementation of this function, the House is empowered to organize the Council of Constitutional Inquiry, approve the rules of procedure for the Council, make final decisions upon submissions for constitutional interpretation by the Council, receive appeals from dissatisfied parties whose cases have been rejected by the Council on grounds of no need for constitutional interpretation and to decide on submissions of the Council within thirty days. Though the House is obliged to give its decision on submissions of the Council within thirty days, in practice, cases are taking longer than that to resolve.

4. THE COUNCIL OF CONSTITUTIONAL INQUIRY

As hinted at in the preceding discussion, the unique aspect of the present system of constitutional adjudication in Ethiopia is demonstrated in the fact that a combined setting of a professional and political approach is formed to handle the task of constitutional adjudication. A similar pattern is also followed at state level where the Constitutional Interpretation Commission, Council of Nationalities and Council of Constitutional Inquiry are envisaged to be engaged in this matter. The Council of Constitutional Inquiry has been established at the federal level as well as in a few regional states. At the regional state level, the states of Amhara, Oromia and Southern Nations, Nationalities and Peoples are those who have already established the Council of Constitutional Inquiry.

---

[1] Fasil Nahum, *Constitution for a Nation of Nations – The Ethiopian Prospect* 59 (Lawrenceville/Asmara: The Red Sea Press, 1997).

At the federal level, the Council of Constitutional Inquiry was established in 1996 and already some of its members are currently serving their second term.

Unlike its counterparts in many other countries, the composition of the Council of Constitutional Inquiry is not confined to judges. The constitution arranged it for the Council to have eleven members of different mix of which six are "...legal experts of proven professional competence and high moral standing..." to be appointed by the head of state upon recommendation of the House of Peoples' Representatives. The federal Council of Constitutional Inquiry (the regional Councils of Constitutional Inquiry have a similar composition) is therefore composed of the president and vice-president of the federal Supreme Court who occupy the position *ex officio* (to serve as chairman and deputy chairman of the Council), six legal experts appointed by the president of the republic on recommendation of the House of Peoples' Representatives for their proven professional competence and high moral standing, and three persons designated by the House of Federation from among its members.

Members of the Council have their terms of office determined according to their way of inclusion in the Council. Hence, the *ex officio* members have their term for as long as the period of their position in the Supreme Court lasts, the six legal experts have a term equal to that of the president of the republic, i.e. six years, and they can also be re-nominated and the term of members designated by the House of the Federation equals the term of this House.

The Council of Constitutional Inquiry proclamation provides some guidance as to the appointment, term of office of members of the Council and removal of their membership. However, the proclamation doesn't seem to have sufficient prescriptions for issues that might arise in some respect. It is provided that the body that appoints them is authorised to remove members of the Council subject to good cause and the removal is effected upon approval of a majority vote of the House of the Federation. The fact that what constitutes a good cause for removal of a member of the Council is not clarified is likely to cause tenure insecurity which as a result could have the effect of undermining the independence of members of such an important institution. Obviously, the *ex officio* positions are not subject to such a threat. In view of strengthening the institutional independence of the organ, this is a point worth considering. At state level, since this organ is not fully established or organised, it is necessary that state authorities be aware of the importance of a clear determination of such issues and address it in a way that helps create a strong and independent institution. Parallel to that, revisiting the working rules of procedure at the federal level is also important.

The unique nature of the mechanism of constitutional interpretation applied by Ethiopia since the adoption of the 1995 constitution is not only reflected in the nature of the organ entrusted with the power of constitutional interpretation but also in the composition of the members of the Council of Constitutional Inquiry. More specifically, as indicated above, non-legal professionals are included as members and this is not a common practice in many systems. Membership in the Council therefore is not restricted to legal experts. Eight of them are obviously legal professionals as the constitution prescribes that six members should be lawyers of proven professional competence and integrity. The other two are judges by their position in the Supreme Court. The remaining members however may or may not be legal experts since their membership is not conditioned on their professional competence but their representative capacity.

The Council of Constitutional Inquiry has the power to investigate constitutional disputes and submit recommendations to the House of the Federation should it find interpretation of the constitution necessary. As stipulated in the rules of procedure of the Council and the Council of Constitutional Inquiry proclamation, the Council may receive cases from the House of the Federation, state legislative and executive organs and from any court or interested party. The Council sits quarterly and an extraordinary meeting may also be called.

Though its rulings are non-binding, as they are subject to approval by the House of the Federation, The Council of Constitutional Inquiry still influences to an important degree the protection of human rights and the sustainment of democracy. Given the level of recognition accorded by the constitution to the respect for and protection of human rights, the role of the Council and the House of the Federation in sustaining democracy and the protection of human rights is immense. Their involvement and interaction in matters of constitutional adjudication is thus of significant importance in ensuring the constitutional guarantees.

The Council of Constitutional Inquiry was established in 1996 to deal with issues of constitutional interpretation. In prior times there was no such arrangement in the 1931 and 1955 constitutions and in the 1986 constitution this was a power vested in the Council of state, the supreme law making organ of the then regime.

Exercising its constitutional powers, the Council of Constitutional Inquiry has adopted its own rules of procedure, which have been approved by the House of the Federation. Along with that, it has determined the persons or organizations that could institute a case before it and the mode of presentation of applications. Guided by the constitution, the Council of Constitutional Inquiry proclamation and the rules of procedure together with the adjudication process as practised by the Council for a decade, have enabled parties to bring their case before the Council and to the House of the Federation on an appeal basis.
Slowly the present constitutional interpretation system in Ethiopia, especially with the advent of some important cases like the Benishangul-Gumuz election

case and the Kedija Beshir case related to adjudication by religious laws and institutions, is moving towards influencing the legal and constitutional system in general. However, the fact that the Council is organised to work in sessions convening on a quarterly basis does not enable it to be as accessible as it should be. Some suggest that the Council cannot deliver what is expected of it unless it is made to work on a full-time basis. Taking account of the level of complexity of cases reaching the Council this appears to be a sound proposition

5. PROCEEDINGS BEFORE THE COUNCIL

Initiation of cases for constitutional adjudication is an important aspect of the constitutional adjudication process. As this is an important aspect of empowering citizens, it holds a key place in the whole process of adjudication. According to the rules of procedure of the Council of Constitutional Inquiry and the Council of Constitutional Inquiry proclamation, the House of the Federation, state legislative and executive bodies, courts and any interested party are allowed to launch the process. These instruments have provided indicative provisions on who has the right to initiate cases for constitutional adjudication and accordingly the aforementioned organs are the ones who are allowed to petition a case with the House of the Federation or the Council of Constitutional Inquiry. Accordingly, in the current system of constitutional adjudication an issue could arise with or in the absence of court litigation.

Compared to the general provision under Article 84 of the federal constitution, the rules of procedure adopted by the Council of Constitutional Inquiry went further in elaborating upon what was stated in general terms in the constitution and gave a list of those who are authorised to launch a constitutional adjudication. Of the listings in the constitution, the Council of Constitutional Inquiry proclamation and the rules of procedure, it is the part that empowers an interested party that has the potential to be the subject of controversy. This could particularly be the case when the issue of constitutionality refers to the exercise of legislative or executive power. Such a situation has the ability to attract parties of direct or indirect interest such as human rights advocacy groups. The scope of those who or which are considered an 'interested party' and entitled to exercise the right to initiate constitutional adjudication is therefore likely to be the subject of controversy.

The way this provision is framed leaves room for its invocation by advocacy groups to initiate a case for constitutional adjudication when especially it involves alleged violations of human rights. That seems to be the reason why the Ethiopian Women Lawyers Association for instance has instituted a case on behalf of a woman who had contested adjudication of an inheritance case by a religious court against her consent as unconstitutional. The association intervened with a view that the way the case under consideration was handled by the religious court as well as by the regular court had a far-reaching effect of jeopardizing women's rights in general. This provision could even open the possibility for extended standing to initiate cases for constitutional adjudication by a number of actors which could among others include human rights NGOs, political parties and moreover that could include the newly established national institutions of The Human Rights Commission and The Office of The Ombudsman.

Records of the registrar of the Council of Constitutional Inquiry and of the House of the Federation reveal that, during its ten-year period of office, the Council has investigated plenty of issues alleged to involve constitutional adjudication. The majority of the cases that reached the Council of Constitutional Inquiry have been rejected on grounds of not meriting constitutional interpretation. Out of the cases recorded in the registrar of the Council, five cases were related to legislative acts alleged to contravene the constitution. These are the Land Law enacted by the Amhara State Council, the Federal Anti Corruption Proclamation, the Election Proclamation, Special Prosecutor Establishment Proclamation and Consolidation of the House of Federation Proclamation; all of which were declared to be constitutional.

A significant number of the cases were rejected for reasons of not exhausting the remedies offered by government institutions having the power to consider and decide on the matter. The Council of Constitutional Inquiry Proclamation requires that a case should first be investigated as to whether it has exhausted all the possibilities for seeking remedies from different and relevant institutions of administrative or judicial structure. Some cases were rejected due to their linkage to a regional constitution and the Council thus decided that their determination was within the competence of the state Council of Constitutional Inquiry. This is interesting when viewed against the situation of the non-operation or non-existence in some regions of state Councils of Constitutional Inquiry. Few cases also arose in relation to adjudication by religious courts against the will of one of the parties and a couple of cases were related to self-determination demands made by applicants claiming recognition as a group of separate ethnic identity. The Denta Debemo, Bahrework Mesmes and the Silte cases of the Southern Nation, Nationalities and Peoples State are the notable cases in this regard. One case that was raised had to do with the contesting of a ruling of the election board and was finally decided by the House of the Federation.

In undertaking its task of determining the constitutionality of an act or practice of the government or of an individual or the constitutionality of a legislative act, the Council is obliged to follow principles of interpretation as determined by the Council of Constitutional Inquiry proclamation and to be developed by it.

6. PRINCIPLES OF INTERPRETATION

An exercise of power of constitutional adjudication has to follow certain guidelines. In the interest of the proper execution of this task, the Council of Constitutional Inquiry and the House of the Federation are supposed to apply certain principles in executing their respective tasks of submitting recommendation to the House of the Federation and interpreting the constitution. Except for what is provided in the constitution in a very general manner, to date it seems that no clear set of principles of interpretation have been established to guide the process of adjudication. With the adoption of the Council of Constitutional Inquiry Proclamation in 2001 there seems to have been some partial move in this direction. By way of confirmation of the principles provided in the constitution, the proclamation authorised and required the Council to develop and implement principles of interpretation, which it believes can help in executing its task of investigating issues of constitutionality and submitting recommendations to the House of the Federation. While authorising the Council to develop principles, the proclamation also requires it to ensure conformity of its work with the principles enshrined in the Universal Declaration of Human Rights, International Covenants on Human rights and International Instruments adopted by Ethiopia. The House of the Federation in similar fashion is authorised to develop and implement principles applicable to constitutional interpretation and ensure conformity of the execution of its task with the principles enshrined in the aforementioned human rights instruments. The fact that both organs are authorised to identify and implement principles of interpretation might cause overlap. However, the fact that the exclusive competence to render final rulings on adjudication is accorded to the House could take care of the possible overlap that might arise in practice.

7. RULINGS OF THE COUNCIL AND THE HOUSE

The Council and the House, over the last ten years have handed down few decisions, but decisions of profound impact. As stated above, the sizable part of cases that reached the Council was struck out at a preliminary stage on grounds of not meriting constitutional adjudication. But there were also a few important cases heard by the Council and submitted to the House of the Federation for a final ruling. Reference to the records of the registrar of the Council of Constitutional Inquiry indicates that to date nearly two third of the cases that reached the registrar of the Council are struck out at first instance and that the Council submitted its recommendation for constitutional interpretation to the House only for a very small number of cases. By case category, the majority of the cases were initiated by private parties and only five cases had to do with contesting the constitutionality of laws adopted by the House of Peoples' Representatives and regional parliaments. The rest of the cases implied contesting the constitutionality of decisions of federal and state executive organs or court rulings. The cases contesting court rulings give the impression that parties to these cases considered this forum as another level of appeal against rulings in cassation or appellate level courts. Therefore, the tasks of the Council and the House in this regard do not seem to be familiar to the public.

In general there are only a limited number of cases that have been entertained by the Council as meriting constitutional adjudication. The following cases can be mentioned as landmark cases where the role of the Council and the House of the Federation as interpreters of the constitution has been exercised:

The election right case

This case was initiated by a group of persons from the Bambasi and Assosa *woreda* of the Benishangul Gumuz state who claimed to belong to and represent the Amhara, Oromo, Agew and Tigray nationalities, residents of the area. They contested the constitutionality of a decision of the Election Board banning them from running for election on grounds of not knowing the language of the electoral district, and of Article 38 of proclamation 111|95. They argued that the decision of the Board and Article 38 of the said proclamation contradicted Article 38 of the constitution, a provision that guarantees the right to vote and to be elected. On reference by the House of the Federation (citing Articles 62 and 84 of the constitution) the Council of Constitutional Inquiry considered the case and submitted its recommendation stating the unconstitutionality of the decision of the board and of the contested provision of the proclamation. The recommendation was passed by a majority vote of five to two and was forwarded to the House of the Federation on 07 July 2000.

The minority opinion argued that the alleged proclamation did not have any inconsistency with the constitution and that the decision of the electoral board, as it had been decided based on the alleged law, was also constitutional. The minority opinion reiterated that Article 38 of the said proclamation, requiring a candidate to know the language of the electoral district as a requirement to qualify and be able to run for election, is not solely aimed at excluding those who do not know the local language, but is inspired by the concern that the candidates have to know the language of their constituency. The minority further argued that language is an important aspect of rights such as the right to self-rule and is an expression of the special place of and recognition accorded to the identity of nations and nationalities. Furthermore, this provision hasn't prohibited someone from running for election because of his membership of a certain language group; it merely requires him or her to know the language of that group he or she is intending to represent. The minority opinion is also of the view that election is not a right without any limit; it is rather subjected to limits that can be imposed by law. Given these facts, the minority opinion argued there is no reason for finding the law and the subsequent decision passed by the Election Board discriminatory and in contradiction with the constitution.

The House of the Federation in its first regular session of the first year of its term referred the opinion of the Council to the legal affairs committee. It instructed the committee to study the recommendation of the Council and propose an opinion for the final ruling by the House. Based on the deliberation of the committee, the House decided the case in its second regular session of the third year term of the House. In delivering its final verdict the House declared the alleged proclamation constitutional and the decision of the board unconstitutional referring to its decision of excluding those candidates who are running for the federal parliament. Accordingly the House decided that the decision of the board shall remain non-enforceable and instructed all federal and state organs of the government to ensure enforcement of this decision.

The Silte case

Two applicants who claimed to represent the community initially filed this case. They filed their case with the House of the Federation and this was later followed by an application from a person who by that time was a member of the House of Peoples' Representatives and of the Silte Democratic Unity Party. The applicants, referring to the fact that their people had been considered as Gurage against their will for a long period in denial of their right to self-determination, requested the House to ensure the exercise of their constitutional right. They stressed that the Silte are not Gurage but people with their own language, territory and history and argued that their being considered Gurage contravened their right to self-determination. The Council of Constitutional Inquiry upon referral from the House considered the case. Upon referral of the case the House asked the Council to deal with issues such as who shall decide on questions that arise in relation to determination of ethnic identity of a community and what procedure should be followed to reach a decision on such matter? Based on an opinion forwarded by the Council the case was referred back to the regional Council.

The Council of Constitutional Inquiry in its opinion to the House has emphasised the principle of exhaustion of local remedies and gave the opinion that the matter should be considered first by the regional mechanisms and indicated that the interested party or parties can bring their case back to the House of the Federation if they feel the decision of the State Council is delivered in a manner that contradicts the constitution. The Council in its opinion forwarded to the House suggested that in dealing with this issue, the State Council needs to observe that the process of determination of this issue is conducted with direct participation of the community that raises the question, by secret ballot, in a free and fair manner and is attended by impartial observers.

Kedija Beshir case

This case was submitted to the Council of Constitutional Inquiry by an application filed by the Ethiopian Women Lawyers Association on behalf of Kedija Beshir. It refers to a decision on an inheritance case by a Naiba court based on the Sharia law. Before its submission to the Council the case had passed through the appeal stages up to the Supreme Sharia Court and finally the federal Supreme Court cassation division of the regular court. The decision of the Naiba court was upheld at all levels. The present applicant (in whose name the Ethiopian Women Lawyers Association filed the complaint) and three other co-defendants together originally filed their objection to the Naiba court itself stating their unwillingness for the case to be considered by this religious court. However the court to which the objection was filed ruled against the objection and proceeded to deal with the merits of the case and delivered its decision according to the laws of the Sharia. The Ethiopian Women Lawyers Association extended its assistance to the applicant with a view that the way this case was handled at all levels of the court it passed through, jeopardised rights of women in general by contravening constitutionally recognised rights of women. The present applicant thus, with the assistance of the Ethiopian Women Lawyers Association, brought the case to the attention of the Council of Constitutional Inquiry challenging the ruling of the Naiba court and the further confirmation of its decision by the highest religious and regular courts of the country as unconstitutional.

The Council of Constitutional Inquiry examined the case and reached the conclusion that the way this case was resolved by the courts at all levels contravened Article 34(5) of the constitution - a provision that recognises the right of the parties to adjudication of disputes by religious or customary institutions. According to this provision, disputes relating to personal and family matters can be handled by religious or customary institutions only with the consent of parties to the dispute. Accordingly, the Council stated that the jurisdiction of religious or customary adjudication doesn't assume a compulsory jurisdiction. Thus the determination of the matter by the Naiba court against the consent of the parties to the dispute was unconstitutional. This was so because the case was tried by the Naiba court (a religious court) against the objection of the parties to the dispute while it was a dispute related to a family matter that needed to secure the consent of the parties as a prerequisite. The Council thus reached the conclusion that the decision of the courts (both the religious and the formal court) in this case contravened the constitution and delivered its opinion to the House of the Federation. The House of the Federation in its second regular session of the fourth year of its term approved the submission of the Council and decided the ruling of the courts was unconstitutional.

Recently the federal Council of Constitutional Inquiry has more cases directly and indirectly related to the exercise of electoral rights. Leaders of the Coalition for Unity and Democracy (CUD) filed a case contesting the decision of the Prime Minster banning demonstration in Addis Ababa city following the post electoral unrest. The Council rejected the case alleging that the contested act was undertaken within the role of the Prime Minister as the chief of the federal government.

In another case the ex-president (who served as the president of the republic from 1995 to 2001) contested the constitutionality of a law promulgated to provide for the administration of the president. He noted that Proclamation 255|2001, which was promulgated to determine the administration of the president, contravened the constitutional rights to opinion, thought and expression and the right to vote and be elected. He pointed to the provision of the said proclamation, which reads "*the president shall be obliged to keep himself aloof from any partisan political movement during or after his presidency.*" Failure to discharge these and other obligations set by this proclamation causes termination of the privileges and benefits that the ex-president is entitled to receive. This, he argued, infringes the constitutional right to vote and be elected. The Council struck out the case as not meriting investigation stating that the contested legislation doesn't prevent the president from exercising his rights but required him to remain non-partisan so that he can claim the privileges and benefits granted to ex-presidents by the contested law.

8. STATE JURISDICTIONS

Owing to the dual setup of the legislative, executive and judicial power and pursuant to Article 52(2)(b) of the FDRE constitution, states have the power "*to enact and execute state constitutions and other laws.*" Accordingly, each member state of the Federal Democratic Republic of Ethiopia does have its constitution and constitutional adjudication is one of the issues addressed by these state constitutions. All the state constitutions, i.e. the revised constitutions of Tigray, Afar, Amhara, Oromia, Southern Nations, Nationalities and Peoples (SNNPRS), Somali, Benishangul Gumuz, Gambella and Harari states, have devoted a part of their text to this issue. These constitutions came up with few, though major, changes to the contents of the constitutions they amend.

As has been hinted at in the preceding discussion, in the previous state constitutions power of constitutional interpretation was entrusted to the single chamber state parliament. One of the changes was that the power to render an ultimate ruling on matters of constitutional adjudication was designated to be the competence of the state Constitutional Interpretation Commission in the constitutions of the states of Tigray, Afar, Amhara, Oromia, Somali, Benishangul-Gumuz, Gambella and of the Council of Nationalities in the Southern Region state constitution. Accordingly the Southern region state constitution provided for the establishment of two Councils, i.e. the State Council and Council of Nationalities. The Council of Nationalities is established by representation from nations, nationalities and peoples of the state and entrusted with the power to interpret the state constitution. This Council is organised almost in a manner identical to the House of the Federation and assumed the authority to render the ultimate ruling on the interpretation of the state constitution.

State constitutions anticipate the establishment of the Council of Constitutional Inquiry to assist the Commission for Constitutional Interpretation or Council of Nationalities in their task of interpreting the constitution. To date, only some states (Amhara, Oromia and Southern Region state) have taken the lead in establishing the Council of Constitutional Inquiry. The composition of the state Council of Constitutional Inquiry is similar to the federal one in all the nine states. Accordingly state Councils of Constitutional Inquiry comprise the president and vice president of the state Supreme Court, six legal experts of proven professional competence and high moral standing to be appointed by the State Council on recommendation by the chief executive and three members to be designated from the Council of Nationalities in the Southern region and from the State Council in all other regions.

The scope of competence of federal vis-à-vis state Councils of Constitutional Inquiry and of the House of the Federation vis-à-vis state Commissions for Constitutional Interpretation or Council of Nationalities remains yet unclear. Whereas, on the other hand, cases seeking determination of constitutionality are rejected on grounds of non-exhaustion of local remedies of which the state Council of Constitutional Inquiry is considered one mechanism. This is being done by the federal Council of Constitutional Inquiry as the Council of Constitutional Inquiry proclamation provides that a case may be submitted to the Council if it has exhausted the local remedies as stated under Article 23 of this proclamation which reads:

"*Any person who alleges that his fundamental rights and freedoms have been violated by the final decision of any government institution or official may present his case to the Council of Constitutional Inquiry for constitutional interpretation*

Any appeal, under sub article (1) of this article, may be made to the Council if the case has been exhausted by the government institution having the power with due hierarchy to consider it

Final decision, under sub article (1) and (2) of this article, shall mean an adjudication that has been exhausted and against which no appeal lies on the same path way"

Because of the degree of similarity exhibited in the contents of the state and federal constitutions (especially part three of the federal and state constitutions) jurisdiction overlap over constitutional adjudication is highly likely to occur between the competent federal and state organs. The fact that the practice of constitutional adjudication is a new practice organised in a unique manner and that sufficient practice has not yet developed poses a problem to which the system has to give an answer.

This dual system of constitutional control could cause the same act of the legislative or the executive to be challenged both at the federal and state Council of Constitutional Inquiry or a case on which ruling is delivered by the federal organ could possibly be instituted as a new case at the regional level.

Thus the system has to look for a way that enables the dual system to work within the confines of the areas of competence delimited for each. One may assume that state organs for constitutional interpretation have jurisdiction only over cases related to state laws and state acts; however there is the possibility that a case can be filed at the federal Council of Constitutional Inquiry while it is a case that has already been disposed of by a state Commission for Constitutional Interpretation. This has already been experienced in the judiciary where cases tried and finally decided by state court of cassation divisions were taken on appeal to the federal Supreme Court cassation division and disposed of by the bench. The constitutional adjudication proceedings are not immune from that. Such possibility implies that this undetermined situation could in the future be a source of debate on matters of constitutional adjudication. As cases of that type have not been encountered yet there is no evidence to prove this arrangement as uniquely problematic but one can however foresee that it is likely to cause a challenge and that is a problem the system has to address.

No matter the reason why this hasn't happened yet and why no case has been registered at state level (even in the regions where the effort to establish the Council has been exerted) it is an issue that seeks attention. This matter is likely to be tested especially when institutions like The Human Rights Commission and The Office of the Ombudsman come to function fully and may launch cases. They have the objective of looking into the compatibility of actions and legislation or directives issued by the government with the standards of human rights and the constitution.

9. EFFECTS OF CONSTITUTIONAL ADJUDICATION PROCEEDINGS

Countries with different mechanisms of constitutional adjudication follow their own approach towards the effect of constitutional interpretation. Under the Ethiopian system it is decided by legislation as to what the effect of a constitutional interpretation decision should be. This was a matter that had not been clarified for sometime. Though the constitution entered into force in August 1995 and the Council of Constitutional Inquiry was established in 1996 and has been operating since then, the proclamation that has clarified this matter (Proclamation no 251|2001; a proclamation to consolidate the House of Federation) was only adopted in 2001. In between this period the Council and the House have entertained plenty of cases in the absence of a clear determination on effects of final rulings on constitutional adjudication.

The proclamation has now made it clear that the decision of the House on constitutional adjudication shall have an effect as of the date of the decision and the decision shall remain applicable to similar issues that may arise in the future. This in a way is a new development in the field as it has introduced a precedent system; a practice peculiar to the common law system has thus been introduced into the predominantly civilian legal tradition. As a country of civil law tradition there is no possibility for the introduction of judge-made laws in Ethiopia. Law making is the sole responsibility of the legislative arm of the state. A sudden departure is exhibited with the adoption of this precedence system for the constitutional adjudication. It is provided in an explicit way that decisions of the House shall apply to future similar cases. Though the constitution was not express in this respect and even if the Council has, for sometime since its establishment in 1996, worked in the absence of a clear determination in this regard, it has now this system to apply.

The proclamation has instructed that the decisions of the House shall be published in a special issue to be issued for this purpose. That arrangement helps to ensure enforceability of decisions of the House. Pursuant to this system of according the precedent effect to final rulings of constitutional adjudication, decisions of the House are going to have the effect of law and seek observance by all concerned persons or organs. For a law to enter into force, publication in the official *Negarit Gazzeta* is required. However this is not required for the rulings of the House in cases of constitutional adjudication. Publication of a special issue is taken as an alternative for that. The House, as the final authority on matters of constitutional adjudication, is required to ensure publication of its rulings in a special publication issued for this purpose. This is an important task that needs to be implemented with due care and with sufficient distribution, as such rulings are going to have significant effect.

In the face of the dual setup of constitutional adjudication, publication will be of significant importance because that will help enable persons and organs authorized to launch cases for constitutional adjudication to check whether the House has considered the case and a ruling has been rendered on it. It is also necessary for the legislative, executive and judicial organs to be kept informed of such decisions that affect their daily work.

The House of Federation proclamation requires that federal and state legislatures have to be consulted especially when the process of constitutional adjudication involves a law the constitutionality of which is contested. With the dual law-making being in place in Ethiopia this appears to be a matter that needs to be considered with care and due diligence. It appears that this is the reason for inclusion of Article 16(2) of the proclamation on the House of the Federation which provides that the federal or the state legislative body may be communicated with within six months so that it amends, changes or repeals the law in question before a final decision of unconstitutionality is rendered by the House.

10. ROLE OF THE JUDICIARY

The judiciary is an institution that assumes a key role in the process of ensuring democracy and the rule of law. The judicial branch of the state is normally charged with the task of ensuring protection of rights and freedoms recognised by the constitution and subsequent legal sources. Hence, constitutional recognition is accorded to the judiciary and to its existence as an organ independent of the control of the executive branch of the state. Through the exercise of its judicial function the judiciary doesn't end up merely resolving disputes between or among parties to a dispute, but also plays a key role in deterring arbitrary exercise of governmental power. In the present system of the judiciary in Ethiopia the supreme judicial authority is vested in the federal and state Supreme Courts in their respective jurisdictions.

The stated task of the judiciary keeps the judiciary closer to the functions of the Council of Constitutional Inquiry, the House of the Federation and the state Constitutional Interpretation Commission or Council of Nationalities. In its daily practice, the judiciary is the primary institution where the constitution is to be under constant consideration. The challenge however is that a clear delimitation of competence in connection to matters that involve determination of constitutionality has not yet been developed to govern the relationship between the Council of Constitutional Inquiry and the House of the Federation on the one hand and the judiciary on the other hand. It is obvious that there are explicit provisions that determine the relationship between those organs in a limited way. The constitution and the proclamation on the Council of Constitutional Inquiry stipulate that a case might be referred by the court for consideration by the Council and the Council can also remand a case to the concerned court when it finds that there is no need to interpret the constitution or may instruct the court to suspend a proceeding or execution of a case which is under consideration. However the matter requires thinking beyond that, as it is impossible to draw a clear demarcation in their scope of competence. Courts cannot avoid consideration of the constitution in disposing cases that come to their attention and no sufficient guidance to that effect is developed. Then cases being handled by the judiciary can reach the Council of Constitutional Inquiry on referral by the courts or when filed by an interested party. So far, only a couple of cases have been referred to the Council of Constitutional Inquiry by the courts. These are cases referred by the North Gonder Woreda

Court and the federal First Instance Court. Else the courts seem inclined to entertain cases that are brought to their attention and are within their competence. In the absence of clear reason, courts tend to avoid blanket referral of all claims of constitutionality or constitutional interpretation to the Council of Constitutional Inquiry.

11. THE PLACE OF TRADITIONAL AND RELIGIOUS RULES AND INSTITUTIONS

Ethiopia is a country of diverse culture, religion, tradition and local institutions. Added to that, the constitutional recognition of the right to be adjudicated by traditional and religious institutions and other related rights implementation poses a challenge in view of constitutional interpretation or adjudication. The traditional or religious laws in some aspects are likely to emerge inconsistent with the principles and rules enshrined in the formal laws, particularly with some of the rights recognised by the constitution. There may therefore arise instances where determination of constitutionality could be at issue, calling for the role of the Council of Constitutional Inquiry and the House of the Federation. That may present a formidable difficulty involving complex issues related to determination of the interaction between the formal laws and religious rules such as the Sharia and the customary rules like in the case of the *ADDA* system in Afar and the *Gadda* system in Oromia. How do these constitutionally recognised and partly institutionalised religious or customary institutions interact with these constitutional organs? Does the Council of Constitutional Inquiry need to consider the rules of these organs in executing its task of interpreting the constitution or determining issues of constitutionality? What should the relationship between rules of these institutions and the constitution be? This could be complicated especially in the absence of detailed rules to guide such an interaction.

Though not many cases have yet arisen in this regard, there was an instance where a case had reached the Council of Constitutional Inquiry and had its root in the right to be adjudicated by religious laws and institutions. If we, for instance, compare this issue with the system adopted in Egypt for similar matters, the Egyptian constitution incorporates explicit provisions that guide the determination by the constitutional court on such issues. These provisions state that Islam is the official religion and that the principal source of legislation is Islamic jurisprudence. At the other end the Ethiopian federal and state constitutions declare the separation of state and religion in an explicit manner. However, no mechanism seems to have been established yet, as no significant literature or precedence has been developed in this regard. Thus if an issue of such a nature arises, its determination won't be easy as there are no developed rules or precedents to guide it.

12. CONCLUSION

It is evident that the present mechanism of constitutional control in Ethiopia is characterized by a dual setup envisaged by the federal and state constitutions. All the state constitutions have addressed this issue while only very few have established the institutions necessary for its execution. Owing to the prevailing ethnic, cultural and religious diversity such mode of arrangement of constitutional adjudication seems necessary. However, the absence of the institutional setting to ensure implementation of this task at state level is undoubtedly affecting the overall process of constitutional adjudication. Considering the complex federal framework that is in place, coupled with the prevailing pluralistic mode of adjudication (i.e. the judiciary in the formal structure and the recognition accorded to religious and traditional institutions by the federal and state constitutions) and the broader recognition of human rights, one can envision the complexity of issues that this process of adjudication is expected to address. Besides, no system has been developed to delimit the scope of competence between the state and federal organs of constitutional adjudication. Consequently some cases, in the event of rejection by the federal Council of Constitutional Inquiry on grounds of non-exhaustion of local remedies, are likely to remain unaddressed.

Since the Council of Constitutional Inquiry commenced its function in 1996, the cases that appear before it are growing in size and complexity. The complexity of issues caused by the dual setup of the system of constitutional adjudication, the multicultural and multilingual background of society and the degree of constitutional recognition accorded to rights and freedoms warrants a full-time Council that is able to execute its task with sufficient time and research. Though the proclamation on the House of the Federation instructs for deliberation of decisions on constitutional adjudication in the shortest possible time, in reality constitutional adjudication is taking longer time than anticipated by the law. The fact that the Council of Constitutional Inquiry is organised to work in sessions has partly contributed to this. Owing to the complexity of issues that call for constitutional adjudication, it appears that the Council of Constitutional Inquiry needs to be organised to work full time and be assisted by full-time experts. This is a matter that the Council of Constitutional Inquiry proclamation has also provided, stating that members of the Council may be assigned to work at the head office permanently. Therefore, considering the precedence effect and the far-reaching consequence of the decisions of the House of the Federation, the Council needs to be institutionalised to be in a shape to assist the House to the level required.

A matter of equal importance in this regard is that the decisions of the House need to be publicized and made accessible. No clear mechanism of communicating rulings of the House is however in place yet. In the absence of this mechanism it will be difficult for respective institutions and parties to identify whether the Council and the House have reviewed the case. Because of the fact that exhaustion of local remedies is adopted as a principle in the process of constitutional adjudication, parties are required to comply with that. However in the absence of publicity of decisions of the House, parties will be faced with difficulty in the exercise of this right.

The role of the judiciary in the present system of constitutional adjudication is not very clear. It however appears that the judiciary in the execution of its daily functions cannot be prevented from applying the constitution as it is difficult to imagine a court case that doesn't involve consideration of the constitution. That seems also to be what is going on in practice as not many cases are being referred by the courts to the Council.

6. Ethiopia and the Right to Secession in International and Comparative Law

Stefaan Smis•

1. INTRODUCTION

Article 39 of the Constitution of Ethiopia proclaims that "*[e]very Nation, Nationality and People in Ethiopia has an unconditional right to self-determination, including the right to secession.*" Knowing that Ethiopia is a state constituted of numerous population groups most of them possessing a strong sense of belonging based on their own traditions, languages or even religion, it seems curious that this state espouses such a progressive approach to self-determination. What makes it even more curious is that Ethiopia has historically played an important role in creating a static African view on self-determination. Since their independence African states have indeed opted for keeping the colonial boundaries unaltered even if this meant that artificial and sometimes unviable states had to be maintained. This obliged them to embark on a long process of building a national consciousness. National symbols were created, history was rewritten, myths were invented but also African states became the champions of interpreting self-determination only as a right to decolonisation while at the same time defending extreme views on the principles of non-interference and territorial integrity in order to bar all meso-nationalistic demands that could threaten the consolidation of these young and fragile states.

This contribution focuses on the reference to the concept of secession in the Constitution of Ethiopia and looks at it from the point of view of international and comparative law. In very general terms, secession can be described as an act or a process by which a part of a state withdraws from that state to become independent without necessarily receiving the consent of the whole or other constituent parts of that state. To understand secession and its position in law one must put it in the broader context of the right to self-determination to which it is related. However, while linking secession to self-determination one must be aware that there are many manifestations and manners to exercise self-determination.[1] We will first look at the development of self-

---

• Professor at the Faculty of Law and Criminology of the Vrije Universiteit Brussel and Reader at the School of Law of the University of Westminster. E-mail: ssmis@vub.ac.be. I am grateful to Stephen Sevidzem Kingah for his valuable comments.

[1] Kirgis, for example, distinguishes eight 'degrees' of self-determination some of them pertaining to international customary law, others not. His eight degrees of self-determination are: (1) the right to be free from colonial domination; (2) the right to remain dependent, if it represents the will of the

determination and how it has been consolidated as a rule of international law. We will then have a closer look at the legal value of secession properly both in the broader international law debate on self-determination and its position in comparative public law as well. This should allow us to formulate some concluding remarks regarding the situation in Ethiopia.

2. THE HISTORY OF SELF-DETERMINATION

Self-determination was accepted as a right under international law during the second half of the twentieth century but its roots can be traced back to the writings of eighteenth century theorists who tried to elaborate views on democracy based on the consent of the governed and the sovereignty of the nation. Closely interacting with the previous ideas and similarly influencing the concept of self-determination were the various theories on nationalism that equally saw the light of day during the eighteenth but mainly the nineteenth century.[2] The word itself, however, postdates the development of the concept and is borrowed from Kant and other radical 'German' philosophers who considered '*selbstbestimmung*' as an individual right to be morally free and thus not to be subjected to anyone or to any authority.[3] This 'right' was quickly transposed from an individual right to autonomy to a collective right to independence to be exercised by a group for that purpose called the nation. The enthusiasm for these ideas made self-determination quickly become a core principle in political philosophy. It therefore played a driving role in the great revolutions of that time.

The American settlers of the eighteenth century found it increasingly difficult to be subjected to Westminster without having the opportunity to be involved in their governance:[4] the colonists were represented neither by the Lords nor by the Commons and thus did not participate in the sovereignty of the nation. When the time came to implement unpopular measures such as the Fiscal Acts, the Declaration Act or the Stamp Act, the colonists rejected them demanding to be represented: "no taxation without representation". But demands were not

dependent people who occupy a defined territory; (3) the right to dissolve a state, at least if done peacefully, and to form new states on the territory of the former one; (4) the right to secede; (5) the right of a divided state to reunite; (6) the right of limited autonomy, short of secession, for groups defined territorially or by common ethnic, religious and linguistic bonds; (7) the right of minority groups within a larger political entity; and (8) the internal self-determination freedom to choose one's own form of government, or even more sharply, the right to a democratic form of government. *See* F. L. Kirgis, The Degrees of Self-Determination in the United Nations Era, 88 *American Journal of International Law* 307-308 (1994).

[2] For the theories on nationalism, see e.g. E.J. Hobsbawm, *Nations and Nationalism since 1780. Programme, Myth, Reality* (Cambridge: Cambridge University Press, 1990).

[3] R.T. De George, The Myth of the Right of Collective Self-Determination, in: W. Twinning (ed.), *Issues of Self-Determination* 4 (Aberdeen: Aberdeen University Press, 1991).

[4] *See* B. Donoughue, *British Politics and the American Revolution: The Path to War: 1773-75,* 1-21 (L. Macmillan, 1964).

met and the subsequent use of force and inflicted suffering convinced the colonists that they had to look outside the British Empire to secure their rights. Inspired by British theorists the leaders of the revolution advanced their claim for independent statehood in a number of documents of which the Declaration of Independence is most renowned.[5] It announced the separation of the 13 colonies from Great Britain and offered a justification for the same:

> *"When in the Course of human events it becomes necessary for one people to dissolve the political bands which have connected them with another, and to assume among the powers of the earth, the separate and equal station to which the laws of Nature and the Nature's God entitle them, a decent respect to the opinions of mankind requires that they should declare the causes which impel them to the separation.*
> *We hold these Truths to be self-evident, that all Men are created equal, that they are endowed by their Creator with certain unalienable Rights, that among these are Life, Liberty and the Pursuit of Happiness. That to secure these Rights, Governments are instituted among Men, deriving their just Powers from the Consent of the Governed, that whenever any Form of Government becomes destructive of these Ends, it is the Right of the People to alter or abolish it and to institute new Government, laying its Foundation on such Principles and organising Powers in such Form, as to them shall seem most likely to effect their Safety and Happiness."*[6]

The colonists considered that secession should not be recognised for 'light and transient causes' but 'when a long train of abuses and usurpations, pursuing invariably the same object evinces a design to reduce them under absolute Despotism, it is their right, it is their duty, to throw off such government, and to provide new Guards for their future security.'[7] The drafters of the Declaration considered it an affirmation of their fight to be delivered from the foreign yoke and legitimating the obtained secession. At the same time, they ensured that the government resulting from this separation became that of the people. They considered the will of the people supreme because it is sovereign. This made the American Declaration of Independence an inexhaustible source of inspiration for subsequent revolutions. It also made it a moral force for legitimisation for the whole decolonisation movement and even the today's timid but growing support for a right of secession.

---

[5] *See generally* C. L. Becker, *The Declaration of Independence. A Study in History and Political Ideas* (New York: Random House, 1942).
[6] American Declaration of Independence (4 July 1776).
[7] Encyclopaedia Britannica, Vol. VII, 161 (1964).

The French Revolution illuminates yet another aspect of self-determination; it was clearly not an instance of secession or an anti-colonial war, but rather a revolution to free France from absolutism: 'freedom, equality and fraternity' was the motto. The revolution was aimed at putting the ideas of liberty and equality into practice. 'All men are born and remain equal in right', proclaims the preamble of the Declaration of the Rights of Man and Citizen. 'No class of people had the inherent right to oppress another: relations between peoples were to be governed by justice and not by the favour of the privileged heredity'.[8] The French representative institutions were, therefore, replaced by direct representation of the people. '[T]he people ceased to be an atomic dust of individuals: it took shape and form, became a *whole*, was called the *Nation*,'[9] empowered with certain rights. In short, the nation became sovereign. Borrowing the words of Abbé Sieyes written in his influential pamphlet, *What is the Third Estate*: 'the nation's will is always legal, it is the law itself... In whatever manner a nation wills, it suffices that it does will; all forms are valid and its will is always the supreme law.'[10] This view was confirmed as Article III of the Declaration of the Rights of Man and Citizen which refers to the nation as the source of all sovereignty: '[t]he nation is essentially the source of all sovereignty, nor shall any body of men or any individual exercise authority which is not expressly derived from it.'[11] In other words, what the French Revolution added to self-determination was the requirement that the state must represent the nation since it is sovereign. The latter was built upon the common interests of the whole people against the privileged interests of the individual classes of the ancient regime.

During the nineteenth and early twentieth centuries, the doctrine of self-determination further developed through the theories of nationalism. It became the motor of the nineteenth-century unification processes all through the European continent but also legitimated all sorts of nationalistic demands of groups fighting for recognition and independence within existing states. At the same time, but on the other shore of the Atlantic, the territories subjugated by the *conquistadores* freed themselves from Iberic rule and proclaimed their independence. Consequently, self-determination developed from a right belonging to all to participate in the governance of the state without distinction to a right reserved for a group that wants to distinguish itself from others within the state in order to claim distinct rights. With the national movements coming of age in Europe (1848), it was indeed postulated that every nation had to be allowed the freedom to choose its political status; that every nation was to form a state and

---

[8] Umozurike Oji Umozurike, *Self-Determination in International Law* 11 (Hamden Conn.: Archon Book, 1972).

[9] A. Cobban, *National Self-Determination* 5 (Oxford: Oxford University Press, 1944).

[10] *Quoted* in D. Heater, *National Self-Determination: Woodrow Wilson and his Legacy* 4 (New York: St. Martin's Press Inc., 1994).

[11] *Quoted* in A.M. Connelly, The Right of Self-Determination and International Boundaries, 14 *Thesaurus Acroasium* 551 (1985).

every state to include just one nation.[12] The consequence of this theory was that states that could not convince the inhabitants that they belong to one nation and thus constitute a nation-state were deemed to disappear or at least would face a difficult time convincing the inhabitants of the necessity to maintain the bounds that unite them.[13] This contradiction between the eighteenth and nineteenth century views on self-determination is the dilemma associated with the concept and will explain the tensions that exist until today between its various implementation forms.

During the first decades of the twentieth century, both Wilson and Lenin gave a new *élan* to the principle of self-determination. U.S. President Wilson championed its application during World War I to rally support for his war policy (e.g. the Fourteen Points Program) and after the war to establish peace in Europe, but also to secure the new balance of power in what his contemporaries called a 'new world order'. Lenin, on the other hand, considered the same principle of self-determination as a means of realising his dream of world socialist revolution. As self-determination had grown many faces, it was not surprising that it could also as easily be invoked by the Bolsheviks in their fight against capitalism as by the U.S. government to unite the political left and right in its attempt to counter the upcoming Soviet threat.

At that time, however, the concept did not yet pertain to the domain of public international law even though at the Peace Conference of Versailles the principle had in many ways a greater influence on the parties than several long established rules of international law.[14] The principle was far from applied universally or consistently but in the name of self-determination, the map of Europe was redrawn, some nations gained their independence, frontier disputes were settled, treaties protecting minorities saw the light of day, and with the incorporation of Article 22 in the Covenant of the League of Nations certain peoples, who lived under colonial domination, could cherish and foster the hope of some day becoming independent.

With the outbreak of World War II, self-determination reappeared on the international agenda and with the United Nations era the concept that had up till then been granted only a status of principle of political philosophy finally transformed into a rule of international law. Even though the word 'self-determination' appears twice in the Charter of the United Nations (Articles 1(2) and 55) it is the UN General Assembly that imposed self-determination as a rule of customary international law by which peoples living under colo-

[12] *See* P. Bastide, La révolution de 1848 et le droit international, 72 *Recueil des Cours de l'Académie de Droit International* 214-234 (1948).

[13] Cobban, *supra* note 9, 6. The most obvious examples were Austria-Hungary and the Ottoman Empire.

[14] I. Brownlie, An Essay in the History of the Principle of Self-Determination, *Grotian Society Papers* 94 (1968).

nial, foreign or racist domination were attributed the right to independence. The 1955 Bandung Declaration paved the way for the UN General Assembly: 'colonialism in all its manifestations is an evil which should speedily be brought to an end.'[15] At the close of the 1950s, the General Assembly espoused this view and hence proclaimed the fight against colonialism, foreign domination and military occupation, as one of the first priorities of the world organisation. The Socialist-Third World coalition within the General Assembly used its newly obtained majority to support and facilitate the independence of colonial territories.[16] This policy found its momentum in 1960 when it adopted Resolution 1514 (XV) known as the 'Declaration on the Granting of Independence to Colonial Countries and Peoples', followed by Resolution 1541 (XV) concerning the 'Principles which should guide Members in Determining whether or not an obligation exists to transmit the information called for under Article 73e of the Charter'. Resolution 1514 (XV) insists upon the inalienable right of all colonial peoples to complete freedom, sovereignty and territorial integrity and asserts that colonialism constitutes a denial of human rights and a violation of the Charter of the United Nations. Resolution 1541 (XV) seeks to establish criteria guiding the Member States in determining whether or not there exists an obligation to transmit information under Article 73(e) of the Charter of the United Nations. At the same time it provides the criteria for identifying non-self-governing territories. According to the Resolution, a territory is non-self-governing when it is "*geographically separate and is distinct ethnically and/or culturally from the country administering it.*" Elements of "administrative, political, juridical, economical or historical nature" are considered secondary elements. These pronouncements of the General Assembly quickly transformed into a rule of customary international law.

A right to decolonization is, however, not the sole dimension that has been propagated by the General Assembly since, through a more consensus-based approach, it adopted Resolution 2625 (XXV) known as the 'Declaration on the Principles of International Law Concerning Friendly Relations and Cooperation among states in Accordance with the Charter of the United Nations'. This resolution has a much broader range than its predecessors as it includes

---

[15] Final Communiqué of the Bandung Conference (First meeting of Asian and African Nations, 24 April 1955). *Reprinted* in Royal Institute of International Affairs, *Documents on International Affairs*, 1958, 429 *et seq*.

[16] For a good overview of the United Nations involvement with decolonisation, see A. Rigo Sureda, *The Evolution of the Right of Self-Determination. A Study of United Nations Practice* (Leiden: A.W. Sijthoff, 1973); M. Virally, Droit international et décolonisation devant les Nations Unies, 63 *Annuaire français de droit international* 508-541 (1963); Hector Gros Espiell, *The Right to Self-Determination. Implementation of United Nations Resolutions*. UN Doc. E/CN.4/Sub. 2/405/Rev. 1 (1980); J. Soubeyrol, L'action de l'O.N.U. en faveur de la décolonisation et contre la discrimination raciale, 16 *Thesaurus Acroasium* 559-589 (1990); M.A. Ajomo, International Law, the United Nations, and Decolonization, in: Emmanuel G. Bello & Bola A. Ajibola (eds.), *Essays in Honour of Judge Taslim Olawale Elias*, Vol. I, 77-92 (Dordrecht: Martinus Nijhoff Publishers, 1992); Frank Abdulah, The Right to Decolonization, in: Mohammed Bedjaoui (ed.), *International Law. Achievements and Prospects* 1275-1289 (Dordrecht: Martinus Nijhoff Publishers, 1991).

aspects of pluralistic representative democracy defended by Western states. Adopted to celebrate the organisation's 25th anniversary, the resolution defines seven principles representing the most fundamental areas of inter-state relations.[17] Of these principles there is one that deals exclusively with the principle of equal rights and self-determination. This principle had to reconcile two divergent opinions. On the one side, Western states, in line with their ideology of popular and national sovereignty, defended internal self-determination for all peoples of all sovereign states.[18] On the opposite side, the Socialist Bloc, more or less followed by the Developing World, tried to restrict, as much as possible, the Western approach to self-determination because the right they considered paramount to free colonial territories from foreign domination and freeze the international balance of powers could turn into a dangerous tool against their autocratic rule if it also contained a reference to representative democracy.[19] They, therefore, tried to limit self-determination to its external dimension of a right to decolonisation.[20] As a result, clarity had to be sacrificed to bring the opposing sponsors to agree on a consensus text.

The Declaration holds that self-determination is a right conferred to all peoples. Self-determination is therein defined as the 'right to freely determine without external interference their political status and to pursue their economic, social and cultural development.'[21] The purpose of self-determination is twofold: to promote friendly relations and co-operation among states and to bring about a speedy end to colonialism.[22] Four modes are accepted as ways to implement the right of self-determination: (a) the establishment of a sovereign or independent state, (b) the free association with an independent state, (c) the integration with an independent state, or (d) the emergence into any

[17] The seven principles are: (1) the principle that states shall refrain in their international relations from the threat or use of force against the territorial integrity or political independence of any state, or in any other manner inconsistent with the purposes of the United Nations; (2) the principle that states shall settle their international disputes by peaceful means in such a manner that international peace and security and justice are not endangered; (3) the duty not to intervene in matters within the domestic jurisdiction of any state, in accordance with the Charter; (4) the duty of states to co-operate with one another in accordance with the Charter; (5) the principle of equal rights and self-determination of peoples; (6) the principle of sovereign equality of states; (7) the principle that states shall fulfil in good faith the obligations assumed by them in accordance with the Charter.

[18] A. Cassese, *Self-Determination of Peoples. A Legal Reappraisal* 109 (Cambridge: Cambridge University Press, 1995).

[19] Ibid.

[20] The external dimension of the right is mainly concerned with the international status of the territory whereas the internal dimension relates to the internal state structure, including certain legal regulations to accommodate population diversity in a more optimal way. Cassese, one of the first to have distinguished the two dimensions defines internal self-determination as 'the right to choose [the] form of government and to determine the social, economic and cultural policies of the state.' External self-determination, however, is the right to 'freely decide on [the] international status, whether to form a new state or to associate themselves with an existing state.' *See* A. Cassese, The Self-Determination of Peoples, in: L. Henkin (ed.), *The International Bill of Rights. The Covenant on Civil and Political Rights* 97-98 (New York: Columbia University Press, 1981).

[21] GA Res. 2625 (XXV), section on self-determination, para. 1.

[22] *Ibid.*, paras. 2 & 3.

other political status freely determined by a people.[23] The latter is important because it makes any political status acceptable if it is the result of the freely determined will of the people concerned. The Declaration further imposes a duty upon every state to refrain from using force against peoples fighting for their right of self-determination. In order to exercise their right to self-determination, peoples are entitled to seek and receive support against any forcible action on the part of a (foreign) state not allowing for self-determination.[24] On the other hand, the Declaration warns states to refrain from actions that are aimed at the partial or total disruption of the national unity and territorial integrity of any other state or country.[25] It is a reaffirmation of the Charter provisions on the issue. The Resolution is also relevant for the question of secession. In fact, pursuant to the wording of Resolution 2625 (XXV), states are protected by the principles of national unity and territorial integrity on the condition that they possess a representative government. If, however, this requirement of representativeness is not realised, the protection of their territory is as we will show below no longer guaranteed.

The end of the twentieth and beginning of the twenty-first century is witnessing a new approach towards self-determination in which the interest of the peoples rather than those of the states and governments has become the focal point of attention. The UN Declaration on the Rights of Indigenous Peoples was the first instrument to be drafted along this new policy orientation.[26] The Declaration asserts that indigenous peoples must be considered as peoples and thus enjoy all rights accorded to peoples including the right to self-determination.[27] It is a right to participate in political, economic, social and cultural life of the state promoting 'the negotiation of arrangements to strengthen states and make them truly representative, democratic, liberal and inclusive.'[28] For indigenous peoples it is important to be able to fully participate in the decision-making process within the confines of existing state boundaries. Only in exceptional circumstances, when "*the right to share power democratically would have been abused 'grievously and irreparably*,'"[29] would it be legitimate to appeal to secessionist self-determination.[30] What is provided here for indigenous peoples can be considered a progressive

---

[23] *Ibid.*, para. 4.
[24] *Ibid.*, para. 5.
[25] *Ibid.*, para. 8.
[26] GA Res. 61/295 of 2/10/2007 adopted with a vote of 144 in favour, 4 votes against (Australia, Canada, New Zealand and the United States of America) and 11 abstentions (Azerbaijan, Bangladesh, Bhutan, Burundi, Colombia, Georgia, Kenya, Nigeria, the Russian Federation, Samoa and Ukraine).
[27] *Ibid.*, Arts. 3 & 4.
[28] UN Sub-Commission on Prevention of Discrimination and Protection of Minorities, *Discrimination against Indigenous Peoples. Explanatory note concerning the draft declaration on the rights of indigenous peoples*, UN Doc. E/CN. 4/Sub. 2/1993/26/ Add. 1 (1993), at 6.
[29] C. Brölmann and M.Y.A. Zieck, Some Remarks on the Draft Declaration on the Rights of Indigenous Peoples, 8 *Leiden Journal of International Law* 107 (1995).
[30] Ibid.

development of customary rules that had already been accepted for peoples. Where the Declaration is really innovative is when it suggests autonomy or self-government for indigenous peoples as a way to exercise self-determination. Articles 3 and 4 of the Declaration combined with other substantive articles attribute indigenous communities the right to govern their most essential matters autonomously.

Besides developing as a rule of customary law, self-determination also became a treaty obligation when the 1966 Human Rights Covenants entered into force.[31] Article 1 of these Covenants is identically framed and deals with self-determination. The article partly reformulated existing customary law. But while reformulating customary law, it clearly added new dimensions by emphasizing that self-determination is inextricably linked to democracy. However, it does not impose uniformity on the manner of implementing such self-determination. Self-determination may thus mean different things to different states. For some states, self-determination equates to independence, for others it means federalism or a state system based on asymmetrical autonomy. Likewise, some states maintain that only the whole population of a state can be considered as the beneficiary of the right, while other states, on the contrary, opt for a system of attributing self-determination to the distinct population groups constituting the state's population.[32] There are, however, certain minimum requirements for which the Covenants provide clear regulations: the main one is that all peoples must be able to participate in the decision-making process without discrimination through regular, genuine, fair and free elections.[33] Self-determination is thus a collective human right that belongs to peoples. The right is, however, essentially exercised through a number of individual human rights.

3. SECESSION AS A MANIFESTATION OF THE RIGHT TO SELF-DETERMINATION

3.1. International Law and Practice

In the whole fabric of international law, there are only a few instruments that explicitly address the question of secession. Traditionally what took place within the confines of states was irrelevant for international law and therefore,

---

[31] International Covenant on Civil and Political Rights, adopted as GA Res. 2200 (XXI), Annex (16. Dec. 1966), 999 U.N.T.S. 171; 6 I.L.M. 368 (1967); International Covenant on Economic Social and Cultural Rights, adopted as GA Res. 2200 (16 Dec. 1966), 993 U.N.T.S. 3; 6 I.L.M. 360 (1967).

[32] *See* state reports submitted periodically by the State Parties of the ICCPR to the Human Rights Committee.

[33] The Committee on the Elimination of Racial Discrimination, for example, stated in its general comment on self-determination that 'there exists a link [between self-determination] with the right of every citizen to take part in the conduct of public affairs at any level.' See UN Doc. CERD/48/Misc. 7/Rev. 3 (1996).

with some notable exceptions such as the decolonisation process referred to above, how states are created is merely a matter of fact,[34] not law. This traditional view of international law was again reconfirmed by the Arbitration Commission instituted in the context of the civil war in the Federal Republic of Yugoslavia to advise the Peace Conference on Yugoslavia on legal issues. This Arbitration Commission stated in its Opinion No. 1 that the 'existence or disappearance of the state is a question of fact.'[35] Consequently, the traditional view is that international law is to a great extent neutral vis-à-vis the question of secession. For most legal scholars secession is not recognised as a right under public international law but it is equally not prohibited.[36] To check the accuracy of this doctrinal position we will review the international and (African) regional sources of law but also the manifestations of state practice at national level.

It has been mentioned above that the Charter of the United Nations refers to self-determination without invoking secession. This does not mean that secession is forbidden the more so since the principle which could have declared secession contrary to international law is construed in the Charter as an obligation imposed on states. States are forbidden to threaten or to use force against the territorial integrity and the political independence of another state (Art. 2(4) of the Charter of the United Nations). This Charter provision is thus limited to 'inter'-state relations and does not extend the obligation formulated in the provision to 'intra'-state situations (addressed to individuals or groups within the state). Therefore, the 'provision does not prevent insurgents from starting a civil war, nor the government concerned from using armed force against them.'[37] This means that, according to the original meaning of the

---

[34] *See*, *e.g.* H. Kelsen, Théorie générale du droit international public, 42 *Receuil des cours de l'académie de droit international* 261 (1932); *Report of the International Committee of Jurists Entrusted by the Council of the League of Nations with the Task of Giving an Advisory Opinion upon the Legal Aspect of the Aaland Island Question*, Special Supplement No. 3 (October 1920), at 5 (stating that "the formation, transformation and dismemberment of states as a result of revolutions and wars create situations of fact").

[35] Arbitration Commission, Opinion No. 1. 31 I.L.M. 1494 (1992).

[36] Akehurst, for example, writes that "there is no rule of international law which forbids secession from an existing state, nor is there any rule which forbids the mother-state from crushing the secessionist movement, if it can. Whatever the outcome of the struggle, it will be accepted as legal in the eyes of international law." *See* M. Akehurst, *A Modern Introduction to International Law* 72 (London: Allen and Unwin, 1970). Several other legal authorities share similar views. *See*, *e.g.* H. Hannum, Rethinking Self-Determination, 34 *Virginia Journal of International Law* 44 (1993); M. Shaw, The Heritage of States: The Principle of Uti Possidetis Juris Today, *British Yearbook of International Law* 144 (1996); T. Franck, Postmodern Tribalism and the Right to Secession, in: C. Brölmann, *et al.* (eds.), *Peoples and Minorities in International Law* 12 (Dordrecht: Martinus Nijhoff Publishers, 1993); R. Higgins, *Problem & Process. International Law and How we Use It* 125 (Oxford : Clarendon Press, 1994); O. Corten, Droit des peuples à disposer d'eux-mêmes et uti possidetis: deux faces d'une même medaille, in : O. Corten, *et al.* (eds.), *Démembrements d'états et délimitations territoriales : l'uti possidetis en question(s)* 426-427 (Bruxelles: Bruylant, 1999); J. Crawford, *The Creation of States in International Law* 266-268 (Oxford: Clarendon Press, 1979).

[37] A. Randelzhofer, Article 2(4), in: B. Simma (ed.), *The Charter of the United Nations. A Commentary* 116 (Oxford: Oxford University Press, 1995); M. Virally, Article 2 paragraph 4, in: J.-P. Cot &

Charter, secession is, with the exception of the intervention by another state, considered a political issue for which international law remains neutral. The references to self-determination in the Charter of the United Nations are consequently of little guidance for the question of secession.

The Charter provisions on self-determination were specified and implemented by the UN General Assembly in a set of resolutions from which the most important have been cited above. In these resolutions the references to self-determination were inextricably followed by 'territorial integrity' clauses. Not all these clauses are, however, as strict as the clause contained in General Assembly Resolution 1514 (XV) which provides that 'any attempt aimed at the partial or total disruption of the national unity and the territorial integrity of a country is incompatible with the purposes and principles of the Charter.' General Assembly Resolution 2625 (XXV), however, requires that for the principle of national unity and territorial integrity to be applicable the state in question possesses a government 'representing the whole people belonging to the territory without distinction as to race, creed or colour.' The 1993 Vienna Declaration and Programme of Action adopted by the United Nations Conference on Human Rights even speaks of 'any distinction' and not only racial or religious discrimination. Some commentators interpret these two latter clauses as suggesting that secession is allowed under international law on the condition that (minority or other population) groups fighting for their independence are driven by the lack of representativeness and are not supported by external powers. Of course, a state threatened by a secessionist movement can use all lawful means to combat it. Other commentators refer to the same wording of the clauses to suggest a narrow reading. The clauses in fact speak of 'the whole people', instead of 'all the distinct peoples'. This leads these commentators to conclude that these instruments did not allow for groups within a state to claim a right of secession, because it is the people of the state as a whole who are entitled to react against minority rule, rather than the distinct minorities or population groups within a state.[38] State practice has, however, been too scarce to prove either of such views.

A. Pellet (eds.), *La Charte des Nations Unies: Commentaire article par article* 121 (Bruxelles, Bruylant, 1985); J. E. Falkowski, Secessionary Self-Determination: A Jeffersonian Perspective, 9 *Boston University International Law Journal* 229 (1991); M. Weller, The International Response to the Dissolution of the Socialist Federal Republic of Yugoslavia, 86 *American Journal of International Law* 572 (1992); T. Christakis, *Le droit à l'autodétermination en dehors des situations de decolonisation* 145 (Paris: La Documentation française, 1999). That the Charter does not address intra-state situations is in stark contrast with, for example, the African Charter on Human and Peoples' Rights. Art. 29 of the African Charter on Human and Peoples' Rights provides that '[e]ach individual shall also have the duty [...] to preserve and strengthen the national independence and the territorial integrity of his country and to contribute to its defence in accordance with the law.'

[38] *See, e.g.* C. Iorns, Indigenous Peoples and Self-Determination: Challenging State Sovereignty, 24 *Case Western Reserve Journal of International Law* 261 (1992); Hannum, *supra* note 36, 16 (writing that 'the use in the same paragraph [of the section on self-determination of Resolution 2625 (XXV)] of the singular "people" suggests that various minorities within a territory may not enjoy the same right of self-determination as that possessed by the people as a whole').

With the end of the Cold War and the subsequent collapse of the Soviet Union, the dismemberment of the Socialist Federal Republic of Yugoslavia and the independence of Eritrea, the relevance of regulating secessions has again been posed. Indeed, most of those involved in the disintegration processes in these countries have frequently endeavoured to legitimise their struggle using self-determination vocabulary. These precedents have again pointed to the lacunae in the international law of self-determination and have forced the international community to show its most creative side in order to find solutions to developments that were previously regarded as purely political or domestic legal questions at best. The dismemberment of Yugoslavia was, for example, too quickly considered a dissolution, a term employed for a process in which all constituent parts of the state agree to extinguish the state and form new entities. That was not really the case with Yugoslavia.[39]

What we can conclude on the basis of international law instruments and international practice is that when a process of secession does not violate the principles of non-intervention and territorial integrity, international law takes a very neutral position and leaves the field for national law or international politics. In such cases, it is currently very likely that the international community will accept a newly formed state entity if the process of secession that led to the separation can be labelled 'remedial secession'. In other words, if it repairs past injustices, i.e. when a distinct people has a legitimate claim to territory that was wrongfully annexed by another state (e.g. the Baltic States or Eritrea) or if it is a reaction against an unfolding act of repression when a distinct group of people or minority is systematically repressed or subjected to ongoing gross violations of human rights and denied equal opportunity to participate in the political process. This is, however, international politics and therefore all cases are not necessarily treated in a like manner. In the current state of affairs, secession must therefore be regarded as an *ultimum remedium* or a solution of last resort when all other options to live together in one state entity have failed.

3.2. African Regional Practice

African states have adopted a more restricted view on secession and have in their regional law attempted to outlaw it by various means (including agreeing on a conservative view on territorial integrity). The Charter of the now defunct Organisation of African Unity (OAU)[40] therefore clearly stated that the aim of the organisation was to promote unity and solidarity between African states, to co-ordinate and intensify inter-state and international co-operation, to eradicate all forms of colonialism, and to defend their sovereignty, their territorial integ-

[39] O. Corten et al (eds.), *Démembrements d'Etats et Délimitations territoriales, l'Uti possidetis en question(s)* (Bruxelles: Bruylant, 1998).

[40] Charter of the Organization of African Unity signed at Addis Ababa on 25 May 1963, which entered into force on 13 September 1963. 479 U.N.T.S. 39 (1963).

rity and independence.[41] It is important to note that, contrary to the Charter of the United Nations, the signatory states of the OAU had thus agreed to 'defend' the territorial integrity of the members of the organisation not only against external aggression but also, and more importantly, against internal secessionist movements. Moreover, by adopting the 1964 Cairo Declaration on Border Disputes Among African States,[42] the principle of intangibility of borders existing at the moment of achieving national independence was recognised with the aim to contribute to continental peace and stability but also had to serve as guardian for the territorial integrity of African states. This principle of intangibility has contributed to contain a second wave of self-determination (through secession this time) by which states would be recreated on the basis of ethnic and religious grounds and military force.[43]

This context explains also that with regard to the right to self-determination recognised in Article 20 of the African Charter on Human and Peoples' Rights,[44] the African Commission on Human and Peoples' Rights remains very cautious as to discuss the taboo subject of secession. In *Katangese Peoples' Congress v. Zaire*, the African Commission on Human and Peoples' Rights was, for example, asked to give its view on a complaint alleging that the people of Katanga who live across Zambia and Zaire (now the Democratic Republic of the Congo) was entitled to an independent and separate state for their history proves that their territory is distinct from Zaire and that members of the Katangese community living in Zambia faced difficulties with immigration authorities in Zambia. The Commission first declared the complaint admissible but finally found it without merit under the African Charter on Human and Peoples' Rights. During discussions in the Commission, the majority found that it was not its task to 'redraw the boundaries of African States' and that it would be inconsistent with the basic principles of the Organisation of

[41] Art. II of the Charter of the OAU. The attainment of these objectives had to be achieved by applying seven principles not always similar in content to those of the Charter of the United Nations. Inasmuch as the principles are concerned, the first three established the basis of the OAU's view on the protection of sovereign state entities. The principles are: (1) the sovereign equality of all Member States; (2) non-interference in the internal affairs of states; (3) respect for the sovereignty and territorial integrity of each state and for its inalienable right to existence; (4) peaceful settlement of disputes by negotiation, mediation, conciliation or arbitration; (5) unreserved condemnation, in all its forms, of political assassination as well as of subversive activities on the part of neighbouring states or any other state; (6) absolute dedication to the total emancipation of the African territories which are still dependent; (7) affirmation of a policy of non-alignment with regard to all blocs. *Ibid.*, Art. 3.

[42] Resolution 16(I) (31 July 1964). *See*, for an account of the events leading to the adoption of the 1964 Resolution, S. Touval, The Organization of African Unity and African Borders, *International Organizations* 103-127 (1967).

[43] *See* S. Smis, The Legal Status of International Land Boundaries in Africa, in: R. Doom & J. Gorus (eds.), *Economics of Conflict and Politics of Identity in the Great Lakes Region* 198-201 (Brussels: VUBPress, 2000).

[44] African Charter on Human and Peoples' Rights, O.A.U. Doc. CAB/LEG/67/3 Rev. 5. 479 U.N.T.S. 39, 72 (1963).

African Unity to entertain the complaint.[45] The fundamental principles to which it referred were those enumerated in Article III of the Charter of the OAU and the principle of intangibility of internal borders existing at the moment of their interdependence which became international frontiers at the moment of independence. African regional practice demonstrates that African states defend a slightly different approach than what is agreed at the international level in the sense that African states are more cautious towards secession.

3.3. National Practice

Quite understandably, states do not like to be confronted with secessionist claims that may threaten their existence. They, therefore, explicitly forbid secession or are silent when it comes to regulating secession. Exceptionally, however, some states have recognized such right.

To illustrate this statement, it is sufficient to look at constitutional law from a comparative perspective. A centralised state such as France very much influenced by its Jacobean heritage unambiguously proclaims in Article 2 of its constitution that "*La France est une République indivisible, laïque, démocratique et sociale.*"[46] Therefore, the French Constitutional Council when asked to give its view on the legal status of Corsica and whether its inhabitants possessed a right to self-determination declared that, with the exception of overseas French peoples who possess a right to self-determination, the French people are indivisible: "*une catégorie unitaire insusceptible de tout subdivision.*"[47] Also in most federal constitutions there is no provision regulating how the relationship between the federation and the federated entities has to be broken down. Accordingly, the U.S. Constitution does not mention the term 'secession'. Nevertheless, in *Texas v. White*, the Supreme Court declared that the American federation was indestructible and secession was only possible through revolution or agreement by the other states constituting the Union.[48] In

[45] Communication No. 75/92. *See also* E. A. Ankumah, *The African Commission on Human and Peoples' Rights. Practice and Procedures* 164 (The Hague: Martinus Nijhoff Publishers, 1996); Umozurike Oji Umozurike, *The African Charter on Human Rights* 53 (The Hague: Martinus Nijhoff Publishers, 1997).

[46] Similar statements can be found in most constitutions of centralised states. Constitutions usually refer to notions such as a unitary, indivisible, inalienable, the prohibition of secession and the immutability of state borders, a state composed of one people or nation, and the principle of territorial integrity.

[47] Décision 91-290 dc (9 May 1991), para. 11.

[48] *Texas v. White* 74 U.S. (7 Wallace) 700, 724-725 (1868). The U.S. Supreme Court interpreted the Constitution as follows: 'By these [the Articles of Confederation] the Union was solemnly declared to 'be perpetual.' And when these Articles were found to be inadequate to the exigencies of the country, the Constitution was ordained 'to form a more perfect Union.' It is difficult to convey the idea of indissoluble unity more clearly than by these words. What can be indissoluble if a perpetual Union, made more perfect, is not?' *Ibid.* at 725.

other words, the only constitutional manner to break the federation is through dissolution, i.e. an agreement of all constituent federal entities to terminate the union. In *Reference re Secession of Quebec*, the Supreme Court of Canada similarly concluded that 'secession of a province "under the Constitution" could not be achieved unilaterally, that is, without principled negotiation with other participants in the Confederation within the existing constitutional framework.'[49] In other constitutions of federal or quasi-federal states, the indissoluble character of their union is explicitly stated (e.g. Australia, Spain, the Russian Federation, etc.).

Even though most states do not want to consider secession as a legal possibility, exceptionally, however, a number of states have (or still) recognise(d) the right of secession in their constitution or by statute. The fathers of Communism adhered to the doctrine of voluntary union and freedom of secession. Therefore, publicists of former Communist states have generally defended an interpretation of self-determination including a right of secession. Lenin, for instance, mentioned that '[t]he question of the object of the right of nations to self-determination is reduced to the question what rights and interests of a nation, people, nationality, etc., are included in their right to self-determination. Undoubtedly, the most important element of this right is freedom of state secession and the formation of an independent state.'[50] As a direct consequence of this doctrinal position, Article 13 of the USSR Constitution of 1936 stipulated that '[t]he USSR is a unionized state established on the voluntary unification of the equal Soviet Republics' and in Article 17 it declared that 'the right freely to secede from the USSR is reserved to every Union Republic.' But the constitution refused to provide for the procedural steps to be followed in case a Union Republic voiced its demand for secession.[51] The 1977 Constitution of the Soviet Union confirmed earlier positions on secession as it stated in its Article 72 that 'each Union Republic shall retain the right freely to secede from the USSR.' While the 1977 Constitution remained silent on the procedural question, the legislator, at the end of the Soviet era, did establish the conditions for the exercise of this right when it became confronted with growing separatist tendencies. The Law on the Procedure for Resolving Questions Relating to the Secession of Union Republics from the USSR was adopted on 3 April

[49] *Re Section 53 of the Supreme Court Act*, R.S.C. [1985] C. S-26; *Re Reference by Governor in Council concerning certain questions relating to the secession of Quebec from Canada, as set out in order in Council P.C. 1996-1497 (30 September 1996)*, paras. 104 & 149.

[50] *Quoted* in L. C. Buchheit, *Secession. The Legitimacy of Self-Determination* 135 (New Haven: Yale University Press, 1978).

[51] It was, however, never the intention that all Union Republics would be able to leave the Federation. In Stalin's Report on the Draft of the U.S.S.R. Constitution three requirements were set before an 'autonomous republic' could become a 'union republic' and thus by implication claim a right of secession. First, the entity in question had to be a borderland and thus not be encircled by Soviet territories. Second, the nationality from which the Soviet Republic in question derived its name had to represent within that state a more or less compact majority. Finally, the territory needed to have a substantial population (more than one million) so that it would 'not be swallowed by the imperialist beasts of prey'.

1990[52] but the procedure in question was so strict that it could not be applied when the Union was dissolved.[53]

The People's Democratic Republic of China was influenced by the same Marxist ideology and initially, when the Chinese Communists had not yet consolidated their power over mainland China, they proclaimed a right of secession similar to that of the USSR.[54] However, they dropped such reference later for the advantage of the formulation 'unitary multi-national State' as can be found in the preamble of the 1975 and the 1982 Constitutions: 'The People's Republic of China is a unitary state built up jointly by the people of all its nationalities.'

The 1947 Constitution of the Union of Burma recognised that the federated entities could secede from the Union 'in accordance with the conditions hereinafter prescribed.'[55] The reference to secession was deleted from the 1974 Constitution of the Socialist Republic of the Union of Burma while reference was made to 'local autonomy under the central leadership' and the prohibition to undermine 'unity and solidarity of the national races.'[56]

Besides these rather historical examples, one can name states that today consider secession as legal under certain circumstances. The present constitution

---

[52] *Izvestia*, No. 97 (6 April 1990). An English translation of the 'Law on Procedures for Resolving Questions Related to the Secession of Union Republics from the USSR' can be found in H. Hannum (Ed.), *Documents on Autonomy and Minority Rights* 753-760 (Dordrecht: Martinus Nijhoff Publishers, 1993).

[53] In accordance with the terms of the 'Law on Procedures for Resolving Questions Related to the Secession of Union Republics from the USSR', any Republic, which wanted to separate from the Union, has to fulfil three main conditions. First, by referendum, two-thirds of the electorate had to express its wish to leave the Union. Second, the Congress of the Peoples' Deputies had to initiate negotiations with the seceding Republic, the Union and the remaining federated and autonomous Republics. Finally, these actors had to conclude agreements with each other laying down the modalities of the separation and had to submit them for approval to the Congress of the Peoples' Deputies. A detailed description of the procedure of the 'Law on Procedure for Resolving Questions Related to the Secession of Union Republic from the USSR' can be found in M. Lesage, La crise du fédéralisme soviétique, *Notes et etudes documentaires* 113-115 (1990).

[54] The first all-China Soviet Congress proclaimed in its Constitution of the Soviet Republic (7 Nov. 1931) that '[t]he Soviet government of China recognises the right of self-determination of the national minorities in China, their right to complete separation from China, and to the formation of an independent state for each national minority. All Mongolians, Tibetans, Miao, Yao, Koreans and others living on the territory of China shall enjoy the full right to self-determination, i.e. they may either join the union of Chinese Soviets or secede from it and form their own state as they may prefer.'

[55] *See* Buchheit, *supra* note 50, 99-100 (As Buchheit mentions, the following conditions can be distinguished: '(1) the right of secession shall not be exercised within ten years from the date on which the constitution comes into operation; (2) a state wishing to exercise the right must have a resolution to that effect passed by two-thirds of the total number of members in its State Council; and (3) a plebiscite will then be taken to ascertain the will of the people of the state concerned, supervised by a Plebiscite Commission.' However, read with other provisions of the Constitution, only two states could exercise that right, namely Shan State and Kayah State.

[56] Ibid., 100.

of the Republic of Uzbekistan allows for the secession of the Republic of Karakalpakstan; Article 74 states that '[t]he Republic of Karakalpakstan shall have the right to secede from the Republic of Uzbekistan on the basis of a nationwide referendum held by the people of Karakalpakstan.' In the Republic of Moldova, the Law on the special legal status of Gaugauzia gives to this minority a possibility to secede from Moldova in the case of unification with Romania: 'in the event of a change in the status of the Republic of Moldova as an independent state, the people of Gaugauzia have the right to external self-determination.'[57]

Finally, as stated earlier Article 39(1) of the 1994 Constitution of Ethiopia provides that 'every nation, nationality and people in Ethiopia has an unconditional right to self-determination, including the right to secession'. The conditions for the exercise of this right are set forth in Article 39(4) of the constitution.[58]

Ethiopia is one of the few countries in Africa that has officially acknowledged ethnicity as an ideological basis for the decision-making process and has recognised it as a basis for the federal power structure enshrined in the 1994 Constitution.[59] Ethiopia adheres to a policy of what has been called 'ethnic democracy'.[60] This policy was initiated with the adoption of a Transitional Charter pending the new constitution with the fall of the Mengistu regime. Regional and local elections were held in June 1992 and a Constitutional Drafting Commission was appointed to draft a new constitution.[61] This Commission tried to include the Ethiopian population as much as possible in the drafting of the constitution. Forums for public discussion were organised in Ethiopia and abroad to discuss the future constitution and to collect the views of both the

---

[57] N.A. Mikhaleva (Ed.), *Novye Konstitucii Stran SNG I Baltii*, 1997, 347.

[58] Article 39(4) of the Constitution of Ethiopia provides as follows: 'The right to self-determination, including secession of every Nation, Nationality and People shall come into effect: (a) when a demand for secession has been approved by a two thirds majority of the members of the Legislative Council of the Nation, Nationality or People concerned; (b) When the Federal Government has organized a referendum which must take place within three years from the time it received the concerned council's decision for secession; (c) When the demand for secession is supported by majority vote in the referendum; (d) When the Federal Government will have transferred its powers to the council of the Nation, Nationality or People who has voted to secede; and (e) When the division of assets is effected in a manner prescribed by law ...'

[59] *See* J. Abbink, Ethnicity and Constitutionalism in Contemporary Ethiopia, 41 *Journal of African Law* 159-160 (1997) (mentioning that unlike South Africa which in one way or another also gives ethnicity official recognition, 'Ethiopia is different in the sense that ethnic identity is the normative identity on the basis of which the new state prefers to deal with its citizens in many spheres of life, especially the political and economic').

[60] Jeremy Skeet, 'Building Myths', *BBC Focus on Africa* (1995), *reprinted* in *De nieuwe Hoorn van Afrika*, Sept./Okt. 1995, 30.

[61] The 1992 elections were the first attempt aimed at holding multi-party elections in Ethiopia. The elections however were marked by several administrative, logistical and political problems. Five political parties, including the Oromo Liberation Front (OLF) even withdrew their participation. *See* Abebe Abdisa, Democratic Elections Held, *Ethioscope* 18 (Sept. 1994).

civic organisations as well as the political parties.[62] The new constitution was adopted on 8 December 1994 and entered into force in August 1995.[63] It established Ethiopia as an ethnic federation attributing far-reaching competencies to the constituent entities including an unlimited right to self-determination. From the outset, the constitution reveals the ambiguity associated with most federal systems regarding the question whether sovereignty is vested in the federation itself or in its constituent entities. The Preamble does declare that '*the Nations, Nationalities and Peoples of Ethiopia*' are "*[s]trongly committed, in full and free exercise of [their] right to self-determination, to building a political community founded on the rule of law and capable of ensuring a lasting peace, guaranteeing a democratic order, and advancing [their] economic and social development.*" This reading of the Preamble is confirmed by Article 8(1), which provides that "*[a]ll sovereign power resides in the Nations, Nationalities and Peoples of Ethiopia.*" It can thus justifiably be inferred that, pursuant to Article 39(1) of the Ethiopian Constitution, the nations, nationalities and peoples are the entities designated as beneficiaries of self-determination. The right to self-determination including secession was an intensively debated issue by the Constitutional Assembly. Opponents of the right argued that the exercise of the right would lead to national fragmentation and disunity. Moreover, there was no democratic precedent accepting such right in their constitution. In addition, some members of the federation possessing rich natural resources would be inclined to secede leaving an impoverished state. In turn, those who favoured the right to self-determination including secession maintained that it constituted a fundamental human and democratic right because it would guarantee the freedom of nations and nationalities from oppression and exploitation. Not including the principle in the constitution would mean a lack of confidence in nations and nationalities and in the democratic process in general. At the end of the debate, the reference to self-determination was adopted with a vote of 508 in favour, seven against and one abstention.[64] Although the constitution recognises a broad right to self-determination based on ethnic affiliation, still many armed and political movements are not satisfied with the constitutional setting and the way it is implemented and have threatened to leave the federation. It is probably the paradox of the present constitution: on the one hand if no federal solution would have been adopted with such a broad right to self-determination, not so many sub-nationalities or centrifugal forces would today claim self-determination or threaten with sepa-

[62] *See* id., 19. Discussion forums were held in Cairo, Paris, New Delhi, Poona, Accra, Seoul, Vienna, Djibouti, Harare, Beijin, New York, Ottawa, Asmara, Assab, Mendefera, Keren, Massawa and Deke Mehari. Moreover, other international NGOs including the Inter-Africa Group, participated in the project of drafting the constitution to enrich the process by sharing their experience. *See* Abebe Abdisa, The Ethiopian Constitution, *Ethioscope* 29 (Jan. 1995).

[63] The 1994 Constitution was the fourth Ethiopian Constitution. Prior constitutions were adopted in 1931, 1955 and 1987. For an account of the drafting of the fundamental aspects of the 1994 Constitution, see ibid., 28-31.

[64] *See* Abebe Abdisa, *supra* note 61, 30.

ration. On the other hand, the recognition of the right to self-determination was probably the only way to hold the country together.

4. CONCLUDING REMARKS

At the present, the world counts more than 4.000 population groups that could be identified as nations or peoples. If all of them were to invoke the theories on nationalism in order to secede, a great number of states would cease to exist but also the world community would be unable to function under the premises of the current understandings in international relations. It is therefore quite understandable that an unconditional right to secession does not exist in international law. At the same time, and since many states have been created on the basis of a successful secession, international law does not forbid a population group to secede on the condition that other principles of international law such as the principles of non-intervention and territorial integrity are respected. These principles are more stringent at the African regional level than at the international level. In the absence of a rule of international law on the issue, states are free to regulate secession. Very exceptionally one will encounter a state that allows secession. Ethiopia is such a state that has adopted a progressive view by accepting secession as a way to exercise self-determination. This means that for groups that want to secede they will not be able to appeal to an international rule on secession since it does not exist but will have to fulfil the conditions of the constitution if they want to remain within the law.

7. Ethiopia: Constitutional Protection of Ethnic Minorities at the Regional Level

Christophe Van der Beken•

1. INTRODUCTION

Like most African states, Ethiopia is ethnically diverse. The Ethiopian population is characterized by considerable diversity in religion (the Ethiopian Orthodox Church, Protestants, Moslems, traditional belief systems), language (there are dozens of different languages), culture, socio-economic activities (pastoral nomadism, sedentary agriculture) and traditional governance structures. But unlike other African states, this diversity is not the result of colonial imperialist designs; instead it resulted from the late 19th century territorial expansion of the empire of Abyssinia. The creation of the Ethiopian state by a process of internal expansion did not, however, give rise to an alternative nation building strategy. Just like the leaders of the postcolonial African states, the Ethiopian power holders, for the largest part of the twentieth century, strived for the creation of one nation within the state, not by the recognition of its national or ethnic diversity, but by the disavowal of and the attempt to erase that diversity. Ethiopian national identity was equated with the ethnic identity of one particular group. The Ethiopian government judged that this nation building strategy offered the best guarantee for the stability of the state. This strategy remained in nature unaltered until the fall of the military dictatorship of Mengistu Haile Mariam in May 1991, when the new power holders, under the guidance of the EPRDF (the Ethiopian Peoples' Revolutionary Democratic Front), a coalition of ethnic-based liberation movements, declared their aim of radically breaking with a strategy of nation building based on ethnic discrimination. Instead they would strive for equal rights for all Ethiopian ethnic groups. According to the new conception, the construction of an Ethiopian national identity was based on the recognition of the ethnic diversity of the population. In other words, unity depended on the recognition of and the respect for diversity. This attention to unity in diversity was legally expressed in the granting of a right to self-determination to all the "nations, nationalities and peoples" (the Ethiopian constitutional term for ethnic groups) of Ethiopia. This right was first incorporated in the Transitional Period Charter (interim constitution) of 1991 and afterwards in the federal constitution of 8 December 1994, which is still functioning today. The right to self-determination as conceived

---

• Postdoctoral researcher at Ghent University Law Faculty, Department of Public Law, Non-Western Law Section. E-mail: Christophe.VanderBeken@UGent.be. The author wishes to thank Ato Tsegaye Regassa for his valuable feedback.

by the Ethiopian constitution is very large and includes language rights, cultural rights and rights of self-administration. It even includes the right of nations, nationalities and peoples to secede from the Ethiopian federation. Thus all ethnic groups have the right to speak and develop their own language, to express and promote their own culture and history; they have the right to self-administration within a particular territory and the right to their own representation at the regional and federal levels of government.[1] As such, the right to self-determination includes both the objectives of unity and that of diversity. To make sure that the granting of this right is more than a mere declaration of intent, the federal constitution provides for a specific administrative organisation and for specific institutional mechanisms. Of course, it is appropriate to make the observation that the effective realisation of the constitutional provisions is partly determined by the political context. This, however, does not mean that an analysis of the constitutional provisions is superfluous. Not all constitutional provisions are context dependent to the same extent. Moreover, if the rule of law is to prevail in Ethiopia, it is necessary that the constitutional provisions have a greater sustainability than the relative political context. Nor should it be neglected that the constitutional provisions have themselves a large impact on political reality.

As the use of the term 'federal constitution' indicates, the constitution of 8 December 1994, which became effective in August 1995, creates a federal state structure. This implies that the Ethiopian territory is administratively divided into nine regional states.[2] These are Tigray; Afar; Amhara; Oromia; Somali; Benishangul-Gumuz; the State of the Southern, Nations, Nationalities and Peoples; Gambella and Harar.[3] The ethnic criterion has played an important role in the creation of the regional states, in the sense that the delimitation of the regional borders is based on ethnic ones. Indeed, the Ethiopian government has tried to realise a match between regional and ethnic borders. As a result, Ethiopian federalism has been called 'ethnic federalism', distinguishing it from federalism in a country such as the United States, where regional borders do not in any way correspond with ethnic ones. Therefore, the ethnic groups of Ethiopia are constitutionally coupled to specific regional states and it is within and through these states that they exercise their right to self-determination. The constitution grants important competences to the regional states. Among these are the power to choose its own working language, the competence to set up its own police force and the competence to adopt its own constitution. This last competence allows the regional states to form their own administrative and institutional structures and, for example, to determine the structure and functioning of their local governments. However, as indicated above, the right to

[1] Article 39 of the Ethiopian federal constitution.

[2] The cities of Dire Dawa and Addis Ababa do not belong to one of the nine regional states. They constitute separate territorial entities that, in contrast to the regional states, are accountable to the federal government.

[3] Article 47 (1) of the Ethiopian federal constitution.

self-determination in the Ethiopian constitution implies not only autonomy rights (diversity), but also the right to representation in the federal government (unity). The federal constitution not only regulates the state structure and the relationship between the regional and federal level, the federal constitution also determines the fundamentals of the federal legislative, executive and judicial institutions. Therefore, in order to realise the right to self-determination, the federal constitution guarantees the representation of the ethnic groups in these federal institutions.

The federal parliament, as is customary in federations, is composed of two chambers: the House of Peoples' Representatives and the House of the Federation. The representatives of the former are representatives of the Ethiopian people as a whole. They are elected by means of general and direct elections under the 'first-past-the-post' electoral system.[4] In practice, this means that the one seat in each electoral district is won by the candidate who gets the most votes in the district. In a state organised on an ethnic basis, the use of such an electoral system runs the risk that the one seat in each electoral district will be won by the candidate who represents the interests of the largest ethnic group in the district. This is particularly problematic for those ethnic groups that are a minority in every electoral district. There is a real risk that those ethnic groups will not have a single representative in the House of Peoples' Representatives. To reduce this risk and to guarantee the representation of all ethnic groups in the first chamber of parliament, the federal constitution provides for a guaranteed representation of "minority nationalities and peoples".

Article 54(3) of the federal constitution stipulates that out of the maximum number of 550 seats in the House of Peoples' Representatives, a minimum of 20 seats is reserved for "minority nationalities and peoples". As such, a representation of a large number of ethnic groups in the House of Peoples' Representatives is guaranteed. Nevertheless, the chosen electoral system leads to the fact that the larger ethnic groups are more strongly represented in the first chamber of the parliament than the smaller ones. This is a common situation in federal states. As indicated before, most parliaments in federal states are bicameral. The first chamber is the representative institution of the federation as a whole, its members being elected pro rata of the population. In Ethiopia, the federal constitution stipulates that the members of the first chamber, the House of Peoples' Representatives, are the representatives of the "Ethiopian People as a whole".[5] This conception of the first chamber and the resultant electoral system lead to a predominance of the larger federated entities in the first chamber. For example, in the United States the large (highly populated) regional states have a larger representation in the House of Representatives than the smaller states. We have the same picture in Ethiopia, where the large ethnic groups are much more strongly represented in the House of Peoples' Rep-

[4] Article 54 of the Ethiopian federal constitution.

[5] Article 54 (4) of the Ethiopian federal constitution.

resentatives than the small ethnic groups. For example, on the basis of the 2000 elections, the Amhara and Oromo ethnic groups jointly held a majority of seats in the House of Peoples' Representatives.[6] However, it is also customary in federations that the preponderance of the large federated entities is compensated for by the overrepresentation of the small federated entities in a second chamber. To stay with the example of the United States, there, the preponderance of the large regional states in the House of Representatives is compensated for by an equal representation of all regional states in the second chamber, the senate (all regional states of the US federation having two senators). This brings us to the second chamber of the federal parliament in Ethiopia: the House of the Federation. The House of the Federation is the representative organ of the diverse Ethiopian ethnic groups or of the diversity in the federation. Article 61(1) of the federal constitution stipulates that all nations, nationalities and peoples have a right to be represented in the House of the Federation. Each is entitled to at least one representative and the members of the House of the Federation are elected either by the regional parliaments or within the framework of direct elections organised by these parliaments.[7] In practice, all members of the House of the Federation are elected by the regional parliaments and, therefore, no direct elections for the House of the Federation take place.[8] The fact that all members of the House of the Federation are elected by the regional parliaments is an expression of constitutional logic. As noted above, ethnicity played an important part in the creation of the nine regional states. More specifically, the government tried to realise an overlap between ethnic and territorial boundaries. As a result, all Ethiopian ethnic groups (more than 80), were, figuratively speaking, coupled to one (or in rare cases several) of the nine regional states. To put it in another way, the habitat of an ethnic group was delimited territorially and this ethnic territory fell within the boundaries of (usually) one of the nine regional states. The parliament of a regional state is therefore the representative organ of those ethnic groups that have been localised in the state concerned. The Amhara ethnic group, for example, has been coupled to the Amhara regional state. In other words, the Amhara regional state has been created for the Amhara ethnic group. From here it follows that the parliament of the Amhara region is the representative organ of the Amhara ethnic group. It is thus logical that the representatives of the Amhara in the House of the Federation are elected by the parliament of the Amhara region. Though all ethnic groups have a right to be represented in the House of the Federation, this does not imply that the House of the Federation corresponds with the traditional model of a federal second chamber. Article 61 (2) of the federal constitution stipulates that the ethnic groups, for each one million of their population, are entitled to an additional representative in the House of the

[6] *Regional Surveys of the World, Africa South of the Sahara 2004* (London/New York: Europa Publications, 2003).
[7] Article 61 (3) of the Ethiopian federal constitution.
[8] Interview conducted by the author with Samuel Alemayehu, Secretary General of the House of the Federation, Addis Ababa, September 2003.

Federation. Because of this, large ethnic groups such as the Oromo and Amhara have 20 and 14 representatives respectively whereas smaller ethnic groups such as the Harari and the Silte have just one representative each in the House.[9] Consequently, the House of the Federation offers an insufficient counterweight to the preponderance of the larger ethnic groups in the first chamber of the parliament.

The Ethiopian constitution of 1994 contains no provisions that guarantee representation for different ethnic groups in the federal executive, thus differing from the interim constitution of 1991.[10] In practice, as seems clear from the example of the federal government, there appears to be an ambition to distribute the most important government positions across members of different ethnic groups. In the current government, formed in October 2005, the 21 ministers (without the prime minister) comprise 7 Oromo, 5 Amhara, 2 Tigrayans, 5 from different groups in the Southern Nations, Nationalities and Peoples state, 1 Somali and 1 Afar.[11]

It is notable that a wide ethnic representativeness is guaranteed in the institution competent for constitutional review. In most federal states the power to monitor the constitutionality of laws and regulations is granted to an independent court. This task can be granted to the highest court in the normal legal organisation (such as in the USA, Canada and Australia) or to a specialised judicial organ (as in Germany and Spain).[12] However, the Ethiopian constitutional drafter did not adopt such traditional mechanisms and opted instead for a remarkable alternative and unique mechanism of constitutional review. In Ethiopia, the constitutional review power is not granted to a judicial organ, but to the second chamber of the federal parliament: the House of the Federation. In the exercise of its constitutional interpretation power, the House of the Federation is assisted by the Council of Constitutional Inquiry.[13] The majority of the members of the latter institution are legal experts, which is not the case for the members of the House of the Federation. However, the Council of Constitutional Inquiry is not itself a constitutional court; it is merely an advisory body to the House of the Federation. It is the latter that has the ultimate authority to interpret the constitution. Although this power of the House of the Federation might appear remarkable, it is nevertheless in line with the overall structure of the constitution. The constitution grants all sovereign powers to the nations,

[9] The composition of the House of the Federation can be found on: http://www.hofethiopia.org/index.html

[10] Article 9 of the Transitional Period Charter stated that the head of state, the prime minister, the vice-chairperson and the secretary of the Council of Representatives had to have a different ethnic identity.

[11] Walta Information Center, 12 October 2005.

[12] R. Ergec, Institutionele analyse van het federalisme (institutional analysis of federalism), in: Interuniversitair Studiecentrum voor Federalisme (ed.), *Federalisme – Staatkundig, politiek en economisch* 47 (Antwerpen/Apeldoorn: MAKLU uitgevers, 1994).

[13] Article 84 of the Ethiopian federal constitution.

nationalities and peoples of Ethiopia and states that the constitution is an expression of their sovereignty.[14] From this perspective it is not surprising that the constitution allocates the constitutional review power to the institution that is composed of representatives of those nations, nationalities and peoples. Since all ethnic groups have a right to be represented in the House of the Federation, the ethnic representativeness of the institution competent for constitutional review is guaranteed.

The above offers a concise overview of the mechanisms developed by the federal constitution in order to ensure the right to self-determination of the Ethiopian nations, nationalities and peoples. The realisation of this right should result in unity in diversity, in the creation of an Ethiopian national identity through the respect for ethnic diversity. In so doing, the Ethiopian constitutional drafter attempted to remedy and prevent ethnic tensions and conflicts and guarantee the stability of the Ethiopian state. If each of the nine regional states of the Ethiopian federation were ethnically homogenous, the mechanisms of the federal constitution would offer a comprehensive approach towards this aim. In that scenario, any one ethnic group could exercise its autonomy rights through the regional institutions and its representatives in the House of the Federation are elected by or through the regional parliament. However, the Ethiopian reality does not correspond with this ideal scenario. This can already be deduced from the fact that though there are more than 80 ethnic groups, only nine regional states have been created. All Ethiopian regional states have, to a greater or lesser extent, an ethnically diverse population. The ethnic diversity that characterises the federal level is therefore also present at the regional level. From here it follows that tensions and conflicts between different ethnic groups can also occur within the borders of one particular region. Ethnic harmony in the Ethiopian state is therefore unthinkable without harmony inside the regions. This fact, in combination with the constitutional autonomy of the regions (the power to adopt their own constitution), makes clear that the capacity of the Ethiopian constitutional framework to ensure unity in diversity is to a large extent determined by the capacity of the regional constitutional mechanisms to do so. In other words, the right to self-determination of all Ethiopian ethnic groups can only be realised if the regional constitutional provisions also develop the necessary mechanisms. This brings us to the objective of this article, which addresses the question of whether the regional constitutions contain provisions to protect the rights of the ethnic groups that live within the territories of their respective regional states. The article studies the constitutional law of four states. The choice of states is, as is explained in the next section, motivated by the ambition to obtain as representative a sample as possible. The article starts with an overview of the ethnic diversity of the nine regional states, on the basis of which the regional states are categorised into four groups - a classification which acts as

[14] Article 8 (1) + (2) of the Ethiopian federal constitution.

the guiding principle for the selection of the regional states for further study. The article then proceeds to the actual study of the constitutional law of the selected regional states. Of course, I do not discuss all aspects of regional constitutional law. Rather I focus on those elements that are related to the regional strategy regarding ethnic diversity. More specifically, I examine whether the regional constitutions, following the example of the federal constitution, have developed specific territorial-administrative and specific institutional mechanisms to accommodate ethnic diversity. This analysis enters an area of Ethiopian constitutional law that has been barely touched upon by scholars. Some thorough analyses of the federal constitution and federal mechanisms for ethnic accommodation already exist, but research on the regional constitutions is very rare.[15] This article therefore results from a personal interpretation of regional constitutional law, based on the author's own analysis of the constitutional texts and on additional interviews conducted by the author with regional politicians and civil servants.

2. ETHNIC DIVERSITY AT THE INTRA REGIONAL LEVEL

As indicated above, Article 47 of the federal constitution provides that the territory of the Ethiopian federation comprises nine regions. These regions are listed in Article 47(1): the state of Tigray, the state of Afar, the state of Amhara, the state of Oromia, the state of Somali, the state of Benishangul/Gumuz, the state of the Southern Nations, Nationalities and Peoples, the state of Gambella and the state of Harar.

Since the constitutional drafter tried to create an overlap between regional and ethnic boundaries, the Ethiopian federal structure can be called an ethnic federation. However, a closer look at the various state populations indicates that none of the nine regions is ethnically homogeneous. A perfect match between ethnic group and territory has thus not materialised. This is not surprising taking into account the presence of more than 80 different ethnic groups in Ethiopia. However, the degree of diversity differs from region to region.

Based on the ethnic composition of their populations, the Ethiopian regions can be divided into four groups.[16]

---

[15] Thorough analyses of the federal administrative organisation and state institutions can be found in "Assefa Fiseha, *Federalism and the Accommodation of Diversity in Ethiopia – A Comparative Study* (Nijmegen: Wolf Legal Publishers, 2005-2006) 460 p." and in "C. Van der Beken, *Decentralisatie en etnische diversiteit in Afrika met casestudy Ethiopië* (decentralisation and ethnic diversity in Africa with a case study of Ethiopia), Universiteit Gent, Doctoral Thesis, 2006, 379 p." A good concise analysis of the Ethiopian regional constitutions can be found in "Tsegaye Regassa, *State Constitutions in Federal Ethiopia: A Preliminary Observation,* *http://camlaw.rutgers.edu/statecon/subpapers/regassa.pdf*" (last visited 14 May 2008).

[16] For the data on population numbers and ethnic composition, see: *The 1994 Population and Housing Census of Ethiopia Results at Country Level – Volume I Statistical Report* (Addis Ababa: Central Statistical Authority, 1998) 377 p.

1) The first five regions, as listed above, form the first group, in which the population group which gives its name to the region dominates. This implies that the first five regions are dominated by the Tigrayan, Afar, Amhara, Oromo and Somali ethnic groups, respectively. These ethnic groups dominate the regions not only because of their numerical predominance; they also have a political dominance through their control over the regional government institutions.[17]

Notwithstanding the clear dominance of one ethnic group, each of these five regions has substantial ethnic minorities.[18] For instance, the Amhara represent about 10% of the population of Oromia (amounting to more than one and a half million people).

2) The second group is formed by regions six and eight as listed above: the Benishangul/Gumuz and Gambella regions. In these regions there is no dominance of a particular ethnic group, but of two ethnic groups jointly. The name Benishangul/Gumuz refers to the two major groups in the region: the Benishangul (also known as Berta) and the Gumuz. In the Gambella region, the two major groups are the Nuer and Anuak.

3) The third category consists exclusively of the Southern Nations, Nationalities and Peoples region (hereafter referred to as the Southern region). The Southern region is characterised by extreme ethnic diversity. According to official sources, there are no less than 56 different ethnic groups (or – to use the official vernacular – nations, nationalities and peoples) in the region.[19] Some of these groups have more than one million members (such as the Sidama and the Gurage), but most are very small, each amounting to no more than some tens of thousands of people. Despite the existence of some larger groups, it is important to note that not a single group has the numerical majority.

4) The fourth category is limited to the Harar region. This region comprises mainly the city of Harar and is not larger than 340 km². As its name indicates, the Harar region is dominated by the Harari ethnic group or, to put it differently, the region has been created to accommodate the Harari ethnic group. However, the Harar region differs from those of the first category in that the Harari do not have a numerical majority in the region. However, they have a political dominance through their control over the regional government institutions.

---

[17] This control is exercised by political parties that have been created specifically for these ethnic groups (respectively the TPLF, the ANDP, the ANDM, the OPDO and the SPDP). More information on this political mechanism can be found in "C. Van der Beken, *supra* note 15."

[18] For the purpose of this article, people belong to an ethnic minority group when they are members of an ethnic group that is not controlling the regional state where they are living.

[19] Hailemariam Desalegn, Experience of Conflict-Handling and –Prevention in SNNPR, in: *First National Conference on Federalism, Conflict and Peace Building* 44 (Addis Ababa: Ministry of Federal Affairs, 2004).

As it was practically impossible for the author to conduct field research in all of the nine regions, a number of regions had to be selected for further constitutional study. To guarantee an as wide and as representative an overview as possible, it was decided to study at least one region from each group. However, the fourth group, consisting exclusively of the Harar region, could not be included. The author was unable to collect the data (such as an official English translation of the regional constitution) necessary to guarantee an accurate analysis of regional constitutional law. Four regions were eventually selected: the Amhara and Oromia regions from the first group, the Benishangul-Gumuz region representing the second group and the Southern region.

3. REGIONAL CONSTITUTIONAL MECHANISMS TO ACCOMMODATE ETHNIC DIVERSITY

3.1. Constitution and Accommodation of Ethnic Diversity in Amhara and Oromia

3.1.1. Ethnic Composition of the Population

The Amhara region has a total surface area of 170 752 km² and a total population of about fourteen million people. The Amhara are by far the largest ethnic group in the region. Notwithstanding this Amhara predominance, there are many other ethnic groups of which the Oromo are the most important. An interesting observation is that the Amhara regional constitution does not deny this diversity. The preamble of the constitution makes reference to the "peoples of the Amhara National Regional State." Furthermore, Article 8 stipulates that: "*The supreme power of the national regional state resides in and belongs to the peoples of the Amhara region.*" As will be discussed below, this constitutional recognition of ethnic diversity is not inconsequential.

With its total surface area of 353 690 km², the Oromia region is the largest region of the Ethiopian federation. It also has the largest population with about nineteen million people. The Oromo people constitute 85% of the population. On the one hand, this implies a numerical dominance of the Oromo, but on the other hand it implies an important presence of other ethnic groups. The most important minority group is the Amhara, who constitute about 10% of the population. As opposed to the Amhara constitution, the Oromia constitution does not refer to ethnic groups other than the Oromo themselves. The preamble, for instance, does not refer to the peoples of the Oromia region, but simply to the "Oromo people". Furthermore, Article 8 of the Oromia constitution provides that "Sovereign power in the region resides in the people of the Oromo Nation…."

3.1.2. Territorial Organisation

The Amhara regional constitution was approved by the Amhara regional parliament on 22 June 1995. In this article, however, we analyse the amended constitution of November 2001.
This constitution organises the administrative divisions of the region into three hierarchical levels: the highest level is of course the regional level. The second administrative level is the level of the *Woreda* (district), these being further subdivided into *Kebele* (the lowest administrative level). However, for the Himra, Awi and Oromo ethnic minority groups, the constitution creates a special territorial entity: the Nationality Administration. Hierarchically, the Nationality Administration is situated between the regional and *Woreda* levels. In February 2005, according to data from the Ministry of Federal Affairs, the Amhara region had 113 *Woreda* and 5264 *Kebele*.

The Oromia regional constitution was approved by the regional parliament on 21 August 1995 and then amended in October 2001. The constitution provides for the following hierarchical administrative structure: the region, the Zone, the District and the *Kebele*. In February 2005, there were 197 Districts and 10676 *Kebele*.

3.1.3. Regional Institutional Structure

At the regional level, the Amhara region has legislative, executive and judicial institutions. Legislative powers are vested in the regional council, executive powers in the Council of the Regional Government and judicial powers in the regional courts.[20]

The Oromia region has a similar structure with a regional parliament (*Caffee Oromia*), an executive organ (regional Administrative Council) and regional courts.

The Amhara regional council is the highest authority of the region.[21] Unlike the federal parliament, it is unicameral. Its members are representatives of the "peoples in the regional state as a whole"[22] and are elected for a term of five years on the basis of direct elections[23] using the so-called first past the post system.[24] The Amhara constitution pays attention to the position of ethnic minority groups by providing for a guaranteed representation of "minority nationalities and peoples."[25]

---

[20] Article 46 Amhara constitution.
[21] Article 46 (1) Amhara constitution.
[22] Article 48 (3) Amhara constitution.
[23] Article 48 (1) Amhara constitution.
[24] Article 48 (2) Amhara constitution.
[25] Article 48 (2) Amhara constitution.

The parliament of the Oromia region, the *Caffee Oromia*, is likewise the highest authority of the region.[26] The *Caffee* is unicameral and its members are representatives of the "peoples of the region as a whole".[27] They are elected for a term of five years.[28] The electoral system that is used is the first past the post system. However, unlike in Amhara, there is no guaranteed representation of minority groups.[29]

At this point we can already see differences between the Amhara and the Oromia constitutions in the ways they handle ethnic diversity. The first significant provisions are in the preamble. The preamble of the Amhara constitution refers to the peoples of the region, whereas the Oromia constitution refers to the Oromo people. This illustrates different constitutional attitudes towards diversity: a positive attitude in Amhara, a negative one in Oromia. The constitutional provisions on sovereignty reinforce this attitude. In the Amhara constitution, sovereign power in the region is exercised by the different peoples, in Oromia by the Oromo people. The same attitudes can be found in the provisions for the composition of the respective regional parliaments. The Amhara constitution recognises that the first past the post electoral system in an ethnically organised state carries dangers for the representation of ethnic minorities, hence its provision for the guaranteed representation of ethnic minority groups. The Oromia constitution pays no attention to the representation of minority groups; the association of the region with the Oromo people leaves no room for it.

As far as the regional executive institutions are concerned, neither of the two constitutions provides for a guaranteed representation of ethnic groups. As such, the regional constitutions follow the example of the federal constitution (as explained in section 1).

To conclude this section on the regional institutions, we focus on the regional judicial organisation and more specifically, on the institution that has the competence to review the constitutionality of regional laws and regulations. As explained in section 1, the federal constitution grants the competence to review the constitutionality of federal laws and regulations to the second chamber of the federal parliament, the House of the Federation. By doing so, it provides for a very special mechanism of constitutional review. The Oromia constitution of 1995, just like other regional constitutions, also provided for a very special mechanism of constitutional interpretation under which the power to interpret the constitution was given to the regional parliament. This was a clear infringement of the *nemo iudex in sua causa* principle. However, the constitutional amendment of 2001 created a new institution for constitutional interpre-

[26] Article 46 (1) Oromia constitution.
[27] Article 48 (3) Oromia constitution.
[28] Article 48 (1) Oromia constitution.
[29] Article 48 (2) Oromia constitution.

tation: the Constitutional Interpretation Commission. This Commission consists of a representative nominated from each district council.[30] Since the districts in Oromia are not ethnically based, there is no guarantee that members of ethnic minorities (non Oromo) will be represented in this Commission.

In Amhara, the constitution also provides for the establishment of a Constitutional Interpretation Commission. However, as opposed to the Oromia constitution, the Amhara constitution does provide for a guaranteed representation of ethnic minorities in this Commission. The Commission consists not only of members nominated from each *Woreda* council, but also from each Nationality Council (this is the legislative council of the Nationality Administration). As indicated above, and as discussed in section 3.1.4. below, the Amhara constitution provides for the establishment of a Nationality Administration for three ethnic minority groups in the region: the Oromo, Himra and Awi. As such, the representation of these three ethnic minority groups in the regional organ for constitutional interpretation is guaranteed.

3.1.4. Institutional Structure of the Nationality Administration and the Zone

As presented above, the administrative level below the regional level in Amhara is the Nationality Administration. The creation of this administrative level results from the constitutional recognition of ethnic diversity in the Amhara region. The Amhara constitution recognises that, although the Amhara region was created for the Amhara people, there are other peoples living in the region as well. Following this recognition, it has developed mechanisms to realise the right to self-determination (in the broad definition of Article 39 of the federal constitution) of these minority groups. One of these mechanisms is the representation of minority groups in the regional institutions as discussed above. Analysis of the federal constitution makes it clear that the preferred mechanism of the Ethiopian constitutional drafter to realise the right to self-determination is the creation of ethnic-based territorial entities. In the federal constitution, this ethnic territorial strategy is expressed by the creation of ethnic-based regional states, such as the Amhara region. Following the example of the federal constitution, the Amhara constitution attempts to ensure the right to self-determination within its boundaries through the creation of Nationality Administrations, territorial entities on an ethnic basis. The Amhara constitution limits the establishment of Nationality Administrations to the Himra, Awi and Oromo. Nonetheless, many other groups are living within the boundaries of the Amhara region. It is thus argued here that the Amhara constitution limits the recognition of ethnic diversity in the region to particular ethnic groups, to those groups that are considered to be endogenous in the region. Endogenous groups are people who have been living in the region for a long time; they are peoples **of** the region. It is only for these groups that protective mechanisms

---

[30] Article 67 (1) Oromia constitution.

(such as the creation of an administrative entity) have been developed. The other groups are regarded as exogenous because they have moved to the region in a more recent past and can therefore be seen as internal migrants or peoples **in** the region. These same exogenous groups are endogenous in another region (where they can exercise their right to self-determination). This thesis has been developed on the basis of an analysis of the regional constitutions and on the basis of the practices in other regions that indicate a certain pattern. The Amhara constitution does not make explicit the difference between endogenous and exogenous groups. Implicitly, however, this differentiation is made in its Article 39 that contains, as is the case with Article 39 of the federal constitution, the formulation of the right to self-determination. This right to self-determination is exercised by the peoples of the Amhara region. The fact that "peoples of the Amhara region" only refers to the endogenous population of the region (the Amhara, Oromo, Awi and Himra ethnic groups) is shown by Article 39(6): "*The national rights stipulated under sub-art, 1-5 of this article hereof shall apply with respect to the peoples of Himra, Awi and Oromo as well.*" The implication is that only the four endogenous peoples can exercise the various aspects of their right to self-determination in the Amhara region.

In the Oromia region there are no intra-regional ethnically organised territorial entities. In the region, the administrative level below the regional level, the Zone, was not created with the exercise of ethnic minority rights in mind.

The powers of the Nationality Administrations in the Amhara region, on the other hand, illustrate that the endogenous groups there have wide-ranging possibilities for self-administration and for the development of their own languages and cultures. The nationality councils have, for instance, the power to determine their own working language.[31]

3.1.5. Constitution and Accommodation of Ethnic Diversity in Oromia and Amhara: an Evaluation

A fundamental point is that Oromia's constitutional provisions pay no regard to the ethnic diversity of the Oromia region. On the contrary, further examination of the Oromia constitution shows an almost complete identification of the Oromia region with the Oromo ethnic group.
This identification is clear even in the preamble, which makes reference not to the population of the Oromia region, but rather to the "Oromo people". Notwithstanding the fact that Article 2(1) of the regional constitution recognises that Oromia is populated by "people of the Oromo nation and other peoples", Article 8 stipulates that "*Sovereign power in the region resides in the people of the Oromo nation.*" The fact that "people of the Oromo nation" refers exclusively to people of the Oromo ethnic group can be deduced from Article 39(6)

[31] Article 74 (3a) Amhara constitution.

of the Oromia constitution: "*For the purpose of this constitution, the expression 'the people of the Oromo nation' shall be construed as meaning those people who speak the Oromo language, who believe in their common Oromo identity, who share a large measure of a common culture as Oromos and who predominantly inhabit in a contiguous territory of the Regional State.*" Thus, the sovereign power in Oromia does not reside in the various ethnic groups of the region, but in the Oromo ethnic group. From here it follows that the regional parliament, the *Caffee*, should not be perceived as the representative institution of the population of Oromia, but as the representative institution of the Oromo ethnic group. Several other elements support this conclusion. First, unlike the Amhara constitution, the Oromia constitution contains no provisions for the guaranteed representation of ethnic minority groups in the regional parliament. Second, we may note that the *Caffee* elects exclusively Oromo representatives to the federal House of the Federation. Consequently, the Amhara living in the Oromia region are represented in the House of the Federation only by members elected by the Amhara regional parliament. Finally, we may note the regional constitutional provisions on the right to secession. Article 39(4) of the federal constitution stipulates that a demand for secession must be approved by the legislative council of the nation, nationality or people concerned. This provision has been included in Article 39 of the Oromia constitution. Article 39(5) of the latter constitution stipulates that the "*Demand for secession is approved by a two thirds majority vote of the* members of the caffee." The legislative council of the Oromo ethnic group is thus equated with the *Caffee* of the Oromia region.
Nor do Oromia's constitutional provisions on the regional executive and judicial organs contain provisions for guaranteed representation. Ethnic minority groups in Oromia have no right to territorial self-administration. The Zonal administrative level is not an ethnic-based territorial entity, but an executive organ of the regional administration.
The identification of the population of Oromia with the Oromo ethnic group is a clear consequence of the ethnic territorial approach to ethnic diversity. The Ethiopian constitution has established the Oromia region for the Oromo people. From here it follows that ethnic minorities within the Oromia region cannot claim group-specific rights.

The approach of the Amhara constitution is *prima facie* completely different. This is apparent from the preamble, which speaks not only of the Amhara people, but also about the different peoples of the Amhara region. Consequently, Article 8 grants the sovereign power to the peoples of the region. It is therefore no surprise that the Amhara constitution provides for guaranteed representation of ethnic minority groups in the regional parliament. Particular minority groups also have guaranteed representation in the regional organ for constitutional interpretation. Additionally, those same minority groups have a right to their own territorial entities. The Amhara constitution provides for the establishment of ethnic-based territorial entities for the Himra, Awi and Oromo.

Thus, contrary to the Amhara in Oromia, the Oromo in Amhara have their own territorial entity. As far as the exercise of the right to self-determination is concerned, there seems to be a fundamental difference between the two regions. On the basis of the Oromia constitution, only the Oromo have such a right. The Amhara constitution, on the other hand, grants this possibility not only to the dominant Amhara, but to the Himra, Awi and Oromo as well. These minority groups have the right to territorial self-administration, to determine their own language and to representation in the regional institutions.

Notwithstanding these apparent differences, it is argued here that the difference between the Amhara and Oromia constitutions is merely a *prima facie* difference and that the two share the same approach to ethnic diversity.

At this point, I would like to come back to my thesis that inside the regions, a differentiation is made between two categories of ethnic minority: i.e. endogenous and exogenous minorities. Endogenous minorities are those ethnic groups that have traditionally lived in the territory of the region. Exogenous minorities are ethnic groups that have migrated to the region in the recent past and are endogenous in another region. We could also call them internal migrants. Endogenous minorities have a right to have a territory of their own inside the region and to representation in the regional institutions. Exogenous minorities do not have such specific protection and can only claim universal rights. The Oromia constitution only contains protective mechanisms for the Oromo, not for the other ethnic groups, since these are considered to be exogenous. The Amhara constitution contains group – specific rights for the Himra, Awi and Oromo who are considered to be endogenous in the region. The conclusion is therefore that the two regions have a similar approach to ethnic diversity. In both cases the constitutional accommodation of ethnic diversity is limited to endogenous groups.

3.2. Constitutional Accommodation of Ethnic Diversity in Benishangul-Gumuz

3.2.1. Geographical Situation and Ethnic Composition of Benishangul-Gumuz

Benishangul-Gumuz, in the west of Ethiopia, is one of its remotest regions. To the north and northeast of the region lies the Amhara region, to the east Oromia, to the south Gambella and to the west Sudan. The region has a total surface of 50 380 km^2 and, with a mere 460 459 inhabitants, is sparsely populated. This, together with its fertile soil, makes the region attractive to many Ethiopian farmers from other regions who wish to leave their own small and exhausted plots behind. This interregional migration is clearly reflected in the ethnic composition of the region's population. Interestingly, the constitution of Benishangul – Gumuz explicitly differentiates between endogenous and other peoples. Its Article 2 classifies the following five ethnic groups as endogenous: the Berta, Gumuz, Shinasha, Mao and Komo. As indicated in section 2 above, none of those five ethnic groups has a numerical majority: the three most numerous (endogenous) groups are the Berta (25.1 % of the population), the Gumuz (23.3 %) and the Shinasha (7%). The Mao and Komo each count for less than 1% of the population. Striking is the large number of Amhara (22.1 %) and Oromo (12.8 %), an illustration of the impact of migration.

3.2.2. Territorial Organisation

The territorial organisation of Benishangul – Gumuz discussed in this paper is the one based on the constitution of 2 December 2002, though it should be mentioned that, at the time of field research in the region (February/March 2005), the territorial organisation based on the 1996 constitution was still in place.

The 2 December 2002 constitution provides for a four-tier administrative structure: the region, the Administration of Nationalities, the *Woreda* and the *Kebele*.

3.2.3. Regional Institutional Structure

At the regional level, the Benishangul-Gumuz region has legislative, executive and judicial institutions. Legislative powers are vested in the state council, executive powers in the executive council and judicial powers in the regional courts.[32]

Legislative power is exercised by the state council, which is the highest authority in the region. State council members are representatives "of the People of the Regional State as a whole"[33] and are elected for a term of five years through direct elections.[34] The constitution provides for guaranteed representation of the Mao and Komo peoples in the state council. Article 48 (2) stipulates: "*The representation of Mao and Komo nationalities shall be given special consideration.*"

Contrary to what is the case for the regional parliament, the constitution does not provide for a guaranteed representation of ethnic groups in the regional government. In reality, however, there does not appear to be a problem with the representation of endogenous groups in this body. In March 2005, the regional cabinet's thirteen members consisted of four Berta, four Gumuz, three

[32] Article 46 Benishangul/Gumuz constitution.
[33] Article 48 (3) Benishangul/Gumuz constitution.
[34] Article 48 (1) Benishangul/Gumuz constitution.

Shinasha and two Mao/Komo.[35] Thus, as it is, the regional cabinet has no representatives of exogenous groups. In the regional administration, however, the situation is the opposite. Due to a shortage of qualified endogenous staff, more than 70% of regional public servants belong to non-endogenous groups.[36] This large representation is facilitated by the continued use of Amharic as the regional working language.[37]

When it comes to the issue of constitutional interpretation, there are important differences between the 1996 and 2002 constitutions. In the former the power to interpret the constitution was granted to the regional parliament, as was the case with other regional constitutions. But the 2002 constitution has transferred this power to a new institution: the Constitutional Interpretation Commission. This new body appears to be based on the example of the federal House of the Federation. As such, it expresses the ethnic diversity in the region. Article 71(1) of the 2002 constitution stipulates that each endogenous nationality has a right to four representatives in the Commission. Therefore, the total number of Commission members is limited to 20. This brings us to two observations. Firstly, it is striking that each endogenous group, irrespective of the size of its population, has the right to the same number of representatives in the Commission. As indicated in section 1, one of our critiques of the federal House of the Federation is related to its composition. The protection of the interests of the small federated entities is one of the objectives of a second chamber in a federation. The House of the Federation does not achieve this objective since the membership of each ethnic group in the House is, just as for the federal House of Peoples' Representatives, also determined by numerical criteria. This critique does not apply to the Constitutional Interpretation Commission in Benishangul-Gumuz. In this institution, each endogenous ethnic group has an equal number of representatives. The non-endogenous groups, however, have no representation.

Another aspect of the commission modelled on the federal House of the Federation is the way its members are elected. Article 71(1) of the Benishangul-Gumuz constitution provides that they are elected by the Council of Nationalities, the legislative council of the Administration of Nationalities. The representatives of the nations, nationalities and peoples in the House of the Federation are elected by the regional parliaments. The premise of the constitutional drafter is that the regions constitute the framework in which the nations, nationalities and peoples exercise the different aspects of their right to self-

[35] Interview conducted by the author with Yaregal Aysheshim, president of Benishangul – Gumuz, Assosa, 2 March 2005.

[36] Information provided to the author by the regional government.

[37] Article 6 (1) Benishangul/Gumuz constitution. For most of the twentieth century, Amharic was used as the official language at central and lower administrative levels. This was part of the nation building strategy as explained in section 1. The coming into power of the EPRDF in 1991 has changed this radically. Although Amharic is today still being used as the working language of the federal government, the regions have the power to choose their own working languages (and many regions have done so).

determination. The regional parliament is therefore considered to be the representative organ of those nations, nationalities and peoples. From here it follows that the representatives of the ethnic groups in the House of the Federation are elected by the regional parliaments. The Benishangul –Gumuz constitution starts from the same premise. The Administration of Nationalities is the territorial framework in which the diverse ethnic groups of Benishangul-Gumuz exercise their right to self –determination. The legislative council of this administrative level is therefore considered the representative organ of the nations, nationalities and peoples and thus has the power to elect the representatives of those nations, nationalities and peoples in the Constitutional Interpretation Commission.

It should be noted that at the time of research, the Constitutional Interpretation Commission had not yet been effectively established. The establishment of this institution depends on the creation of the administrative level of the Administration of Nationalities and, as indicated above, in March 2005 this administrative level had yet to be created.

3.2.4. *The Institutional Structure of the Administration of Nationalities*

The Administration of Nationalities is a new administrative level that has replaced the Zone. It is an application of the territorial strategy based on the belief that the nations, nationalities and peoples can best realise their right to self-determination within their own territories. Therefore, the nations, nationalities and peoples in Benishangul-Gumuz have a right to establish their own territorial entity. The question now is whether this right pertains to all ethnic groups or whether it is limited to those endogenous to the region. The answer to this question can only be speculative since, so far, no Administration of Nationalities has been established.[38]

Taking into account the philosophy of the constitution and political practice in Benishangul – Gumuz, it is argued here that only the endogenous groups have a right to their own Administration of Nationalities. This position is supported by the composition of the Constitutional Interpretation Commission and the way it is elected: the legislative council of the Administration of Nationalities only elects members of endogenous groups as representatives in the Commission. The position is also supported by the administrative structure of Gambella. The regional constitution of Gambella provides for the administrative level of the Nationality Zone. In Gambella, this new structure is already in place and we can observe that the region is divided into three Nationality Zones, one for each of the three major endogenous groups: the Anuak, Nuer and Mejenger. The Amhara and Oromo, even though numerically more important than the Mejenger, do not have separate Zones in the region. *Mutatis mutandis* we may argue that in Benishangul – Gumuz only the endogenous groups have a right to create their own Administration of Nationalities. This

[38] Interview with Yaregal Aysheshim, *supra* note 35

position is further supported by Article 39 of the Benishangul-Gumuz constitution that, similar to the Amhara constitution, limits the exercise of the various aspects of the right to self-determination to endogenous groups. In the Southern region (discussed below) it is also only endogenous groups that have been granted their own territorial entities. The same is true for the Amhara region. However, this situation does not imply that the exogenous groups have no right to be represented in the Administration of Nationalities. The Benishangul – Gumuz constitution does not guarantee such representation, but the example of the Southern region illustrates that the exogenous groups can be represented in the ethnically organised sub-regional territorial entities.

The competences of the Administration of Nationalities in the Benishangul-Gumuz region are similar to those of the Nationality Administration in the Amhara region.

3.2.5. Benishangul-Gumuz and the Accommodation of Ethnic Diversity

The 2002 constitution pays more attention to the ethnic diversity of the regional population than the constitution of 1996. It introduced fundamental changes to the regional administrative and institutional structure. Particularly significant for our purposes is the disappearance of the administrative level of the Zone (the administrative level hierarchically placed between the region and the district) and the introduction of the Administration of Nationalities as a new territorial administrative entity. The nations, nationalities and peoples of Benishangul–Gumuz have the right to their own Administration of Nationalities. Within the Administration of Nationalities, the nations, nationalities and peoples or ethnic groups have self-administration and the possibility of protecting and developing their own cultures and languages. Two considerations must be made here. Firstly, some ethnic groups in Benishangul – Gumuz (such as the Gumuz) are dispersed over the regional territory. For them, it seems impossible to establish their own territorial entity in the region.[39] Secondly, and this partially results from the first remark, the new ethnic-based administrations will inevitably have their own minorities. The example of the Mao Komo Special *Woreda* can illustrate this. Though this *Woreda* has been established for the Mao and Komo ethnic groups, a large number of different ethnic groups are living in the area.[40] For these reasons, the territorial strategy for the accommodation of ethnic diversity (the creation of ethnic based territorial administrative entities) is not appropriate for the Benishangul-Gumuz region.

It is furthermore not clear whether the right to a territorial entity applies to all ethnic groups in the region or whether it is limited to the Berta, Gumuz, Shi-

[39] This argument was mentioned by President Yaregal Aysheshim as one of the reasons why the new administrative structure had not yet been introduced.
[40] Remark based on a field visit of the author to the Special *Woreda* in March 2005.

nasha, Mao and Komo. The constitution defines the latter groups as endogenous groups, implying a hierarchy of ethnic groups. The impression exists, as remarked above, that the non-endogenous groups do not have a right to their own Administration of Nationalities. The distinction between endogenous and non-endogenous groups is expressed much more clearly in the provisions on the regional institutions. The small endogenous ethnic groups (the Mao and the Komo) have a guaranteed representation in the regional parliament. The exogenous groups have no such guarantee. Furthermore, all endogenous groups are represented in the regional cabinet whereas none of the exogenous groups is represented at that level. The same goes for the Constitutional Interpretation Commission. In this last institution, all endogenous groups are equally represented while the exogenous groups have no representatives.

We may conclude that the 2002 constitution has strengthened the position of the endogenous ethnic groups of the region by providing for their guaranteed representation in the regional parliament and in the regional Commission for Constitutional Interpretation. The right of the ethnic groups to their own territorial entities (the Administration of Nationalities), however, is not appropriate for the situation in Benishangul-Gumuz. Because they lack territorial concentration, the ethnic groups of Benishangul-Gumuz cannot exercise their right to self-rule through the creation of ethnic-based territorial administrative entities (the Administration of Nationalities). Furthermore, although the exogenous groups can claim universal human rights in the region, no regional administrative or institutional mechanisms are in place to allow for the exercise of their group-specific rights.

3.3. Constitution and Accommodation of Ethnic Diversity in the Southern Nations, Nationalities and Peoples Region

3.3.1. Ethnic Composition of the Population

The Southern Nations, Nationalities and Peoples Region (the Southern region) has a population of more than 13 million people who live in an area of 113 539 km^2. As the name of the region indicates, a particular feature of its population is its enormous ethnic diversity. According to official sources, there are no less than 56 different ethnic groups, or to use the official vernacular, nations, nationalities and peoples in the region. Some of these groups (such as the Sidama and the Gurage) have more than 1 million members, but most are very small, each amounting to no more than some tens of thousands of people.
Notwithstanding the existence of some larger groups, it is important to note that not a single group has the numerical majority. Therefore, it is contended that there are clear similarities between the population composition of the Southern state on the one hand and the Ethiopian society *in toto* on the other

hand, the latter being also characterised by the presence of a few large and many small ethnic groups.

3.3.2. The Territorial Organisation of the Southern State

The Southern state ratified its own constitution on 22 June 1995. On 12 November 2001, this constitution was replaced by the "Revised Constitution, 2001, of the Southern Nations, Nationalities and Peoples Regional State Proclamation No. 35/2001". This revision introduced several institutional reforms that, as can be seen below, reflect the particular ethnic diversity of the Southern population and that, therefore, in the context of this article, merit our particular attention.

Article 45(1) of the Southern constitution provides a four-tier internal administrative structure: the regional/state level, the Zonal/Special *Woreda*, the *Woreda* level and finally the *Kebele* level. As discussed further below, the Zone in the Southern region is not the same as the Zone in the Oromia region. In the latter case, the Zone is a deconcentrated organ of the regional administration whereas the Zone in the Southern region is an ethnically based territorial entity. The Special *Woreda* has the same status as the Zone, but is used for smaller and territorially strongly concentrated groups. Therefore, the Zone/Special *Woreda* in the Southern region can best be compared to the Nationality Administration in Amhara and Benishangul – Gumuz.

February 2005 data provided by the Ministry of Federal Affairs show that the Southern region currently consists of 13 Zones, 8 Special *Woreda*, 104 *Woreda* and 3772 *Kebele*.

3.3.3. Regional Institutional Structure

Article 46(1) of the Southern state constitution designates the legislative body, the State Council, as the highest authority of the regional state. The State Council has been profoundly reformed by the constitutional revision of 2001, which created a second chamber, the Council of Nationalities, in addition to the State Council. Thus today, the Southern state parliament is – like the federal parliament – composed of two chambers. Further analysis clearly reveals many other similarities between the regional and the federal parliaments.

The members of the first chamber, the State Council, are representatives "of the people of the state as a whole"[41] and are directly elected for a term of 5 years.[42] These representatives are elected by the plurality electoral system. But again, the full consequences of this system are compensated for by the guaran-

[41] Article 50 (3) Southern constitution.
[42] Article 50 (1) Southern constitution.

teed representation for "minority Nationalities and Peoples".[43] This latter mechanism was not included in the original constitution of 1995 but was incorporated in the 2001 revision.

It is, however, the Southern state's second chamber, created by the 2001 constitutional revision, which is of particular interest for this article. An analysis of the relevant constitutional provisions concerning this second chamber, the Council of Nationalities, clearly demonstrates its similarities with the federal House of the Federation.

Article 58(1) of the Southern constitution states that the Council of Nationalities is composed of representatives of nations, nationalities and peoples, each with at least one member. This implies that every ethnic group in the Southern region has the right to be represented in this institution. Furthermore, Article 58(2) stipulates that each nation, nationality or people shall be represented by one additional representative for each one million of its population. As most ethnic groups in the Southern state are small, this means that only some groups will be able to claim more than one representative. The Council of Nationalities' list of members (see Table 1 below) shows that six ethnic groups have more than one representative: the Sidama (3), the Gurage (2), the Wolayita (2), the Gedeo (2), the Hadiya (2) and the Gamo (2).

Table 1 The Council of Nationalities
Members of the Council of Nationalities[44]

	Zone/Liyu (Special) Woreda	**Ethnic Composition (No. of Representatives)**
1	Gurage	Kabena (1), Gurage (2), Mareqo (1)
2	Kembata Timbaro	Timbaro (1), Donga (1) Kembata (1)
3	Alaba Liyu Woreda	Alaba (1)
4	Kaffa	Kaffa (1), Nao (1), Chara (1)
5	Gedeo	Gedeo (2)
6	Sidama	Sidama (3)
7	Burji Liyu Woreda	Burji (1)
8	Hadiya	Hadiya (2)
9	Konso Liyu Woreda	Konso (1)
10	Dawro	Dawro (1)
11	Bench Majji	Bench (1), Shaka (1), Dizi (1), Surma (1), Zelmam (1), Miniyit (1)

[43] Article 50 (2) Southern constitution.

[44] This list is adapted from: C. Van der Beken, *The Ethiopian Federal State Structure and the Accommodation of Ethnic Diversity: A View from the Southern Nations, Nationalities and Peoples Region,* Ghent University Faculty of Law, Non - Western Law Working Paper, 2003, 53 p.

	Zone/Liyu (Special) Woreda	Ethnic Composition (No. of Representatives)
12	Amaro Liyu Woreda	Amaro (1)
13	Konta Liyu Woreda	Konta (1)
14	Shaka	Shaka (1)
15	Silte	Silte (1)
16	Gamogoffa	Gamo (2), Zeiss (1), Gedicho (1) Aida (1) Goffa (1)
17	Debub Omo	Ari (1), Male (1), Benna (1), Tsemay (1), Biraili (1), Hamar (1), Arbore (1), Karo (1), Dasenech (1), Gnangatom (1), Murill (1), Muguji (1), Dimm (1), Bodi (1), Mursi (1), Bacha (1)
18	Derashe Liyu Woreda	Derashe (1), Masholle (1), Kusumme (1), Msiye (1), Dobass (1)
19	Yem Liyu Woreda	Yem (1)
20	Basketo Liyu Woreda	Basketo (1)
21	Wolayita	Wolayita (2)

Thus the Southern constitution guarantees the representation of all ethnic groups in the regional parliament. However, this representation is limited to the endogenous groups of the Southern region. Notwithstanding the fact that hundreds of thousands of Amhara and Oromo live in the Southern region, they do not have representatives in the Council of Nationalities. This is further confirmation of our theory about the distinction between endogenous and exogenous groups, which states that the regional constitutions have developed mechanisms to protect ethnic diversity exclusively for endogenous groups. From here it follows that exogenous groups have no right to be represented in the Council of Nationalities. This is not explicitly stated in the Southern constitution, but we can deduct it from the list of members of the Council of Nationalities and the Deputy Speaker of the Council of Nationalities confirmed it to the author.[45]

Members of the Council of Nationalities are elected from among members of Zonal and Special *Woreda* councils. Nationalities that do not have representatives in Zonal Councils are represented by members elected for *Woreda* Councils.[46] This indirect system of election is a result of the territorial approach towards ethnic diversity that characterises the Ethiopian state structure. The federal constitutional objective to accommodate ethnic diversity by creating eth-

[45] Interview conducted by the author with the Deputy Speaker of the Council of Nationalities, Awassa, 16 March 2005.
[46] Article 58 (3) Southern constitution.

nically based regional states has been, in a sense, adopted on the regional level. Article 45(2) of the Southern constitution says, "*The Nations, Nationalities or Peoples in the Region shall have their own Zonal or Special Wereda administration.*" Following the theory on endogenous and exogenous groups, we can assume that "nations, nationalities and peoples in the region" refers exclusively to its endogenous groups. Of course, notwithstanding the exclusion of exogenous groups, a large number of ethnic groups have the right to their own territorial entities in the Southern region. As indicated above, the region has 56 nations, nationalities and peoples. However, by 2005, only 13 Zones and 8 Special *Woreda* had been created in the Southern region. As a result, the largest ethnic groups in the Southern region (such as the Sidama, the Gurage, the Hadiya, the Gedeo and the Wolayita) have their own Zone and a number of Special *Woreda* have been created for small and territorially concentrated groups. All other groups constitute a minority within one of these entities or live together in multi-ethnic Zones such as the Southern Omo Zone and the Bench-Majji Zone. One can observe in this territorial organisation of the Southern state clear similarities with that at the federal level. In both cases, a number of large and territorially relatively concentrated ethnic groups have their 'own' administrative entities while the remaining groups are a minority in those entities or are brought together into multi-ethnic entities. Given this fact, it is not surprising that the members of the Council of Nationalities – in accordance with the practice that the members of the House of the Federation are elected from the regional councils – are elected from Zonal and Special *Woreda* Councils.[47]

Article 59 of the Southern constitution lists the powers and functions of the Council of Nationalities. These competences were clarified in regional Proclamation No. 60/2003, "The consolidations of house of council of nationalities and definition of its powers and responsibilities proclamation" of 29 June 2003.

- The Council of Nationalities is the authoritative interpreter of the regional constitution.[48] This is a departure from the Southern constitution of 1995, which allocated this power to the State Council, but is in line with the global structure of the Southern state constitution. Article 8(1) of this constitution stipulates "*All power of the regional state resides in the peoples of the Southern Nations, Nationalities and Peoples' Regional State.*" Therefore, following an internal logic, the constitution allocates the power to interpret the constitution to the Council of Nationalities - the representative organ of the same nations, nationalities and peoples. The exact procedure by which this is done is explained in Proclamation No. 60/2003.

[47] Official sources in Awassa indicate that no members of the Council of Nationalities have been elected by (ordinary) *Woreda* councils.

[48] Article 59 (1) Southern constitution.

- It is the Council of Nationalities which organises the regional Council of Constitutional Inquiry,[49] the structures and competences of which are regulated and enumerated in Articles 78 and 79 of the Southern constitution. A close reading of these provisions reveals that the regional Council of Constitutional Inquiry is a regional copy of the federal Council, a mere advisory organ to the Council of Nationalities, this latter having the ultimate power to interpret the Southern constitution.

- It is the Council that decides on issues relating nations', nationalities' or peoples' rights to Zone, Special *Woreda* or *Woreda* administration according to the state constitution.[50] Here, a significant divergence between the federal and the regional constitution can be noted. Article 62(3) of the federal constitution states that the House of the Federation shall decide on issues relating to the rights of nations, nationalities and peoples to self-determination. The Southern constitution, on the other hand, does not speak – in its Article 59 (3) – of the right to self-determination but about the right to Zone, Special *Woreda* or *Woreda* administration. The right to self-determination appears to have been reduced to the right to have one's 'own' administrative entity. This can be seen as another expression of the territorial approach towards ethnic diversity, according to which the right to self-determination of nations, nationalities and peoples can best be realised through territorial autonomy. However, Southern Proclamation No. 60/2003 again gives a wider definition to the right of self-determination, a definition that is identical to the definition in the federal constitution. Therefore, the procedure is as follows. When an ethnic group in the Southern region believes that its right to self-determination has been violated, it can submit a complaint to the Council of Nationalities. An important protection for such a group is that, if it is not satisfied with the decision of the Council or the Council does not reach a decision within two years, it can submit its case to the federal House of the Federation.

- The Council of Nationalities promotes and consolidates the unity and the equality of the peoples of the region, based on their mutual consent.[51] Not only does it have the responsibility to ensure the right to self-determination of the various Southern peoples but also the duty to foster unity between them. In this context, the former president of the Southern state, Hailemariam Desalegn, had the following to say: "*The mission* (of the Council of Nationalities) *is not only to resolve conflicts once they happen but also to advocate unity, advocating unity and peaceful coexistence. The peaceful coexistence of the Southern peoples is important. When you become unified, you become strong. It is up to*

[49] Article 59 (2) Southern constitution.
[50] Article 59 (3) Southern constitution.
[51] Article 59 (4) Southern constitution.

this institution to advocate unity and create awareness about the need to strengthen the unity of the southern peoples."[52]

- The Council of Nationalities has the duty to strive for solutions to disputes or misunderstandings that may arise between administrative hierarchies.[53]

- It also has the duty to create favourable conditions for the study of the history, culture and languages of the nationalities.[54]

- The Council of Nationalities studies disputes between neighbouring states and questions of border delimitation, submits its findings to the House of the Federation and follows up for implementation.[55]

- The Council of Nationalities has an important role to play in the procedure for amendment of the regional constitution.[56] This procedure was thoroughly revised by the 2001 constitutional revision. On this subject the 1995 Southern constitution merely stated, "*the provisions of this constitution shall be amended when the idea of amendment is supported by a three-fourth majority vote of the members of the State Council.*" The 2001 Southern constitution, on the other hand, lays out a much more detailed procedure that is inspired by the federal constitution amendment procedure. It reserves an important role for the Zones and Special *Woreda.* They participate in the process both directly (through their respective councils) and indirectly (through the Council of Nationalities). The amendment procedure can be found in Articles 124 and 125 of the Southern constitution.

Article 124 provides that a constitutional amendment can be initiated in one of three ways:

1) An amendment proposal can be supported by a two-thirds majority vote in the State Council;
2) It can be supported by a two-thirds majority vote in the Council of Nationalities;
3) Finally, it can be supported by one-third of the Zonal or Special *Woreda* councils by majority vote.

As for the actual approval of the constitutional amendment, two procedures are incorporated in Article 125. The first procedure has to be followed in the case

[52] Interview conducted by Walta Information Center with the president of the Southern region, Hailemariam Desalegn, Walta, 20 April 2002.
[53] Article 59 (5) Southern constitution.
[54] Article 59 (6) Southern constitution.
[55] Article 59 (8) Southern constitution.
[56] Article 59 (7) Southern constitution.

of a proposed amendment to Article 125 itself (the article on the amendment). This article can be amended only when:

a) All Zonal and Special *Woreda* Councils, by majority vote, approve the proposed amendment(s) and;
b) Both the State Council and the Council of Nationalities, by a two-thirds majority vote, approve the proposed amendment(s).[57]

The second procedure has to be followed in the case of a proposed amendment to any other constitutional provision, which can be amended only when:

a) The State Council and the Council of Nationalities, in a joint session, approve a proposed amendment by a two-thirds majority vote and;
b) Two-thirds of the Councils of Zonal and Special *Woreda* also approve it by majority vote.[58]

However, Article 125(2) of the Southern constitution goes on to stipulate that the provisions of chapter two ("the fundamental principles of the constitution") and chapter three ("fundamental rights and freedoms") can be amended only if the – corresponding – provisions of chapter two and three of the federal constitution are similarly amended. This is to prevent an infringement of the federal constitution, since the regional constitutions have to be in conformity with it.

This concludes the analysis of the regional parliament of the Southern state. It is worthwhile to summarise the most relevant points. The analysis has shown that the ethnic diversity of the Southern population is clearly reflected in the constitutional provisions on the regional parliament. It is obvious that the constitutional revision of 2001 has resulted in a profound reform of the Southern state parliament. This reform was clearly guided by the example of the federal parliament. Firstly, in order to assure the representation of all ethnic groups, the representation of ethnic minorities in the State Council is guaranteed. However, the most important reform is the creation of a second chamber which, with regard to both its composition and its powers, is modelled on the second chamber of the federal parliament: the House of the Federation. The establishment of the Council of Nationalities resulted from the ambition to develop in the Southern state appropriate institutional mechanisms for the prevention and regulation of ethnic conflicts. Taking into account the parallels between the Southern state and the Ethiopian state as a whole concerning population composition, it is not surprising that the development of these institutional mechanisms was guided by the federal example. Once again a statement from Hailemariam Desalegn can be cited: "*There was need for an institution which can resolve conflicts democratically and amicably, thereby con-*

[57] Article 125 (1) Southern constitution.
[58] Article 125 (3) Southern constitution.

tributing to the consolidation of the democratic unity among the diverse peoples of the south. So from the exercises of the federal House of the Federation we came to learn the need to establish a similar institution in our region. The House of Nationalities or the Council of Nationalities is the result of that realization."[59]

With this new composition, the Southern state parliament has become a truly representative assembly. By guaranteeing the representation of ethnic minorities, all ethnic groups, no matter how small, are assured of representation in the first chamber of the regional parliament. And although the number of members representing each ethnic group in the first chamber is proportionate to the size of its population so that large ethnic groups have a larger representation than smaller ones, their preponderance is not as pronounced as on the federal level, where a few ethnic groups dominate the first chamber. Moreover, the larger representation of the large groups is compensated for by the composition of the Council of Nationalities. This institution does not offer a numerically equal representation of ethnic groups, but because of its specific composition (one representative per group and one additional representative per one million people), even the largest ethnic groups do not have more than two or three representatives. For this reason, the equality between the different ethnic groups in the Southern Council of Nationalities is much larger than in the federal House of the Federation.

It should be stressed however that this representation in the regional parliament applies only to the endogenous groups. The composition of the parliament confirms our thesis about the exogenous and the endogenous groups. Even though the difference between endogenous and exogenous groups is not made explicit in the constitution, it can be deduced from the composition of the Council of Nationalities. Notwithstanding the fact that the number of Oromo and Amhara in the Southern region is much larger than that of many other ethnic groups, they do not have a single representative in the Council of Nationalities.

There is no guaranteed representation of ethnic groups in the regional government. Obviously, given the sheer number of ethnic groups, representation of all of them in the regional government is not possible. However, in view of the attention paid to representation in the regional parliament, we can assume that attempts are normally made to ensure that the composition of the regional government reflects the region's wide ethnic diversity.

As far as constitutional interpretation is concerned, the Southern constitution of 1995 had established a mechanism also included in the other regional constitutions. As indicated above, this mechanism implied that the ultimate power to interpret the constitution rested with the regional parliament. Today, after the constitutional amendment of 2001, the procedure for constitutional inter-

[59] Interview with Walta Information Center, *supra* note 52.

pretation is regulated by the Articles 78 and 79 of the regional constitution and in Southern Proclamation No. 60/2003 of 29 June 2003. These documents still do not give the power of interpretation to a judicial institution. The revised procedure for constitutional interpretation enshrined in the constitutional amendment of 2001 has followed the federal model. This implies that the power to interpret the constitution now rests with the Council of Nationalities. The nations, nationalities and peoples thus have representation in the organ for constitutional interpretation. However, only the endogenous groups are represented. As such, this organ in the Southern region resembles the Constitutional Interpretation Commission in Amhara, Oromia and Benishangul-Gumuz. In these institutions as well, only endogenous groups have guaranteed representation.

3.3.4. The Institutional Structure of the Zone/Special Woreda

The Zone/Special *Woreda* is the administrative level just below the region.

Article 80(2) of the Southern constitution stipulates that a Zone/Special *Woreda* comprises: the Zonal/Special *Woreda* Council, the Zonal/Special *Woreda* Administrative organ (the executive organ) and the judiciary.

The competences of the Zonal and Special *Woreda* Council are listed in Article 81(3) of the Southern constitution. One of these is the power to determine its working language. This creates the possibility for the Zonal/Special *Woreda* Councils to do away with the use of Amharic as the working language within their respective territories. At the regional level, however, Amharic continues to be the working language.
Again, a clear parallel with the federal constitution can be observed. Article 5 (2) of the federal constitution stipulates that Amharic shall be the working language of the federal government. Article 5(3) of the federal constitution, however, states that the members of the federation (the regions) may by law determine their respective working languages. Some regions have made use of this provision, resulting, for example, in the adoption of Tigrigna and Oromifa as working languages in the Tigray and Oromia regions respectively. Nor has the constitutional right of the Zones/Special *Woreda* in the Southern state to determine their working language remained theoretical either. By August 2003, five Zones had introduced a local language as the working language of their respective Zone.[60]

Another competence of the Zonal/Special *Woreda* Council is the power, without prejudice to the powers vested in the State Council, to issue laws on mat-

[60] These are the Sidama, the Wolayita, the Hadiya, the Kembata and the Gedeo Zones; interview conducted by the author with Fikru Gnakal, Speaker of the Southern state Council, Awassa, 18 August 2003.

ters uncovered provided that they are consistent with state and federal laws.[61] For the time being, this provision will probably remain theoretical. It is presently unclear what residual legislative powers are left to the Zonal/Special *Woreda* Councils.[62]

3.3.5. The Southern Region and the Accommodation of Ethnic Diversity

As the above constitutional analysis has demonstrated, the constitutional provisions of the Southern state take into account the ethnic diversity of its population. Although the ethnic element was to some extent recognised in the 1995 Southern constitution, it is primarily the 2001 constitutional revision that has designed institutional mechanisms to incorporate and accommodate the enormous diversity that characterises the Southern population.

It is clear that the Southern constitutional provisions on this matter were inspired by the federal constitution. The constitutional revision of 2001 has created a state structure that has many similarities with the ethnic-based federal state structure of the federal constitution. Firstly, all nations, nationalities and peoples of the Southern state have the right to form their 'own' Zone/Special *Woreda*, with the power to issue laws and to determine its working language. These competences are specified in the constitution and this constitution – as the above discussion of the constitutional amendment procedure has shown – cannot be revised without the participation of the Zones/Special *Woreda*. Furthermore, the Zones/Special *Woreda* can influence policy-making at the regional level through their representation in the Council of Nationalities. But ultimately – notwithstanding many similarities – the Zones and Special *Woreda* cannot be described as federated entities. Such a designation does not accord with the hierarchical relationship between the regional level and the subordinated Zonal/Special *Woreda* level.

The question that has to be answered now is whether the mechanisms developed by the Southern constitution have the potential to make the right to self-determination of all ethnic groups in the region a reality. The answer is not straightforward. On the one hand, the constitution does contain mechanisms that can accommodate the wishes of particular ethnic groups. On the other hand, the available mechanisms will undoubtedly give rise to new expectations.

The most important mechanism is without any doubt the creation of a Zone/Special *Woreda*. All (endogenous) nations, nationalities and peoples in the Southern region have the right to form their own Zone/Special *Woreda*. So

---

[61] Article 81 (3.c) Southern constitution.

[62] Interview conducted by the author with Dr. Kebede Kanchula, Deputy Chief Administrator Sidama Zone, Awassa, 20 August 2003.

far, a number of ethnic groups (such as the Gurage, Gedeo, Sidama, Hadiya and Wolayita) have made use of this right. Therefore, these groups can exercise their right to territorial self-administration and have the possibility of taking steps to protect their own languages and cultures. However, most of the Southern state's 50+ ethnic groups do not have their own Zone/Special *Woreda*. These groups either live in a multi-ethnic Zone (examples of which are the Debub (South) Omo and the Bench-Majji Zones) or are a minority group in a Zone dominated by another group. The question now is whether there are mechanisms in the Southern constitution to enable these groups to realise their right to self-determination.

Obviously, there is the availability of the territorial mechanism. The Southern constitution grants all ethnic groups in the Southern state the right to form their own Zones/Special *Woreda.* In recent years, some new Zones and Special *Woreda* have been created effectively and this appears to have assuaged the demands of particular ethnic groups. However, this approach has many defects. First, the establishment of a new Zone/Special *Woreda* for a particular ethnic group requires the territorial concentration of the group under consideration. The territorial mechanism is therefore no solution for territorially dispersed groups. Second, it should be stressed that any newly created Zone will probably not be ethnically homogenous either. It is very likely that the new Zone will have its own minorities and this could then result in new ethnic problems and demands. Finally, the creation of more Zones/Special *Woreda* conflicts with the objectives of good governance. The creation of additional administrative entities will, for instance, result in a dispersion of scarce resources, thus undermining government efficiency.

In this context, it is important to note that neither the federal government nor the Southern regional government have been very enthusiastic about further pursuing this territorial strategy. The Silte/Gurage dispute illustrates this point. Traditionally, the Silte were considered to be part of the Gurage ethnic group. The ethnic-territorial approach that characterises the Ethiopian decentralisation process resulted in the creation of a Gurage Zone within which the Silte were accorded their own *Woreda.* The Silte, however, increasingly manifested themselves as a separate ethnic group – not merely as a Gurage sub-group – and accordingly they requested their own Zonal administration. Finally, their demand was met, but only after the government had reluctantly realised that this was the only way to prevent escalating ethnic tensions and conflicts.[63]

Recent political developments in the Southern state could make the creation of additional Zones and Special *Woreda* even more unlikely. The ruling party in the Southern state, the Southern Ethiopia Peoples Democratic Front (SEPDF), has recently been dramatically transformed. The 20 ethnic-based member parties of the SEPDF have merged and formed a united party: the South Ethiopian

[63] Aklilu Abraham, *Federalism, State Restructuring and Rights of Ethnic Minority Groups in Ethiopia,* unpublished paper.

Peoples Democratic Movement (SEPDM). The former ethnic-based parties will now become branches of the new one. According to the Vice-Chairman of the SEPDM this merger was necessary in order to intensify the fight of the southern nations, nationalities and peoples "*against poverty, backwardness and anti-democratic elements in a unified and more integrated way.*"[64] The question now is whether this political centralisation will also have an impact on the administrative structure. It is the author's impression - taking into account the overwhelming majority of the SEPDM in the Southern state council (even after the 2005 elections) – that the creation of the SEPDM will in fact have an impact on the administrative structure in the Southern state. Though some SEPDM party officials have refuted this likelihood, others have indicated that in the future no new territorial entities would be created. In fact, they have even suggested the possibility of merging existing *Woreda*. Therefore, there is absolutely no guarantee that the government will in fact allow any new Zone or Special *Woreda* to be established.

The above illustrates the limited capacity of the ethnic-territorial strategy to solve possible future ethnic tensions and conflicts. However, this conclusion should not be interpreted as a suggestion to the Ethiopian and Southern governments to completely abandon the territorial strategy when trying to accommodate ethnic diversity. Granting territorial autonomy can certainly result in a relaxation of ethnic tensions. However, what the above does indicate is that the right to self-determination of all nations, nationalities and peoples in the Southern region can only be realised if the territorial strategy is complemented by other mechanisms. Such non-territorial mechanisms are not included in the Southern constitution. For instance, the constitution could have provided for mechanisms of non-territorial autonomy[65] and for guaranteed representation of minority groups in the Zonal councils. At the same time, as far as the representation of minority groups is concerned, it should be pointed out that the Zonal councils, notwithstanding the lack of a constitutional obligation thereto, are reasonably ethnically representative. Also important is that at this level, not only endogenous but also exogenous groups are represented. The latter, who cannot claim their own territorial entities, are thus represented in these entities. To illustrate the latter point, we give an overview of the ethnic composition of 20 of the 21 Zonal/Special *Woreda* Councils.[66]

---

[64] Walta Information Center, 16 September 2003.

[65] Non-territorial autonomy deviates from the paradigm where an automatic association between autonomy and territory is made. In the case of non-territorial autonomy, autonomy is not granted to a certain territorial entity, but to the ethnic group itself. As such, ethnic groups can exercise self-government irrespective of whether they live concentrated in a certain territory or not; J. Mc Garry, Federal Political Systems and the Accommodation of National Minorities, in: A.L. Griffiths and K. Nerenberg (eds.), *Handbook of Federal Countries, 2002* 425 (Montreal & Kingston/London/Ithaca: McGill-Queen's University Press, 2002).

[66] Information on the Konso Special *Woreda* could not be obtained. I would like to thank Ato Darota Dejamo (Deputy Speaker of the Southern state Council) and Ato Simon Aldada (advisor to the

Table 2 Ethnic Composition of the Zonal/Special *Woreda* Councils in the Southern Region

Gurage	Gurage (60), Kabena (5), Mareqo (6), Amhara (1)
Hadiya	Only Hadiya representatives
Kembata Timbaro	Kembata (23), Timbaro (3), Donga (2)
Sidama	Only Sidama representatives
Gedeo	Only Gedeo representatives
Debub Omo	Amhara (3), Ari (7), Male (2), Karo (1), Bana (2), Tsemay (2), Hamar (2), Arbore (2), Dime (2), Bodi (2), Mursi (2), Dasenech (2), Muguji (1), Gnangatom (2)
Kaffa	Kaffa (29), Nao (1)
Sheka	Shekicho (11), Sheko (2), Mejenger (1), Kaffa (1), Amhara (2), Tigray (1), Bench (1), Oromo (1)
Bench Majji	Bench (15), Kaffa (3), Sheko (6), Dizi (7), Surma (8), Miniyit (9), Amhara (2)
Silte	Only Silte representatives
Wolayita	Only Wolayita representatives
Gamogoffa	Gamo (22), Goffa (14), Zeiss (1), Gedicho (1), Oida (1)
Alaba Liyu (Special) *Woreda*	Only Alaba representatives
Dawro	Only Dawro representatives
Yem Liyu *Woreda*	Only Yem representatives
Derashe Special *Woreda*	Derashe (35), Oromo (1), Amhara (5) Kusumme (5), Musie (10), Masholle (7), Dobass (26)
Amaro Special *Woreda*	Only Amaro representatives
Burji Special *Woreda*	Only Burji representatives
Konso Special *Woreda*	No data
Konta Special *Woreda*	Only Konta representatives
Basketo Special *Woreda*	Only Basketo representatives

Although many Zonal/Special *Woreda* councils are ethnically inclusive, table 2 also indicates that in some councils only the dominant ethnic group is represented. This does obviously not imply that those Zones are perfectly ethnically homogenous. The cities are particularly ethnically diverse with a large presence of exogenous groups. There is a concern for the rights of those groups. However, recently an interesting development has occurred that grants ethnic minority groups, in those regions dominated by a particular ethnic group, the possibility for self-administration. The Southern Proclamation No. 51/2002 of 19 August 2002 grants cities, which comply with criteria determined by the regional executive council, an important degree of autonomy.[67] These cities

Southern regional government) for providing me with the data on the Zonal/Special *Woreda* Councils.

[67] According to regional government sources, city autonomy implies the power to determine the working language. This could mean that cities, geographically located in a particular Zone, could choose a working language that differs from the working language of that Zone.

are administered according to the Council-Mayor system whereby the Council determines policy and takes the important decisions and the Mayor performs the executive functions.[68] The members of the City Council are directly elected by the citizens of the city.[69] The members of the Council elect the mayor.[70] This development offers groups who are in a minority in Zonal terms but may have a numerical majority in the city important guarantees of representation and self-administration. In this Proclamation, we again notice the great care shown for the protection of the endogenous groups. Ethnic groups endogenous to a particular city enjoy a specific legal protection. The endogenous group that can be a minority in the city is assured of 30% of the seats in the City Council. Moreover, the law stipulates that the Mayor must also be elected from the representatives of the endogenous group. By taking these measures, the law attempts to assuage the fears of endogenous groups about losing control over 'their' city. That these fears are very real was illustrated by the serious riots in Awassa, the Southern regional capital, in May 2002. These riots, which caused the deaths of many people, resulted from the fear of the Sidama people that they would lose influence in 'their' city.

The Southern constitution pays attention not only to the possibility of self-administration. It also provides for different mechanisms of guaranteed representation at the regional level. Through the guarantee of reserved seats for minority groups, all (endogenous) groups are assured of representation in the first chamber of the regional parliament. But it is primarily the second chamber - the Council of Nationalities - that guarantees ethnic representation in the regional parliament. In this organ, all the endogenous ethnic groups have at least one representative. Such guaranteed representation is not assured in the executive council, but there are as yet no indications to doubt the ethnic representativeness of the executive. Finally, we may note the inclusive ethnic representation in the organ competent for constitutional interpretation (the Council of Nationalities).

3.4. Regional Accommodation of Ethnic Diversity: An Overview

The analysis presented in this article has clearly indicated that the regional constitutions do recognise the ethnic diversity of the regional populations. Notwithstanding the major differences between the regional constitutional mechanisms, it is argued that all regions basically share the same approach to ethnic diversity.

[68] Article 13 Proclamation No. 51/2002.
[69] Article 15 Proclamation No. 51/2002.
[70] Article 16 Proclamation No. 51/2002.

An important outcome of the analysis is that we have been able to show that different routes are taken towards endogenous and exogenous groups. Some regional constitutions (such as that of Benishangul–Gumuz) explicitly provide for this differentiation, but most constitutions only recognise this implicitly. The analysis of constitutions and practice shows that in the regions studied only endogenous groups enjoy specific protective mechanisms. Endogenous groups are people who have been living in the region for a long time; they are peoples **of** the region. Exogenous groups have moved to the region in a more recent past and can therefore be seen as internal migrants or peoples **in** the region. These exogenous groups cannot enjoy specific protection in the region. These same exogenous groups are endogenous in another region and it is there that they can enjoy such protection. In those regions, where next to the dominant group, no other endogenous groups are recognized (as in Oromia), the regional constitution does not include mechanisms for ethnic minorities. However, the lack of group-specific rights for exogenous minorities does not preclude the fact that all Ethiopian citizens, no matter where they live on the Ethiopian territory, can claim equal universal rights.

In those regions where ethnic minorities are recognized, the regional constitutions contain protective mechanisms that can be divided into two categories.

The first category aims at creating self-administration for ethnic minorities on a territorial basis. Within their own territories (Zone, Special *Woreda*, Nationality Administration), these minorities have a right to self-administration. These territorial entities have their own councils and executive organs and have important competences such as the power to choose their own working languages.

The second category of protective mechanisms is the inclusion of representatives of ethnic minorities in the regional institutions as in the guarantee of seats in regional parliaments granted to ethnic minorities. In the Southern region this guarantee goes further: the Southern constitution additionally creates a second chamber of the regional parliament wherein all (endogenous) groups have a right to be represented. With regard to the executive power, the regional constitutions do not provide for guaranteed representation. Finally, the interests of ethnic minority groups are protected by the guaranteed representation of ethnic minorities in the organ competent for constitutional interpretation.

8. Ethiopia before the United Nations Treaty Monitoring Bodies

Eva Brems[•]

1. INTRODUCTION

The current international system for the protection of human rights was born on 10 December 1948, the date of the adoption of the Universal Declaration of Human Rights by the General Assembly of the United Nations. Yet, as a resolution of the General Assembly, the Universal Declaration does not have formal binding force. Hence, while the Universal Declaration remains the mother text of human rights and a constant reference point in international relations, lawyers prefer to work with the binding texts that have been adopted since 1948. Among the many human rights conventions adopted by the United Nations, seven are known – together with their additional protocols - as the 'core international human rights instruments': the International Convention on the Elimination of All Forms of Racial Discrimination (ICERD, adopted 21 December 1965), the International Covenant on Civil and Political Rights (ICCPR, adopted 16 December 1966), the International Covenant on Economic, Social and Cultural Rights (ICESCR, adopted 16 December 1966), the Convention on the Elimination of All Forms of Discrimination against Women (CEDAW, adopted 18 December 1979), the Convention against Torture and Other Cruel, Inhuman or Degrading Treatment or Punishment (CAT, adopted 10 December 1984), the Convention on the Rights of the Child (CRC, adopted 20 November 1989) and the International Convention on the Protection of the Rights of All Migrant Workers and Members of Their Families (ICRMW, adopted 18 December 1990).

The main international control mechanism under these conventions is what may be considered the standard mechanism in international human rights protection: state reporting before an international committee. An initial report is due usually one year after joining the treaty, and afterwards reports are due periodically (every four or five years). The Committee on the Elimination of Racial Discrimination (CERD), the Human Rights Committee (HRC), the Committee on Economic, Social and Cultural Rights (CESCR), the Committee on the Elimination of Discrimination Against Women (CEDAW), the Committee Against Torture (CAT), the Committee on the Rights of the Child (CRC) and the Committee on Migrant Workers (CMW) are each composed of

[•] Professor of Human Rights and Non-Western Law, Ghent University, Faculty of Law, Department of Public Law. E-mail: Eva.Brems@UGent.be

10 to 23 independent experts. They examine the reports submitted by the State Parties. In the course of this examination they include information from other sources, such as the press, other United Nations materials or NGO information. They also hold a meeting with representatives of the state submitting the report. At the end of this process the Committee issues 'concluding observations' or 'concluding comments'. Drafted in diplomatic language, these nevertheless point out problematic issues from a human rights perspective and include recommendations for change.

In addition to the examination of state reports, the main functions of the supervising Committees are the formulation of General Comments – these interpret the content of specific treaty provisions – and the examination of individual complaints. An individual complaint mechanism exists under the ICERD, the ICCPR (additional protocol), the CEDAW (additional protocol) and the CAT. In all these cases, the individual complaint mechanism is optional, because it depends on the state's ratification of an additional protocol or making of a special declaration.

This paper focuses on the experience of one state – Ethiopia – with the seven core human rights treaties. This should allow the reader to gain insights both into the human rights situation in Ethiopia and the functioning of the United Nations human rights protection system.

2. ETHIOPIA AND THE UN HUMAN RIGHTS COMMITTEES

2.1. Ethiopia's Ratification Record

Ethiopia has been a member of the United Nations since 1945. It is a party to six of the seven core human rights treaties. Ethiopia joined the ICERD in 1976, but did not make the declaration under Article 14 that would allow individuals to submit complaints to the CERD. It ratified the CEDAW in 1981, but not the 1999 Optional Protocol. In 1991, Ethiopia joined the CRC, but it has not yet taken any action with respect to the 2000 Optional Protocols on the sale of children, child prostitution and child pornography and on the involvement of children in armed conflict. In 1993, Ethiopia joined both the ICCPR and the ICESCR. It has not joined the Optional Protocols to the ICCPR on an individual complaint mechanism (1996) and on the abolition of the death penalty (1989). Ethiopia became a party to the CAT in 1994, but did not make the declaration under Article 22 that would allow individual complaints, nor did it join the 2002 Optional Protocol establishing a system of regular visits. Finally, Ethiopia has not taken any action with respect to the ICMW.
This can be considered a good ratification record. The ICMW has been ratified by few states and the substantive protocols that Ethiopia has not ratified are – with the exception of the ICCPR protocol abolishing the death penalty – recent

ones, hence ratification may still occur in the near future. It should be noted furthermore, that Ethiopia has not made any reservations under the substantive provisions of any of these conventions.
Successive Ethiopian governments have consistently refused to accept individual complaint mechanisms before the United Nations Committees of independent experts. Since there are no decisions on individual complaints to be examined, this paper will focus on the Committees' concluding observations relating to state reports.

2.2. Ethiopia's Reporting Record

One of the problems that is noted in the literature with respect to the reporting mechanism before the UN Committees[1] is the huge delay that builds up because states report late or not at all. This pattern can be recognised in the case of Ethiopia. Until now, Ethiopia has delivered 11 reports, but 17 reports are overdue. Under the CERD, Ethiopia delivered reports in 1978, 1979, 1981, 1984, 1985 and 1988, but since then, 8 reports are due. Under the CEDAW, Ethiopia submitted three combined reports in 1993 and two combined reports in 2002. Currently one report is due. Under the CRC, Ethiopia has submitted reports in 1995, 1998 and 2005. Ethiopia has not yet reported under the ICCPR (3 reports due), the ICESCR (3 reports due) and the CAT (3 reports due).

This is a very mixed record, with an excellent performance under the CRC and a fair one under the CEDAW, but very poor under the other treaties. It is remarkable to see regular reporting under the CERD at first, but none under the current regime. And it is troubling to find that Ethiopia has now been a party for over a decade to the ICCPR, ICESCR and CAT, yet has not bothered to submit a single report.
An explanation for this would require an analysis of the national political context as well as of the organisation and dynamics of the relative administrations. An evaluation of Ethiopia's reporting record would have to conclude, first, that it is very positive that activities are currently going on in the field of human rights reporting, as the most recent reports were submitted in 2002 (CEDAW) and 2005 (CRC). Yet, the total lack of reporting under three treaties is a serious shortcoming. The ICCPR and ICESCR may be considered the main human rights treaties, because they include general human rights catalogues, applicable to all individuals and together protect almost all human rights. Moreover, the Convention Against Torture concerns what is arguably the most serious human rights violation that should be on top of the list of any state's priorities.

---

[1] P. Alston, *Effective functioning of bodies established pursuant to United Nations human rights instruments*, Final report on enhancing the long-term effectiveness of the United Nations human rights treaty system, UN Doc. E/CN.4/1997/74.

This unbalanced picture might be due to the fact that Ethiopia joined the CEDAW and CRC earlier, and hence, responsibilities for reporting have been assigned and procedures have been set in motion that may not yet have been cleared out for the other conventions.
On a substantial level the result is remarkable: it appears that the Ethiopian government accepts being challenged by the international community concerning questions with the inclusion of all its citizens, especially the most vulnerable members (women and children), in its policies, but it is more reluctant to see its overall policies and practices challenged in the same way. It is clear that the ICCPR and CAT address issues that do not explicitly come to the fore when discussing women's or children's rights (in particular political freedoms and the prohibition of torture and ill-treatment by state agents). Yet, the ICESCR is different: a state that accepts monitoring under the CRC and CEDAW should not fear the ICESCR Committee, as relatively few issues not covered under the former conventions can be expected to come up under the latter.
The apparent lack of commitment to the CERD is surprising, as this is the treaty that explicitly addresses issues of ethnicity, which take a central place in Ethiopian constitutional law and institutional arrangements.[2] It remains to be examined whether it might be the case that the Convention's focus on non-discrimination is experienced as problematic in a system based on collective self-determination.[3] In March 2006, the CERD Committee sent Ethiopia a list of issues to facilitate the drafting of a report: an answer to this list was due by 31 December 2006.
The eleven reports submitted by Ethiopia to the UN Committees, have all been examined – typically two or three years later – by the relevant Committees. Five of these eleven 'concluding observations' are the object of the analysis in this paper.
Not included are the six reports that have been commented upon by the CERD. The most recent one among these was submitted in 1988 and considered by the Committee in 1990. This is too long ago, especially in the light of recent Ethiopian history.[4]
The five documents that are included are:

- the Concluding Observations of the CEDAW Committee issued in 1996 on the combined first, second and third report of Ethiopia submitted in 1993;[5]
- the Concluding Observations of the CEDAW Committee issued in 2004 on the combined fourth and fifth report of Ethiopia submitted in 2002;[6]

---

[2] See C. Van der Beken, *Decentralisatie en etnische diversiteit in Afrika met casestudy Ethiopië*, Ph.D. Thesis Ghent University, 2006.
[3] In that case the situation might be comparable to Belgium's reluctance to ratify the European Framework Convention on National Minorities, because it would upset institutional arrangements expressing a fragile political consensus.
[4] From 1974 until 1991, Ethiopia was governed by the socialist *Derg* regime. The current majority party EPRDF has been in power since then.
[5] UN Doc. A/51/38, paras.134-163 (hereafter: CEDAW 1996).
[6] UN Doc. A/59/38 (Part I) paras. 226-273 (hereafter CEDAW 2004).

- the Concluding Observations of the CRC Committee issued in 1997 on the initial report of Ethiopia submitted in 1995;[7]
- the Concluding Observations of the CRC Committee issued in 2001 on the second report of Ethiopia submitted in 1998;[8]
- the Concluding Observations of the CRC Committee issued in 2006 on the third report of Ethiopia submitted in 2005.[9]

3. THE UN HUMAN RIGHTS COMMITTEES' CONCLUDING OBSERVATIONS ON ETHIOPIA: AN ANALYSIS

3.1. General Observations

The CEDAW Committee labelled the first state report in 1996 as 'frank and honest'[10] and used the term 'frank and constructive' for the dialogue with the state in 2004.[11] Yet it noted both times that the state report did not follow the Committee's Guidelines and in 1996 found that these shortcomings were 'obstacles to constructive dialogue'.

This problem did not exist under the CRC. The CRC Committee noted in 1997 that the guidelines for reports were respected, even though not all questions asked were answered. It appreciated the 'open and constructive dialogue' and the 'self-critical approach' of the report.[12] In 2001 it noted 'frank and constructive efforts' in the course of 'high quality dialogue'.[13] In 2006, the CRC Committee welcomed "the detailed written replies to its list of issues … and the constructive dialogue with a high-level, cross-sectional delegation".[14]

3.2. Obstacles to the Implementation of the Conventions

The format of 'concluding observations' sometimes provides for a specific section dealing with so-called 'factors and difficulties' - elements that are recognised by the supervising body as obstacles to full implementation of the Convention and as elements explaining a slow rate of progress.

The CEDAW Committee in 1996 mentioned: "poverty, deep-rooted customs and traditions, illiteracy, high birth rates and unemployment"; it stated that these were "compounded by the existence of different kinds of laws, national as well as a variety of customary and religious ones".[15] Hence the existence of

[7] UN Doc. CRC/C/15/Add.67 (hereafter CRC 1997).
[8] UN Doc. CRC/C/15/Add.144 (hereafter CRC 2001).
[9] UN Doc. CRC/C/ETH.CO.3 (hereafter CRC 2006).
[10] CEDAW 1996, § 138.
[11] CEDAW 2004, § 236.
[12] CRC 1997, § 2.
[13] CRC 2001, § 2.
[14] CRC 2006, § 2.
[15] CEDAW 1996, § 139.

legal pluralism in Ethiopia is seen by the Committee as one of the obstacles for the realisation of women's rights.
The CRC Committee in 1997 mentioned: "civil war, transition to democracy, interregional and urban/rural disparities in particular with regard to the availability of resources and infrastructure, and the prevalence of certain traditional practices and customs."[16] The Committee also recognised the impact of poverty on the situation of children, pointing amongst others at indicators such as mortality rates, malnutrition, low levels of school enrolment and immunization coverage.[17]
In 2001, it noted "the continuing incidence of natural disasters, including droughts and floods", [18] as well as the period of armed conflict with Eritrea and "the State party's continuing serious socio-economic problems".[19] Under the same heading, the CRC Committee also expressed "its concern at the situation of human rights in general" in Ethiopia.[20]

3.3. Positive Aspects

Concluding observations on state reports are targeted in the first place at identifying shortcomings in state policy and practice (expressed as 'concerns' of the Committee), and at making recommendations to remedy these. Yet care is always taken to start with a number of positive observations with respect to measures taken and progress made.

Under the CEDAW, these positive aspects are:
- political will, noted with respect to international commitments in the Beijing Conference,[21] and expressed in a national policy for the advancement of women, policies with gender perspective, and women's focal points in decision-making bodies;[22]
- affirmative action policies for women at university level[23] as well as in the civil service;[24]
- in 1996, the Committee noted a high percentage of women participating in local government;[25]
- in 2004, it mentioned the revision of the family code and penal code to eliminate discriminatory provisions and also gender mainstreaming in the school curriculum.[26]

---

[16] CRC 1997, § 8.
[17] *Ibid.*
[18] CRC 2001, § 10.
[19] CRC 2001, § 11.
[20] CRC 2001, § 11.
[21] CEDAW 1996, § 141.
[22] CEDAW 1996, § 140; CEDAW 2004, § 239.
[23] CEDAW 1996, § 143; CEDAW 2004, § 240.
[24] CEDAW 2004, § 240.
[25] CEDAW 1996, § 142.

Under the CRC, the following points were mentioned:

- a similar political commitment to improve the situation of children, expressed in the establishment of committees at different levels as well as a national plan of action;[27]
- a number of elements in the legal framework: in 1997, the Committee noted the fact that the constitution and domestic law both incorporate children's rights standards,[28] and in 2001 it mentioned the translation of the Convention (by state and NGOs) into 11 official languages, the ratification of the ILO Conventions on child labour and the new family code amending some problematic provisions;[29] in 2006, the Committee mentioned the ratification of several other conventions[30] and the Revised Family Code setting 18 years as the minimum age for marriage for both girls and boys;[31]
- in 1997, efforts by the government together with international and non-governmental organisations in the field of information campaigns on HIV/AIDS as well as on harmful traditional practices;[32] in 2006, Ethiopia was congratulated for its free anti-retroviral programme and for the criminalization of harmful traditional practices in the 2005 Criminal Code, as well as the criminalization of most forms of human trafficking;[33]
- also in 1997, the Committee welcomed the fact that primary education had been made free (but it regrets that it is not compulsory);[34]
- in 2001, the Committee noted some general measures for human rights including children's rights: review of legislation, establishment of the Commission on Human Rights and of the institution of Ombudsman.[35] It noted Ethiopia's significant efforts in the assistance to refugees;[36]
- It also mentions a number of specific measures: the interim prohibition of corporal punishment in schools, efforts for child participatory education and integrating children's rights into school curricula; AIDS awareness clubs in high schools and childcare and protection units in 10 police stations in Addis Ababa.[37]

---

[26] CEDAW 2004, § 238 and 240.

[27] CRC 1997, § 5; CRC 2006, § 3 (national Plan of Action for Children 2003-2010).

[28] CRC 1997, § 3.

[29] CRC 2001, §§ 3-4 and 8.

[30] CRC 2006, § 5: The Convention of the International Labour Organization No. 29 concerning Forced or Compulsory Labour and No. 182 concerning the Prohibition and Immediate Action for the Elimination of the Worst Forms of Child Labour, both on 2 September 2003; The African Charter on the Rights and Welfare of the African Child on 2 October 2002; The Convention on the Prohibition of the Use, Stockpiling, Production and Transfer of Anti-Personnel Mines and Their Destruction on 17 December 2004.

[31] CRC 2006, § 3.

[32] CRC 1997, § 6.

[33] CRC 2006, § 3.

[34] CRC 1997, § 7.

[35] CRC 2001, §§ 3 and 5.

[36] CRC 2001, § 9.

[37] CRC 2001, § 6.

3.4. Most Urgent Concerns

Concluding observations on state reports do not normally use the language of 'violations'. They express 'concerns' – although some matters of concern would manifestly constitute human rights violations if they were considered by a court. The Committees establish a certain hierarchy in their observations by occasionally using the term 'great concern' or 'deeply concerned'. Or they make certain recommendations 'as a matter of priority'. From the examination of the concluding observations of the CRC and CEDAW Committees on Ethiopia, the following appear to be the most urgent and most serious matters in the eyes of the Committees.

a) Certain Harmful Cultural Practices

Widespread *FGM* (*Female Genital Mutilation*) is a 'great concern' of the CEDAW Committee in 1996[38] and of the CRC Committee in 2001;[39] the CEDAW Committee also noted *early marriage* as a great concern[40] and the CRC Committee in 1997 recommended as a matter of priority the abolition of the minimum age of marriage for girls at 15 (as opposed to 18 for boys).[41] Both Committees later welcomed the fact that the minimum age of marriage had been set at 18 years for both sexes,[42] but the CEDAW Committee expressed concern about the persistence of this practice[43] and the CRC Committee stated it was 'specifically concerned' over the high percentage of early marriages and early pregnancies, as these have a negative impact on girls' health.[44]

b) Gender-based Violence

The incidence of violence against women and girls and the insufficiency of measures to eradicate it was another great concern of the CEDAW Committee in 1996.[45] This concern was repeated in 2004 (though not with the same emphasis).[46] The Committee pointed at the lack of specific legislation and systematic data collection, in particular on domestic violence. It noted the incidence of rape and mentioned in addition that the crime of abduction was not systematically prosecuted, but was rather addressed through discriminatory customary laws and practices. The CRC Committee in 2001 stated that violence against women has a negative impact on children and may lead to child abuse.[47]

---

[38] CEDAW 1996, § 148.
[39] CRC 2001, § 64.
[40] CEDAW 1996, § 149.
[41] CRC 1997, § 27.
[42] CEDAW 2004, § 253; CRC 2006, § 3.
[43] CEDAW 2004, § 253.
[44] CRC 2006, § 57.
[45] CEDAW 1996, § 148.
[46] CEDAW 2004, §§ 255-256.
[47] CRC 2001, § 46.

c) Juvenile Justice

In 1997, the CRC Committee showed itself 'deeply concerned' about the system of juvenile justice, in particular about the age of criminal responsibility at 9 years and the treatment of children as adults from the age of 15.[48] This concern was repeated (though not with the same emphasis) in 2001 and 2006.[49] The Committee then added the issue that there was only one specialised youth court, fearing that international juvenile justice standards may not be available before adult courts.

Moreover, the Committee 'particularly recommended' the abolition 'as a matter of priority' of a number of legal provisions, concerning the sentencing of children to *corporal punishment*, the acceptance in the Civil Code of 'light bodily' punishment as an educational measure within the family, and the limitation of the *child's right to counsel* when he or she may be represented in legal proceedings by parents or a legal guardian.[50] The concerns with respect to corporal punishment were repeated (though not with the same emphasis) in 2001 and 2006: the Penal Code still allows "reasonable chastisement" and in practice corporal punishment is still widespread at home, in schools and in other settings.[51]

d) Health

The CRC Committee in 2001 was deeply concerned about the extremely high infant mortality rates and low life expectancy, "in particular, at the high incidence of malaria and tuberculosis and their effects upon children, at the fragile health infrastructure, limited health awareness among the public … that implementation of health policies has been slow and that only limited progress has been achieved in this area." [52] In 2006, the same Committee expressed deep concern "that infant, under-five and maternal mortality remain very high".[53] The high incidence of malaria also remains among its (ordinary) concerns. Moreover, an additional deep concern was expressed "over the HIV/AIDS infection rates, and that children and women of child-bearing age remain highly vulnerable to contracting HIV/AIDS. Specifically, the Committee is concerned that testing and counselling are lacking as well as a strategy on how to support and counteract discrimination against children who have contracted or lost their parents to HIV/AIDS".[54]

[48] CRC 1997, § 20.
[49] CRC 2001, §§ 28-29, §§ 76-77; CRC 2006, §§ 77-78.
[50] CRC 1997, § 27.
[51] CRC 2001, §§ 38-39; CRC 2006, §§ 33-34.
[52] CRC 2001, § 52.
[53] CRC 2006, § 53.
[54] CRC 2006, § 55. A concern about HIV/AIDS had earlier been expressed by both committees (CEDAW 1996, § 161; CRC 2001, §§ 58-59)

e) Education

In 2001, the CRC Committee showed deep concern "at the very low rates of primary and secondary school enrolment, at the especially low rate of enrolment among girls and the very high drop-out rate".[55] In 2006, the same Committee welcomed the improved enrolment rate in primary schools, as well as increased budget allocation for education, but remained "seriously concerned that primary education is still not free nor compulsory and that net enrolment is still very low".[56] The dropout rate remains one among many other concerns in the area of education.[57] Other concerns raised by the Committees in the area of education included sexual harassment of girls at school and lack of vocational training programmes,[58] school fees in primary education, overcrowding of schools, low transition rate to secondary school, insufficient number of trained teachers and available school facilities, absence of budget allocations for pre-primary schools and the poor quality of education.[59]

f) Sexual Exploitation

In 2001, the CRC Committee was "deeply concerned at reports of sexual exploitation, prostitution, rape and other sexual abuse of children".[60] In 2006, the Committee welcomed initiatives by the state to combat sexual exploitation, but a deep concern remained concerning the lack of information on the extent of the problem and the number of children affected by sexual abuse and exploitation,[61] as well as the sale and traffic in children.[62] The CEDAW Committee, dealing with adult women, used the term 'prostitution' rather than 'sexual exploitation', and expressed concern – not 'deep concern'- at its prevalence.[63]

g) Discrimination and Vulnerable Groups of Children

The CRC Committee recommends in its most recent observations that Ethiopia should make combating discrimination against vulnerable girls a national priority. The Committee identifies many groups of children that suffer discrimination,[64] but emphasises in particular the vulnerability of girls, who "remain victims of harmful traditional practices, deprived of education (primary and secondary), victims of sexual and physical violence as well as commercial exploitation."[65]

---

[55] CRC 2001, § 66. Before being thus raised as a priority concern, these issues had already emerged as a shared concern of the CRC Committee (1997, § 17) and the CEDAW Committee (1996, § 151).
[56] CRC 2006, § 63.
[57] *Ibid.*
[58] CEDAW 1996, § 151.
[59] CRC 2006, § 63.
[60] CRC 2001, § 72.
[61] CRC 2006, § 73.
[62] CRC 2006, § 75.
[63] CEDAW 1996, § 149.
[64] CRC 2006, § 24: "girls, children with disabilities, children living in poverty, refugee children, children affected by and/or infected with HIV/AIDS and children belonging to ethnic minorities".
[65] *Ibid.*

In addition, a serious concern is expressed about torture, cruel and degrading treatment by the police and the military of vulnerable groups of children, such as children belonging to ethnic minorities.[66] In 2006, the CRC Committee was also deeply concerned about the fate of street children[67] and about the prevalence of child labour.[68]

h) Birth Registration

The registration of children at birth may seem like a simple administrative matter, but it is in fact important leverage for the enjoyment of many rights – children who are not registered, do not officially 'exist' and hence cannot receive social nor other benefits. In 2006, the CRC Committee was "deeply concerned that a very large number of children are neither registered at birth nor at a later stage".[69]

i) Poverty

The CRC Committee is deeply concerned about the widespread poverty in Ethiopia and the impact of extreme poverty on children, in particular "the increasingly large numbers of children who do not enjoy the right to an adequate standard of living, including access to food, clean drinking water, adequate housing and latrines"[70] and children living in extreme poverty as a result of their being deprived of parental care, because of AIDS or other reasons.[71]

j) Human Rights Institutions

In 2006, the CRC Committee recommended as a matter of priority that the state should ensure "the efficient operation of both the Human Rights Commission and Ombudsman", in full compliance with all relevant international principles.[72] These institutions were established by law in 2000. The Committee "understands that the Offices commenced operation in 2005 but regrets the lack of information on their work".[73]

k) Police and Military Behaviour in a Context of Political Upheaval

The CRC Committee "is deeply concerned over the information concerning the direct impact on children of events following the November 2005 demonstrations which involved arbitrary mass detentions, excessive use of force by

---

[66] CRC 2006, § 35.

[67] CRC 2006, § 69. This was already an ordinary concern in CRC 1997, § 19 and CRC 2001, §§ 74-75.

[68] CRC 2006, § 71. This was already an ordinary concern in CRC 1997, § 19 and CRC 2001, §§ 74-75.

[69] CRC 2006, § 31. Before being thus raised as a priority concern, registration had already emerged as a common concern of the CRC Committee (1997, § 15; 2001, § 34 – 'deep concern') and the CEDAW Committee (2004, § 253).

[70] CRC 2006, § 61.

[71] CRC 2006, §§ 37-38.

[72] CRC 2006, § 15.

[73] CRC 2006, § 14.

the police and the military causing deaths and physical injuries, including by gunshots, of numerous children. The Committee is particularly disturbed to learn that schools were attacked under the pretext that children were involved in demonstrations. Among the children affected, the Committee notes an elevated number of vulnerable children belonging to ethnic minorities as well as street children. The Committee urges the State party to take urgent measures to ensure respect for the civilian population and protect vulnerable groups, such as children of ethnic minorities and street children, from excessive use of force." [74]

In addition, the Committee "is especially concerned at the lack of awareness of children's rights displayed by the police during the post-election events, despite having received considerable relevant training". [75] Moreover, in this context, children's rights issues are to such an extent intertwined with general human rights issues that the CRC Committee's serious concerns do not remain restricted to the field of children's rights: "the Committee is seriously concerned over restrictions placed upon civil society since the elections in 2005 and, in particular, regrets the arbitrary mass detentions, including of children, that place severe restrictions upon the freedom of expression which is a fundamental element of a free civil society". [76]

l) Lack of Government Commitment

The most remarkable deep concern is one of a general nature, expressed by the CRC Committee in 2001, casting doubt on the Ethiopian government's authentic commitment to children's rights "particularly in the context of high military expenditure, the Committee is deeply concerned that the State party has not sought to implement the Convention to the maximum extent of available resources". [77] This implies insufficient budgetary allocation to implement policies and plans in favour of children's rights. In the preceding paragraph, the Committee had noted that some relevant budgets had been decreased since the submission of the initial report.

3.5. Shared Concerns of the CEDAW Committee and the CRC Committee

Several among the priority concerns enumerated above were raised by both the CEDAW Committee and the CRC Committee, though not necessarily with the same strong emphasis. This is specifically the case for the issues of birth registration, education rights and HIV/AIDS. Below are some other issues that have been mentioned by both Committees.

---

[74] CRC 2006, § 27.
[75] CRC 2006, § 20.
[76] CRC 2006, § 22.
[77] CRC 2001, § 18.

Harmful Cultural Practices

Two practices – female genital mutilation and early marriage – are raised as priority concerns (cf. *supra*). Yet the CRC Committee also mentions some harmful practices against children that do not exclusively affect girls: one is the persistence of discriminatory social attitudes against vulnerable groups of children, such as the girl child, disabled children, children born out of wedlock and children affected by HIV/AIDS.[78] In 2001, it added the practices of uvulectomy, milk-teeth extraction and forced marriage.[79] In 2006, the concern about forced marriage was specified as being about the widespread practice of "forced and early marriages of girls through abduction".[80]

The CEDAW Committee additionally mentions some harmful practices against adult women: widow inheritance and "strong stereotypical attitudes in respect of the roles and responsibilities of women and men in the family and society".[81] In 1996 it added that all existing customary laws should be reviewed in view of their compatibility with international and national law.[82]

Health Care

Health care affects all people, including of course women and children. Both Committees have stressed the importance of primary health care. The CEDAW emphasises access to reproductive health, family life education and family planning services,[83] adding in 2004 a concern about maternal mortality and clandestine abortion.[84] The CRC Committee in 1997 proposed to give budgetary priority to the development of a primary health care system, which would develop a culture of nutrition, hygiene and sanitation.[85] In 2001, it also pointed at insufficient provision of mental health care facilities and in both 2001 and 2006 at the situation in adolescent health care, in particular the high incidence of early pregnancy and sexually transmitted diseases.[86] In 2006, the CRC Committee added concern at "the low coverage of vaccinations, the prevalence of malaria, low breastfeeding rates and the high incidence of malnutrition".[87] It noted moreover that medical facilities are concentrated in the urban areas, resulting in exclusion of the majority of the population from necessary health services.[88]

---

[78] CRC 1997, § 14.
[79] CRC 2001, § 64.
[80] CRC 2006, § 59.
[81] CEDAW 2004, § 251.
[82] CEDAW 1996, § 154.
[83] CEDAW 1996, § 160.
[84] CEDAW 2004, § 257.
[85] CRC 1997, § 28.
[86] CRC 2001, §§ 60-63. CRC 2006, §§ 57-58.
[87] CRC 2006, § 53.
[88] *Ibid.*

State Responsibilities in a Federal Structure
An interesting issue that is alluded to by both Committees is the impact of the federal state structure on human rights protection. On the one hand, this is an issue because some matters are within the powers of regional authorities; hence legislation and policies have to be adopted in all regions. The CEDAW Committee in 2004 was worried that the federal state structure might slow down changes to improve women's rights: "The Committee urges the State party to enforce the supremacy of the Constitution over regional laws and encourages it to proceed, as a matter of urgency, with the full implementation of the provisions of the Convention throughout the country, including through enhanced cooperation between the federal and regional governmental bodies and institutions, so as to achieve uniformity of results in the implementation of the Convention. Also, the federal government must ensure that all regional governments adopt and duly implement the revised Family Code."[89] In 2006, the Committee was concerned that the newly created Ministry of Women's Affairs "lacks sufficient resources and the ability to establish coordination at the regional, zone and Woreda levels".[90]

On the other hand, the structure itself might mean a risk for some rights, in particular those of ethnic minorities. The CRC Committee in 2001 expressed concern "that children and their families who are members of ethnic groups which are in a minority in a particular region, or which are not in control of the region's administration, face discrimination".[91]

Other Concerns
In addition, both Committees complain about a lack of statistical data that are the basis for evaluating a situation and for measuring progress and making comparisons. This lack of data includes lack of information on specific categories of women or children.[92]

Both Committees worry that the mechanisms and institutions that have been created (and that are noted under 'positive aspects') might have too little power and too little resources to actually make a difference.[93]

Both Committees encourage the state to increase its cooperation with NGOs. The CEDAW Committee states that they should be consulted in the preparation of the state report.[94] The CRC Committee says that the legislative network governing the work of NGOs is to be updated.[95]

[89] CEDAW 2004, § 242.
[90] CRC 2006, § 10.
[91] CRC 2001, § 30.
[92] CEDAW 2004, § 249; CRC 2001, §§ 22-23; CRC 2006, § 18.
[93] CEDAW 1996, § 145; CEDAW 2004 §§ 245-246; CRC 2001, §§ 17-21; CRC 2006, §§ 10-17.
[94] CEDAW 2004, § 270.
[95] CRC 2001, § §§ 26-27. Also CRC 2006, §§ 22-23.

3.6. Additional Concerns of the CEDAW Committee

While the CRC Committee abstains from comments on the general development of rights protection in the state, the CEDAW Committee in 2004 commented with concern on the "slow progress in the implementation of the provisions of the Convention" since the consideration of the previous report in 1996.[96]

Specific issues taken up by the CEDAW Committee and not by the CRC Committee usually affect mostly adult women: political rights and economic rights.

In the political sphere, the Committee regrets the low representation of women at higher decision- making levels.[97] In the economic sphere, the Committee mentions discrimination in the labour market, especially in the emerging private sector. It recommends temporary special measures to remedy this.[98] The Committee is also concerned about the increasing number of women migrating in search of work and their vulnerability to violence, exploitation and trafficking.[99] Finally it emphasises poverty reduction for women; the Committee insists on the integration of gender perspectives in poverty reduction programmes and the participation of rural women in the formulation, implementation and evaluation of such programmes. In addition, it calls upon the state to put in place policies to protect women's right to property and to ensure that women have access to land and water resources on an equal basis with men.[100]

3.7. Additional Concerns of the CRC Committee

First, there are a number of general remarks that the CRC Committee has made in each of its reports on Ethiopia. One is the lack of publication of the CRC in the Official Gazette, which makes it difficult even for legal professionals to have access to it.[101] Another is the lack of awareness and understanding of the principles and provisions of the Convention. In order to remedy this, the Committee recommends among other things, the training of relevant personnel.[102]

In addition, there are numerous child-specific human rights violations that have been highlighted in one or several concluding observations of the CRC on the state reports of Ethiopia. The list below summarises these issues and thus provides a sorry account of many challenges facing Ethiopia with respect to children's rights.

---

[96] CEDAW 2004, § 240.
[97] CEDAW 1996, § 150; CEDAW 2004, §§ 263-264.
[98] CEDAW 2004, §§ 261-262.
[99] CEDAW 2004, § 265.
[100] CEDAW 2004, § 260.
[101] CRC 1997, § 9; CRC 2001, § 14; CRC 2006, § 8.
[102] CRC 1997, § 10; CRC 1997, §§ 24-25; CRC 2006, §§ 20-21.

Children's rights are usually subdivided into three categories (the so-called "three P's"): *protection rights*, *participation rights* and *provision rights.*

- In the field of *protection rights*, the Committee has expressed concern that the lack of conformity of adoption systems with CRC requirements may make children vulnerable to human rights abuses,[103] that widespread unofficial (illegal) adoption leads to discrimination and that the possibility to revoke adoption may leave children without care.[104] It has remarked on the insufficiency of measures taken for the recovery and social reintegration of children victims of war[105] and has urged that children's concerns be taken into account in all post-war efforts.[106] In 2006, the Committee was still "concerned at the lack of physical and psychological recovery for all children affected by armed conflict, in particular those who were displaced and separated from their parents and those affected by land mines".[107] Moreover, it expressed a fear that the recruitment of child soldiers might be possible despite legal arrangements to the contrary, on account of "possible gaps within the recruitment process due to a lack of adequate birth registration".[108] It also emphasised the needs of refugee and internally displaced children and their families.[109] In the context of population displacement caused by natural disasters and armed conflict, the Committee has stressed the importance of family reunification.[110] In the area of juvenile justice, the Committee is concerned that contrary to international standards, children are not separated from adults in detention,[111] at least during pre-trial detention.[112] It fears "that deprivation of liberty is not used as a measure of last resort", as it should be with respect to children, and it "regrets the absence of a child-friendly juvenile justice system in most of the country and the lack of legal aid representatives for child victims of offences as well as accused children".[113] Moreover, it is "concerned over the large number of young children, including infants, in prison with their mothers".[114] The Committee has also made detailed recommendations to improve state response to child abuse.[115] In 2006, the Committee included for the first time an entry on the rights of children belonging to a minority or indigenous group. It noted the absence of information on this topic in the state's report and expressed concern "over the situation of children belonging to minorities, in particular Oromo and Anuak, as they suffer stigmatization and persecution by the armed forces,

[103] CRC 2001, §§ 44-45.
[104] CRC 2006, §§ 39-44.
[105] CRC 1997, § 21.
[106] CRC 2001, § 69.
[107] CRC 2006, § 67.
[108] *Ibid.*
[109] CRC 2001, §§ 70-71; CRC 2006, §§ 65-66.
[110] CRC 2001, §§ 42-43.
[111] CRC 2001, § 76.
[112] CRC 2006, § 77.
[113] CRC 2006, § 77.
[114] CRC 2006, §§ 49-50.
[115] CRC 2006, §§ 45-48.

including torture, rape and killings, due to the presence of opposition groups within their territories".[116]

-With respect to *participation rights*, the Committee noted in 1997 that children's right to adequate recourse (in particular against abuse or neglect within the family) is hampered by the requirement that a complaint can be lodged only through their parents or legal guardians[117] and that systems of adoption were not in conformity with the best interests principle and the principle of respect for the child's views.[118] In 2001, the Committee expressed concern that children's right to be heard is insufficiently respected, as well as their right to express their opinions freely – including through peaceful demonstrations; in this respect the CRC Committee also recommends that the State Party make additional efforts to guarantee general respect for the human rights of adults.[119] In 2006, the Committee appreciated efforts that had been undertaken such as a 'child forum', but remained concerned "that traditional societal attitudes appear to limit children in freely expressing their views in the community, the schools, the courts, or within the family".[120]

- In the area of *provision rights*, the Committee expressed concern about the shortage of teachers and about school curricula that are divorced from cultural and social realities[121] and about discrimination against girls and children with disabilities *inter alia* with respect to access to education,[122] as well as about insufficient education and training for children in institutional care[123] and the allocation of insufficient resources for schools. In this respect, the Committee recommends that the state assist children with insufficient means with the costs of education, including school uniforms and school fees.[124] Among the concerns enumerated in 2006 were school fees in primary education, overcrowding of schools, low transition rate to secondary school, insufficient number of trained teachers and available school facilities, absence of budget allocations for pre-primary schools and the poor quality of education.[125] In addition to this range of concerns relating to education, the Committee has also noted the absence of social welfare services.[126]

[116] CRC 2006, § 79.
[117] CRC 1997, § 16.
[118] CRC 1997, § 18.
[119] CRC 2001, §§ 36-37.
[120] CRC 2006, § 29.
[121] CRC 1997, § 17.
[122] CRC 2001, § 30; CRC 2006, § 51.
[123] CRC 2001, §§ 50-51.
[124] CRC 2001, §§ 66-67.
[125] CRC 2006, §§ 63-64.
[126] CRC 2001, §§ 54-55.

4. CONCLUDING COMMENTS

Backlog

Ethiopia's serious backlog in reporting under the United Nations human rights conventions illustrates a generally recognised problem with the reporting system. According to UN figures, on 16 February 2006, 70% of all reports that were due had in fact been submitted. The remaining 30% represented a total of 1442 reports that were overdue at that date.[127] 585 reports were 5 years overdue and 225 reports were 10 years overdue.[128] In fact, only 8 of the 194 states that are party to one or more of these mechanisms were up to date with all their reports.[129] States have to submit extensive reports to a large (and increasing[130]) number of Committees at different intervals. A state that has ratified all nine treaties and protocols imposing reporting obligations must produce a report to a treaty body on average once every five and a half months.[131] Moreover, different Committees have adopted different working methods and overlaps between the fields covered by the conventions are not taken into account. Nor is there any coordination among the Committees with respect to the scheduling of state reports. "A State party may be asked to present several reports to several Committees in the period of a month or sometimes a week and many States parties appear before several Committees in the same year… A State party may be asked the same question by several of the treaty bodies, and find that less time is devoted to treaty-specific issues."[132] For states that are confronted with resource constraints, both in terms of human capacity, time and finances, this proves to be a difficult challenge. Moreover, the average time from submission to consideration of State Party reports by the treaty bodies (measured in 2005) varies between 12 months (Human Rights Committee) and more than 23 months (CEDAW Committee).[133] This delay reduces some of the positive effects to be expected from the reporting mechanisms. In particular the momentum built when civil society actors contribute information to a Committee, may be lost again by the time the Committee issues its comments on the report. Moreover, changes in the political environment may result in some of the information in the report being outdated, or in a situation in which a report drafted by one political majority has to be defended by another political majority.

---

[127] Concept paper on the High Commissioner's proposal for a unified standing treaty body, UN Documents HRI/MC/2006/2, 19.

[128] *Id.,* 26.

[129] *Id.,* 7.

[130] When the new Convention on the Rights of Persons with Disabilities enters into force, a UN Committee on the Rights of Persons with Disabilities will be created. Likewise, when the new Convention on Enforced Disappearance enters into force, it will be monitored by a UN Committee on Enforced Disappearance.

[131] Concept paper on the High Commissioner's proposal for a unified standing treaty body, UN Documents HRI/MC/2006/2, 19.

[132] *Id.*, 8.

[133] *Id.*, 27.

The United Nations High Commissioner on Human Rights has expressed the ambition to reform the United Nations human rights machinery and replace the existing Committees by one unified standing treaty body. If this is realised, states would have to submit only one integrated report on which they can focus their resources. To the extent that resource constraints explain the current backlog, the situation might improve substantially. Ethiopia's practice under the CRC and CEDAW shows that it has the capacity to submit timely reports. However, to the extent that the backlog is to be explained by political concerns rather than resource constraints, there is a risk that this procedural innovation would halt Ethiopia's current good reporting practices under the CRC and CEDAW. If the lack of reporting under the ICESCR, ICCPR and CAT reflects a deliberate government refusal to report on general human rights issues, the same government may also refuse to submit the integrated report in order to avoid questioning about these issues.

Effects of State Reporting

The main functions of state reporting procedures are: initial review, monitoring, policy formulation, public scrutiny, evaluation, acknowledging problems and information exchange.[134]

The analysis of Ethiopia's experiences under the treaty monitoring bodies offers clear indications that the 'monitoring function' and 'policy formulation function' are working. In order to write a report, a state has to set in place mechanisms to monitor its domestic human rights situation. Moreover, the reporting exercise may act as a catalyst for the proposal of legislative changes and the formulation of long-term policies. Through the Committees' concluding observation, it is clear that policies have been formulated and monitoring bodies and mechanisms have been created. It is however problematic that after formulation, policies are not necessarily implemented and that monitoring bodies once created are not necessarily effective.

The 'public scrutiny function' refers to reporting as an opportunity for broad consultation with relevant sectors of society and hence as an instrument of government accountability toward its citizens. In the case of Ethiopia, this function appears to be hampered, as the government apparently does not use the reporting procedure as an occasion for dialogue with civil society.

Finally the 'evaluation function' offers a mixed picture. Regular state reporting allows monitoring progress, and is supposed to keep pressure on governments to realise progress. Yet both the CEDAW Committee and the CRC Committee have expressed concern over the lack of sufficient progress.

---

[134] P. Alston, The purposes of reporting, in Manual on human rights reporting, Geneva, United Nations, 1997, 19-24.

9. Federalism and Autonomy Conflicts in the Benishangul-Gumuz Region, Ethiopia

Asnake Kefale•

1. INTRODUCTION

Ethnicity has been used as a central instrument of restructuring the Ethiopian state since 1991. The first decade since the institutionalisation of ethnic federalism in 1992,[1] by the Ethiopian Peoples Revolutionary Democratic Front (EPRDF)[2] - which came to power in May 1991 after its victory over the previous military government (*Derg*)[3] - debates about Ethiopia's ethnic federalism and its impacts on peace and conflict were largely normative and polarised. On the one hand, some believed that ethnic federalism would reduce ethnic conflicts by tackling its core cause - ethnic inequality[4] while others held the view that, instead of reducing conflicts ethnic federalism would exacerbate them by encouraging secessionism and fragmenting the political space along ethnic lines.[5]

Understanding the impact of Ethiopia's federalism on ethnic conflicts, however, requires going beyond these polarised debates and examining the impacts of the federal restructuring exercise on inter-group relations at regional and local levels. This article discusses how the top-down restructuring of the

---

• Lecturer, Department of Political Science and International Relations, Addis Ababa University, currently Ph.D. candidate, Department of Political Science, Leiden University, The Netherlands. Some of the materials for this chapter were derived from my Ph.D. project on federalism and ethnic conflicts in Ethiopia. E-mail: asnakek@fsw.leidenuniv.nl

[1] Ethiopia officially adopted a federal constitution in 1994, but the political structure which was created since the 1992 reorganisation of local and regional administration could be termed as federal as significant legislative, judicial and executive authority was transferred to the fourteen regions which were created in 1992.

[2] The Ethiopian Peoples' Revolutionary Democratic Front (EPRDF) is a coalition of four ethnic organizations, i.e. the dominant Tigray People's Liberation Front (TPLF), the Amhara National Democratic Movement (ANDM), the Oromo People's Democratic Organization (OPDO) and the Southern Ethiopian Peoples' Democratic Front (SEPDF), which was established in 1989 under the leadership and control of the TPLF.

[3] The military regime, which ruled Ethiopia under the leadership of Colonel Mengistu Haile Mariam from 1974-1991, is popularly known as the *Derg*, which in Amharic means 'committee'.

[4] Kidane Mengisteab, New Approaches to State Building in Africa: The Case of Ethiopia's Ethnic-Based Federalism, 40 (3) *African Studies Review* 111-132 (1997); J. Young, Ethnicity and Power in Ethiopia, *Review of African Political Economy* 531-542 (1996).

[5] M. Ottaway, The Ethiopian Transition: Democratization or New Authoritarianism, 2(3) *Northeast African Studies* 67-84 (1995); Walle Engedayehu, Ethiopia: Democracy and the Politics of Ethnicity, 40(2) *Africa Today* 29 – 52 (1993).

Ethiopian state into an ethnic federation led to 'autonomy conflicts'[6] among the several ethnic groups, which are found in one of the newly constituted regions, i.e. the Benishangul-Gumuz region (B-G). Autonomy conflicts in the context of this study refer to those conflicts, which emerge between or among different ethnic groups within the new regions over such issues as 'resource sharing', 'representation', 'identity', 'citizenship', 'administrative boundary' and others. These conflicts are distinct from the more traditional centre-regional conflicts[7] as the main protagonists of these conflicts are regional actors and the conflicts are also largely over resources which were made available due to provision of autonomy.

This article examines two aspects of autonomy conflicts. First, conflict between two indigenous[8] ethnic groups (Berta and Gumuz). Second, dispute between the indigenous and the non-indigenous[9] groups over political representation. The article has six parts. The first consists of the introduction. The second section provides a brief background to the history and ethnic makeup of the Benishangul-Gumuz region. The third discusses some of the reasons that led to political instability at the formative years of the region. The fourth section examines the dispute between the Berta and the Gumuz regarding distribution of power and economic resources in the new region. The fifth examines the demand of the non-indigenous people of the region to have political representation and how their demand was addressed. Finally a brief conclusion will be drawn.

2. ETHNICITY AND HISTORY: BRIEF BACKGROUND TO THE BENISHANGUL GUMUZ REGION

The Benishangul-Gumuz region was established in 1992 when the Transitional Government of Ethiopia (TGE) reorganised the country's regional administration into fourteen regions.[10] It was established by the merger of parts of the

---

[6] The concept 'autonomy conflict' is adopted from S. E. Cornell who in his study about the Caucasian conflicts suggested that ethnic federalism and autonomy, even if they are widely promoted as instruments of resolving and reducing conflicts, they generate conflicts. S. Cornell, Autonomy as a Source of Conflict: Caucasian Conflicts in Theoretical Perspective, 54(2) *World Politics* 246 (2002).

[7] Centre-regional conflict was the dominant form of conflict in Ethiopia prior to the reorganization of regional administration in 1992. In this conflict different regional forces ranging from spontaneous rebellion to organised ethnic insurrection clash with the forces of the central government.

[8] The term indigenous in the context of this paper refers to those five ethnic groups, i.e. Berta, Gumuz, Shinasha, Mao and Komo who inhabited the area, which is now designated as Benishangul-Gumuz region for a longer duration of time. In addition to this, their status as 'indigenous' and 'owner' nationalities has been recognised by the regional constitution.

[9] The term non-indigenous refers to any ethnic group or individual who does not belong to the five 'owner' nationalities of the region.

[10] In 1992, by proclamation no. 7/1992, the EPRDF restructured the regional administrative structure of the country into fourteen regions, which were largely constituted along ethno-linguistic lines.

former Assosa and Metekel administrative regions.[11] Presently, the region is one of the nine members of Ethiopia's ethnic federation.

The B-G region is one of the frontier and peripheral regions of the country with poor integration into Ethiopia's political economy. The peripherality of the region is not limited to Ethiopia. Even if almost all of the indigenous ethnic groups of the B-G region are found within the Sudan, they remain peripheral to the Sudanese state like their ethnic kin and kith in Ethiopia. That is why this frontier region has been described as a "double periphery".[12] More importantly, the historical association of the indigenous ethnic groups, which today constitute the B-G region, with both Ethiopia and the Sudan, was painful. For instance, in the last decades of the nineteenth century and during the first three decades of the twentieth century both Christian Ethiopia and Islamic Sudan raided many of the ethnic groups, which today constitute the B-G region, for slaves.[13]

The history of this frontier region has been shaped by political developments both in Khartoum and Addis Ababa. The collapse of the Mahdist Sudanese State at the end of the nineteenth century precipitated the extension of Ethiopian sovereignty to the region.[14] Similarly, the fixation of the boundary between Ethiopia and British occupied Sudan in 1902 resulted in the division of some of the indigenous ethnic groups of the region between Ethiopia and the Sudan.[15]

Presently, the Benishangul-Gumuz region is a truly multiethnic region of multiple minorities. No single ethnic group constitutes more than fifty percent of the region's total population. The B-G constitution recognises the Berta, Gumuz, Shinasha, Mao and Komo ethnic groups as indigenous and 'owner' nationalities of the region. In accordance with the 1994 census, the population of the B-G region is estimated to be around 460,000. From among this total population, the share of the indigenous ethnic groups is as follows: the Berta (26.7%), Gumuz (23.4 %), Shinasha (6.9 %), Mao (0.6 %) and Komo (0.24%).

---

[11] In 1987, when the military regime established the People's Democratic Republic of Ethiopia (PDRE), it restructured the regional administration of the country into 25 administrative regions and 5 autonomous regions. The Assosa and Metekel *awraja* (sub-province) of the former Wolega and Gojam provinces became Assosa and Metekel administrative regions. In 1992 when fourteen regional administrations were established on the basis of ethnicity and language, the two were joined to establish 'Region six' which was later named the Benishangul-Gumuz region.

[12] A. Triulzi, *Salt, Gold and Legitimacy: Prelude to the history of a no-man's land Bela Shangul, Wallagga, Ethiopia (ca. 1800 – 1898)* (Napoli: Instituto Universitario Orientale, Seminario Di Studi Africani, 1981).

[13] Abdussamad H. Ahmad, The Gumuz of the Lowlands of the Western Gojjam: the Frontier in History, 50(1) *Africa/Istituto Italo-Africano* 57 (1995).

[14] Bahru Zewde, *A History of Modern Ethiopia 1855-1974* 66 (London, Athens, Addis Ababa: James Currey, Ohio University Press, Addis Ababa University Press, 1991).

[15] Abdussamad H. Ahmad, Trading in slaves in Bela-Shangul and Gumuz, Ethiopia: border enclaves in history, 1897-1938, 40 (3) *The Journal of African History* 436 (1999).

The region has also a large non-indigenous population, which accounts for about 47% of the total population. The majority of the non-indigenous communities are from the politically and economically dominant ethnic groups of the country, i.e. Amhara and Oromo who respectively account for 22.2% and 12.8% of the total population of the B-G region. A significant portion of this population came to the region during the 1980s as a result of a controversial resettlement programme that was carried out by the previous military regime.[16] That is why the non-indigenous communities in the region are alternatively called 'settlers'. After the creation of the new region, the non-indigenous ethnic groups have been transformed into 'new minorities'.

The identity of the indigenous groups of the region has been largely shaped by the relationship which each of them maintained with its ethnic neighbours and with other dominant groups ranging from the Sudanese Arab migrants to the neighbouring Amhara and Oromo. In this regard, the identity and internal differentiations of the Berta were defined by the historic relationships of the group with the Sudanese Arabs. Accordingly, Berta traditions maintain that the ruling families of the Berta, i.e. the 'half cast' Witawit,[17] were descendants of marriage associations between the ruling families of the 'pure'-Berta'[18] and the Arabic and Islamic preachers who came to the region from the Sudan.[19] This cleavage within the Berta is not clear to the outsider, as there are no linguistic, religious and other distinctions between the Witawit and the 'pure' Berta. The Witawit, however, differ from the 'pure' Berta not only because of their fluent Arabic and Islamic faith but also because of their "*...unshakable belief [in their]...racial, cultural and political superiority over the Bertha*".[20] What followed from this division was the development of an exploitative relationship between the Witawit and the latter in which the 'pure' Berta along with other minority groups like the Mao, Komo and the Gumuz formed the bulk of the nineteenth century slave trade in the region. The Witawit partici-

[16] The military regime during the 1980s implemented a controversial resettlement programme of peasants after the 1984 famine that hit the northern provinces. With the professed aim of alleviating the problem of food security, hundreds of thousands of highland peasants were forcefully relocated to the fertile and sparsely populated lowland regions of the country. Both the Metekel and the Assosa *awraja* that today constitute the Benishangul-Gumuz region received thousands of settlers.

[17] In the tradition of Berta, the 'mixture' of the kings of the 'indigenous' Berta with Arabic-Islamic preachers and traders from the neighbouring Sudan gave birth to the development of a class cleavage within the Berta between the 'half-cast' Witawit and the 'pure' Berta: the 'half-cast' or 'Witawit' have been historically the dominant group within the Berta. See Triulzi, *supra* note 12.

[18] 'Pure Berta' refers to the large majority of the Berta (excepting the ruling families) who were not mixed by marriage with the Arabic preachers and merchants coming from the Sudan. They are pure simply because of the fact that they were not mixed with Arab blood.

[19] A. Triulzi, Trade, Islam and the Mahdia in northwestern Wallagga, Ethiopia, 16(1) *The Journal of African History* 59 (1975).

[20] Triulzi, *supra* note 12, 7.

pated in this not only as conduits but also as slavers.[21] Moreover they used the slave labour of the 'pure' Berta for extracting alluvial gold.[22]

This hierarchal division within Berta between the so-called aristocratic Witawit families and the 'pure' Berta encapsulates the somewhat complex and controversial nature of Berta ethnicity. This division was reinforced by alien forces ranging from the Turco-Egyptians who ruled the Sudan from 1820 until 1881 to the Ethiopians who in the twentieth century controlled the area for its resources, notably gold and slaves.[23] Because of the hierarchical relationship that prevailed within the Berta, its ethnic identity is presently contested. There are some within the Witawit who resent the naming of their ethnic group as Berta.[24] This is because of the fact that in the past the name Berta was used interchangeably with the Arabic term for slave '*Abid'*.[25] Today, many educated descendants of the Witawit who still control important offices within the B-G region not only support the designation of their ethnic group as Berta, but also seek to capitalise on the victimisation of the Berta in the past as an important platform to advance their political career within Ethiopia's ethnic federation. In this context, Berta politicians promote a 'new' Berta identity, which includes both the 'half cast' and the 'pure'.

Like that of the Berta, the ethnic history and identity of the Gumuz could be explained by its rather painful relationship with its more powerful neighbours. Historically, slaving raids and eviction mainly characterized relationships between the Gumuz and their dominant neighbours.[26] Moreover, the settlement of the Oromo from the south crossing the Blue Nile in the Metekel area during the early twentieth century displaced "…the Gumuz … to the hot and inhospitable lowland areas".[27]

The continued pressure that was placed on the Gumuz from several sides not only shaped their settlement patterns but also left an indelible mark on their identity and the manner in which they relate with their neighbours. For instance, the Gumuz of the Dedessa Valley even accepted the derogatory name of *Shankilla* (slave) as their own self-name in order to forge unity between various Gumuz groups.[28] The flight of the Gumuz to the malaria infested low-

---

[21] Abdussamad H. Ahmad, *supra* note 15.
[22] Triulzi, *supra* note 12, 8.
[23] Triulzi, *supra* note 19, 59.
[24] Personal Interview, former high official of the B-G region from the Berta ethnic group, 18 April 2005.
[25] Triulzi, *supra* note 12, 8.
[26] W. James, Lifelines: exchange marriage among the Gumuz, in: D. Donham and W. James (eds.), *The Southern Marches of Imperial Ethiopia* 124 (Cambridge: Cambridge University Press, 1986).
[27] Abdussamad H. Ahmad, *supra* note 13, 54-55.
[28] James, *supra* note 26, 121.

lands in order to escape pressures that were coming from both the Sudan and Ethiopia helped the survival of their cultures.[29]

The Shinasha, one of the indigenous ethnic groups of the B-G region, also had a painful historical relationship with its more powerful neighbours. Like the Gumuz, they faced slave raiding by the highlanders of the Ethiopian empire. R. Pankhurst, citing the Jesuit patriarch André de Oviedo, for instance, wrote that the forces of Emperor Sarsa Dengel raided the Shinasha in the sixteenth century.[30] As a result of raiding and displacement, which the Gumuz and Shinasha collectively encountered, they retreated to the hot inhospitable lowlands. This collective plight led to tensions and conflicts between the two groups, as they had to compete for land in the lowlands.[31] In the lowlands of Metekel, where the Shinasha and the Gumuz reside intermixed, the Shinasha, managed to exercise some power over the numerically superior Gumuz claiming that they had supra-natural power (spirit mediums) and made them "*yield up to them part of their scanty store of grain, meat or honey.*"[32] Another traveller who visited the Metekel region in the nineteenth century reported that due to the precarious condition of their security, the Shinasha fortified their villages in an inaccessible cliff to fend off unwanted intruders.[33] It was also reported that the Shinasha, because of the repeated threat they faced from the highlanders (Agaw and Amhara), were assimilated to the Oromo who crossed the Blue Nile and settled in the Metekel area since the eighteenth century.[34]

In more recent times, the relationship between the Shinasha and their ethnic neighbours kept on changing depending on the conditions on the ground. For instance, during the 1980s when the military regime settled thousands of people in the fertile lands of Metekel, the Shinasha, the Gumuz and the Agaw, who considered the move as a threat to their livelihood, improved their relationships. Similarly, after the formation of the B-G region a new alliance seemed to have emerged in the Metekel region between the Gumuz and the Shinasha against the settlers.[35]

---

[29] F.J. Simoons, *Northwest Ethiopia: Peoples and Economy* 53 (Madison: University of Wisconsin Press, 1960).

[30] R. Pankhurst, *The Ethiopian Borderlands: Essays in Regional History from Ancient Times to the end of the 18th century* 267-268 (Lawrenceville: Red Sea Press, 1997).

[31] Tsega Endalew, *Conflict Resolution through Cultural Tolerance: An Analysis of the Michu Institution in Metekkel Region, Ethiopia* 15 (Addis Ababa: OSSREA, 2002).

[32] O. T. Crosby, Notes on a Journey from Zeila to Khartum, *the Geographical Journal* 54 (1901).

[33] W. James, G. Baumann and D. Johnson, *Juan Maria Schuver's Travels in North East Africa 1880-1883* 180-181 (London: Hakluyt Society, 1996).

[34] Tsega Endalew, *supra* note 31, 10.

[35] Gebre Yntiso, Resettlement Risks and Inter-Ethnic Conflicts in Metekel, Ethiopia, *Ethiopian Journal of the Social Sciences and Humanities* 61 (2004).

The Mao and Komo are little studied small minority groups within the B-G region. Both groups are located along the Ethio-Sudanese frontier.[36] The Mao ethnic group is presently located within the B-G and Oromia regions. In contrast, the Komo are found within B-G region, Gambella and the Sudan. The Komo language is a member of the Nilo-Saharan linguistic family, whereas the classification of the Mao language into one of the linguistic families of Ethiopia is not yet established.[37] The naming of the Mao is still controversial. Some scholars argue that the Mao call themselves and their language Mao and that this name is not derogatory.[38] In contrast, in an earlier study W. James noted that the Mao do not call themselves Mao. Their neighbours, particularly the Oromo, instead call them Mao.[39] Similarly, Bender said that the Oromo used the term Mao in a derogatory fashion like that of the term *Shankilla.*[40]

In contrast, the Komo are called by various names: Kwama, Koma and Komo.[41] Presently, the majority of the Komo in Ethiopia are located within the newly created Mao-Komo special district of the B-G region. Because of their scattered settlement, there are internal differences within both the Mao and the Komo in terms of language.[42]

The Mao and Komo have a long history of settlement in the former Assosa *awraja.*[43] Their settlement patterns were, however, affected by population movements.[44] For instance, when the Berta initially emigrated from their homeland in the Sudan, they settled in the Assosa region by displacing the Mao and Komo.[45] Like the Gumuz, the Mao and Komo had difficult relationships with their powerful neighbours. The pressure on the Mao and the Komo became more intense after Sheik Khojele of Assosa peacefully submitted to

---

[36] E. Cerulli, *Peoples of South-West Ethiopia and its Borderland* 12 (London: International African Institute, 1956).

[37] Ethiopian languages are broadly divided into the following categories: Semitic, Cushitic, Omotic and Nilo Saharan.

[38] R. Siebert, K. Siebert and K. Wedekind, *Sociolinguistic Survey Report on Languages of the Asosa – Begi – Komosha area, part I* 5 (SIL International, 2002).

[39] W. James, *Kwanim Pa: the Making of the Uduk People* 8 (Oxford: Claredon Press, 1979).

[40] M.L. Bender, The Beginnings of Ethnohistory in Western Wellega: the Mao Problem, in: R.K. Herbert (ed.), *Patterns in language, culture, and society: Sub-Saharan Africa; proceedings of the Symposium on African language, culture, and society*, held at the Ohio State University, Columbus, April 11, 1975, 128.

[41] A. Gonzales-Ruibal and V.M. Fernandez, Exhibiting cultures of contact: a museum for Benishangul Gumuz (Ethiopia), in: *Cultures of Contact: Archaeology, Ethics, and Globalization*, Stanford Archaeology Centre at the Stanford Humanities Centre (2005); James, *supra* note 39; D.H. Johnson, On the Nilotic frontier: Imperial Ethiopia in the Southern Sudan, in: D. Donham and W. James (eds.), *The Southern Marches of Imperial Ethiopia* (Cambridge: Cambridge University Press, 1986); Siebert, *supra* note 38.

[42] Gonzalez-Ruibal and Fernandez, *supra* note 41; Siebert, *supra* note 38.

[43] An Amharic term for a sub-provincial administrative structure.

[44] H.C. Fleming, The importance of Mao in Ethiopian history, in: S. Rubenson (ed.), *Proceedings of the Seventh International Conference of Ethiopian Studies, University of Lund, 26-29 April 1982* 31 (Addis Ababa: Institute of Ethiopian Studies, 1984).

[45] Triulzi, *supra* note 12, 22.

the Ethiopian Emperor Menelik at the beginning of the twentieth century and became a loyal vassal. Khojele's autonomy was contingent upon his regular payment of tribute in gold and slaves to the crown in Addis Ababa and the lavish gifts that he used to give to imperial retainers. Maintaining the flow of the so-called 'recruits' to the palace in Addis Ababa at the beginning of the twentieth century required Khojele the use of a harsh tactic which led to the development of the notorious *'lij gibir'* (child tribute) through which the Mao were coerced to 'contribute' their children to be sent as 'recruits'.[46] All these pushed the Mao and the Komo further into the fringes of the periphery.[47] Though powerless in the face of their dominant neighbours, the Komo used to play one predator against the other. They also exploited the frontier aspect of their location by alternating their residence between the Sudan and Ethiopia.[48]

Because of their proximity in location and shared plight, these groups over the years developed several common cultural values. For instance, the Komo influenced the social organisations of the Mao.[49] The establishment of the Mao-Komo special *woreda* since the 1990s is expected to further strengthen the development of shared cultural values between the two groups. Indeed, the formation of a local government organisation, a political party and a development association under the newly invented identity of Mao-Komo may accelerate the amalgamation of the two ethnic groups into this invented identity and both groups seem to have found it expedient to use their new identity in order to defend their interests within the B-G region.[50] The newfound autonomy has yet to change the life of the Mao and the Komo. For instance, a project paper, which was produced by the Mao-Komo special *woreda*[51] officials with the help of experts of the Ministry of Federal Affairs in Addis Ababa to solicit international financing for development projects in the special *woreda*, characterises the Komo as follows:

"*...people [who] wander in the remote and border areas of the B-G region where the climate is hazardous and infrastructure; social and economic services are only in words. In general, their mode of life is comparable to the primitive communal society of the old days.*"[52]

In order to change this situation, what the new local administrators in the Mao-Komo special district pursue is no less than a social engineering aimed at

[46] Abdussamad H. Ahmad, *supra* note 15, 437.
[47] Cerulli, *supra* note 36, 16; Johnson, *supra* note 41, 229.
[48] Johnson, *supra* note 41, 239.
[49] Cerulli, *supra* note 36, 20.
[50] Gonzales-Ruibal and Fernandez, *supra* note 41, 10.
[51] *Woreda* is the Amharic word for district.
[52] Mao-Komo Special *Woreda* Administrative Office, 2004, *Let's support the Komos: Community Based Integrated Livelihood Transformation Project for the Komo people in Mao-Komo Special Woreda of BGNRS.*

changing the mode of livelihood of the Komo from hunting and gathering into sedentary farming.

In addition to the above five indigenous ethnic groups, the B-G region contains a large non-indigenous population which constitutes 47% of the total population. The proportion of the non-indigenous population to the total population of the region is so significant that there is a considerable sense of anxiety among the leadership of the region. Hence, the new indigenous political elite sought to reduce the citizenship role of the non-indigenous. For instance, the constitution of the region declares the five indigenous ethnic groups as 'owner nationalities of the region'. The non-indigenous communities did not, however, accept the decision to exclude them from political representation and have mounted a struggle to ensure their citizenship, which is discussed in section five of this article.

3. AUTONOMY AND INTRA-REGIONAL INSTABILITY: THE RISE AND DECLINE OF THE BPLM

The Benishangul People Liberation Movement (BPLM) was the first political organisation to be established in the region in 1989 in the Sudan.[53] The aim of the BPLM was to mount a guerrilla war against the then Ethiopian military government. The political objectives of the organisation were not, however, clearly outlined. The BPLM was predominantly composed of Berta, though it had some members from other ethnic groups of the region, notably from the Gumuz.

During its formative years, the BPLM sought the assistance of other larger ethnic 'liberation' movements, which were then fighting against the military regime in Ethiopia in order to have access to weapons, ammunition and other supplies.[54] To this end, it first approached the Oromo Liberation Front (OLF),[55] which was operating in the border region. This was, however, unsuccessful, as the OLF required the BPLM to recognize the territory, which the latter aimed to 'liberate', as part of the territory of Oromia, which the OLF was planning to establish.[56] The BPLM, which refused to accept OLF's precondition, had to search for another 'patron'. This was realised when the TPLF

---

[53] J. Young, Along Ethiopia's western frontier: Gambella and Benishangul in transition, 37 (2) *The Journal of Modern African Studies* 327 (1999).

[54] Personal Interview: Head, Culture and Information Bureau, Assosa, 13 April 2005.

[55] The Oromo Liberation Front (OLF), which was established in 1975, is an ethno-nationalist movement that aims at the realisation of an independent state for the Oromo ethnic group (Oromia). The OLF participated in the formation of the EPRDF dominated Transitional Government of Ethiopia in 1991. Because of differences with the TPLF/EPRDF regarding elections and the freedom of non-EPRDF affiliated political parties to independently operate within the country (and mainly their ethnic constituency), the OLF left the TGE in 1992 and resumed armed insurgency.

[56] Young, *supra* note 53, 327.

agreed to provide support to the BPLM. Hence, the TPLF in 1990 gave military training to BPLM's combatants at Agereselam, which was then a TPLF 'liberated' territory in Tigray.

The decision of the TPLF to provide support to the BPLM could be seen from two angles. Firstly, the desire of the TPLF to undermine the military regime by proliferating armed opposition. Secondly, TPLF's need to cultivate allies which would help realise its aspiration of playing a prominent role in Ethiopian politics after the downfall of the military regime. Indeed, TPLF's assistance to the BPLM coincided with the period in which it was preparing for a national role after its successive major military victories against the *Derg* in northern Ethiopia at the end of the 1980s. The question of getting support from stronger liberation fronts was, however, divisive to the Berta. While the leaders of the nascent BPLM rejected the OLF's territorial claim, another faction of the Berta, under the leadership of Atom Mustafa, sought the partnership of the OLF.

After the May 1991 military defeat of the *Derg*, the BPLM participated in the July 1991 Addis Ababa Conference[57] and got representation at the interim non-elected legislative assembly, the Council of Representatives (CoR) and formed the first B-G regional government. The B-G region, nonetheless, faced political instability in its initial years due to the conflict that emerged between the EPRDF, OLF and BPLM in western Ethiopia and later because of the divisions that occurred within the political parties that emerged in the region. Initially, the BPLM was promoted by the EPRDF as an ally and a regional 'vanguard' party, which would take charge of the B-G region. This was not, however, realised because of the differences that emerged between the EPRDF and the BPLM on the one hand, and internal divisions that emerged within the ranks of the latter on the other. As a result of the differences that emerged within the BPLM, some Gumuz members left the organization and established their own ethnic political party called the Gumuz People Liberation Movement (GPLM) in 1992. Similarly, the other indigenous ethnic groups of the region established their own ethnic parties, which included: the Shinasha People Democratic Movement (SPDM), the Mao People Democratic Movement (MPDM) and the Komo People Democratic Movement (KPDM).[58] This undermined the multiethnic character of the BPLM, as ethnic political parties were formed in the names of all of the ethnic groups that existed within the new region.

---

[57] The July 1991 'Peace and Democracy Conference' was held in Addis Abba under the leadership of the TPLF/EPRDF. The conference adopted the Transitional Charter and inaugurated the Transitional Government of Ethiopia (TGE) under the Presidency of TPLF/EPRDF's Meles Zenawi.

[58] Ministry of Federal Affairs appointed Ad Hoc Committee, *Report and Recommendation on Political Instability and Security Problems in the BGNRS,* MoFedA (Amharic text), Addis Ababa, 2002.

Because of the conflict between the OLF, EPRDF and BPLM, the inauguration of the region was delayed by about a year. When the regional government was eventually established in 1993, the Berta and the Gumuz, who emerged as the two major ethnic groups in the regional assembly, differed on the naming of the regional president and the capital of the new region. After some wrangling, a compromise was struck which gave the position of president to the Berta and the regional capital to the Gumuz, i.e. Pawe in Metekel.[59] Later on, the regional capital was moved to Assosa due to inter-ethnic conflict between the indigenous Gumuz and the settlers in Metekel. After sorting out these controversial questions, the regional government was established in 1993/1994 under the leadership of a newly formed regional party called the Benishangul North-West Ethiopia People Democratic Unity Party (BNWEPDUP). Though the BNWEPDUP served as a joint front for all the ethnic parties, which emerged in the region, it was under the control of the BPLM.

The regional government, which was led by the BPLM, was riddled with factional infighting. As a result, three regional presidents all from the Berta ethnic group were changed in quick succession. Atom Mustafa, who was elected as the first president of the region in 1993 was sacked by the Berta dominated executive committee of the regional government three months after his election to the post. Atieb Ahmed who replaced the first president was also removed from office after working for about nine months. Another Berta politician, Abdu Mohammed who came to power in 1994 was replaced by a Gumuz politician in 1995. The rivalries and internal divisions that were the hallmark of the Berta political class in the first few years of the post-*Derg* period could be explained by several interrelated factors.

Firstly, lack of experience in self-administration. Many of the regions, which emerged after devolution of power in Ethiopia, faced enormous administrative challenges in carrying out their functions. The problem was much more profound in the peripheral parts of the country where there was a severe shortage of a well trained and educated elite which could easily fill the new administrative and political vacancies that ethnic federalism made available at regional and local levels. In the case of the Benishangul-Gumuz region, the new indigenous elite who suddenly came to control the region suffered from lack of party discipline and a uniting vision.[60]

Secondly, the formation of the region seemed to have revitalised frozen inter-familial conflict among the descendants of the three former dynastic families of the Witawit Berta. Hence, the political instability of the region under the leadership of the Berta could partly be explained by the enduring infighting among prominent families of the Berta notably between the descendants of

[59] Personal Interview: Ex-President of the BGNRS, Assosa, 18 April 2005.

[60] Personal Interview: Official in the BGNRS administrative council, Assosa, 21 April 2005.

Dejach[61] Mustafa of Menge and Sheik Khojele of Assosa. Indeed, some Berta informants allege that Berta officials removed the first president of the region, Atom Mustafa, unceremoniously from the regional presidency due to the long running grudge that existed between the two prominent Berta families.[62]

As the internal division within the Berta (BPLM) made the region unstable, the political landscape within the region was restructured by the direct intervention of the EPRDF. First, at the instigation of the federal government, Yaregal Aysheshim from the Gumuz ethnic group was installed as regional president in 1995. The Berta did not, however, happily greet the election of Yaregal. This was evident in a comment of one Berta official:

"*When Yaregal was elected as president, we were not happy with the decision; we opposed his election. The authorities of the federal government after listening to our complaints told us that as there were divisions when we [the Berta] were given the presidency during the transitional period, the chance should now be given to a Gumuz. Moreover, we were given an indication that the position would in the future rotate between the Berta and the Gumuz. Thus we accepted the election of Yaregal.*"[63]

Secondly, in 1996, the EPRDF purged and reconstituted all the ethnic political parties that existed within the region. As a result of this, the BPLM was officially changed into the Ethiopia Berta People Democratic Organization (EBPDO). Similarly, the Gumuz People Liberation Front (GPLF) was renamed the Gumuz People Democratic Organisation (GPDO) and the Mao and Komo political organisations were united to create the Mao-Komo People Democratic Organisation (MKPDO). The newly created political parties were brought together in a new regional front, i.e. the Benishangul People Democratic Unity Front (BGPDUF) that was made an affiliate of the EPRDF. Following these there was relatively better political stability in the region from 1995-2000.

4. THE BERTA-GUMUZ DISPUTE: BERTA DOMINANCE OR EXIT?

The Berta-Gumuz dispute was largely a non-violent localised autonomy conflict as the dispute was about sharing of political and economic resources. The dispute did not challenge the authority and ideology of the political centre (the EPRDF) in Addis Ababa.

---

[61] Traditional military rank.

[62] Personal Interview: Official in the BGNRS administrative council, Assosa, 21 April 2005.

[63] Personal Interview: Executive Committee member of the EBPDO, Assosa, 15 April 2005.

4.1. First Stage of the Dispute: Berta Demand for the Regional Presidency

In September 2000, the founding conference of the second regional government of the Benishangul-Gumuz region was held in Assosa. In the poorly contested May 2000 elections, the BGPDUF emerged as the winner of the regional election with a commanding majority. The main purpose of the September conference was to elect the executive officers of the second regional government.

Before the regional council proceeded to elect the new regional president, the Berta members of the council demanded the holding of an informal consultation among the executive committee members of the BGPDUF about the naming of the new regional president. In this separate meeting, the Berta demanded that the offices of the president and the secretary should be given to them. Berta politicians tried to justify their demands by two points: their greater contribution to the dismantlement of the *Derg*[64] and their larger population size as compared to the Gumuz.[65] These demands were, however, rejected by the Gumuz and the other members of the executive committee of the ruling BGPDUF. The Gumuz and their supporters argued that executive positions of the regional government were elective and could not be apportioned on a quota basis.

The Berta whose demands were not accepted walked out of the conference. Despite this, the regional council proceeded with the founding conference and re-elected Yaregal Aysheshim as president for a second term (2000-2005). To express their protest, the Berta officials withdrew from different structures of the regional government including *woreda* councils. The stalemate between the Berta and the Gumuz-dominated regional government led to political tensions and instability.

4.2. Second Stage of the Dispute: Berta's Demand for Exit

At the second stage of the dispute, Berta officials whose quest to ensure their dominance over the region was rebuffed, advanced a demand for the formation of a new region for the Berta in accordance with Article 47 of the federal constitution, which provides for the formation of new ethnic regions out of the existing ones through a referendum. The 'exit' demand of the Berta from the B-G region was presented as an opportunity, which would provide the Berta a chance to administer themselves in their own geographic area and help develop their culture and language.[66]

[64] This refers to the establishment of the BPLM by Berta and their partnership with the TPLF/EPRDF in the armed struggle against the military regime.
[65] Ministry of Federal Affairs, *supra* note 58.
[66] Personal Interview: Top Berta official, Assosa, 12 April 2005.

The demand for setting up a separate region for the Berta seems to have had popular support at the height of the crisis. The popular support, however, was eventually weakened because of two main reasons. Firstly, internal divisions emerged within the Berta. Accordingly, some Berta officials changed their position, joined the regional government and provided key support to its president, Yaregal Aysheshim. Moreover, the somewhat endemic Berta interfamilial dispute resurfaced at one point of the crisis when the leaders of the EBPDO presented a list of persons whom they wished to be appointed in the regional government. Apparently this list did not include the Berta from Menge.[67] This created resentment by the Berta of Menge against officials of the EBPDO watering down the united demand of the Berta for the formation of a separate region.[68]

Secondly and most importantly, federal authorities were lukewarm to the idea of creating a new region as they feared allowing the Berta to have their own ethnic region by breaking away from B-G would trigger unstoppable similar demands throughout the country. In this respect, some senior officials of the federal government alleged to have told the protesting Berta that "the demand for separation and to create a new region was not the demand of the Berta people; it was only the demand of the Berta ethnic elite".[69] The federal government thus proceeded in two important ways to foil the demand. Firstly, it ordered the regional parties to undertake '*gimgema*'[70] which led to mutual recrimination among Berta officials undermining the quest for a separate region. Secondly, it sought to address the crisis through mediation. The task of mediation was given to the House of the Federation (HoF) of the federal parliament.

When the HoF began the mediation process, the Berta produced a well-articulated list of grievances. In other words, the blunt desire of the Berta to play a dominant role in the region by controlling the office of the president and the secretary was now couched in democratic terms of 'fair' representation and 'equitable' resource distribution. First, the Berta complained that although they had a larger population size than the Gumuz, the Gumuz had more seats in the regional council. This anomaly happened due to the fact that when the regional council was initially established, each of the *woreda* was made to have equal representation, without considering population size. As a result, the Gumuz who inhabit larger territory and have more *woreda* than the Berta emerged with more seats in the regional council (see table 1 below). According to one top Gumuz official, the National Electoral Board of Ethiopia (NEBE) in Addis

[67] The previous Witawit Sheikdoms under Dejazmach Mustafa.

[68] Personal Interview: Resident of Assosa, Assosa, 26 April 2005.

[69] *Ibid.*

[70] *Gimgema* (evaluation) is an important instrument of the ruling party (EPRDF) through which it evaluates the activities of individual members of the party. The institution of *gimgema* is particularly important to 'cleanse' the party of those who do not toe the official line. *Gimgema* is also used by EPRDF affiliate organisations for similar purposes.

Ababa made the decision about the size of ethnic representation in the regional council, and the issue only appeared as a problem after the emergence of the Berta-Gumuz dispute after the 2000 elections.

Table 1: Ethnic Composition of BG regional council before the Berta-BG dispute

Ethnic group	Population	% total Population	No of representatives	% of representatives
Berta	122,883	26.7	28	35
Gumuz	107,495	23.4	35	43.75
Shinasha	32,105	6.9	6	7.5
Mao-Komo	3,843	0.83	4	5
Others	194133	42.17	7	8.75
Total	460,459	100	80	100

Source: CSA 1994 and HoF appointed non-partisan Committee (2001)

Secondly, the Berta contended that more regional financial resources were directed to the Gumuz as they had more *woreda* and administrative zones[71] than the Berta, although the former had a lower number of people. In fact, as presented in table 2 below, the Gumuz have two zones, i.e. Metekel and Khamashi and eleven *woreda*, while the Berta have one zone (Assosa zone) and seven *woreda*.

Because of the presence of more *woreda* in the Gumuz inhabited territories, there was bigger inflow of financial resources from the regional government to the Gumuz. This was because of the fact that the population size of each of the *woreda* was not given consideration when budgetary allocations were made. However there was no disagreement within the regional council about *woreda* budget allocation before the emergence of the Berta-Gumuz dispute over political power.

The introduction of the '*woreda* block grant formula'[72] since the beginning of the 2000s is expected to address such grievances. Even after this, aggregate financial flows to Gumuz inhabited *woreda* are still larger than the aggregate of the *woreda* under the Berta. For instance, in the 2004/2005 fiscal year, the administrative budget that was allocated to the Gumuz inhabited zones was higher than the total that was allocated to the Berta inhabited Assosa zone (see table 3).

[71] In the prevailing regional administration setup zones are administrative divisions below regions.

[72] The *Woreda* block grant refers to a mathematical formula that regional governments use in order to calculate the amount of budget (capital and recurrent) each *woreda* receives from the regional government. The formula takes into account a) population size, b) revenue generating capacity, and c) level of development as expressed by a set of social and economic indicators. The purpose of the *Woreda* block grant is to ensure a 'fair' and 'just' distribution of finance on the basis of a standard formula.

Table 2: Distribution of Woreda and Zones in the Benishangul – Gumuz region

No	Zone	Name of Woreda	No of zonal population
1	Assosa (Berta)-7 *Woreda*	Oda Sherkole Kumruk Komosha Menge Assosa Bambassi	194,084
2	Metekel (Gumuz)-6 *Woreda*	Guba Dangur Wenbera Mandura Dibate Bullen	165,663
3	Khamashi (Gumuz)-5 *Woreda*	Khamashi Agelo Meti Belo Jigan-foy Sirba Abay Yaso	50,783
4	Special *woreda*-2 *Woreda*	Mao-Komo	14,071
		Pawe Special *Woreda*	35,858
5	Total 20		460,459

Source: CSA 1994

Table 3: Budget Summary for the 2004/5 regular budget

No	Explanation	Human services	Procurement of goods and services	Durables and construction	Other payments	Total
1	Regional Bureaus	36, 969, 020.00	20, 881, 29.00	322, 739.00	4,581, 21.00	62, 754, 009.00
2	Assosa zone (Berta)	25, 174, 952	3, 670, 604.00	80, 574.00	486, 777.00	29, 412, 907.00
3	Khamashi zone (Gumuz)	9, 120, 551.00	2, 434,891.00	161, 283.00	655, 773.00	12, 372, 498.00
4	Metekel zone (Gumuz)	26,069, 912.00	5, 658, 031.00	485, 606.00	1,030,963 .00	33,244, 512.00
	Total	97,334,435.00	32,644, 718.00	1,050,202.00	6,754,634 .00	137,783, 926.00
	%	70.65	23.69	0.76	4.90	100

Source: B-G BoFED (Bureau of Finance and Economic Development) 2005

In addition to this, the Berta contended that office buildings and infrastructure that were built in Assosa could not be considered as development work for the Berta as Assosa serves as the capital of the region. Furthermore, Berta politicians complained that they were put at a disadvantage in terms of appointment to the regional government and provision of training opportunities at the Ethiopian Civil Service College (ECSC)[73] in Addis Ababa and foreign scholarships.

Thirdly, the Berta demanded that the smaller minority ethnic groups in the region, i.e. the Shinasha and the Mao-Komo, should only be represented at the *woreda* level. The EBPDO seemed to have been particularly incensed by the disproportionately higher presence of the Shinasha. The Shinasha, who appear to have more qualified personnel, came to disproportionately assume more executive offices. Hence, one of the slogans of the Berta activists during the height of the crisis was: the "Shinasha should be reduced to its size".[74] The Berta furthermore demanded the exclusion of the non-indigenous groups from representation in the regional assembly.[75] While the legality of these demands could easily be doubted, the aim of the demand was more explicit to ensure the dominance of the Berta with the regional administration.

4.3. Federal Mediation: neither Dominance nor Exit for the Berta

For nine months the Berta remained out of the regional government. There was widespread agitation for the formation of a separate region. There was also some violence involving the Berta and the settlers in the Assosa zone. The House of the Federation (HoF), which received the complaint of the Berta, attempted to resolve the crisis through mediation. In an agreement, which was brokered by the HoF, the EBPDO and the regional government agreed on some basic principles to resolve the conflict. Accordingly, it was agreed to revise the size of the representation of the indigenous ethnic groups in the regional council in which the Berta and the Shinasha were given additional seats. After this change, the Berta emerged as the largest ethnic group within the regional council. Moreover, the distribution of seats in the regional executive committee was revised. Hence, the Berta and the Gumuz were given four and three seats respectively and the smaller minority ethnic groups, i.e. Shinasha,

---

[73] The Ethiopian Civil Service College (ECSC) was established in 1995 to train national, regional and local officials of the ruling party and its affiliates in such fields as law, economics and business administration. It was an institution, which was set up to train particularly local officials who are going to fill the new vacancies created by the formation of regional government.

[74] Personal Interview: Official of the Mao-Komo party, Assosa, 12 April 2005.

[75] House of the Federation, Non-partisan Committee, *Report and recommendation on the question of the Berta nationality of the BGNRS on rights and representation,* Addis Ababa, 2001 (Amharic text).

Mao and Komo and the settlers of the Pawe special *woreda* were each given a single seat.[76]

The demand of the EBPDO for a quota distribution of regional bureau heads was, however, dismissed. Both parties reportedly agreed that appointment of bureau heads should be made on the basis of professional competence and ethnic composition.[77]

In addition to these measures, on the basis of the demand of the Berta, the 2002 revised constitution of the region provided for the establishment of a "council of nationalities" following the model of the enormously diverse Southern region, where ethnic groups are given different levels of self-administrative structures largely on the basis of their size and where the regional council includes an upper house called the "council of nationalities" in which all ethnic groups of the region are represented. This reform has not been, however, put into practice due to the following problems. Firstly, the difficulty of creating compact nationality administrative structures that geographically correspond to the indigenous ethnic groups of the region: for instance, the Shinasha are widely spread in the Metekel zone within Gumuz.[78] Secondly, there is an apparent half-heartedness among the Gumuz to the idea as its implementation may lead to a reduction of the number of zones they control into one.[79] Thirdly, the formation of 'nationality zonal councils' would bring the problem of providing an adequate administrative framework for the non-indigenous communities. It may as well strengthen the demand of the Assosa settlers to have their own special *woreda* in the region. Lastly, some senior officials of the region feared that nationality councils may weaken the unity of the five ethnic groups of the region and endanger the authority of the regional government, as zonal and other lower authorities could be tempted not to implement what has been decided by the vote of the majority at the regional level.[80] Because of all these reasons, the issue of organising nationality councils has not been implemented so far.

Regarding distribution of political appointments in the region, an 'informal arrangement' seemed to have emerged after the crisis. Accordingly, if one of the two dominant ethnic groups (Berta or Gumuz) takes the presidency, the office of the vice president of the region and the chairman of the regional ruling Front would be left to the other. Hence, Yaregal who is from the Gumuz has been maintained as president and the head of the EBPDO serves as both

[76] BGNRS, *Agreement between the BGNRS executive committee and the representatives of the Berta nationality,* 2001 (Amharic).
[77] *Ibid.*
[78] Personal Interview: Deputy Speaker, BGNRS Council, Assosa, 25 April 2005.
[79] Personal Interview: Official in the BGNRS administrative council, Assosa, 21 April 2005.
[80] Personal Interview: President of BGNRS, Assosa, 24 April 2005.

vice president of the region and chairman of the regional ruling party, i.e. the BGPDUF.

In sum, the attempt of Berta activists to assert their dominance within the new region was not successful. The appointment of Yaregal for a third term after the controversial May 2005 elections might have also dismayed the Berta political class which has been trying to carefully follow EPRDF's lines after the 2000 political crisis so that it would be allowed to claim the regional presidency again.

5. AUTONOMY AND CONFLICT BETWEEN THE INDIGENOUS AND THE NON-INDIGENOUS

The formation of the Benishangul-Gumuz region has led to changes in inter-ethnic relations not only among the so-called 'owner' nationalities of the region but also between the indigenous and the non-indigenous. The right of the indigenous ethnic groups has been enshrined in the regional constitution and political parties, which claim to represent the indigenous ethnic groups, are now in charge of the new region. In contrast, the political rights of the so-called non-indigenous communities in the region were limited.

Consequently, the two groups within the region accepted the formation of the Benishangul-Gumuz region differently. The historically marginalised indigenous ethnic groups not only warmly embraced the new system but also seek to use their newfound autonomy to ensure their economic and political development.[81] The non-indigenous in contrast "*…felt that they were treated as second-class citizens with restricted rights to live and work...*" in the new region.[82]

As a result, relationships between the indigenous and the non-indigenous ethnic groups seem to have been strained. There are tensions and conflicts between the new 'owners' of the region and the previously dominant highlanders in the region.

5.1 Representation for the Non-indigenous in the Benishangul-Gumuz Region

In terms of citizenship and representation, the formation of the B-G region has a differential outcome for the two groups. In other words, the creation of the region transformed the hitherto marginalized minority groups at the fringes of the Ethiopian periphery into 'owner' nationalities, while members of the so-

[81] Gebre Yntiso, *supra* note 35, 63.
[82] Ibid.

called non-indigenous groups were turned into new minorities. For the EPRDF, which oversaw the reorganisation of the Ethiopian state into an ethnic federation, the presence of a relatively large number of non-indigenous people in some of the new ethnic regions seemed to have been considered as an anomaly. That is probably why no systematic mechanism was put in place in the federal constitution to look after the interests and citizenship rights of the non-indigenous groups who are found out of their presumed 'ethnic homelands'. Thus with the formation of the B-G region, acrimonious relationships between the new regional authorities and the non-indigenous communities emerged on a range of issues such as the rights of the non-indigenous to have representation in the political institutions of the new region and the protection of their economic and political interests.

The right to be represented for the 'new minorities' in the B-G region was thus limited until 2002. The legal basis for the exclusion of the 'new minorities' from representation was the electoral law of the country which provided that people who cannot speak the language of the electoral district/region where they wish to stand for election cannot run as candidates (proclamation no 111/1995). This controversial provision of the electoral law seemed to have emanated from the very core policy of the ruling party, which considers ethnicity as the most important instrument of state organisation. In this respect, the constitution provides that each and every ethnic group has the right to exercise self-determination in its 'geographic location'.[83] The implicit understanding of this provision is that all ethnic groups within the country exercise their right of self-determination in their own 'ethnic homelands'. The government argues that the linguistic criterion was put in the electoral law for the sake of reducing 'communication problems' in local and regional assemblies.[84] This controversial provision and the overall political dispensation in the country implicitly, however, hint at the presence of two levels of citizenship, i.e. national (federal) and regional (local). Indeed, the establishment of language competence as a requirement for election is more about 'ethnic/regional citizenship' than about easing problems of communication.

As a result of this implicit notion of regional citizenship, the non-indigenous communities in the Benishangul-Gumuz region were partially disenfranchised. They were allowed to vote but not to run as candidates unless they knew one of the five languages of the indigenous ethnic groups of the region. The barring of the non-indigenous ethnic groups from running as candidates became even more controversial as the regional government itself uses Amharic, the language almost all of the settlers speak, as a 'working language'.

---

[83] Article 39(3) federal constitution.

[84] House of the Federation, *Decision on the constitutional question of the right to elect and to be elected from the BGNRS,* 1995 EC (Amharic).

Hence, both the regional and the federal government initially attempted to exclude the participation of the non-indigenous ethnic groups from the political process as exemplified by the tacit attempt of constructing two levels of citizenship. This was, however, undermined because of the conflict that emerged in the region between two groups. One of the outcomes of the intense conflict that happened between the Gumuz and the settlers in Metekel during the beginning of the 1990s was the formation of the Pawe Special *Woreda* for the settlers.[85] It was made directly accountable to the regional government bypassing the Gumuz-dominated Metekel zone. Moreover, the Pawe settlers were allowed to have some representation in the assembly and executive committee of the regional government, though their level of representation was far from their population size.

The situation in the Assosa zone was, however, different. The substantial non-indigenous community in the Assosa zone was only allowed to have some representation at *woreda* and *kebele*[86] levels. Accordingly, when *woreda* councils were established in 1995, each of the settler *kebele* was allowed to have two representatives in the Assosa *woreda* council. Moreover, the *woreda* executive committee was composed of seven settlers and eight Berta. But the representation of the settlers has been steadily declining. For instance, in 1996, when the Assosa *woreda* was split into two (Assosa and Bambassi), the ethnic composition of the *woreda* executive committees was dramatically changed. From among fourteen seats ten were reserved for the Berta, while four were given to the settlers. This makeup of *woreda* executive committees is still maintained.

The regional authorities also devised another way to reduce the proportion of the settlers in the Assosa and Bambassi *woreda* councils. In the 2003 *woreda* elections, irrespective of their population size, the *kebele* which were constituted by the Berta were made to have more representatives in the *woreda* council than the *kebele* composed of settlers.[87] This was again engineered to make the Berta the majority in the *woreda* councils. At the same time the settlers of Assosa were not allowed to have representation at regional level.

Following several petitions, the regional government decided to allow the candidates of the settlers to run for seats of the regional assembly in the 2000 elections. According to the office of the president of the BGNRS, the decision to provide representation for the non-indigenous peoples was made to: "*ensure the sustainability of the prevailing peace and security in the region; expedite*

---

[85] Pawe special *Woreda* was created to defuse the conflict between the settlers and the Gumuz in 1994. It had three representatives at the regional council and one representative at the executive committee of the region. Since 1995 EC, there has been no non-indigenous member at the executive committee of the regional executive committee.

[86] *Kebele* literally means neighbourhood, it is the lowest tier of local government.

[87] Focus Group Discussion: with former settlers, Assosa, 13 April 2005.

the development of the region in unison and cooperation and strengthen the increasing unity among peoples."

Nonetheless, the representation, which was suggested for the non-indigenous communities, was on a quota basis. Accordingly, the BGPDUF agreed to provide 12 seats at the regional council for the non-indigenous ethnic groups from the Assosa zone. The proposed representation was not, however, proportionate to their population size. Moreover, the candidates of the settlers were to run on the party ticket of the regional 'vanguard' political front, i.e. the BGPDUF, as the EPRDF of which many of the settler candidates were members refused to field its candidates in a region which was run by its affiliate political organization.[88]

With the apparent agreement of the BGPDUF and of the functionaries of the EPRDF in the region, the candidature of the prospective representatives of the non-indigenous who were recruited by the EPRDF field cadres were registered by the National Electoral Board of Ethiopia (NEBE) for the May 2000 regional elections. Nevertheless, on the basis of a complaint that some Berta officials submitted to it, the NEBE cancelled the candidacy of the non-indigenous. The then Secretary General of the NEBE, Assefa Birru, explained the reason for the cancellation of the candidacy of the non-indigenous in the following words:

"*The Ethiopian Electoral Board in its extraordinary meeting held on February 18, 2000 considered the complaint it received from some Berta officials and the EBPDO regarding the candidacy of individuals who do not know the national language of the electoral district in which they stand as candidates. The Board in accordance with article 38/1b of proclamation 111/87(EC), which provides that prospective candidates must know the national/regional language of the region in which they stand for election, has decided to nullify the candidacy of those who have registered as candidates in the Assosa zone without knowing the language.*"[89]

The cancellation of the candidature of the settlers, however, precipitated tensions and violence between the Berta and the settlers. It also polarized the political organisations of the indigenous ethnic groups. While the EBPDO opposed the candidacy of the settlers, the other members of the BGPDUF did not approve this opposition. In fact, EBPDO's decision to appeal against the candidature of the prospective representatives of the settlers was considered by the other members of the BGPDUF as reneging on a collective decision of the Front. Thus the president of the region, Yaregal Aysheshim, and the leaders of

[88] Focus Group Discussion: with former settlers, 13 April 2005.

[89] Assefa Birru, *Letter to Assosa Zone Electoral Coordinator,* (reference No. A64-01/K6/134/7), dated 10.06.1992 EC, Addis Ababa (Amharic).

the other parties not only opposed the position of the former but also supported the effort of the settlers to ensure their representation in the regional council. For instance, the president of the region, right after the decision of the NEBE to cancel the candidacy of the settlers, protested against the decision as follows:

"*The National Electoral Board of Ethiopia in its meeting of February 18, 2000 decided to cancel the candidacy of the members of other ethnic groups from the upcoming national and regional election. We found the decision of the electoral board not clear. We are afraid that it would endanger the peace and stability of our region. We demand explanation from the electoral board and also request the House of Peoples Representatives, the House of the Federation and the Council of Constitutional Inquiry (CCI) to look into the issue considering the constitution and provide a sustainable solution to the problem.*" [90]

The settlers who were denied representation mounted a sustained legal challenge against the decision of the NEBE. Thus they wrote a series of petitions to several regional and federal authorities claiming that the decision of the NEBE that prohibited them from running for election was unconstitutional and violated Article 38/1/b of the constitution which provides, "*Every Ethiopian national, without any discrimination based on colour, race, nation, nationality, sex, language, religion, political or other opinion or other status, has the right to vote and to be elected at periodic elections to any office at any level of government.*" [91]

After the cancellation of the candidacy of their prospective representatives, the settlers who were initially interested in getting representation at the regional council later on elevated their demand to the provision of a special *woreda* or zonal administration, which would be directly accountable to the regional government surpassing the Berta dominated Assosa zonal administration. In one of those grievance letters the settlers wrote to the officials of the federal government - they stated that as the officials of the EBPDO consider them 'refugees' in their own country, and do not respect their human and democratic rights, it would be impossible for them to get fair and just administration under the EBPDO. They, moreover, threatened that if their demand for representation was rejected and if they were forced to accept the leadership of the EBPDO, they would not be responsible for any conflict that could emerge be-

[90] BGNRS, Office of the President, *letter to the National Electoral Board of Ethiopia, the House of Peoples' Representatives, the House of the Federation, the Council of Constitutional Inquiry on cancellation of candidacy,* 1992 EC (Amharic).

[91] Amare Asefa *et al.*, *Letter to the Benishangul Gumuz national regional state council,* Assosa, 31/05/2001 (Amharic); Belayneh Ashenafi *et al.*, *Letter to the Benishangul Gumuz national regional state council on cancellation of candidacy,* Assosa, 17/06/1992 EC (Amharic); Dereb Chane *et al.*, *Petition to the House of the Federation, the House of Peoples' Representatives, the National Electoral Board of Ethiopia, the Office of the Prime Minister, the Council of Constitutional Inquiry and others*, 16/06/1993 EC (Amharic).

tween the two groups.[92] Understandably the relationship between the settlers and the Berta during this period became tense and at times violent. Thus there were outbreaks of violence in Assosa and Bambassi in 2000/01 in which some lives were lost.[93]

5.2. Economic Dimensions of Conflict between Settlers and the Indigenous

The settlers' demand for political representation has also economic dimensions. In this respect, they argue that political representation within the region would help them address their socio-economic problems.[94]

Since the 1991 change of regime, the settlers particularly have grievances regarding access to land and land resources. When the settlers were brought to Assosa, they were given 1,000 square metres of land for their individual residential quarters and private vegetable gardens. The main farming land was, however, jointly owned by the cooperatives, which were established following socialist principles. Many of the villages had 500 hectares of farming land, which used to be collectively cultivated by the settlers up until the 1991 change of government. After the 1991 change of regime, the communally held land was distributed among the peasants. In many of the villages, the average household land holding after land distribution became small. For example, in one of the settler villages close to Assosa town, the average household land holding of the settlers became 0.5 hectares.[95]

While the settlers are facing severe shortages of land, since the establishment of the region their prospect of having access to the virgin lands of the region has become increasingly limited. At the same time, the Berta who have been emboldened by the new changes have become more assertive about their ownership of the region's land resources.

The economic grievances of the settlers could broadly be discussed from the following three dimensions. Firstly, the settlers resent the development of a new land tenure system in Assosa, i.e. the leasing out of land by the indigenous Berta to the settlers in which they give a third of their produce to the Berta. The settlers consider this as the development of an exploitative relationship between a 'tenant' (settler) and 'landlord' (indigenous/Berta). The settlers also seem to be dismayed by the 'failure' of the EPRDF to ensure 'just' distribution of land which it 'attained' in the Tigray and Amhara regions.[96] Sec-

[92] Dereb Chane *et al.*, *supra* note 91.
[93] Both the officials of the EBPDO and the EPRDF who were alleged to have participated in the inter-ethnic violence were arrested and tried by the regional government.
[94] Focus Group Discussions: with settlers of Amba 4, Assosa, 14 April 2005.
[95] Focus Group Discussion: with former settlers, 13 April 2005.
[96] *Ibid.*

ondly, the settlers complain that they were made to pay for forest resources of the region, which were freely available to them before the 1991 change of regime.[97] Thirdly, the settlers who are located in the vicinity of Assosa town have grievances regarding the taking away of their farming land for urban development without compensation.[98]

Another reason for the disquiet amongst the settlers is the preferential treatment of the members of the indigenous ethnic groups for college and university admission. The Ethiopian government provides preferential treatment to members of minority ethnic groups and women to be admitted to government colleges and universities. The rationale for this policy of affirmative action is to redress the disproportionately low level of participation of minority ethnic groups and women in institutions of higher learning and also to ensure a balanced development within the country. In fact there is still an acute shortage of professionals from the indigenous ethnic groups in the B-G regional bureaucracy that the attempt of both the regional and federal government to increase the participation of the indigenous ethnic groups in higher education appears to be justifiable. To this end, the following sets of preferences were used.[99] Firstly, if admission to a college preparatory school after completing high school is set at 2.5 on a scale of 4.00 for all students, indigenous students will be allowed to be admitted at 2.4. Secondly, after completion of two years of college preparatory courses, all students from indigenous groups who have completed the programme will be admitted to colleges and universities, while there will be a cut off point for students coming from non-indigenous ethnic groups. Thirdly, there is a heavy preferential treatment of students coming from the indigenous ethnic groups to be admitted to regional technical and teacher training institutes and colleges. For instance, there is a one hundred percent reservation of places in the regional teacher training college for students coming from the indigenous ethnic groups.

As the majority of the students from both the indigenous and the non-indigenous groups compete for few places in post-secondary colleges like teacher training institutions, the settlers are apprehensive of the heavy preference (100% reservation) given to the indigenous.[100]

[97] Amare Asefa *et al.*, *supra* note 91.
[98] *Ibid.*
[99] Personal Interview: Official BGNRS, Education Bureau.
[100] Focus Group Discussions: with settlers of Amba 4, Assosa, 14 April 2005.

5.3. Viewpoints of the Indigenous Political Class on the Representation of the Settlers

Political parties of the indigenous ethnic groups generally seem to support the idea that political representation within the region should be a preserve of the indigenous ethnic groups. There were, however, differences among them regarding the need to provide a 'limited' representation to the numerically significant non-indigenous groups in the region. For instance, Berta politicians opposed the representation of the Assosa settlers at the regional council, while the Gumuz supported the provision of a limited representation. Despite such differences, all of the indigenous political parties seem to be apprehensive of the demands of the non-indigenous to have a political role in the region, which is expressly created for them to exercise self-determination.

Because of the explicit and implicit desire of the regional government to limit the political role of the non-indigenous, it put a 'linguistic' restriction on the right to be elected. Hence, Article 39(1)(d) of the 1995 regional constitution provides that it is only '*those who speak the languages of the nationalities of the region [who] would have the right to be elected*'. Though the 2002 revised constitution of the region dropped the 'linguistic' requirement, it did not include a provision on universal suffrage. It instead contained a provision, which states that '*representation of other people of the region shall be given special consideration*'. So far, the particular laws that specify the implementation of this provision have not been put in place yet.

The unwillingness of the new indigenous political class in the Benishangul-Gumuz region to allow proportional representation for the non-indigenous communities could be seen from two angles. Firstly, some regional officials argue that the formation of a federal system of government was intended to provide self-rule to ethnic groups in their own 'geographic space' and as such the settlers who were brought to the region without the consent of the indigenous ethnic groups should not be allowed to have equal political representation on the basis of one-man-one vote.[101] In line with this some even suggest that settlers who wish to have a political role should go to their own ethnic region as political power is given to their own ethnic groups in their home territories.[102]

Secondly, there is nervousness among the 'new' elite of the region because of the relatively large volume of the non-indigenous people in the region. There is fear among some officials of the region that allowing the non-indigenous

[101] Personal Interview: Top Berta official, Assosa, 12 April 2005.

[102] Personal Interview: Ex-*Woreda*, Awraja, Administrator, Assosa, 11 April 2005.

equal representation undermines the status and role of the indigenous within 'their own' region. One regional official for instance underscores that:[103]

"*As everybody agrees there was ethnic domination in the past. The culture of one group was presented as superior to that of others. The regions were established to reverse this. Representation in this region should not be on the basis of one-man-one vote, there is an affirmative action element in the formation of this region for the hitherto marginalized groups. Migration of people from one region to the other should not undermine the self-determination right of ethnic groups in their own 'geographic space'. The question of providing representation for the 'non-indigenous' communities should consider all these problems. It should not be done in a manner that would compromise the right of the 'owner' nationalities to exercise their self-determination. If the 'outsiders' were provided equal representation on a one- man- one-vote basis what would happen if a question of secession is to be raised? Who is going to decide? Could the settlers demand secession in a region, which does not belong to them? Could they prevent the secession demand of the indigenous ethnic groups, which is provided in the federal and regional constitution? The constitutional principle of self-administration is geographic specific and ethnic groups should exercise their right of self-determination in their own geographic regions.*"

5.4. The House of the Federation Constitutional Interpretation on the Representation of the Settlers

The settlers put their application to the House of the Federation - which is constitutionally responsible for interpreting the constitution - claiming that the provision in the electoral law which prohibits the candidacy of people who do not know regional/local languages and the decision of the NEBE which cancelled the candidature of their prospective candidates were unconstitutional and violated the constitution which provides universal suffrage with no discrimination. Once it received the case, the House of the Federation referred the case to the Council of Constitutional Inquiry (CCI). The CCI, which has the duty of advising the HoF, ruled that:

"*The constitutional article (Article 38) provides that citizens without any distinction should participate in public administration through representatives whom they elect freely and independently. The constitution provides that: 'Every Ethiopian national, without any discrimination based on colour, race, nation, nationality, sex, language, religion, political or other opinion or other status, has the right to vote and to be elected at periodic elections to any office at any level of government'. On the other hand, the electoral law, article*

[103] Personal Interview: Top Berta official, Assosa, 12 April 2005.

38/1/b says that any candidate should know the national regional language of the region where he/she is appearing as a candidate. We believe that the approach of the electoral law to tie knowledge of a regional language to the right to be elected does not conform to the constitutional principle. Thus we found that the decision of the National Electoral Board to use ones knowledge of language as one criterion of candidacy violates the constitution."[104]

The House of the Federation (HoF) did not, however, agree with the recommendation of the CCI. It, therefore, ruled that the provision of the electoral law (art. 38/1/b) does not violate the constitution, as knowledge of the language used by the local people is an important element that fosters self-administration.[105] The HoF has, nevertheless, found that as the working language of the Benishangul-Gumuz region was Amharic and the applicants knew that language, the decision of the NEBE to cancel their registration as candidates because of their lack of knowledge of one of the five indigenous languages of the region (Berta) was 'unconstitutional'.[106] This meant that the non-indigenous people in the B-G region who do not know the languages of the indigenous ethnic groups could run as candidates.

The decision of the HoF has a precedent effect and applies to other similar cases throughout the country. Nevertheless, this ruling only applies to those regions, which use Amharic as their 'working language' such as Gambella, and the Southern region. In other words, the linguistic criteria, which the electoral law provides, are still valid in regions such as Tigray, Afar, Amhara, Oromia and Somali where there is congruence between the language of the dominant regional ethnic group and the 'working language' of the regions.

Following the 2003 decision of the HoF, the right of the non-indigenous communities in the Assosa zone to elect and to be elected was ensured. On this basis, the regional government endorsed a new quota for the representation of all the ethnic groups in the region for the 2005 third parliamentary and regional elections. According to Yaregal Aysheshim,

"*In order to make the elections more just and balanced and in consultation with the electoral board, the necessary modification has been made to have a proportionally representative regional assembly on the basis of the composition of nationalities and also considering the participation of other peoples. On this basis, the regional assembly would have 100 seats. These seats will be divided in the following manner, 40 for Berta, 35 for Gumuz, 11 for Shinasha, 5 for Mao and Komo and 9 for other peoples. The presentation of the indige-*

[104] Council of Constitutional Inquiry, *Recommendation to the House of the Federation,* 1992 EC.
[105] House of the Federation, *supra* note 84.
[106] *Ibid.*

nous ethnic groups at the federal parliament would be 4 for Berta, 3 for Gumuz, 1 for Shinasha, and 1 for Mao and Komo."[107]

There was also a tacit agreement among the different players that the non-indigenous people would only be represented at the regional level. Representation at the federal level was reserved for the indigenous ethnic groups. As the EPRDF has again declined to field its candidates in the region, an understanding was reached between the settlers, EPRDF functionaries in the region and the regional ruling front that the prospective representatives of the settlers should run on the party ticket of the BGPDUF. These arrangements were made on the assumption that the main contender in the regional election would be the regional 'vanguard' party, i.e. the BGPDUF. This assumption, however, proved wrong as nationwide opposition parties, particularly the Coalition for Unity and Democracy (CUD) managed to register their candidates using the opening up which the EPRDF government for the first time provided for competitive elections in the 2005 elections.

The coming of national opposition parties to contest seats both at the regional and federal levels threatened to undermine the 'carefully' worked out 'balance' of ethnic representation in the regional council in which the indigenous ethnic groups should hold the commanding majority. Thus the pre-voting period in the region was characterised by anxiety. The indigenous political parties and the field operatives of the EPRDF were directly and indirectly urging the settlers to vote for those who had been nominated by the EPRDF and had been endorsed as candidates of the BGPDUF. The regional officials even promised to expedite the provision of new farming land to the settlers, if they would vote for 'democracy' and 'peace'.

The relatively better contested election of May 2005 affected the 'balance' which the regional officials sought to bring about. Firstly, from among the nine seats allocated to the region for representation at the federal level and preserved to the indigenous groups, the CUD took one seat. Secondly, the CUD won eleven seats at the regional council again affecting the 'proportional' ethnic 'balance', which the regional government wanted to bring about at the regional level. More importantly, the limited competitive election of 2005 showed how a 'quota' arrangement, which was worked out with the assumption that the 'vanguard' party would always win, could easily founder. The May 2005 elections have also left an important lesson—the need to clarify the 'basis' and 'framework' in which the 'equal' or 'unequal' representation of the 'outsiders' in the region is ensured.

---

[107] BGNRS, Office of the President, *Performance Report on the first half of 1997 presented to the seventh session of the regional council*, Assosa, 1997 EC.

6. SUMMARY AND CONCLUSION

This article demonstrated how the federal restructuring process in Ethiopia has in several and interrelated ways changed relationships among the different ethnic groups within the B-G region.

Firstly, the formation of the region has enabled the hitherto marginalized minority ethnic groups at the north western Ethiopian periphery for the first time in their history of association with the Ethiopian state to participate in their own administration, though at a limited level. Nevertheless, as the politics of the region is structured on the basis of ethnicity, competitive and often conflictive relationships are developing among the ethnic groups, which are now constitutionally recognised as 'owner' nationalities.

Secondly, two important categories of ethnic groups, i.e. indigenous and non-indigenous, having implications on citizenship and representation emerged after the formation of the region. The 'new' political class of the indigenous ethnic groups emphasises the right of the ethnic groups to self-administration in their own 'geographic space' and seeks to limit the representation of the non-indigenous communities in the region. In this respect, the regional government attempted to limit the participation of the non-indigenous ethnic groups through (a) prohibition of the right to be elected for those who do not speak the languages of the indigenous groups of the region (b) determination of a quota for representation and (c) gerrymandering for *woreda* councils in which the *kebele* of the settlers would have lesser number of representation than the *kebele* of the indigenous. The settlers nevertheless mounted a protracted struggle to ensure their representation in the regional council.

Thirdly, the demand of the settlers to have representation led to the first 'major' constitutional interpretation by the House of the Federation. The House of the Federation's ruling led to the recognition of the right of the settlers to be represented in the region. The decision of the House of the Federation, however, seemed to have sought a pragmatic solution to the question by ruling that if one speaks the 'working language' of any region, he/she should not be prohibited from standing for election. In effect, the decision of the House of the Federation maintained the controversial provision of the electoral law, which ties the right to be elected to linguistic fluency. By doing so it maintained the prevailing two levels of citizenship, national and regional. This means that one would have full citizenship that includes the right to vote and to be elected when he/she resides in a region where he/she speaks the regional ethnic or 'working language'. If he/she does not know the language, his/her citizenship right is limited to voting.

The confrontation between the indigenous and the non-indigenous in the Benishangul-Gumuz region over such issues as 'resources' and 'representation' shows the problem of federal restructuring on the basis of ethnicity. As there will always be a lack of convergence between a given ethnic group and an administrative structure, it is important to devise ways in which devolution of power would not create incentives for conflict and violence between 'titular' ethnic groups for whose sake the region is created and those who find themselves outside the ethnic region created for their ethnic kin and kith. Unless the necessary legal and political measures are taken which ensure the rights of both the indigenous and the non-indigenous ethnic groups, there could be recurrent violent conflicts.

10. Traditional Governance Systems and their Operational Linkage with Formal Governing Structures in Aba'ala Woreda, North Afar

Mengistu Hailu, Getahun Kassa and Mulubrhan Balehegn[•]

1. INTRODUCTION

This study has been initiated by the request of the Project AIPDP (Afar Integrated Pastoral Development Programme) to have a better understanding of the operational linkages of the informal and formal governance structures that prevail in the Aba'ala *Woreda* of the Afar Regional state.

2. OBJECTIVES

The study was intended to achieve the following objectives:

- Map out local governance institutions that operate in Aba'ala *Woreda* of the Afar state;
- Identify and analyse the value transfer mechanisms in society;
- Appraise the current formal governance structures of the *woreda*;
- Analyse the interface between formal and informal governing structures;
- Conduct SWOT analysis on the formal and informal governance structures in managing natural resources and conflict;
- Synthesize findings and give recommendations for the project.

3. METHOD OF STUDY

The study mainly employed qualitative data collection methods. A Literature review was performed to better understand the socio-economic and political tradition of the people and to comprehend the agro-climatic transformation of the area.

Primary data was collected through semi-structured interviews with key informants and through focused group discussions with several cross-sections of the society.

[•] Mengistu Hailu and Mulubrhan Balehegn are both lecturers at Mekelle University, Faculty of Agriculture. E-mail Mulubrhan Balehegn: mulubrhanbg@yahoo.com. Getahun Kassa is Executive Director of the Ethiopian Human Rights Commission and former Dean and Lecturer, Mekelle University, Faculty of Law. E-mail Getahun Kassa: ateykg96@fastmail.fm

The study team identified the following categories of people for the interviews and focused group discussions:

- Project staff
- Clan leaders
- Elders
- Governmental officials (civil servants)
- Political administrators
- Highlanders
- Youths

The selection of individuals for the interviews and focused group discussions was done in consultation with the AIPDP project staff and the authorities in the *Woreda* and of course taking into consideration their status as per the above categories. The team wanted to identify interviewees based on their clan affiliations, but later dropped the idea for it found it unproductive in certain ways. The issue of women interviewees was similar, because the *Asayamara*[1] were a bit uncomfortable when we raised the issue of interviewing their women. They said women don't participate in the *ADDA* institution, and there was no need to interview them.

4. THE STUDY AREA

The study was conducted in Aba'ala *Woreda* found some 50km south east of Mekelle – the capital town of the Tigray regional state. Aba'ala is the capital of the zone two of the Afar regional state. It constitutes about 12 villages/Tabiyas/ namely: Adi-Haremedi; Murga; Hidmo Wuhdet; Gelaeso; Haridan; Wesema; A'tkul; Gube; Aba'ala; Asengola and Enda-Asengola. Most of these villages are found within a near distance from the capital town, Aba'ala.

4.1. Population

According to the census undertaken by the Central Statistics Authority the Aba'ala *Woreda* has a population of 26,094 out of which 14,100 are males and 11,994 are females.[2] The majority of the people in the *woreda* are Muslims with a small number of Christians who emigrated from the neighbouring highlands. Afar, Tigrayan highlanders and other Ethiopians of various ethnic ori-

---

[1] **Asayamara** is a clan leader (usually from Damohoita clan). It is a prestigious position that offers power and recognition by the community. But it also entails hard work in managing the clan, especially during conflict resolution. *Asayamara* receive no payment for the service.

[2] *The 1994 Population and Housing Census of Ethiopia – Results at Country Level – Volume I: Statistical Report.*

gins inhabit the town. The majority of the inhabitants rely on subsistence livestock rearing with a few engaged in cultivation and salt trade along with livestock rearing.[3]

4.2. Climate

Aba'ala is climatically categorized as semi-arid receiving an annual rainfall of less than 500mm, with evapo-transpiration exceeding precipitation during most parts of the dry months of the year. The rainfall pattern is bimodal with the main rainy season falling in the months of July-August and the short rains usually come in March and April.[4] The high rainfall in July and August usually leads to high run-off rates, which coupled with high evapo-transpiration rates, make the rainfall insufficient for crop production.[5]

The dominant soils are sandy in texture developed from alluvial deposits resulting from flood coming from upland nearby areas. Exposed rocks and gravel dominate most of the hills and ridges. Deposits of silt and fine sand particles occur in the plain flat areas where cultivation is practised.[6]

4.3. Land Use

The Afar practice grazing and cultivation as their main land use schemes in addition to settlement. The Aba'ala plains are areas of cultivation that receive some floodwater and spring water for irrigation. The Afar sharecrop their land for the traditional highland farmers who prepare the land, saw and harvest and finally share the harvest with the land holding Afar in different modalities. These could be sharing a half or one quarter of the harvest.

Free grazing is the main mode of grazing in the area. Kelemework[7] mentions that Afar nomadism was founded on the pastoral philosophy of individual ownership of livestock in communal land, which enabled them to move freely to different available grazing lands.

---

[3] Fassil Kebebew, Diress Tsegaye and G. Synnevag, *Traditional Coping Strategies of the Afar and Borana Pastoralists in Response to Drought* 4-17 (Drylands Coordination Group Report No. 17, November 2001).

[4] (Hunting, 1976) as cited by Yayneshet Tesfay and Kelemework Tafere, *Indigenous Rangeland Resources and Conflict Management by the North Afar Pastoral Groups in Ethiopia* 9 (Drylands Coordination Group Report No. 31, November 2004).

[5] Mitiku Haile and Diress Tsegaye, *Water Harvesting for Crop Production in semi-arid Areas of North Eastern Ethiopia: A Case Study of Floodwater Diversion in Aba'Ala Agro-Pastoral Area* (Mekelle: Mekelle University).

[6] (Hunting, 1976) as cited by Yayneshet Tesfay and Kelemework Tafere, *supra* note 4, 9.

[7] Yayneshet Tesfay and Kelemework Tafere, *supra* note 4, 34.

Most informants say that there was no serious shortage of grass in the Afar territories and that there was no need to have a regulated grazing system. They also mention "the Afar values appreciate sharing what you have" hence there was no ground to reserve what one has; rather the prevailing value is sharing what is available. But in reality the Afar have shortages of grass and water sources and the free grazing tradition is re-inforced to avoid conflict propelled by shortages of grass and water.

The Afar are not ignorant of restricted grazing. Especially the Damohoitas had a tradition of reserving grass and water only for themselves and they also periodically closed some of their mountains for the dry seasons. They had a fining system to punish those who violated the closures. But recently the *Asayamara* have decided to abolish most of the closures and those areas that were kept for restricted grazing. This was mainly because these areas are causes for continued conflict when neighbouring Afar come in search of grass and water. Now there is an understanding among the Afar that there is no restricted area for grazing. But some of our interviewees mentioned that there are still some areas that are reserved for the bad times.

In Aba'ala town the Afar together with other ethnic groups have permanent houses. But in many villages the Afar have mobile houses.

4.4. Livelihood

Out of the 1.1 million people in the Afar region, over 90% are primarily pastoralists who depend on livestock. Livestock are sources of food, income, security and insurance.[8]

The Afar around Aba'ala are developing an agro-pastoral system. Aba'ala being at the confluence with the farming highlanders, there is a significant influence of the highlanders on the Afar and *vice versa*. In fact Aba'ala town is a host for both the Afar and the Tigrayan highlanders. Recently there is a developing pattern of depending on food aid. This is attributable to the recurrent shortage of rain in the area. But still it seems that the issue of aid is an area worth investigation since the growing dependence syndrome is enormous.

4.5. Social Organization

The Afar organize themselves around a patrilineal descent. Their patrilineal descent system defines a man as belonging to his father's clan. Descent groups that claim common ancestry – who trace their origin to the same man - make up a group that grows into a clan. Hence the clan is an important concept in the

---

[8] Fassil Kebebew, Diress Tsegaye and G. Synnevag, *supra* note 3, 4.

Afar social organization. It is a functional institution that plays an important role in wealth distribution, granting security and insuring identity.

Afar settlements are composed of a mixture of clans although each locality is identified with a major clan. This makes it easier to organize social, economic and political support in times of crisis.[9]

There are numerous clans in the Afar social organization. In Aba'ala *Woreda* itself our interviewees mentioned that there could be more than 200 clans. But some are more influential than others and affect the social fabric of the Afar. This is because some clans have a distinct function. For instance, Damohoitas are known for their role in conflict resolution. They serve as *Asayamara* among which the Asmeroras and Alietos are people who are entrusted with the power to give the last blessing to the settlement of a conflict. The Seka clan is known for making prayers. In the old days, and even now to some extent, they used to pray for rain and good health for their cattle and people. The Dahimela and the Hadarmo clans are also entitled to conduct *Fatiha*[10] in the absence of the Damohoitas. On the other hand there are some clans that are not allowed to make the *Fatiha*. These clan functions are accompanied with status and access to resources.

The clan functions are diminishing with the advent of modern administration and because of the revolution that has been going on in Tigray, a neighbouring regional state. The Afar have been members of the armed struggle and have been influenced much by the political orientation of the struggle, which actually was a communist view that rarely entertains much of the kind of social structure the Afar have. However, this does not mean that the Afar have completely lost their traditional social organization.

5. CONFLICT AND INSTITUTIONS OF CONFLICT RESOLUTION IN AFAR

5.1. Sources of Conflict in Afar

There are basically two types of conflicts that involve the Afar in Aba'ala. Firstly, there are the conflicts between the Afar and their Christian neighbours in the highlands - which might be described as inter-ethnic conflict while the second is the conflict among the Afar themselves, which may be described as intra – Afar conflict.

[9] Yayneshet Tesfay and Kelemework Tafere, *supra* note 4, 10.
[10] **Fatiha** is a final word and procession made to indicate the resolution of a conflict peacefully.

Given their nomadic tradition and major dependence on livestock, there is a perceived opinion among outsiders that natural resources like grass and water are likely to be the major causes of conflict in the area. This opinion is true when we look at the inter-ethnic conflicts between the Afar and the neighbouring highlanders. Most of these conflicts have been caused by competition for resources like grass, water and charcoal.

But, looking into the intra-Afar conflicts, we find that resources are not the major sources of conflict. According to our interviewees, resource conflicts among the Afar are mainly limited to clashes of herders who mainly come from neighbouring *woreda* and those conflicts get resolved easily through elderly people's intervention. But the main conflicts are attributed to traditional animosity between clans.

Given the sedenterization of the Afar around Aba'ala, there are some new reasons of conflict. These include: farming, land holding and irrigation water.

5.2. Institutions of Conflict Resolution in Afar

Defining an institution

There are a lot of definitions of institutions. The DFID (www.dfid.gov.uk) makes a working definition of institutions by contrasting them to organizations: "*Institutions are the rules, norms and values that shape our behaviour.. ...They are rules of the game, ...while organizations are players of the game…*"

There are two diverging views as to why institutions exist. The first view considers institutions as objective things with their own regularities. Arnold Gehlen argues, "*Well functioning institutions ... are objective and collective patterns of behaviour that have their own regularities ... and even their own value ... They don't have to be justified and legitimated.*"[11] The mere fact of existing, and having existed for such a long time, is the justification and legitimation of their controlling function. Gehlen defined institutions as "empty forms" … which can and indeed will be filled in the transition of time by motives and aims that were not theirs to begin with.

The second view is the functionalist view that attributes the existence of institutions to the functions they exercise. They serve the satisfaction of human needs. "*... there are basic biological and social needs which are satisfied through actions. These actions are permanently needed for the satisfaction of*

[11] Arnold Gehlen, as cited in A.C. Zijderveld, *The Institutional Imperative – The Interface of Institutions and Networks* 32 (Amsterdam: Amsterdam University Press, 2000).

the needs, and will in time become schematic. That is, they gradually grow into collective habits and patterns of behaviour. There is, for example, the biological need for sexual intercourse. The behaviour that satisfies this need grows into a regular pattern - the institution of marriage."[12] In this paper, institutions have been treated taking the second view into consideration i.e. taking their function.

5.2.1. The ADDA Institution

The Afar have a traditional institution locally called the *ADDA*. The *ADDA* is a council of clan leaders and elderly people who are nobility in the area and who are known for their skill in conflict resolution. This council of elderly people is locally called the Mekabons.

The *ADDA* mainly operates in post conflict dispute settlements. It does not pro-actively act to prevent potential conflicts. The organization of the Mekabons comes into existence after a crime is committed.

The *ADDA* has no fixed structures. There are no constantly elected or nominated people who run the *ADDA*. Rather there is a kind of constantly imprinted thinking that these people are "elderly members of the Afar nobility" who are thought to be well versed and skilled in conflict resolution. This means that, though the Afar social structure makes it clear who are the likely persons to participate in the *ADDA*, it is not delineated who exactly are the members of the *ADDA* council.

The *ADDA* has, however, a kind of "fixed" set of rules upon which it gives its rulings. These rules describe the only way of litigation and ways of compensation. There is no alternative way of settling a dispute, except for very minor disagreements that can be contained at clan leader level. Every Afar would like to see the implementation of these rules as prescribed. And the Afar say that the fact that the rules are fixed and don't change according to circumstances is a strategy for protecting the rules from erosion.

The Afar *ADDA* rules are not written, but the Afar elders say that they have not been changed ever since they have been drawn. The guarantee for their stability is that they are open and accessible to any one so that everyone can easily learn them and defend himself and/or anyone else in case there is a miscarriage of justice. The Afar also claim expedient dispensation of disputes.

The rules of the *ADDA* administrative institution are based on respect for human life, irrespective of the cause for hostility. This is to say the Afar discourage bodily and property offences by levying heavy punishment despite the

[12] A.C. Zijderveld, *supra* note 11, 33.

strength and weakness of the reason for the offence: all guilt is rebuked severely through serious compensation so that it conveys an instructive message to other potential offenders. For example, one component of the *ADDA* compensation package for a murder case is a payment of 3,000 birr. This 3,000 birr is equal to 4,500 current Ethiopian birr.♦ Of this money the convict is supposed to pay half of it in money and half of it in livestock. So the 1,500 birr is to be given in cash while the remaining is paid in camels and goats. This compensation is accompanied by strong social pressure. The wisdom here is that the Afar have their own pricing system. A camel in the actual market costs between 1,500 to 3,000 birr, but the traditional value (for compensation purposes) of a camel, according to the Afar *ADDA*, is 40 birr for male camels and 50 birr for pregnant female camels. The Afar prefer to stick to this price with the logic that 1,500 birr remains a heavy fine for offenders. If the convict were made to pay only the 1,500 in cash, the fine would be very light and would not discourage a second crime. The Afar believe that the compensation should coercively castigate the convict in a way that others should learn a lesson. Thus the convict is expected to pay about 37 camels and some more goats in addition to the 1,500 birr and other things within the compensation package. In reality 37 camels cost a fortune, even for a rich Afar family. So it does serve the purpose the Afar intend – creating a deterrent for would-be offenders. But the other side of this coin is that there is no penalty like imprisonment imposed on offenders; forgiveness followed by compensation and respect for the *ADDA* are the only things done in the conflict settlement process.

The *ADDA* institution includes a right to appeal. This means that when an offender feels that the verdict is biased he has the right to appeal and he will choose some *Asayamara* from a different clan to constitute a new *ADDA* council. These clan leaders will see the case and give their verdict based on the previous cases they have settled. Hence they refer to the previous settled cases to support their judgments. Appeal is however discouraged in general terms. In case the new *ADDA* members reject the offender's appeal, the latter is liable for further punishment. But if the new *ADDA* council accepts the appeal and gives a ruling contrary to the ruling of the former *ADDA* council, there are two scenarios: the second ruling is endorsed or a third *ADDA* council, composed of quite influential *Asayamara* from other clans, is constituted to decide on the judgement of the first two *ADDA* councils. This is a final and binding ruling. The operation of the *ADDA* institution is an interesting case and shows how the Afar abide to their traditional judicial system.

The Afar mention that their traditional administration has prevailed since ancient times, passing the test of time with "no change" in content. The Afar claim that this institution and its laws have sustained different shocks and im-

♦ This is because the Afar calculate 1.50 birr as one. Hence the total compensation of 3,000 birr awarded to the victim is 4,500 birr in actual calculation.

positions of different regimes that installed their own institutions. Literally speaking they believe that the rules of the *ADDA* have not been changed when time and regimes have changed. They say ***Nigusi memarta Afari mebata***: translated as "the king and its rules pass but the Afar laws never pass." The Afar think that their institution is uniformly accepted in all regions where Afar live - from the coast of Eritrea to the coast of Djibouti. They place a strong emotional attachment and solid conviction on its impartiality and capability of dispute settlement.

The above *uniformity* and *non–changing* features of the *ADDA* rules are subject to debate. There are some elements that indicate that the rules have been adapted to the socio-economic realities of the Afar. For example, the *ADDA* rules for a murder case obligate the culprit to pay compensation to the victim's clan. This compensation is effected by payment of half in cash and half in livestock (mainly in camels and goats) in the tradition of the Afar that live around the Aba'ala area, which is adjacent to the Christian highlands. This same rule is however implemented differently in other parts of Afar – compensation only through payment of livestock. This disparity in mode of compensation payment has been caused, firstly by the fact that the groups of Afar that neighbour the Christian highlands are poorer than the other Afar who live in the central part of the region and who still possess significant volumes of livestock. Secondly, being nearer to the Christian highlanders who make extensive use of money as a means of transaction, the Afar in Aba'ala have been significantly influenced by their relations with these highlanders. For instance their mechanism of conflict resolution with the highlanders includes the payment of cash as compensation.[13]

Another example is that when an offender is very poor and/or if he is from a relatively poorer clan so that he cannot pay the compensation, the *Asayamara* negotiate so the 'price' of the camel increases.
The above examples challenge the solid assumption of the Afar that the *ADDA* rules are uniformly applied and have not been changed since their construction.

But this conviction of the Afar has a positive implication for the settlement of their intra-Afar disputes. The fact that they believe that the *ADDA* rules don't change and are applicable to every Afar equally, highly influences the acceptance of the rules by the people. This is something that is worth promoting. The erosion of this belief may need a proper functioning of an alternative institution – like the formal judiciary system. But the institution of a properly functioning judiciary system that is accepted by the people will no doubt take time.

---

[13] Yayneshet Tesfay and Kelemework Tafere, *supra* note 4, 42.

Operation of the *ADDA* institution in settling intra-Afar conflicts

The Afar traditionally classify crimes into the following categories:

1. Murder
2. Physical injuries caused by:
    a. Stick
    b. Stone
    c. Knife
    d. Gun
3. Animal killings
    a. Camel
    b. Cow
    c. Ox
    d. Goat
    e. Sheep
    f. Etc.

The Afar emphasize that there are specific recipes for resolving inter-clan conflicts that arise as a result of any of the offences listed above.

Rules and process of solving a murder case

Whenever an intra-Afar murder is committed, concerned elders of the community, the "*Asaya-mara*" that constitute the *ADDA* council, gather and summon the leaders of the clans as soon as the clans of both the murderer and the deceased are identified. The *Asayamara* are often drawn from clans other than those involved in the conflict. Traditionally the *Asayamara* are composed of the leaders of the Damohoita and Seka clans.[14] But currently the *Asayamara* constitute mainly clan leaders and elderly who are believed to be wise and skilled enough to solve complex matters. What is interesting is that the Damohoita still have the power of conducting the last blessing that marks the reconciliation of the disputants and the settlement of the conflict. This is called *Fatiha*. The persons who give the *Fatiha* are supposed to come from sub-clans of the Damohoita clan called Asmerora/Alieto. The council of the *Asayamara* – the *ADDA* council – is called "*Mekabons*" in the local language.

- The pre-verdict stage – Investigation and fact-finding

According to our informants the first step in the traditional judicial procedure is the bringing of ***Waidal***. This is the sacrifice of a camel (or at times a cow) offered by the offending individual's clan to the victim's clan. This is an important step and a precondition for the commencement of the settlement procedure. The Afar allege that the victim will not be buried before sacrificing the

[14] Id., 39.

animal. The provision of *Waidal* confirms that the clan that brought it is officially responsible for the murder and is willing to litigate. If there is no provision of *Waidal* it signifies that the assumed killer has not accepted responsibility.

Following *Waidal*, the *Mekabons* will be engaged in investigating and identifying the real causes and nature of the crime like how the incident took place, the type of weapon used and whether or not it was intentional. The nature or the strength and weakness of the justification for the committed crime - especially with intention - is said to affect the smooth and easy acceptance of the litigation by the members of the deceased clan. But lack of intention does not affect the final verdict on compensation. However, if the murder was intentional it costs the killer and his clan much more to convince the clan of the deceased to come to the *ADDA* litigation. On top of the customary amount of the compensation or blood money, the *Mekabons* decide that an additional amount of 165 birr (equivalent to 247.5 birr) will have to be paid, in the form of camels. This is called *BATIL*, which means additional payment for unfair deed.[15] A period of 40 days '*Moretemta*' is given to finalize the investigation of a murder case. In the meantime clan and family members of the deceased remain under oath that they will not attempt to retaliate.

If the reason for casualty is identified to be an unintentional or accidental crime, the Asayamara will continue to give the final judgment or punishment, which always takes place according to pre-existing rules.

- *The verdict –the Meda*

The *ADDA* always requires that anyone who has committed murder of any kind should pay:

- 3,000 (=4,500 birr) to the family of the deceased. It is common practice that an amount of 300 (= 450 birr) be considered as an amount that has already been spent in the previous stages of the settlement for food and other bureaucratic expenses of the *Asayamara* and the clan leader of the deceased. Therefore, the clan members of the convict will normally be expected to pay only 2,700 (= 4050 birr).
- The latter amount will be divided into two halves. The first half, 1350 (=2050 birr) will be paid in terms of camels (assuming that a pregnant camel costs 50 (=75 birr) and a male one 40 (=60 birr). Therefore, 30-40 camels are commonly paid as a compensation for a single murder. This

[15] **Batil** means unfairness (wrongness) that results in punishment. If a person is convicted of it, he is liable to the following payments: level 1: 6 birr, misbehaving during the *ADDA* procedure; level 2: 18 birr, insulting someone; level 3: 165 birr, if someone sues an offender through the formal institutions without consulting the *ADDA* and if someone killed a person intentionally.

form of payment is called *Fur*. The second half is paid in cash. It is mandatory that the *Fur* is paid before *Fatiha*, while the cash can be paid over a longer period of time at the convenience of the offender. Yayneshet and Kelemework indicated that out of these 30 or 40 camels, one will be given to the clan leader of the deceased.[16]

After all these procedures, the families of both the convict and the deceased will agree and promise not to attempt any retaliation. This is known as "*Fatiha*". *Fatiha* is therefore a peaceful and formal ending of a murder case settlement according to the procedures of the *ADDA*. Our interviewees from both the traditional institutions and the formal judicial system confirmed that after *Fatiha* no Afar attempts to reinitiate the issue nor does he retaliate. This shows a strong compliance to the *ADDA* ruling. What is equally interesting is that the Afar show loyalty to the *ADDA* institution by undermining the formal judicial process. If an Afar files charges in the formal court without going to the *Asayamara*, the convict can sue him for that and they call it *Cafiruna,* which means *'he accused me in the Christian court',* and some of our interviewees mentioned that there is a fine (165 birr) for that. This definitely undermines the workings of the formal court.

During the *Fatiha* a sheep is slaughtered in the presence of all the *Mekabons* (*Asayamara*) as a sign of the achievement of reconciliation.

Failing to accept the final verdict (*Meda*) and declining to offer forgiveness (*Fatiha*) at the inception of the procedures or afterwards is very uncommon. However, in case of such obstinacy, some members of the murderer's clan may assemble to exercise further begging (*Dubarity*). The clan leader would then normally seek to exert pressure to influence the person(s) threatening to take revenge. A person who resorts to retaliation in spite of all these cultural procedures would be denied clan membership and would be an outcast.[17]

Traditionally *Fatiha* has been the last stage of the *ADDA* procedure. But since recent years in the *woreda*, the Mekabons are reporting to the formal judiciary organs (the police, court and woreda administration) about the status of the settlements.

5.2.2. The Clan as a Basic Unit of the Afar

Afar society structures itself around a functional social institution called the clan. The clan performs a lot of social functions. It functions as a centre of a social capital: the famous cooperative sprit of the Afar operates through the clan system. For instance, an Afar has a right to sue another Afar to the clan

[16] Yayneshet Tesfay and Kelemework Tafere, *supra* note 4, 39.
[17] Id., 39-40.

leader for denying him money or some need. Thus the clan functions as an institution that regulates wealth distribution among clan members.

The clan also acts as a guarantee for the individual during times of need and as an effective instrument to apply the verdict of the *ADDA*. For instance, if someone is convicted of murder or something else, the clan is an instrumental institution in the litigation process represented by the clan leader and in applying the verdict (locally called *Meda*).

The clan is a centre of value transfer in Afar.

The most important thing an Afar should know since his childhood is his clan. A person who does not know or who is alien to his clan is exposed to danger. At an early age a child is expected to know the genealogical lines of his father's line. Additionally, he/she learns all the strengths, roles, status or social position, friends and enemies of his clan. The father, elder brothers and/or uncles are responsible for the transfer of values to the child.

Marriage arrangements and issues of dowry are all arranged through the clan. The clan is also a central organ for information exchange, organization of labour and other related mobilization activities.

5.2.3. ABO ESRA – Head of Twenty

ABO ESRA, as the name indicates, is not a native Afar institution. It means the head of twenty people in Tigrigna. It has been introduced to the Afar during the armed struggle of the Tigray People's Liberation Front (TPLF), to politically organize the Afar. This institution has been used for political training and to mobilize for military operations and later for development campaigns like terrace construction, weeding, pest control and road construction.
Currently the Afar use the *ABO ESRA* to manage irrigation water. The water source called MAI – ABA'ALA is managed through this institution. We found this institution interesting since there is a particularly strong concern for water at Aba'ala right now and because it is a small institution that can be controlled easily by the people. We inquired if this institution could also be applied to regulate other sources of water for livestock and for human consumption. Paradoxically, many of our interviewees felt that it was not worth using this institution for other water sources since they believed that there was no water shortage. This is contrary to our observation and to the observation of some experts who work in the area.

Formal Institutions

Dispute resolution in Afar follows a dual approach. With the *ADDA* system being the major mechanism in this regard, the formal dispute resolution structures also exist side by side with this indigenous system. From the discussions held with interviewees in the study area it appears that people usually prefer to resort to the local system rather than to the formal one. Nevertheless, as part of the over all system of governance the formal institutions of the Police, Prosecutor, Sharia Courts and the Regular Courts exist and are functioning in the *woreda*. Each of these institutions is charged with a certain jurisdiction aimed at ensuring observance and enforcement of laws that have their source in formal law making as well as in religious sources. These institutions exist and function both at the federal and regional levels. In the study area, being a part of a member state of the existing federal arrangement, these institutions have been organized as an expression of the decentralized system of governance.

5.2.4. The Police

The institution of the police is part of the formal system of governance that operates in this area. It has been made evident that the participation of this institution at local level (i.e. the study area) is limited in practice to complementing the enforcement of rules and procedures as developed by the local system. As part of the formal system, the police institution is established to undertake tasks of preventing and investigating crime. This role has however been significantly diminished by the long established tradition of local dispute investigation and resolution. The role of the police is thus mainly confined to controlling inter-clan or inter-community clashes that could be fierce and difficult to manage by local mechanisms. Such mode of intervention by the police is the practice in the operational reality in this area while the formal system expects a much higher level of involvement of the police in dealing with disputes. This limited intervention of the police is mainly due to the role of elders, who in many instances substitute the police. The local people believe that the role of the police should not be any bigger than this. Despite what the laws of the nation and the region expect from this institution, the practice and the belief of the people in the study area are that the police are there to complement the function of the traditional governance system.

5.2.5. The Prosecutor

The office of the prosecutor among other things has the task of framing and instituting charges of criminal offence and brings it to the attention of courts on behalf of the public to ensure conviction and punishment of offenders. This institution exists and functions also in the Aba'ala area of the Afar region. Despite its existence in the formal system, the prosecutorial institution has a role that is much more limited than what is expected of it under ordinary circumstances. This is mainly due to the fact that the practice of settlement of disputes in this area is guided primarily by a clan-based approach and by rulings of the Afar elders that consequently significantly substitute the role of the prosecutorial institution.

5.2.6. The Sharia Courts

The Sharia Court system is a system that functions on the basis of religious sources of authority drawn from the Quran and other related sources. In Ethiopia, law has recognized the Sharia Courts since 1942. Unlike the jurisdiction of Sharia Courts in some countries, the main function of Sharia Courts in Ethiopia is to hear and determine disputes in civil matters (disputes related to marriage, divorce and inheritance) and no criminal jurisdiction is accorded to these courts. The Sharia Court is therefore a body with judicial authority to hear and determine disputes that arise in these specific areas with reference to religious sources of authority. Structurally the Sharia Courts are organized in three tiers, i.e. from *woreda* to the Supreme Court. All levels of the Sharia Courts are manned by Kadis (judges) appointed for their knowledge of the Quran and other related sources of the Sharia; and clan membership is not a requirement for this position. Compared to the regular courts, Sharia Courts have demonstrated a stronger presence in the Afar area. Jurisdiction of the Sharia Courts is confined to matters related to marriage, divorce and succession between Muslims. Its decisions are equally enforceable as rulings of the regular courts. The Afar regard the Sharia Courts and *ADDA* as timeless institutions that have existed unchanged for generations and that will remain operational in the future. This view, coupled with the dominance of the Muslim religion in the area, indicates a significant role for these courts in the actual dispute resolution exercise. Statistical data from the Aba'ala *Woreda* shows that in this *woreda* the Sharia Court deals with up to 100 cases a year. In handling these cases it often faces an overlap with the *ADDA* system and sometimes it claims jurisdiction over particular cases that arise in the regular court. The dispute resolution mechanism in this area therefore represents a diversified feature with the *ADDA*, Clan Elders, the regular court and the Sharia Courts exercising their respective roles.

5.2.7. The Regular Courts

These are part of the formal state structure and function based on the judicial authority vested in them by major laws of the country. The tasks of the regular courts are carried out by judges appointed by the regional council and on the basis of laws enacted by the formal system of law making. These institutions are not supposed to make reference to the unwritten customary or religious sources of law. However, in actual practice, particularly in this area, the regular courts in a number of instances tend to encourage disputants to settle their disputes outside the regular court system. Local disputants also usually tend to take their cases to the local institutions rather than to the regular courts. It is only in rare circumstances that individual disputants prefer to file their cases in the regular courts. Disputants who prefer to resolve cases through the regular courts rather than through the *ADDA*, will be considered in breach of the traditional system and siding with Christianity; hence these people could face social sanctions. In the Afar region the regular courts are organized in three tiers from the *woreda* to the Supreme Court level. Unlike the neighbouring regions of Amhara and Tigray the small-scale claims courts (Social Courts) are yet non-existent in the region. The latter courts that are organized at *kebele* level, the lowest administrative unit within the current administrative structure, play a key role in the administration of justice in the regions where they are made functional. They have an important place within the justice system in general because they provide the outlet for the disposition of a substantial number of disputes that arise in the daily life of the community. In the *woreda* bordering the study area (Enderta *Woreda*, in Tigray region) for instance, statistics show that over a six-month period, the Social Courts in nine *kebele* of this *woreda* had disposed of 233 small-scale civil matters and petty contraventions. This indicates that the Social Courts could be important institutions for this area, as they provide easy access to justice with their simple and flexible procedures. Owing to the stronger ties of the Afar to the *ADDA* and the Sharia Court systems, dispute resolution by regular courts is believed to have remained less effective in this area.

6. DISCUSSION

6.1. Comparison

The field studies we conducted in the area revealed that there is a great deal of interface between the functions of the formal and traditional systems of governance. The level of recognition the traditional system has acquired on the ground further strengthens this fact. The interviews conducted in the area appear to show that the traditional system of governance is embedded in the Afar tradition and that it is regarded as expeditious and fair. It is noteworthy that the supreme law of the land also recognizes the parallel existence of the traditional and the formal systems of governance. Owing to the fact that the traditional system of governance is embedded in the Afar tradition and that these institutions are recognized by the Ethiopian constitution, the two systems are operating side by side. Their being operating that way has thus caused an interface between their respective roles, which can be illustrated by some examples as indicated hereunder.

6.2. Criminal Offence, Punishment, Compensation and Appeal

The formal system provides a long list of commissions or omissions classified as offences and determines a respective punishment for each. The *ADDA* system on the other hand, though unwritten, provides a list of acts that are considered contraventions to the customary rules and has an impressive system of imposing liability for the offences, where the amount and the mode of calcula-

tion seem to be well known to an ordinary Afar. However the list of acts that are considered offences is mainly restricted to acts related to causing physical injury, murder and resource management. In a similar fashion to the formal system, rulings of the Afar *ADDA* institutions are subject to review by appeal. An Afar dissatisfied with the ruling of the *Asayamara* can appeal for review by an *Asayamara* from another (any) part of the Afar region. The verdict they render might end up upholding the previous decision against which the appeal is made or instructing the *Asayamara* to reconsider and decide the case differently. The interesting aspect of this appeal process is that the appellant will face a penalty if the appeal is found to be without merit, which is not the case in the formal system.
In the formal system crime is individual and it is only the offender who stands liable for it. This is different in the traditional system as it renders the clan of the offender collectively liable for the commission. Interestingly enough it is only the patrilineal line from the offender's side that stands liable for the act. The calculation of the compensation the offender's clan should pay is calculated differently, where the rate for a female victim is half of the amount that could be awarded in the case of a male victim. In the Afar tradition a case has to be settled between the clans of the offender and the victim. In the absence of it the case will remain outstanding even when the offender has served the sentence prescribed by the formal laws. The case will be considered settled only after it passes through the proceedings before the *Asayamara* and the *Asayamara* have said *Fatiha*. No concept of limitation of period exists as is the case in the formal system. The two clans have to settle the case even when the offender has served/is serving a long formal sentence.

Compensation is awarded in the formal system for damages caused as a result of fault by the person liable or without fault in the case of individuals who have the responsibility for persons under their guardianship or for a property they own. The amount is not fixed; it rather varies depending on the nature of the case and the degree of harm sustained by the victim in which sometimes a person might not be obliged to pay compensation while facing punishment for the same act. Punishment and compensation are thus different in the sense that they can be applied either separately or concurrently against the same person and for the same act. In the *ADDA* system punishment and compensation for an offence are merged in a fixed amount to be paid. Compensation for damage is the main instrument of conflict resolution accompanied by forgiveness. All damage is compensated by pre-existing rules for compensation. This compensation and sense of forgiveness are believed to bring lasting reconciliation and better social harmony among the disputants. But it leaves offenders physically unpunished.

Though the Afar social organization and the tradition of revenge♦ puts pressure on the offenders to strictly adhere to the judgments and advice of the *ADDA* institution (regretting what they have done), the compensation based punishment does not recommend physical punishment or exclusion to punish the offender. Theoretically, if the culprit is from a strong and dominant clan while the victim is from a weak clan that cannot take revenge, there is a possibility that the compensation may not prevent a second crime. But all of our interviewees strongly objected to this idea, saying that the economic pressure that the family of the culprit and his clan faces is beyond tolerance to commit a second murder. In addition the *Asayamara* had to undergo a severe begging and reconciliation process that places another social and religious pressure on the part of the culprit – because he knows that all this hassle is because of him and religiously the Quran instructs that a person who kills another person is a sinner.

The amount (half of the fixed payment rate) which is to be paid in kind by camels and goats (in case of murder) is very heavy by the standard of the pastoralist Afar. Interviewees indicated that the payments imposed by the *ADDA* for offences and damages are much harsher for an Afar than what he might face if it was in the formal system. Though addressed in a way that merges the compensation and punishment, the liabilities that an offender's clan might face in the *ADDA* system could be as much a deterrent as the formal system.

6.3. Institutional Interface

It is evident that in exercising their respective roles both systems face an interface quite often. Primarily the Afar believe that the *ADDA* system is the ideal institutional set up to govern their local affairs and the formal system should only function to supplement the function of the traditional system. They claim that it is a system that has been established and has remained unchanged since their great-great grandparents and that it has proved to be more effective (though the effectiveness of the *ADDA* system is contested by some). This attitude is rather strengthened by the fact that the administrators also tend to use this channel when the disputes/clashes are inter-clan and fierce. It has been experienced in different instances that the formal government organs also leave cases for settlement by the local institutions. In a number of instances this has even been the case in clashes that involve highlanders.

Our investigation has highlighted that there is a kind of tacit recognition of the role of the traditional institutions by the formal institutions. The prosecutor or the police usually don't allow the withdrawal of a case that has reached their hands but they don't tend to investigate alleged offences that they happen to

♦ When an Afar killed another and escaped or did not submit himself to the verdict of the *ADDA*, a relative of the victim kills any relative of the culprit who is related to the father's line of the killer.

know of in the absence of any complaint. The formal system expects its organs to deal with cases that reached them on complaint or in the absence of complaint. In this area however the formal institutions seem to have modified their role by confining themselves to dealing with cases that reach them on complaint and to restoring peace and order during fierce inter-clan clashes alone. It is even believed that the formal institutions sometimes allow cases that have already reached them to be settled through the local mechanisms. They don't follow the provisions of the law in a very legalistic way; rather they try to accommodate the local system that in many instances could not be accepted with the legalistic approach. The interface between the formal and traditional systems is further complicated by the fact that formal, religious and traditional systems of governance exist side by side in the study area. The Sharia Courts operate with the powers vested in them by the formal law and having the Quran and other related sources as bases of authority. The fact that followers of Islam dominantly inhabit the area makes the role of the Sharia Courts important and that gives way to overlap of jurisdiction with the traditional as well as the formal system.

7. CONCLUSION

Dispute resolution in Afar follows a dual approach. The *ADDA* system is the major mechanism in this regard and the formal dispute resolution structures exist side by side with this indigenous system. According to the long established local tradition, Afar disputants with their mutual consent will first try to resolve their dispute through mediation by local elders. In the absence of agreement they will take their case to the clan leader and when that happens to be non-acceptable to either side one may take the case to the attention of the *Asayamara.*

The indigenous local governance institutions in Afar include the clan leaders, *Gereb*, *Abo Esra* and *ADDA*. According to the tradition in the study area, these institutions are charged with separate tasks.

The *Gereb* is an institution handling cases that involve an Afar and a highlander/non-Afar/a Christian party. In the operational reality there is quite often an interface between the *Gereb* and the formal institutions. In the highland parts of Tigray, that border the study area, disputes - especially criminal offences - are handled by the formal institutions. This however poses difficulty when such cases involve an Afar. In that case, especially the Afar and sometimes the highlanders as well prefer to settle their matter by the *Gereb* as this is part of their joint tradition. However this has never been easy as it clearly contradicts the criminal law principle that obliges the responsible state organ to ensure prosecution of a criminal offence on behalf of the public.

Abo Esra is another local institution in this regard but is an institution of a distinctively different background compared to the other local institutions, which are mainly based in the Afar tradition. This institution is believed to have a political background related to the involvement of Afar in the TPLF led political movement against the military regime. Initially it was used mainly for mobilizing the local people for political movement, community work and food aid distribution. Despite its origin, later this institution, to some extent, began to function as part of the local governance system. This has been mainly demonstrated in administering water use for small-scale irrigation in Aba'ala town that is fully dependent on a small water source located in the north end of the town. It seems that, pertaining to the arid nature of the area, the *Abo Esra*, even if it originates in the highlands, has emerged as an important institution. It should however be noted that the operation of the *Abo Esra* is limited to Aba'ala town's irrigation water use only. Water use is one major source of dispute in this area. Although our interviewees reiterated that, since all the resources in Afar belong to all Afar, water and pasture are not as such sources of dispute, they also indicated that the local elders have a certain role in determining prioritizing water use whenever a scarcity of the resource is experienced. It is therefore clear that the Afar local governance system has a role in regulating matters related to water use. In the belief of the Afar in the study area, the traditional governance system should have the ultimate say in every matter that involves Afar. The formal system of governance is not that important except for settling fierce clashes that could go out of control in the absence of its involvement. As has been discussed above, the Afar traditional system seems quite well recognized by its subjects. From the discussions held with interviewees in the study area it appears that members of the community usually prefer to resort to the local system rather than to the formal one. Nevertheless as part of the over all system of governance the Police, Prosecutor, Sharia Courts and the Regular Courts exist and function in the region as part of the formal governance system. Each of these institutions is charged with a jurisdiction aimed at ensuring observance and enforcement of laws that have their source in the formal law making as well as in religious and customary sources. These institutions exist and function both at the federal and regional level. In the study area, being a part of a member state of the existing federal arrangement, these institutions have been organized as an expression of the decentralized system of governance.

The Afar people comply with the decisions of the *ADDA*, but they don't take the final rulings of the formal courts seriously and they don't consider them as final, if they are not supplemented by the *ADDA*'s *Fatiha*. Even after 20 years of imprisonment, the members of the clans of the deceased and the murderer negotiate to end the hostility through the *ADDA* procedures. Hence, there is a double punishment for the offender if the formal institutions penalize him. Retaliation can even be initiated after many generations if the issue is not settled through the *ADDA* procedures.

In Afar free grazing is a practice. This practice is damaging the resource base of the Afar. Interestingly most of our informants recognized that the free grazing practice is harmful and they recognize the need for the introduction of some form of range management techniques. *Asayamara* interviewees believe that they can make a difference in the current land use system. They understand that free grazing is causing a problem to their rangelands and agree with the presence of rangeland management. On the other hand these *Asayamara* see that the Afar tradition of 'sharing what one has' and lack of full awareness on resource management could be a bottleneck for immediate intervention. But the *Asayamara* fully subscribe to the idea that they can contribute to educating the people to introduce new management practices, which they think is possible given their traditional influence. They have a high social and political status, which can be exploited for the good of the Afar. This idea has also been confirmed by most of our interviewees from the formal institutions.

8. RECOMMENDATIONS

Creating an institutional interface

There is a need to create a transitional interface (institution) between the formal judicial system and the traditional one, till the date people comply with the decisions of the formal system. This interface can be created by legitimizing the *ADDA* institution through the formation of a semi-formal *ADDA*. In this institution, it is wise to use most of the important values that Afar believe and practice, while adding some element of the formal system. This will facilitate a smooth transition of the Afar wisdom to the enriched formal institutions.

We have mentioned that institutions like the Social Courts that operate in the highlands are non-existent in the Afar area. We believe that the *ADDA* institution, with some modification, can serve the function of these institutions.
This institution, however, should avoid the nuisance of some practices of the *ADDA* institution. A case in point is that it should discourage gender discrimination and make appropriate changes in the concept of penalty and compensation. But since these values are deep-rooted in the tradition of the Afar, they should be approached systematically and handled with care.

Natural Resource Management

As mentioned above, the Afar are not ignorant of what is happening to their rangelands. They agree that free grazing is a bad practice that is facilitating the rapid deterioration of their pasture and water. Hence introducing appropriate technologies with proper extension work is of paramount importance. But they practise free grazing to prevent hostility and resulting conflict. Given the Afar attitude of respecting their *Asayamara* and their value of abiding by the decisions of the *ADDA* we suggest that the *Asayamara* be trained to positively influence and train their people to bring attitudinal change and introduce workable range management practices.

Documentation

Afar rules and values are all oral. Despite the fact that they think that their values are well preserved through oral communication, it is imminent that they will be eroded fast given the introduction of communication technologies and given the over all social transformation. Hence there is a need for documentation of these values not only for the sake of documenting them but also to contribute to the local development that bases itself on local realities. Development should benefit from local culture and local realities if it is to sustain itself.

11. The Protection of Land Rights in Ethiopia

Montgomery Wray Witten•

1. LAND RIGHTS: DELINEATION

For many people, land rights and their protection are central to life. But what are 'land rights'? More particularly, in the setting of this seminar, what human rights are recognized *to* land, or *related to* land?

The international farmers' movement La Via Campesina[1] has often articulated the need for a human right *to* land, particularly for subsistence farmers. Just as clearly they have demonstrated that there is none recognized internationally.

Instead, what we find are a variety of general and specific (e.g. for women[2]) human rights *related* to land (or the more ambiguous 'home' or 'property'[3] which may or may not include land). These international rights related to land are all in the nature of more general human rights to due process of law,[4] equal protection of law[5] and non-discrimination[5]. That is, if a person has land or if some right to land *is* recognized (as when a government-sponsored land redistribution occurs), then the right to land should not be taken, lost or denied without due process and equal protection of law, and no other recognized rights should be dependent on whether the person has land or not.

However, domestic land rights are rarely affected by international instruments. We must look to domestic systems. In Ethiopia, both by incorporation of international agreements (Article 9.4) and inclusion of specific provisions (often identical in language to the international instruments), the current constitution[7] includes both general human rights related to land, i.e., to due process, equal protection and non-discrimination (Article 25), and specific rights for women (Article 35.5) and other groups (Article 40).

• Start-up Dean of Mekelle University Law Faculty until 2003. E-mail: wrayw2@yahoo.com

[1] *See*, <www.viacampesina.org>.

[2] Convention on Elimination of All Forms of Discrimination Against Women (CEDAW) Article 14.2(g).

[3] Universal Declaration of Human Rights (UDHR), Articles 12 and 17, respectively.

[4] UDHR Art. 8, 17; International Convention on Civil and Political Rights (ICCPR) Art. 17, 26.

[5] UDHR Art. 7, 17; ICCPR Art. 17, 26.

[6] UDHR Articles 2, 7, 17; ICCPR Art. 17, 26.

[7] Proclamation No. 1/1995. It should be remembered that the Amharic version is the official version (Article 106).

But, quite unusually among the nations of the world, Ethiopia's constitution also grants actual rights *to* rural[8] land (Article 40).

Of course, as soon as that is said, it is necessary to ask what such a right entails. And, more generally, in order to provide the most elementary basis for this paper, we must distinguish between different 'rights' in land. For the bizarre and diverse nature of land rights, and the ability to fragment them in novel ways, appears to be limited only by failure of human imagination. In addition, each of these rights may be held by one or more different parties. For example, the right to use the surface[9] may be owned by one party, granted conditionally to another, leased on to several others, future interests assigned to yet others, and taken at any time in whole or part by the state. Thus, what is sometimes called the 'bundle' of land rights is, in almost all cases, fragmented and distributed over many holders so that an individual's rights in a particular parcel of land are actually quite restricted and limited by the rights of the state and other parties. Conflicts between all those holders of rights are, of course, common.

Similarly, the current laws establishing and allocating land rights in Ethiopia distribute those rights among various holders. Most fundamentally, the Ethiopian Constitution places certain rights in the hands of the state:

> "*The right to ownership of rural and urban land, as well as of all natural resources, is exclusively vested in the State and in the peoples of Ethiopia.* (Article 40.3)

But then reserves to three classes of people specific rights to land:

> *40.4. Ethiopian peasants have the right to obtain land without payment and the protection against eviction from their possession. The implementation of this provision shall be specified by law.*
> *40.5. Ethiopian pastoralists have the right to free land for grazing and cultivation as well as the right not to be displaced from their own lands. The implementation shall be specified by law.*
> *40.6. Without prejudice to the right of Ethiopian Nations, Nationalities, and Peoples to the ownership of land, government shall ensure the right of private investors to the use of land on the basis of payment arrangements established by law. Particulars shall be determined by law.*"

---

[8] This paper focuses on rural and peri-urban land because urban land is under a different administrative system and almost all land in Ethiopia falls outside the urban category.
[9] Never mind rights to use the air above and subsurface, or the right to decide what use may be made of any of these – likely to be held by a local government.

It is important to note that each of these rights is hedged by the last provision in each paragraph, that the particulars of each right are to be determined by law. To date, these constitutional provisions have been further delineated by two federal laws[10] and the different laws and regulations of each of the federal states (see below).

By the federal land laws, the federal government's constitutional authority to proclaim laws related to land (Article 51.5) has been partially delegated, within specific though broad guidelines, to the states.[11] This has allowed significant differences in state laws. The constitution also allocates the authority to administer land and other natural resources in accordance with federal laws directly to the states (Article 52.6).

But, so far, how much the basic constitutional rights may legally be modified by such laws is quite untested in the courts. For example, the right of children to inherit rural land has been both specifically acknowledged in the successive federal land laws[12] and subject to limitations in state laws[13]. As a specific example, the laws of Tigray state both assure and limit inheritance of land. The state's goal is clearly to balance increased certainty of an adequate payback period and, thus, the holder's investment in land,[14] with the social welfare principle that the most needy descendants obtain the parents' very limited land. The need to balance such competing policy principles is prevalent in land rights legislation, but when eventually challenged the basic right may be determined by the courts to limit policy choices.

---

[10] Proclamation No. 89/1997, Rural Land Administration Proclamation of The Federal Democratic Republic of Ethiopia (FDRE); and Proclamation No. 456/2005, FDRE Rural Land Administration and Land Use Proclamation.

[11] As can be seen by the fact that three states, Amhara, Oromia and Tigray, passed laws before authorized, the first federal law was clearly an effort to catch up with state initiatives.

[12] Proclamation No. 89/1997, Rural Land Administration Proclamation of The Federal Democratic Republic of Ethiopia (FDRE), Article 2.3; and Proclamation No. 456/2005, FDRE Rural Land Administration and Land Use Proclamation, Article 8.5.

[13] State laws and regulations vary greatly. Tigray state adopted Proclamation No. 23/1997, Rural Land Utilization Proclamation of The Tigray National Regional State, replaced in 2004, and Rural Land Utilization, Investment, Agricultural and Natural Resources Development Regulation, Proclamation No. 15/2001/02, also with amendments. State proclamations issued before federal devolution were legitimised by the federal land laws inclusion of "savings clauses" that recognize earlier state laws that conform to specific guidelines.

[14] Gebremedhin, B., J. Pender, *et al*, Policies for Sustainable Land Management in the Highlands of Tigray, Northern Ethiopia, in: *EPTD Workshop Summary Paper* No. 14, IFPRI/ILRI, Washington/Nairobi; D. Atwood, Land registration in Africa: the impact on agricultural production, 18(5) *World Development* 659-671 (1990); R. Barrows and M. Roth, Land Tenure and Investment in African Agriculture: Theory and Evidence, 28 (2) *The Journal of Modern African Studies* 265-297 (1990).

2. PROTECTION OF LAND RIGHTS: A SCHEMATIC INTRODUCTION

From the Land in Africa Conference,[15] we may take some lessons: economy, history, perspective, alignment of interests and structural details all matter in the protection of land rights. In Tigray state, northern Ethiopia, where the detailed research on which this paper is based has been centered and in the literature concerning land rights and our less in-depth research in other parts of Ethiopia, we have found the same to be true.

A) Despite relatively rapid economic growth since 1991, Ethiopia remains one of the very poorest nations on earth and, within Ethiopia, Tigray state is the poorest area of the settled rural population. Ethiopia has 70 million people and a Human Development Index placing it 170th out of 177 nations (UNDP 2005). Tigray has 4 million people, of whom 85% are smallholder subsistence farmers; of these 75%, the largest proportion in any settled farming area in Ethiopia, do not have enough land to produce a living.

B) Focusing on land rights, one of the striking differences between Ethiopia and other nations is its recent history. The current forms of land rights and the systems for protecting them, exist today as the most recent iteration of a sequence of radical changes. Ancient customary laws were amended by, *inter alia*, Emperor Haile Selassie's mid-twentieth century efforts at modernization through introduction of a Constitution and a new Civil Code, and then again by the *Derg* (the Soviet Union-backed military dictatorship from 1974 to 1991) Constitution and proclamations. The latter nationalized all land, redistributed the majority of rural land, and, in the process, created new forms of land rights and, quite probably, extinguished almost all former land rights[16]. If we were to consider the protection of land rights during that transformation period, we would find, particularly from the perspective of the establishment, many people's land rights badly abused.[17] But today – thirty years after the

---

[15] J. Quan, S. Tan and C. Toulmin, Land in Africa: Market Asset or secure livelihood?, Proceedings and summary of conclusions from the Land in Africa Conference held in London November 8-9, 2004 (2005).

[16] The Provisional Military Government of Ethiopia (1975), Proclamation No.31 of 1975, A Proclamation to Provide for the Public Ownership of Rural Lands, Addis Ababa. Whether the "extinguished" rights to interests in land might be revived, either politically or through judicial action, is unknown. Efforts in other countries, from Kenya to the USA, have had very mixed results. In addition, for example, some villages in Tigray have reallocated land to the church (e.g., in Felig Daro *tabia*, Tigray state, a plot of traditionally irrigated land that is leased to a local farmer each year by auction), perhaps reducing pressure to reinstating prior rights.

[17] In addition, the *Derg* prohibited the renting out of land, and other transactions (sales, mortgages, sharecropping and hiring in labour) were severely restricted. The current FDRE Constitution reinstates some (renting land in and out, sharecropping, and hiring in labour) but not all (sales and mortgages are still prohibited) of these rights. There has been some debate about how extensive the changes really were: H. Marcus, *A History of Ethiopia* (Berkeley: University of California, 1994).

Derg transformation – the problems entailed by overlapping historical and regional land tenure systems in other nations[18] are relatively mild in Ethiopia.

C) There are many perspectives from which the success of a land rights protection system may be judged quite differently, e.g., those of the poor, rich, rural or urban citizens, as well as the administrators', politicians and 'disinterested' observers. But the perspective of the economic historian Douglass North,[19] in terms of institutions, both formal and informal, provides particularly penetrating insights to the protection of land rights.

Simply put, North uses the word 'institutions' to mean 'the rules of the game', rather than organizations, with formal rules including constitution, laws and regulations and informal rules including a variety of other rule-like constraints on behaviour, such as customs, traditions and even habits. Of particular importance is the finding that formal rules are relatively easy to change while informal rules are much harder. Using these concepts, 'administrative discretion' may be understood as one important place where formal and informal rules meet, sometimes producing innovative solutions to unforeseen problems, as intended, but also providing fertile grounds for various forms of abuse of power.

D) Alignment of interests is not always possible. To demonstrate this, let us consider rural Tigray,[20] where demand far outstrips available land. Past land redistributions – in some villages in Tigray as many as a dozen times between 1974 and 1989, 'trying to get it right' – created uncertainty, undercut investment in land and created hard feelings. The land registration and certification undertaken in the mid-90s were desired by farmers to clearly mark the official end of redistributions.

But, when massive land redistributions were stopped, access to land suddenly changed from primarily[21] village allocation to mostly family allocation. And, because family land holdings were already too small, many young people reaching the age when they should receive access to rural land found none available either from their family or the village. They saw registration and cer-

---

[18] E.g., B. Cousins and A. Claassens document the complicated and contentious results in South Africa: B. Cousins and A. Claassens, *More than simply 'socially embedded': recognizing the distinctiveness of African Land rights,* Keynote address, Montpellier, May 17-19, 2006.

[19] D. North, *Institutions,Institutional Change and Economic Performance* (Cambridge: Cambridge University Press, 1990).

[20] There is evidence from family land holding size that the conditions in other areas of Ethiopia are not as pressured: Ethiopian Economic Association/Ethiopian Economic Policy Research Institute (EEA/EEPRI), *Land Tenure and Agricultural Development in Ethiopia*, Addis Ababa (2002); Mersha, G. and wa Githinji, M., Untying the Gordian Knot: The Question of Land Reform in Ethiopia, *ISS/UNDP Land, Poverty and Public Action Policy Paper* No. 9 (2005).

[21] As discussed below, some land also still returns to the village local government and is available for distribution to adults returning to the village and youths coming of age.

tification as the end of any possibility of obtaining land and made their disquiet known.

Their demand for land, together with improved malaria control, eventually formed the primary motive force behind the government's recent opening of unsettled land along Ethiopia's western border to new voluntary settlements. In this way, over time, the alignment of interests has evolved and, by some measures, improved, but not without large social changes and costs.

E) Comparison of the Tigray land rights protection efforts with the subsequent efforts of the Amhara state to implement a similar program illuminates how systemic differences arise. As is more fully described below, the 'Tigray Model' of land rights preservation is embedded in the village local government. When the Amhara state subsequently began a similar system, fresh in the minds of the citizens were the more recent (1996/1997, compared to 1989 in Tigray) and probably punitive[22] land redistributions that had left many people afraid of the local governments that had administered them. Therefore,[23] the administrative portion of the Amhara state land rights protection system was set up as an independent line organization, intentionally removing land issues from the grasp of local government. Whether this change in the 'Tigray Model' will be followed in Tigray is not clear. Some of the new parallel structure has recently been put in place in Tigray, but the benefits of the system operating through the local government, described below, are also well appreciated.

More generally, this is but one structural difference among a very large possible number.[24] Still, though land rights are handled in very different ways in different nations,[25] all land rights protection systems seem to entail a combina-

---

[22] A. Hoben, *Ethiopian Land Tenure Revisited: Continuity, Change and Contradictions,* a paper presented at the IDR Conference on Land Issues, April 6-7, Addis Ababa (2001); Y. Adal, *Rural land holdings readjustment in West Gojam, Amhara region,* a paper presented at the Workshop on Access to Land and Resource Management in Ethiopia, organized by the land tenure project of Addis Ababa University, Nov. 28-29, Addis Ababa (1997); Debele, B., *Review of Land Distribution Procedures in Tigrai and Amhara regions and Proposals for Study in Oromia region, Part I – Review of Experiences,* a paper for the Land Use Planning and Resource Management Project in Oromia Region, GTZ, Addis Ababa (1997); S. Ege, The Promised Land: The Amhara Land Redistribution of 1997*, Working Papers on Ethiopian Development* No. 12, Norwegian University of Science and Technology, Center for Environment and Development, Trondheim (1997).

[23] Personal communication, Legal Advisor to the President of Amhara state, February 2005.

[24] The definition of 'rural land administration' in the current federal land law recognizes this: "… means a process whereby rural land holding security is provided, land use planning is implemented, disputes between rural land holders are resolved and the rights and obligations of any rural land holder are enforced, and information on farm plots and grazing land holders are gathered, analyzed and supplied to users." Proclamation 456/2005, Section 2.2.

[25] The current efforts just within the European Union to reduce institutional barriers to land transactions has also found this. Personal interview with UK member of the Commission, February 2006. Official websites of nations and states are particularly useful for understanding the different func-

tion of institutions and organizations in the following functionally defined niches. We call this an Ecology of Land Rights Protection:[26]

- *Identification* of a piece of land: This may be done with simple (and often cheap) or sophisticated (and usually more expensive) technologies. For example, a piece of land within a small community may be defined simply by the name of the holder or the names of the neighbours; it may be marked on the ground (e.g. with natural landmarks, stone walls, steal pins or fabricated monuments); or it may be described with various types of more or less accurate measurements so that the land can be located on the ground when there is a dispute.
- *Creation* of rights: Over time, various rights in the piece of land are created and allocated to individuals, groups, the state and other levels of government. Various social institutions and organizations create the initial rights and the many limitations on them (e.g. royal or state grants, federal and state laws, local land-use plans, community bylaws or even customs) and their allocation. Cognisance of all sources of rights is important if their interaction is to be predictable.
- *Transformation* of rights: Changes in the initial rights and the person or persons or organizations holding them, occur through private intentional transactions (e.g. sales or leases) but also through more complex transactions (e.g. enactment of new laws, government regulation or takings, or adjudication of divorce or inheritance or incompetence or dissolution) accomplished through one, or some combination of, forums – legislative, administrative or judicial; government or private sector; local and community-based or distant and centralized, cheap or costly.
- *Preservation* of evidence of the original rights and the transformations (documentary or witnesses): For example, the original of documents, or a copy or certified summary, may be lodged in collections (one or more, publicly accessible or not), kept safe from natural elements and human tampering, and, often, helpfully indexed by the names of the actors, the dates of the transactions or events, the piece(s) of land affected, or all of these. The collection may be entrusted to the interested parties, the state, private enterprise, or a combination. Preserving the evidence of aging witnesses is more difficult.
- *Registration* of 'title': The rights held by various parties in the piece of land may[27] be recorded in some form. But it is essential to understand that 'title' is a legal conclusion, based on available evidence, interpreted in light of current rules – a conclusion that may be in error or, even

---

tions of the essential components, e.g., http://www.ros.gov.uk/index.html (Scotland); http://www.landregistry.gov.uk.html (England and Wales).

[26] The Ecology relies heavily on: Haile, M., W. Witten, *et al*, Research Report 2, Land Registration in Tigray, Northern Ethiopia, *Securing Land Rights in Africa Series,* IIED, London (2005).

[27] As an example, apparently only about 30% of English land is so registered, and even that is often registered in ways that hide the true owners.

though never actually in error, may change from time to time as a result of changes in the rules (e.g. a wife's rights to her husband's property on his death changed by a new law) or in legal reasoning (e.g. a new local government land-use plan, or judicial abandonment of prior reasoning), or the ever-occurring transformations resulting from births, deaths and divorces. Keeping the records of conclusions about title up-to-date is a key element of such systems if trust in the accuracy of the recorded conclusions is to be fostered. It may be accomplished by placing the burden on interested private parties, disinterested private organizations (e.g. for-profit title insurance companies or otherwise insured legal experts in the USA), some part of government, or some combination (e.g. Ghana).

- *Assurance* for reliance on system errors: Insurance, or some other guarantee of, or mechanism for providing compensation or rectification is often provided for those who rely on what turn out to be errors in the system. Sometimes the compensation mechanism is provided by government, sometimes by private insurers; sometimes government does not compensate but provides a different solution – e.g., redistribution; and sometimes there is no recourse at all.
- *Protection* of land rights: Protection rests on the foundation of the other parts of the ecology. The functions may be accomplished through a single specialized body or a combination of informal and formal forums; administrative or judicial; government or private sector; local and community-based or distant and centralized, cheap or costly; it may be done periodically and all at once or episodically and individually. Without real and effective protection, land rights loose much of their certainty and, often, their value.

Thus, the environment in which land rights must be protected is complex, populated by interconnected domestic organizations and institutions, with quite variable configurations. It is also common – even in highly developed, long-standing systems – for one piece or another of the system to be in transition from one type to another in order, ostensibly, to improve it from one perspective or another. Often, however, such changes benefit some at the expense of others.[28] All of these statements are true of the complex Ethiopian land rights protection ecology, including as it does, federal, state and local levels.

[28] N. Kanji, L. Cotula *et al.*, *Research Report 1, Can Land Registration serve the Poor and Marginalized Groups? Summary Report*, IIED, London (2005).

3. PROTECTION OF LAND RIGHTS IN ETHIOPIA: FINDINGS

Mekelle University's recent land rights research, with IIED and DfID[29], was concentrated in the state of Tigray, where systematic post-*Derg* land rights protection reforms were first undertaken in Ethiopia. The resulting 'Tigray Model' of universal rural land registration and certification has subsequently been the starting point for all the other states' current efforts,[30] though many changes and improvements are underway in those other states, and in Tigray, as well, in part as a result of the feedback from Mekelle University's research.

What did we find? Too much to report in a short paper like this, but examples of various strengths and weaknesses can be given. The most general finding is that since 1989[31] a multi-faceted and largely effective effort has been made throughout Tigray to create a configuration of inexpensive, local, practical institutions and organizations to protect land rights, one that could be and was put in place across the state expeditiously, uniformly and with available resources.

It doesn't take very long to describe that remarkable achievement, compared with the pages and pages of more extensively detailed problems that follow, but in large measure the effort has been quite successful when considered as a comprehensive system. In terms of the ecology of land rights protection, we find:

Land Identification: When we look at the technology selected in Tigray for identification of a piece of land on registration forms and personal certificates, we find very low cost, locally available and locally well-understood choices: land is quantified using traditional measures (time required to plow) and demarcated primarily by the names of the family head, four neighbours, and a neighbourhood within the village. Sometimes physical markers (most often stones) are also used. When large-scale registration was first undertaken anew (1996-1998), minimally trained high-school students (fulfilling their civilian national service) assisted. But the primary evidence of land rights came from local people, confirmed in open general meetings.

These choices of technology, understandably cost-based though they are, have consequences for the protection of land rights: In the positive, such land descriptions were and continue to be easy, cheap and quick to generate uniformly

---

[29] Mekelle University, Mekelle, Tigray, Ethiopia; International Institute for Environment and Development, London; funded by the United Kingdom's Department for International Development. For the full report, *see* Haile, M., W. Witten, *et al*, *supra* note 26.

[30] Adenew, B. and Abdi, F., Research Report 3, Land Registration in Amhara Region, Ethiopia, *Securing Land Rights in Africa Series,* IIED, London (2005).

[31] And before 1989 in areas controlled earlier by the Tigray People's Liberation Front (TPLF) during its struggle against the *Derg*.

across the state,[32] and in most every-day situations, serve adequately. But, in the negative, such simple descriptions are of little use in the most common land disputes when they do occur – encroachments (e.g., plowing or grazing) by one farmer into the land of a neighbour. Evidence from the traditional witnesses who laid out the parcels is, therefore, still necessary when disputes over plot boundaries arise.

This, in turn, we found, has two corollaries. First, it corresponds to a difference in the way men and women tend to think about their land title certificates: though men initially sought registration to mark the end of redistributions, and expect plot-incursion conflicts, they do not generally fear challenges to their 'title'. As a result, after the initial recording of title, the language men used to refer to their registration and certificates changed and did not reflect a continuation of high valuation. By contrast, women feel most threatened on fundamental title issues (and recent evidence indicates that they are, indeed, targeted in land title disputes more often than men, primarily because of their more limited defensive resources) and continue to highly value their title certificates.

Second, as the traditional witnesses age and die, landholders in some areas (i.e., Samre), including men, express an increasing reliance on, and valuation of their land registration certificates, and have begun demanding better land description technology. This is also occurring in areas where land values are rising (most notably in peri-urban areas[33]) and attendant disputes are also increasing.

These findings provide part of the support for the conclusion that, just as in richer countries, most land holders in Ethiopia do not value land rights protection on conceptual grounds, but, instead, on very functional grounds – grounds that often take some time to manifest themselves, or some particular change in the environment to be noticed. They also demonstrate that, especially for the citizens of a poor country, the cost of better quality government service – here more accurate measurement technology – is a very real barrier.

Creation and allocation of rights: In Tigray, and elsewhere in Ethiopia, this niche in the ecology of land rights protection displays an appearance of sim-

---

[32] In Amhara state a pilot project in four villages has tested GPS and other more expensive and more precise technologies. But, so far, these have not been extended beyond the pilot area, principally for two reasons: 1) the expense and 2) the fact that their use removes control from the local people to experts in more distant locations, one of the great and common dangers of 'modernizing' land rights protection: Adenew, B. and Abdi, F., *supra* note 30; J. Quan and C. Toulmin, Formalizing and Securing Land Rights, *Overview Paper,* Working Group 1, Land in Africa Conference, IIED, London (2004).

[33] There have long been more exact (and expensive) land identification technologies at use in urban areas, primarily theodolite and tape measure.

plicity because the *Derg*[34] extinguished past rights and created a new set of simpler, locally rooted, uniform land rights granted by the state. As a result, inadequate consideration has been given to exactly how land rights actually arise and are allocated.

For example, after the EPRDF liberalized the very restrictive *Derg* landholding laws – allowing leases and sharecropping – many leaseholds were created anew. But in the Tigray land registration system no provision was made for registering the new leasehold and sharecropping rights, only the original state-granted rights. As is so often the case with economic actors, farmers then invented other forms of pseudo-registration, such as signing the leases before the head of the village council or a village Social Court judge and leaving a copy with that authority. Thus, when the formal system failed, the people created an informal system that did much of what they deemed important.[35]

The creation and allocation of land rights is further complicated by the fact that several land rights systems other than the rural land system actually persist side-by-side in Ethiopia today, e.g., the urban land system vs. the rural land system; rural communal vs. rural individual; and rural peasant vs. rural pastoralist vs. rural investor. As a result, conflicts arise at each of these interfaces when rights in the same land are recognized in the different but unconnected systems.

For example, investors in southeast Tigray were allocated (by village leaders, *Woreda*-level administrators, and a lease with the State Agriculture Bureau) 'unused' land in the Mehoni Plain. They borrowed heavily and invested in clearing the land for commercial farming. Then they discovered the land was registered in a separate registry[36] as communal grazing land for a group living in a neighbouring village. When the dispute was administratively adjudicated at a higher level of government – the Zone that included both village areas – the land was reallocated to the use of the neighbouring claimants. The investors were then given a different piece of land to clear and most went bankrupt.

The adverse effect of parallel land rights systems that is most obvious to urban-based researchers is at the urban vs. rural interface – the peri-urban areas. Because the urban and rural land rights systems are separate in Ethiopia, as a municipal area grows rural land is transferred into the urban system. The natural uncertainties of such transfers (i.e., differing evaluations and expectations) are compounded by the 'ownership' of the land by the government, the lack of

[34] Or, in areas under control of opposition movements, like the Tigray People's Liberation Front (TPLF) in Tigray, the rights were effectively extinguished by both the *Derg* laws and the movements' enforcement.

[35] The federal land law now requires leases be registered. Proclamation No. 456/2005, Article 6.6.

[36] Similarly, reforestation and natural regeneration areas are usually described, together with agreed management rules, in written documents kept in a separate registration system.

a clear set of rules for compensation when land and improvements are 'taken', the often limited capacity of local civil servants to follow available rules, and the coincidence that at exactly the time when rural citizens need their local government's protection of land rights, the land is transferred to the jurisdiction of a new, unknown and often more distant municipal government.

The result of all these factors is that the outcomes in 'takings' situations of all types, but particularly in the peri-urban areas, vary tremendously – a sure sign of a poorly functioning system. Complicating the picture even more, the holders of rural land near expanding municipalities have invented clever[37] defensive strategies that further enlarge the variance in outcomes, making it hard to tell at any particular time whether the municipal administration or the land holders are more successful.

But a much larger scale weakness of the post-*Derg* allocation of land rights resulted from increasing population that caused demand for rural land to far exceed local supplies. Thus, as mentioned in the introduction, not many years after the last land redistribution the constitutional right to obtain and hold rural land could no longer be fulfilled for youth coming of age and for adults returning to Tigray villages.[38] Though serious efforts were made in villages to discuss the problem, prioritise those without land, and find unused land within the village boundaries for allocation, the problem grew inexorably worse.

In addition to the severe limitations of already too small family holdings, only very small amounts of land were returning to the local government for reallocation – primarily when villagers with land died without eligible heirs.[39] And because the problem existed at the local level, as a result of the policy choices that emphasized local control, no solution could be found. Eventually, however, when the problem reached a politically sensitive extent, with a large portion of rural people state-wide being landless, new land was located – a good example of different solutions being available to different scales of government.

[37] 'Moon houses' and even 'moon churches', appearing over night on urban sized plots of rural land adjacent to municipal boundaries, in some cases have been construed as entitling the owner of the house to rent the plot from the municipality under the urban land leasing system, thus enabling the rural land holder to "sell" land, which is constitutionally prohibited. However, most often the municipality knocks the illegal moon houses down, though not the moon churches, compensates the rural owner with a small urban sized plot around the family home, and then leases the land to the many urban land seekers.

[38] Returning from, among other places, forced resettlement by the *Derg* in southern Ethiopia, refugee camps in the Sudan, and the TPLF's combatant ranks.

[39] A smaller source of new land to meet demand has been the enforcement of two rights in rural land reserved to the state by the Federal land laws, triggered when landholders abandon or mismanage their land. See Transformation, below.

The largest source of new land has now come from higher levels of government searching larger areas for unused land. In the western 'borderlands' of all of the large highland states, great swaths of land have been located that have never been settled, primarily because of malaria. With improved malaria control these areas have been opened to voluntary settlement, including the slow and sometimes clumsy establishment of the same local institutions and organizations to protect land rights as are found in the highlands.

Transformation of rights: Just as the origins and allocation of land rights were over-simplified, transformation and reallocation of land rights have received insufficient consideration in Tigray and elsewhere in Ethiopia in the post-*Derg* period. At the village level, transforming events, such as births, deaths, marriages, divorces, determinations of incapacity, loans, and myriad others, are well known. But until 1996, little of this information was systematically noted in any permanent form. And if it was, for example, written down, the records were scattered in a variety of traditional and more-modern individual, religious, administrative and judicial systems. The only place the information came together and was tied to land was in people's minds, and often they had different and conflicting interests and agendas and drew different conclusions. The uncertainty that resulted caused disputes to slowly become more common again until, in 1996, the new system was put in place – see Registration of Title, below.

But, as well as these record-keeping issues, transformation of land rights also has direct ramifications. For example, the federal land laws identify two special rights in all rural land, allocate them to the state government and mandate that the states enforce them. First, the state should take the land of rural landholders who leave their land for more than a period of years fixed by the state.[40] Second, the state should take the land of anyone who has 'environmentally mismanaged' their land.[41] In each of these cases, the land taken returns to the local village council for reallocation to the landless.

[40] FDRE proclamation No. 456/2005, Article 9.1. Exceptions to this rule in the Tigray state proclamations, currently highly criticized by rural communities and being considered for state legislative change, protect the rights of some ex-fighters and early urban migrants to maintain rural land even though they live in urban areas. In Tigray, the period is two years if traditional farming technology is in use, ten with modern. In Amhara the period has now been set at twenty years. The difference seems to correlate most strongly with differences in unfilled demand for rural land. The assumption behind this right seems to be that anyone able to stay away from their village for the specified number of years has another viable source of income and their land should be made available to those with no land and no other source of income. In cases where this is demonstrably not the case (i.e., Ethiopians detained in Eritrea during the recent war), the rule has not been applied. There is a correlation between Tigray's 2 year loss-through-absence provision and a limitation on leasing rural land that limits small holder lease periods to 2 years for "traditional technology" and 10 years for "modern technology". Unfortunately, the two quoted terms are not defined.

[41] FDRE proclamation No. 456/2005, Article 10.1.

In determining whether the land has been 'left' or 'environmentally mismanaged', the local village government's administrative discretion plays a major role. It can, therefore, be either helpful, harmful, or some mixture. For example, there is some evidence that 'environmental mismanagement', even with large extension programs to help landholders comply, allows too much room for traditional biases and has been misused to take the land of people a local government wants to punish.[42] Interestingly, the state cabinet-member who oversees the Tigray state land rights system[43] points out that Tigray has never allowed this form of land reallocation, specifically because it is too open to such mischief.[44]

A different result from administrative discretion is found when considering the second state right, at least in Tigray. There women often move to their husband's village where there is no land to be allocated to them. A strict application of the land-abandonment law would probably dictate that these women lose any land they have in their home village and become landless. However, one of the common outcomes in Tigray villages has been to allow women to hold land in their home village until they receive land in their new village. This is generally considered a beneficial outcome, despite pressure from the landless for land.

A related, but as yet unquantified, transformation effect has been more difficult to study because it occurs over a longer period of time. As noted in the Delineation section above, the right to inherit land is also subject to limitation in state constitutions and proclamations. In Tigray, for example, where land pressure is very high and many family holdings are already below the size necessary to produce a living, the right to inherit has been limited by social welfare principles applied by the local government in accordance with state regulations. Principal among these are that not all children have equal rights to inherit; that children with another source of income shall not inherit, even if that means there are no qualified heirs; and that children who have stayed on the land to help the parents farm shall have a better right to inherit.

One result of this intersection of principles is that women who marry men with land and income in another village, and thus do not stay to help their parents farm, are less likely to inherit than their brothers, even though they usually cannot obtain their own land in their husband's village. Thus, despite the official policy and laws providing equal rights to land to men and women, despite

---

[42] A. Hoben, *supra* note 22; Y. Adal, *supra* note 22; Debele, B., *supra* note 22; S. Ege, *supra* note 22.

[43] Now EPLAUA, Environmental Planning, Land Administration, and Use Authority. In 2004, amendments to the Tigray state land proclamation reorganized the role of government in land administration, creating this dedicated Authority as part of the changes to correct past deficiencies, modeled at least in part on the Amhara changes to the 'Tigray Model'.

[44] Personal communication, February 2005.

effective implementation of those policies when there was adequate land, and even despite the local governments' efforts to allow women to keep their own land in their home village, land holdings may slowly become concentrated in male hands. This is a good example of formal and informal institutions interacting with what appear to be entirely unexpected and unintended consequences.

Preservation of evidence: In an impoverished agricultural society like rural Ethiopia, efforts to improve preservation of evidence include a wide range of administratively-complex undertakings, from general education so people can read and value documents to patching the roof on the agricultural extension agent's office to improving record keeping in the courts, and much more. Perhaps most important, however, is to create the understanding that these pieces must all be tied together in one way or another.

It is not an accident that the demand for better preservation of land-rights evidence grew with every passing year after the last land distribution occurred. As events affecting land rights accumulated over time without a systematic way to connect them to resolution of disputes, uncertainty of outcomes increased. Thus, it is that the introduction in 1996 of a statewide land title registration system in Tigray was conceptualised as a way to preserve evidence in a simplified form – as opposed to a way to record legal conclusions based on evidence preserved in separate archives. Those who set up the system did not adequately consider that changing laws (e.g., concerning who inherits) affect how the legal conclusion of title is determined, and may require reassessment of the evidence of original or transforming events.

This misconceptualization led to some of the weaknesses of the Land Title Registration system. One of these is the failure to adequately improve the preservation of the underlying documentary evidence on which the legal conclusions of title are based.

Registration of 'title': Between 1996 and 1998 a new system designed to increase the security of rural land was designed and put in place throughout Tigray state. Of particular importance was the policy choice to accomplish this by building on other aspects of local governance that had been subject to vigorous improvement under the TPLF (Tigray People's Liberation Front) even during the *Derg*, including village councils and the judiciary.

Using simple forms, the traditional land description technology noted above, the local language, minimally trained technicians, negligible per-family charges (US $00.25 for a certificate), and a review of all evidence of then existing land rights, legal conclusions about title were determined and recorded at the village level. The record books were kept in the local village government offices (either the Council President's office or the Agricultural Extension Agent's office, whichever seemed better protected against rain, rodents, mold and people) and a certificate was provided for each family. The entire system was administered locally by the village council, with planning and oversight from more distant levels of government at the *woreda* (County) and state levels.

On the positive side, the speed and even-handedness of implementation across the entire state, and its acceptance by the people with very little controversy, stand out. The source of the systems strength most often mentioned by farmers was that it was established as part of 'their' existing effective local government.

Unfortunately, on the negative side, issues that a more thorough study of the ecology of land rights protection might have made clear were not adequately addressed. Most importantly, no provision for keeping the written records of the legal conclusions about title up-to-date was institutionalised. After only a few years, many of the records of title became unreliable. There is conflicting evidence as to whether up dating was countenanced in Tigray (though it is now clearly on the agenda in all state programs, with USAID assistance focused on it). A second problem – that the registration and certification forms ran out and were not resupplied – compounded the problem.

These systematic failures would have most adversely affected women, particularly on divorce, because of the then state rule (clearly derived from traditional practice, and now changed by federal law[45]) of registering and certifying a family's land rights in the name of the head of the family – a male if present. Upon divorce, fairly common in highland Ethiopia, no new certificate or registration page in the woman's name was issued. Had the records been the sole source of land rights, women might have lost their land, as has been well documented during formalization of land rights systems in other countries.[46]

But because the land title registration system had been established as part of the existing relatively effective local government system, administrative discretion again provided a solution to the potentially harmful consequences of these apparently unforeseen events. As a result, we found no evidence that women's rights to their share of their family's land were ever compromised as a result of this failure.

Assurance for reliance on system errors: In Ethiopia, there is no public (as in Europe) or private (as in the USA) provision for insurance for those who rely on errors (e.g., out-of-date or incorrect records) in the rural land rights protec-

---

[45] Proclamation No. 456/2005, Article 6.4.

[46] J. Quan and C. Toulmin, Formalizing and Securing Land Rights, *Overview Paper*, Working Group 1, Land in Africa Conference, IIED, London (2004).

tion system. Instead, because both the allocation and protection systems are nearly completely local, there are very few rural landholders who do not reside where their land is, and information is easily available, the community provides assurance, at least to community members.

Thus, in many cases, as in the case of divorced women noted above, the local councils were able to address unforeseen problems through administrative action, providing a kind of assurance system. It is this last finding that has required couching the overall research results as: a simple inexpensive local registration system can work well, even with major oversimplifications, if it is established within an existing system of effective local governance.[47] This is the reason the adjustment of the 'Tigray Model' following the Amhara state experience is being watched closely.

But, unfortunately, assurance and administrative discretion have two sides. We also found cases where local village councils colluded with a non-governmental credit association in the use of the threat of loss of land rights to enforce credit repayment. This is, of course, formally prohibited because mortgages, and transfers due to foreclosure, are specifically banned by the constitution for the specific policy objective of ensuring that rural farmers do not lose their land through default on loans.

However, we also found another of the tools of good governance at work: oversight. When *woreda*- (County) and state-level administrators learned of the illegal collusion they promptly reversed the local decisions and instituted further training for local government administrators. Similar oversight results, as with several changes noted above induced by the federal land laws, were found in other cases where what state and local administrators thought were innovative solutions turned out to be ill-advised, or plainly illegal, and were corrected.

Are all such problems corrected through administrative and legislative solutions? Clearly not. This leads us to consider the full range of correctives.

Protection of rights: Particularly for the poor, protection of land rights depends upon local systems. Protecting land rights from private or public attacks can be expensive, mounting in cost as distance, time away from home, and the need for expertise increase. One reason people in Tigray give for favouring local administrative solutions is that through them the government subsidizes the expense of enforcement. Of course, where the local government is the problem, as in the case mentioned above of collusion with debt collectors, local relief may not be available.

[47] What is a system of effective local government? This is a good but complicated question, unfortunately far beyond the limitations of this study. The term is used here simply to mean a system of local government that effectively solves most problems that arise in the community in a way the community accepts, and as such, the term has the weakness of being suspiciously tautological.

In Tigray, and subsequently elsewhere in Ethiopia, a sustained government effort has attempted to supplement more traditional dispute resolution methods. Prior research by Mekelle University Law Faculty into the village Social Courts and *Woreda* (District) Courts compliments its land research and underscores both the popularity and the weaknesses of the dispute resolution options available to rural landholders.

Thus, rural land rights disputes are usually resolved within the village using a) traditional social dispute mechanisms (e.g., elders and/or those witnesses who participated in the last land distribution); b) local government administrative dispute resolution mechanisms, or c) the village Social Court – a 'hybrid[48]' judicial system.

These dispute resolution mechanisms are all within the village and therefore are relatively inexpensive to access; but each also has its problems and limitations. For example, the traditional systems are, as almost the world over, sometimes biased in favour of men or the powerful. When the administrative systems err, formal appeal can be difficult because administrative law is a very under-developed, and even less-utilized, area of Ethiopian law. And the village Social Court, because it applies somewhat more technical rules with less training, is often perceived as less reliable.

All three local forums may also be subject more generally to local community pressures, political pressure, abuse of power, and corruption. It is this which makes the availability of appeal from the Social Court to the *Woreda* (District) Court, away from village forces, very important. But while that appeal is necessary, it is, unfortunately, not sufficient: for the poorest the extra cost favours the rich. For all of these reasons together, forum shopping among the three can be an issue. Though the hierarchy of jurisdiction is clear, with each party able to opt out[49] of the traditional in favour of the administrative, and with the administrative giving way to the judicial, that ultimate step can favour the rich. Thus, though efforts have been made to balance the attributes of the different forums, the balance is not yet completely satisfactory.

In any case, a threat to land rights that requires enforcement is costly and uncertain for the poorest, those already living very much on the edge. Defending rights requires and taxes scarce resources. And there is, for example, now at

[48] 'Hybrid' because the people elected locally to serve, voluntarily and without pay (until July 2005, when they were voted small reimbursements), as Social Court judges are much like the kinds of people who serve as mediators in the traditional dispute resolution forums and, as traditionally, they encourage parties to settle disputes amicably before eventually exercising their authority to decide the case; yet the Social Court also operates with a clear set of rules of procedure and a simplified version of the same law applied in higher courts, and there is an appeal to the *Woreda* Court.

[49] Of course, rights to 'opt out', as with Ethiopia's Sharia Courts, must be known and those with the rights must be free and able to use them.

least anecdotal evidence in Tigray that women's land rights are attacked more frequently than men's because women have fewer resources available for defending.

These considerations have lead to discussions[50] about how to strengthen subsidized administrative dispute resolution, while at the same time providing more oversight. Getting the balance right requires constant attention as institutions and organizations evolve. At this time, throughout Ethiopia these issues appear to be high on the agenda of the government but good information about how the systems are working, or not working, is not always available and solutions, as in every society, are often partial and subject to further adjustment.

4. CONCLUSION

Several different types of conclusions may be drawn.

Systematically, we can certainly conclude that international human rights instruments, *per se*, have little direct impact on domestic land rights. Protection of land rights takes place in a complex and constantly evolving environment of interconnected domestic institutions and organizations. The public legislative, administrative, and judicial functions, as well as the more obvious private transactions, all play a role in protecting land rights. In Ethiopia's federal system, this ecology also includes the diversity of the federal level and multiple states. Changes in the ecology occur constantly as a result of learning, exercise of appeals, democratic forces and transitions, 'civil society' activism, and, unfortunately, violence; often both the land rights ecology and the effects of changes to it, are not well understood and usually changes benefit some people more than others.

Still, there are some principles which can be abstracted because in many cases the domestic institutions and organizations have well-known – though not well-calibrated and easily-achieved – general balance points and trade-offs. For example, we have seen the strengths of local government from high-quality and low-cost information versus their susceptibility to discrimination and abuse of power, whether intended or not. And we have seen how larger scale solutions are only possible at larger scales of government, as with the opening of new state or national lands to settlement, with the unfortunate inverse correlation of larger scales of government being further removed from the concerns of the people. Yet, while interesting, such abstractions don't help us understand the complexity of improving the land rights protection system.

[50] Personal communications with the Tigray state cabinet member overseeing land issues, February and July, 2005.

And it cannot be denied that there is much room for improvement in Ethiopia. In fact, we have seen that many changes are indeed currently underway as a result of both state and federal initiatives. However, these efforts to improve, as everywhere, require an understanding of the complexity and interdependent nature of the system; collection of good quality information about current affairs; mechanisms to inform and train the huge number of politicians, civil servants, and judges involved in legislation, administration and judicial review; and frequent exercise of those systems, like the judiciary, that are internally designed to improve through the exercise of appeals.

Thus, within the hard realities, protecting land rights is not very different from protecting other human rights that can only effectively be protected through domestic systems. Progress is slow and requires great effort at the federal, state and local levels. Cost is always an issue. How the system should be changed is always subject to debate and – particularly in poor countries constantly bombarded with 'experts' from different countries, with their insular knowledge of one or a few ways of doing the thing – that debate is often a confusing and frustrating milieu, sometimes undermined by piecing together contrary methods that don't work together.

So, instead of ending with abstractions about land rights protection, on this particular occasion I would like to consider the specific efforts of the Mekelle University Law Faculty (MULF) towards improving human rights protection in general and land rights in particular. By considering these specific efforts, we may gain a perspective on how the protection of human rights in general may be improved.

From its inception MULF has undertaken practical field research on the strengths and weaknesses of human rights protection; formulated, funded and provided continuing education and shorter tailored trainings for civil servants and Social Court and *Woreda* Court judges; provided advisory services and legislative drafting services for the state parliament; and engaged regularly with all these organizations through workshops and performance reviews.
But this is not enough. Citizens, too, have a role to play and an obligation to do so. Many of the systems by which we expect human rights protection to be improved require that citizens exercise the system. And perhaps here a topical analogy to the right to free and fair elections is appropriate. As the Carter Center, in its Final Statement on the May 2005 Ethiopian elections concluded, "*If parties decide not to file court appeals, the* [National Election Board of Ethiopia's] *announced results should be accepted as final and legitimate*."[51] Just as in challenges to elections in Florida, USA, or in Birmingham, UK, or in the Ukraine, there are, in the end, only the existing domestic institutions and organizations to turn to for protection of human rights. If citizens do not exercise

[51] The Carter Center, September 15, 2005, <www.cartercenter.org/documents/2199.pdf>, 3.

the appeals by which many improvements, by design, must occur, then those improvements will not happen, and society will suffer.

Of course, that so many of the citizens of Ethiopia are as poor as they are means that they need assistance to exercise the systems. Which is why the MULF Legal Aid Clinic, the first in Ethiopia based in a university, and housed in the same off-campus building as the MULF Human Rights Center, provides legal services to poor land holders.

Finally, that some states in Ethiopia are slower, and clumsier, than others to improve should not surprise Europeans any more than it does this American author. There are plenty of well-known examples among the states of the European Union (e.g., the results of Italy's late Twentieth Century devolution of power to regional states[52]). And that is why MULF also, through every possible means, from participating in the design of a USAID land rights security project to participating in the Capacity Building Ministry's committee to strengthen legal education (including research) in all of Ethiopia's law schools, seeks to improve and spread its broad approach to strengthening the Ethiopian domestic institutions and organizations that are all that can, in the end, protect human rights.

Thus, I would like to take this opportunity to encourage MULF to continue and strengthen all these programs, and to ask that those who support them in these endeavours continue their vital support.

---

[52] See R. Putnam, *Making Democracy Work, Civic Traditions in Modern Italy* (Princeton: Princeton University Press, 1993).

12. Press Freedom: European Lessons for Ethiopia

Hassen Mohammed Ibrahim•

1. INTRODUCTION

The Constitution of the Federal Democratic Republic of Ethiopia under Article 9 provides:

"All international agreements ratified by Ethiopia are an integral part of the law of the land."

Article 13 also states that:

"The fundamental rights and freedoms specified in this chapter (chapter 3, on fundamental rights and freedoms) *shall be interpreted in a manner conforming to the principles of the Universal Declaration of Human Rights, International Covenants on Human Rights and international instruments adopted by Ethiopia."*

This guarantees that all human rights provisions, including freedom of expression, should be interpreted according to these instruments. Article 10 of the European Convention on Human Rights (ECHR) is more or less similar to Article 19 of the ICCPR (International Covenant on Civil and Political Rights)[1] for the purpose of this paper but without ignoring some differences like freedom of information.

Accordingly, one can use the interpretation of Article 10 by the European Court of Human Rights for Article 19 of ICCPR.[2]

"ECHR has considerable influence outside Europe in that its provisions are consulted in construing similar provisions of the International Covenant on Civil and Political Rights..."[3]

• LLM Ghent University. E-mail: hassenmoha@fastmail.fm

[1] ECHR 24 May 1988, *Müller and others v. Switzerland*, para. 27 where the Court refers to the ICCPR.

[2] S. Coliver, Press Freedom under the European Convention of Human Rights, in: S. Coliver (ed.), *Press Law and Practice. A Comparative Study of Press Freedom in European and Other Democracies* (London: An Article 19 Report, 1993).

[3] Id. 218.

It has to be noted that the ICCPR is "*...not as extensively or authoritatively interpreted as those mandated by Article 10 of the ECHR.*"[4] Thus, the robust case law of the European court of Human Rights (the Court) makes it very attractive for transplanting higher standards of freedom.

The start of free expression in Ethiopia was marked by 'A proclamation to provide for freedom of the press' of 1992. Even though it is a short history, commentators believe that the evolution has been very slow. Ethiopia's record on abuse of press freedom has been showing no improvement. According to Reporters sans frontières (RSF), Ethiopia ranks 112th in the world press freedom index.[5] This article tries to find out the obstacles in the law that are taking this young process backwards in light of the rich experience of the European Court of Human Rights and forward possible solutions accordingly.

This article does not discuss the broad topic of freedom of expression and focuses only on press freedom. In doing that, it does not rely on the experience of the press, since it is obvious from the ranking of Ethiopia by RSF and other such organisations that there is a serious problem. However, the question is whether the source of the problems lies with the laws related to press activity. To answer the question, this article approaches the topic through interferences, for example Article 10(2) of the European Convention of Human Rights, in order to examine whether or not the laws are justified as they are always claimed to be.

In fact, the writer believes that a good approach to freedom is through the interferences allowed because they are legally open doors for infringement. The Court in Strasbourg also does not raise the issue of whether a particular speech is protected by paragraph one or not but rather addresses "*... primarily the question whether a given limitation on freedom of expression was justified under paragraph 2 of Article 10...*"[6]

Based on the purpose indicated above, the questions to be addressed by the subsequent parts are three in number. One is about identifying the fundamental achievements of the ECHR with regard to press freedom based on some key cases. The second concerns identifying problems of press freedom under Ethiopian law. The third draws lessons from the ECHR so that they can be used for change in Ethiopian law. This writer hopes this work will contribute to the ongoing public discussion on the issue in Ethiopia as well as other similar jurisdictions and draw the attention of stakeholders to the profound experience of Europe.

---

4 Ibid.

5 WWW.rsf.org

6 R. Ryssdal, *The Case-law of the European Court of Human Rights on the Freedom of Expression Guaranteed under the European Convention on Human Rights* 4 (Strasbourg: Conseil de L'Europe, 1996).

2. DRAWING THE LINE: THE EXPERIENCE OF THE EUROPEAN COURT OF HUMAN RIGHTS

Article 10 Freedom of expression[7]

"*1. Everyone has the right to freedom of expression. This right shall include freedom to hold opinions and to receive and impart information and ideas without interference by public authority and regardless of frontiers. This article shall not prevent states from requiring the licensing of broadcasting television or cinema enterprises.*
2. The exercise of these freedoms, since it carries with it duties and responsibilities, may be subject to such formalities, conditions, restrictions or penalties as are prescribed by law and are necessary in a democratic society, in the interests of national security, territorial integrity or public safety, for the prevention of disorder or crime, for the protection of health or morals, for the protection of the reputation or rights of others, for preventing the disclosure of information received in confidence, or for maintaining the authority and impartiality of the judiciary."

The first paragraph of Article 10 provides for expression as a negative freedom because the authorities are prohibited from interfering in the spheres provided. The spheres of expression are freedom of opinion, of receiving information or ideas and imparting information or ideas. The justification for this is that expression is indispensable for democracy and personal development.[8] In one of its pioneer judgments, the European Court of Human Rights provides its justification as follows:

"*Freedom of expression constitutes one of the essential foundations of (a 'democratic society'), one of the basic conditions for its progress and for the development of every man. Subject to paragraph 2 of Article 10, it is applicable not only to 'information' or 'ideas' that are favourably received or regarded as inoffensive or as a matter of indifference, but also those that offend, shock or disturb the state or any sector of the population. Such are the demands of that pluralism, tolerance and broadmindedness without which there is no 'democratic society'. This means, amongst other things that every 'formality' 'condition' 'restriction' or 'penalty' imposed in this sphere must be proportionate to the legitimate aim pursued.*"[9]

The second paragraph of Article 10 provides the legitimate restrictions. While interpreting these restrictions, *"the court is faced not with a choice between two conflicting principles but with a principle of freedom of expression that is*

---

[7] The European Convention of Human Rights, 4 November 1950, in force 3 September 1953.
[8] E. Barendt, *Freedom of Speech* 7 – 30, second edition (Oxford: Oxford University Press, 2005).
[9] ECHR 7 December 1976, *Handyside v. The United Kingdom*, para. 49.

subject to a number of exceptions which must be narrowly interpreted."[10] Accordingly, a restriction on freedom of expression must fulfil three criteria in order to be within the permissible grounds under paragraph 2. These are: one, it has to be prescribed by law; two, it has to have one of the legitimate aims listed under paragraph 2 and three, it has to be necessary in a democratic society in order to achieve the legitimate aims.[11]

2.1. Prescribed by law

The Court defined this requirement in *The Sunday Times* case. The particular issue in the case was whether a common law rule of contempt is a law and the Court concluded that "prescribed by law" includes common law as well. The important thing is whether the following requirements are met:

"In the court's opinion, the following are two of the requirements that flow from the expression 'prescribed by law'. Firstly, the law must be adequately accessible: the citizen must be able to have an indication that is adequate in the circumstances of the legal rules applicable to a given case. Secondly, a norm cannot be regarded as a ' law' unless it is formulated with sufficient precision to enable the citizen to regulate his conduct: he must be able - if need be with appropriate advice - to foresee, to a degree that is reasonable in the circumstances, the consequences which a given action may entail."[12]

States usually can show that they have the mandate to impose the restriction under national law but this requirement goes further than that. It requires states to make their laws precise in terms of providing the criteria of their application and "accessible" to ordinary people. Many cases show that the indicator is whether people had legal advice or not. This being the case, if the restrictions on freedom of expression and information do not offer the minimum degree of protection against arbitrariness required by the rule of law, such restriction will not be regarded as "prescribed by law". In the case *Herczegfalvy v. Austria,*[13] the Court said that a rule, which prohibited a psychiatric patient from getting information, was vague and cannot fulfil the "prescribed by law" requirement. This shows that the manner in which laws are written may lack precision and can be a source of arbitrariness.

---

[10] ECHR 26 April 1979, *The Sunday Times v. The United Kingdom*, para. 65.

[11] D. Voorhoof, Guaranteeing the freedom and independence of the media, in X (ed.), *Media and Democracy* 51 (Strasbourg: Council of Europe Publishing, 1998).

[12] *Supra* note 10, para. 49.

[13] ECHR 24 September 1992, *Herczegfalvy v. Austria.*

2.2. Legitimate aim

In order to be considered as having a legitimate aim, a restriction on freedom of the press has to be covered by one or more on the list provided under paragraph 2 of Article 10.
The list includes the following:

- Protection of national security, territorial integrity or public safety;
- For the prevention of disorder or crime;
- For the protection of health or morals;
- For the protection of reputation or rights of others;
- To prevent the disclosure of information received in confidence or
- To maintain the authority and impartiality of the judiciary.

These aims protect private and public interests. Protection of national security, territorial integrity, public safety, health, morals, prevention of crime and disorder are public interests that have to be protected by the state because on the one hand, if they are not protected, the foundation of the system of rights will be in jeopardy. On the other hand, they are traditional aims for which society formed states. The private interest that needs to be reconciled with freedom of the press is the right to privacy under Article 8 of the Convention. The independence and authority of the judiciary is protected because of Article 6(1) of the Convention: "*A restriction on the freedom of expression can be aimed at the protection of the proper administration of justice and, in particular, of the individual's right to fair trial.*"[14] This protects the reputation of the court system and the accused person.

The Court usually addresses these aims in terms of the necessity and proportionality test. States usually claim that their interference is furthering one of the legitimate aims but
"*The Court has never ruled that the contested interference failed to pursue one of the legitimate aims....*" Rather these aims claimed by states have to be weighed against the principle of the freedom of the press and accordingly, the Court "*has sometimes disagreed with the respondent Government as to what aim was relevant in the circumstances.*"[15] To pursue these aims, states are allowed to interfere in the exercise of freedom of the press under paragraph 2 of Article 10 using "formalities", "conditions" or "penalties". These measures have to go through the necessity and proportionality test developed by the Court while interpreting the requirement "necessary in a democratic society".

[14] Voorhoof, *supra* note 11, 52.
[15] Ryssdal, *supra* note 6, 6.

2.3. Necessary in a democratic society

This test is the "ultimate and decisive criterion" of whether any measure taken by a state is a restriction on freedom of the press.[16] The importance of this test stems from the role of democracy in society on the one hand and its ultimate dependence on deliberation. The reason for this is the nature of democracy. Democracy is a system of governance where many different, often opposite, views and interests are accommodated and coexist with tolerance with each other but with continuous debate and deliberation. All these interests and views are given a chance to win the favour of the public through elections, which also require deliberation and debate. The press as an institution and with its members is an indispensable channel through which this deliberation is conducted. It has also a crucial role of controlling and exposing governments to make their actions transparent and accountable to the public. All these functions make the press an indispensable institution for a democratic society governed by the rule of law. The Court's case law also consistently testifies to this fact.

In one of the famous passages, the Court says:

"Freedom of the press affords the public one of the best means of discovering and forming an opinion of the ideas and attitudes of their political leaders. In particular, it gives politicians the opportunity to reflect and comment on the preoccupations of public opinion, it thus enables everyone to participate in the free political debate, which is at the very core of the concept of a democratic society."[17]

Here the Court is affirming the indispensable position of debate and deliberation, especially on political matters. This special protection is not limited to political speech only. The role of the press now is "*to impart information and ideas*" not only on political topics but also any "*...other issue of public interest. Not only does the press have the task of imparting such information and ideas; the public also has a right to receive them.*"[18]

It is very difficult for a state to justify interference with this regard. However, what if the conflicts are deep and one side doesn't accept the other? What about minority opinions and interests? In order to solve this, limits of tolerance in a democratic society should be as wide as possible, not as wide as the majority. This means that as long as ideas and opinions are not direct threats to the democratic system that protects them and other human rights, they have to be tolerated. The standard the Court sets in the *Handyside* case is that freedom

---

[16] Voorhoof, *supra* note 11, 52.

[17] ECHR 23 April 1992, *Castells v. Spain*, para. 43.

[18] ECHR 8 July 1986, *Lingens v. Austria*, para. 41.

of the press includes "information" or "ideas" "that offend, shock or disturb". "*This means*", according to D. Voorhoof, "*that Article 10 has to be interpreted from a perspective of a high level of protection of freedom of expression, even if this information is harmful to the states or some group, enterprises or organizations and public figures, such as politicians and even judges.*"[19] The following are some examples of this requirement of high level of tolerance, in particular of politicians and judges.

In *Lingens v. Austria*[20] a journalist was convicted by an Austrian court for defamation of the Austrian Chancellor because he published two articles criticising the chancellor for being an 'opportunist' by protecting former SS members and having association with former Nazis. Lingens could not prove the truth of his statement in his defence as required by the law. According to the Court, the conviction violated Article 10 of the Convention because of two reasons, one being:

Freedom of press...affords the public one of the best means of discovering and forming an opinion of the ideas and attitudes of political leaders. The limits of acceptable criticism are accordingly wider as regards a politician as such than as regards a private individual. Unlike the latter, the former inevitably and knowingly lays himself open to close scrutiny of his every word and deed by journalists and the public at large, and he must consequently display a greater degree of tolerance.[21]

The other reason is that "*careful distinction needs to be drawn between facts and value- judgments. The existence of facts can be demonstrated, whereas the truth of value –judgments is not susceptible of proof.*"[22] Thus, the requirement that Lingens has to prove the truth of this claim violates freedom of opinion, the journalist's right to impart ideas and the public's right to receive them.

In another case, *Thorgeirson v. Iceland*[23], the Court extends the same requirement to a matter of "public concern". Mr. Thorgeirson was convicted and sentenced for defaming police officers in his article about police brutality. The article uses such reference to the police as "brutes in uniform" and includes some facts that are not true. However, it depends on rumours and public opinion of police misbehaviour. It also calls for the establishment of an independent body to investigate such matters. For his innocence, he has to prove the truth of the content of the article under Iceland law. The Court again reaffirmed the importance of the press, as a "public watchdog" not only in political matters but also in all matters of public concern and thus, the limit of accept-

---

[19] D. Voorhoof, *supra* note 11, 47.
[20] *Supra* note 18.
[21] *Ibid.* para. 42.
[22] *Ibid.* para. 46.
[23] ECHR 25 June 1992, *Thorgeir Thorgeirson v. Iceland.*

able criticism is still high. It is also impossible for the journalist to prove the truth of his statements because he relied on public opinion and he wrote it in good faith as he recommended institutional reform. His highly critical language was directed to "the police" but no police officer was named in the article. The Court was also concerned about the sentencing of a journalist and suggested that it would have a "chilling effect" on further contributions of the press on issues of public concern. This was also made clear by the Court in a case against Spain in which a senator, Mr. Castells, was convicted of a criminal offence because he published an article that accused the government of failing to investigate (or covering up) the murder by police of people who allegedly belong to a Basque separatist group. The Court said:

"*...the dominant position, which the government occupies, makes it necessary for it to display restraint in resorting to criminal proceedings, particularly where other means are available for replying to the unjustified attacks of its adversaries or the media.*" [24]

In *De Haes and Gijsels v. Belgium,*[25] the applicants were convicted of insult and defamation against four members of the judiciary because they published articles, which accused the judges in a custody and sexual abuse case of being partial and cowards. The Court found that the journalists conducted "thorough research" and thus, fulfilled their professional duty. Even claims about the political lineages of the judges should not be considered defamatory, according to the Court. It concludes:

"Looked at against the background of the case, the accusations in question amount to an opinion, whose truth, by definition, is not susceptible of proof ...... Although Mr. De Haes' and Mr. Gijsels' comments were without doubt severely critical, they nevertheless appear proportionate to the stir and indignation caused by the matters alleged in the article. As to the journalists' polemical and even aggressive tone, which the court should not be taken to approve, it must be remembered that Article 10 protects not only the substance of the ideas and information expressed but also the form in which they are conveyed. ... Journalistic freedom also covers possible recourse to a degree of exaggeration, or even provocation." [26]

In connection with the judiciary, we also have to look at how the Court deals with trial publicity and journalistic sources. The Court established the principle for publicity in *Sunday Times* and *Goodwin* for journalistic sources. In *Sunday Times* the Court held that "*the injunction did not correspond to a social need sufficiently pressing to outweigh the public interest in freedom of expression.*"

[24] *Supra* note 17, para. 46.
[25] ECHR 24 February 1997, *De Haes and Gijsels v. Belgium*, para. 37-49.
[26] *Ibid.* para. 47 and 48.

The strict prohibition of 'trial by newspaper' under English law did not take democratic interests into consideration. In the Courts words:

"There is a general recognition of the fact that the courts can not operate in a vacuum. Whilst they are the forum of the settlement of disputes, this does not mean that there can be no prior discussion of disputes elsewhere, be it in specialized journals, in the general press or amongst the public at large. Furthermore, whilst the mass media must not overstep the bounds imposed in the interest of the proper administration of justice, it is incumbent on them to impart information and ideas concerning matters that come before the courts just as in other areas of public interest." [27]

In *Goodwin v. United Kingdom*[28], the Court concluded that an order of source disclosure violates Article 10 as long as it is not justified by an overriding public interest. The reason is as follows:

"Protection of journalistic sources was one of the basic conditions of press freedom. ... Without such protection, sources could be deterred from assisting the press in informing the public on matters of public interest. As a result, the vital public watchdog role of the press could be undermined and the ability of the press to provide accurate and reliable information may be adversely affected."

On professional independence in *Jersild*, a conviction of a journalist who broadcast an interview with a racist group was found to violate Article 10 since it was not his ideology and he was informing the public. On the issue whether the report was balanced or objective, the Court said:

"*It is not for the court, nor the national courts for that matter, to substitute their own views for those of the press as to what technique of reporting should be adopted by journalists. ... Article 10 protects not only the substance of the ideas and information expressed, but also the form in which they are conveyed.*" [29]

Article 10 does not prohibit prior restraint on publication by the press. However, the Court considers the proportionality and effectiveness of such restraint. In the *Spycatcher* case, an injunction against the publication of newspaper articles, which contained extracts of a book called Spycatcher, was sustained even after the book hit the market in the USA. The UK argued that the book and the newspaper articles to be published contained confidential information vital for national security and that of its allies since it was written by a

---

[27] *Supra* note 10, para. 65.

[28] ECHR 27 March 1996, *Goodwin v. The United Kingdom*, para. 39-46.

[29] ECHR 23 September 1994, *Jersild v. Denmark*, para. 31.

former member of MI5. The Court found that the injunction was unnecessary in democratic society since it is not effective while the book is still in the market. The Court emphasised:

"*The dangers inherent in prior restraints are such that they call for the most careful scrutiny on the part of the court. This is especially so as far as the press is concerned, for news is a perishable commodity and to delay its publication, even for a short period, may well deprive it of all its value and interest.*"[30]

Finally, on the issue of sanctions the Court has a jurisprudence that outlines that states must always take into consideration the "chilling effect" of penalties particularly criminal ones. We have already seen in *Castells* that the Court does not approve of criminal sanctions for journalists while there are other options or means available for the states. In *Cumpana and Mazare v. Romania,* Romanian courts convicted two journalists on the ground of defamation and insult. The Court reiterated:

"Investigative journalists are liable to be inhibited from reporting on matters of general public interest ... if they run the risk ... of being sentenced to prison or to a prohibition on the exercise of their profession. The chilling effect that the fear of such sanctions poses on the exercise of journalistic freedom of expression is evident. ...... The court considers that the imposition of a prison sentence for a press offence will be compatible with journalists' freedom of expression as guaranteed by Article 10 of the convention only in exceptional circumstances, notably where other fundamental rights have been seriously impaired, as, for example, in the case of hate speech or incitement to violence."[31]

One can easily see from the Courts' jurisprudence that sanctions save in exceptional circumstances, have to be conceived as informative but not deterring when it comes to journalists.

3. FREEDOM OF THE PRESS UNDER ETHIOPIAN LAW: WHY THE EXCEPTIONS PREVAIL

After the fall of the totalitarian regime in 1991, a transitional government was formed based on a Transitional Charter, which recognised basic human rights. Subsequently, the transitional government issued a 'Proclamation to Provide for Freedom of the Press' (press law).[32] Following that, a large number of pri-

---

[30] ECHR 26 November 1991, *Observer and Guardian v. The United Kingdom*, para. 60.
[31] ECHR 17 December 2004, *Cumpana and Mazare v. Romania*, para. 113 – 115.
[32] A Proclamation to Provide for the Freedom of the Press: No. 34/ 1992, 21 October 1992.

vate newspapers and magazines proliferated in Addis Ababa (the capital), which was unprecedented in the long history of the country. In 1995, a new constitution[33] came into force. Under Article 29, it provides for freedom of opinion and expression. Though some of the wording is vague, this does not pose any serious problem since the constitution requires under Article 13 that all human rights provisions have to be interpreted according to the UDHR (Universal Declaration of Human Rights) and ICCPR. Even though the constitution cemented press freedom as a fundamental political freedom, it is still, even more than ever, a highly controversial and debatable matter in legal, political and social circles. In what follows, we will try to find out why.

3.1. Press Law

The Proclamation to Provide for the Freedom of the Press (No. 34/1992) was adopted based on the Transitional Charter of Ethiopia. Even though a new constitution was adopted on 8 December 1994 (in force from 21 August 1995), the press law has not been changed. The government recently proposed three drafts of the press law. However, these proposals were unsuccessful because of huge criticism from the press, civil society and international human rights organisations as the drafts were unworkable, even by the standards of the current press law. The current press law contains certain unnecessary provisions like defining a journalist and the purpose of the press. These are matters of the press itself. The law may state what such purpose cannot include and that is already governed by criminal law. Other than that, each member of the press defines its purpose. Leaving such provisions aside, we will try to focus on others entailing serious restrictions and sanctions on the press.

Article 5 of the press law extends the right to engage in press activities to any Ethiopian. That being commendable, it depends on what requirements are imposed for registration and licensing procedures. According to international practice, technical requirements for registration of the press do not undermine freedom of the press as long as they fulfil the following conditions:[34]

"*There is no discretion to refuse registration, once the requisite information has been provided; the system does not impose substantive conditions upon the media; the system is not excessively onerous; and the system is administered by a body, which is independent of government.*"

---

[33] The Constitution of the Federal Democratic Republic of Ethiopia: Proclamation No: 1/1995, 21 August 1995.

[34] ARTICLE19, *The legal Framework for Freedom of Expression in Ethiopia* 19, http://www.article19.org/pdfs/publications/ethiopia-legal-framework-for-foe.pdf (last visited 01 April 2008).

Coming back to the press law, Article 6 requires anyone who wants to carry out a press activity to be registered. This being simple, Article 7(1) provides for the requirement of licence to be obtained from the Ministry of Information or regional Information Bureau, as the case may be, by providing certain information such as the names of the owner, editor, publisher, the press and its address. According to Article 7(4), whenever there is change in such information, the press must inform such change to the licensing authority. When we consider this requirement in terms of the international standard, they pose two problems. The first one being that these licensing requirements apply to small print outlets like pamphlets just as they do to large and regular press. The second is that the licensing authorities are not independent but are rather part of government. The proclamation seems to address the second problem since it provides in Article 7(2) that the authorities should give the licence within 30 days from the date of application by the press. If they fail to do so, the provision continues, the licence is deemed to have been given. That appears to avoid any abuse by these authorities but it is not clear why it should take 30 days to acquire a licence. Article 7(5) provides for renewal of the licence annually and without any precondition but upon payment for such renewal and "*... unless suspended or cancelled by an order of the court...*" The amount to be paid is not determined, thus it is left for the authorities to do so. This provision also gives an indication to the possibility of suspension or cancellation of licences but it is not indicated how and why under the proclamation. All these seem to be manageable until one reaches to the back of the proclamation. Article 20(2) states:

"*Where any press is found to have contravened the provisions of Articles 6 and 7 of this proclamation; the proprietor, the publisher or the editor – in – chief of the press shall be punishable with imprisonment not exceeding two (2) years or with fine not exceeding birr Ten Thousand (Birr 10,000).*"

The amount of 10,000 Birr is equivalent to 1,000€ or a little more. Not only is the fine extremely high considering the 'wrong' (when most democracies abolished such system, let alone to punish it harshly) but attaching a criminal penalty to such simple technical failure sends the message that the press performs a dangerous activity to be seriously regulated by government. In addition to that, it has nothing to do with freedom of the press, which the preamble promised to advance.

Freedom of information

Freedom of information is considered an important component of freedom of expression by many democracies and international human rights organizations such as ARTICLE 19 (XIX). In a way, it is also an important part of the principle of democracy because at the heart of freedom of information are transparency and accountability. The constitution guarantees freedom of information in Article 29(3)(b), as we have already seen. It also obliges (under its Article 12.1) government to ensure that all its conduct and affairs must be transparent. Considering such constitutional guarantees and international experience, freedom of information needs to be addressed in separate legislation rather than in one provision of the press law.

This being the case, Article 8(1) of the press law provides for freedom of information from government sources. The limitations include: information declared secret by the House of Representatives or the Council of Ministers, information which is secret by virtue of other laws, information from a court hearing in camera (unless the court decides otherwise), information on a pending case and information private to a victim of a crime without his/her consent. If these are the only exceptions, a large amount of information seems to be free to be acquired by the press. However, there is no guarantee that it would be read like this even though Article 19 of the proclamation imposes a duty on government officials to cooperate with the press. Still, the authorities like the Council of Ministers are left with indefinite margin to say whatever is secret. The law provides no conditions under which secrecy is determined and which other laws provide for secrecy of what information and for what aim is not clearly outlined. Other than that, court reporting is totally prohibited. It is strange to see that for a hearing in camera there is an exception (the court may decide otherwise) and none at all for a regular case pending in court. Without going far, the constitution guarantees a public trial under Article 20 (the rights of persons accused) except for cases where there is an overriding interest to protect privacy, public morals and national security.

Right of Reply

Article 9(1) of the press law states:

"Where any information or matter concerning any person is reported in a press, such person shall have the right to reply in the press in which the report appeared."

It is clear that the right in this provision is very wide because it allows a person to respond to material that is about him/her, that refers to him/her in any way or that is critical of that person. In addition, it does not matter whether the report of the press is a matter of fact or of opinion. Right of reply is pure interference in editorial independence but to make up for that it can be designed to redress certain harm caused by the press on the right of an individual. This provision is far from providing such a balance and totally puts the pressure on the press.

Responsibilities of the press and penalties

Part four of the press law includes Articles 10 to 14. One can say that this part symbolizes the press law more than any other part. We will summarise this part in relation to its penalty provided under Article 20. Article 10(1) lays down that every member of the press has to make sure that their product is free from anything that may give rise to criminal or civil liability. The second sub-Article provides some details:

a) *Any criminal offence against the safety of the state or of the administration established in accordance with the charter or of the national defence force;*
b) *Any defamation or false accusation against any individual, nation or nationality, people or organization;*
c) *Any criminal instigation of one nationality against another or incitement of conflict between people; and*
d) *Any propagation of war.*

However, it says "*without prejudice to the generality of sub-Article 1*" which means that the list is not exhaustive and may include others not mentioned here. When a member of the press fails to insure this, its editor, journalist or publisher will be punished with 1 – 3 years of imprisonment or a fine of not less than 10,000 Birr and not more than 50,000 Birr (over 5,000€) or with both such imprisonment and fine (Art. 20.1 press law). According to Article 14 of the press law this does not affect those criminal and civil liabilities that may arise from acts of the press. The same Article also provides that the press as an organisation has joint liability and that damages for civil suits could reach twice the registered capital of that organisation. Other responsibilities of the press include:

- Keeping a record of the name and address of authors or editors of every press product (Article 11, 1)
- When a penname is used, it has to be indicated in a clear manner (Article 11, 2)
- Printing the name and address of the proprietor, including residence, the editor-in-chief, deputy editor-in-chief and the publisher (Article 12, 1)
- When there is change in the above, declaring the same for the substitute (Article 12, 3)
- Declaring the author and proprietor of any source of news or report (Article 12, 2)
- When it runs any press product for payment, this has to be put under "classified" or such section (Article 12, 4)

- Submitting two copies of every press item to the licensing authorities for free within 24 hours after publication (Article 13)

Failure to indicate the penname specifically and failure to fulfil all or any of the above responsibilities listed in part four would entail punishment with one year of imprisonment or with a fine not exceeding 5,000 Birr (more than 500€) or with both to the owner, publisher or editor, according to Article 20(3).

Prior restraint

There is a very fine line between censorship and prior restraint. For this reason it has to be construed very narrowly and exceptionally for serious danger in matters of highly crucial public interest. Article 15(1) of the press law provides for prior restraint in the following words:

"The prosecutor of Central Government or of a region as the case may be, may where he has sufficient reason to believe that a press is ready to disseminate any illegal press product which may cause serious damage, enjoin the dissemination of such press product."

It is not clear what constitutes "sufficient reason" or "serious damage", i.e. to whom or what interest the damage is directed. However, "illegal press product" obviously can cover anything made illegal by law, which gives wide possibility to prosecutors to stop publication by the press. In an effort that seems to reduce the likelihood of abuse, Article 15(2) requires the prosecutor to submit the matter to the High Court within 24 hours of taking the measure and the Court has to give its decision within 48 hours of submission, according to Article 16(2). Article 16(3) also requires the decision to be executed within 72 hours of submission unless there is an appellate order against it. While considering the matter, Article 16(1) states, the Court may concur with the prosecutor and order "confiscation and destruction" of the press product or quash the measure taken by the prosecutor. The order of the Court for the destruction of the press does not affect any civil or criminal suit against the press, as provided by Article 16(4).

Finally, in the last part of the press law, Article 20(4) forwards another serious warning. It says that any person who "*violates or obstructs the implementation of this proclamation... shall be punishable in accordance with the criminal code.*" This applies to any violation not covered by the penalty provisions discussed above. This provision ensures that any act that violates any part of this proclamation or that is considered to "obstruct" its implementation is to be punished even though it is not clearly provided. This is the vaguest provision in the press law and considering its punitive nature, it is also the most treacherous. The excessively penalising provisions, including using the criminal law, indicate that the press law is suspicious of the exercise of press freedom rather than encouraging and promoting it. To conclude this section, ARTICLE 19 provides a concise observation of Ethiopian press law:

"*There can be little doubt that the penalty regime in the Ethiopian press law is excessively harsh and that it exerts a serious chilling effect on media freedom. Indeed, it is often described as one of the harshest press laws in the world.*"[35]

3.2. The Civil Code

The Civil Code of Ethiopia,[36] which followed the model of the Code Napoleon, defines defamation in the part that deals with torts. The principle of defamation is provided by Article 2044:

"*A person commits an offence where by his words, his writings or by any other means he acts in such a way as to make another living person detestable, contemptible or ridiculous and to jeopardize his credit, his reputation or his future.*"

There are a number of exceptions to this principle but they do not go that far since they have their own exceptions as well. Here is the list of exceptions:

- If the author did not intend to refer to any particular person then there is no defamation committed but this does not apply if he could have reasonably foreseen his writing would cause injury (Art. 2045 Civil Code).
- "*A person shall not be deemed to have committed an offence where he confined himself to expressing his opinion on matters of public interest, notwithstanding that opinion inflicts injury on another by bringing him under public obloquy.*" However, if the defendant, to his certain knowledge, made false charges then this exception does not apply (Art. 2046).
- Where a defendant proves the charges he made then he did not commit defamation but if he acted "solely with intent to injure" he will be liable of defamation (Art. 2047).
- Speeches in parliamentary debate and legal proceedings are immune to charges of defamation but if someone repeats or reports "with intent to injure" then he will be liable (Art. 2048).

Concerning the press, Article 2049 provides justification, which says that there is no liability if the press acted "without intent to injure and without gross negligence". Nevertheless the same press has to publish a "withdrawal and an apology" if the plaintiff so wishes. Nevertheless, in other situations of defamation Article 2109 imposes compensation to be paid but fails to determine the amount. In addition, opinions of someone as being of 'low morals' or 'incom-

---

[35] *Id.* 22.

[36] Proclamation No. 165/1960, 5 May 1960.

petent' or 'criminal' are punished. These provisions substantially reduce the area of public discussion because they do not distinguish the type of person who is the subject of discussion, for example politicians or any public figure. This law requires the truth and only the truth to be reported and published on any topic of discussion or on anyone. In court, the press has to prove the truth of their writings and that is a test that cannot be fulfilled. Another heavy test that is inescapable is 'intent to injure'. Any criticism of a public figure falls into this test. Freedom of opinion is not protected at all since one can only get away with it by providing the truth of writings. Reporting parliamentary or legal proceedings with 'intent to injure' can be punishable. The law seems easy on public interest issues but they have to be true too and if so, they cannot be opinions. In limited cases the press can get away with it easily by publishing an apology but that is made impossible since they have to prove they did not act with intent to injure and with gross negligence. In general, the law of defamation is designed without any consideration of press freedom.

3.3. The Criminal Code

The Criminal Code, as revised in 2004,[37] markedly identifies press-related offences in a separate section. The definition of crimes relating to the mass media is provided by Article 42 and they "*...may be committed against the honour of other persons, public or private safety or any other legal right protected by criminal law, and are committed where communication is made to the public through the mass media.*" Article 43 lists liabilities for crimes committed through the mass media. The list includes journalists, editors and publishers. Article 43(5) also warns against any defence by members of the press to be not responsible by stating that they are presumed so.

The special chapter provided for press-related offences and also this last presumption against the press show the spirit of the penal code as parallel to the press law discussed above which also imposes a duty on the press to check their publications to be free of anything that gives rise to criminal or civil liability. The same spirit seems to be behind the above provision. This being the case, any person outside the press could also be held liable in accordance with Article 44 (1) of the Criminal Code. This provision is also important because it lists the type of offences (not mentioned as press-related) that the press could be held liable for such as incitement, breach of secrecy laws, etc. The punishment for the incitement of such offences ranges from three months up to ten years with or without a fine and in some cases like incitement for riot it could be more. Other than these, crimes related to the press (as defined by Article 42 above) are generally classified as petty offences under Articles 740-47. The purpose of classifying them as petty offences might be to reduce the punitive

[37] Proclamation No. 414/2004, 9 May 2005.

burden on the press but obviously, these should not even be included in the penal law. The range of punishment for such petty offences is one day to three months arrest with or without a fine of one to three hundred Birr. However, according to Article 46, the press organisation or company as a juridical person is also responsible for any crime committed, as it is under the press law. Article 761 lists principal cases where confiscation and suspension are applicable. This is defined as withdrawal of licences or closing of an establishment and the list in sub-heading b includes press and publication matters. The last article in this chapter related to offences of the press is Article 47 and it deals with immunity.

"*The author, publisher or diffuser of a true record or representation, which is correct in form, of public debates or acts of legislative, administrative or judicial authority the diffusion of which is not expressly prohibited by law or by a specific decision shall not be liable to punishment.*"

It is clear from this that the position of the criminal law is similar to the Civil Code since both give protection, or immunity, to be exact, to an author of a true statement. The provision also prohibits a wide area of information since the secrecy requirement is so open ended that somebody might give a "specific decision" for it. The punishment, as provided under Article 435 of the Criminal Code, can be simple imprisonment not exceeding three years or a fine, the amount of which is not mentioned.

In the chapter on 'crimes against honour' Article 607 states as its principle the fact that such crime is punishable irrespective of the position or social status of parties and the determination of punishment takes into consideration the extent of circulation. Obviously, the press has a relatively large circulation and consequently the punishment will be heavier on them. Article 609 includes juridical persons as punishable by fining and states that this does not stop the punishment of their members. The compensation may include material and moral damages, according to Article 610, the determination of which is left for the courts but it may include the publication of the judgment or part of it. Ironically, public officials are immune to such charges in the normal discharge of their duty. Article 612 clearly provides an encroachment in the professional work of journalists with the following.

"*The following are not punishable as injury to honour*:

a) Considered opinions and well-founded criticism, couched in proper and moderate terms, concerning personal aptitudes or artistic, literary, scientific, professional or social activities, creations or productions; or

b) Averments, statements or comments uttered or repeated... by a journalist or by any other person acting in good faith in the discharge of his duties, especially by way of investigations, reports or depositions, ...by way of authorized public information service, where the alleged facts are germane to and remain within the confines thereof and where they are not uttered with express intent to discredit."

This provision provides an unnecessary interference in freedom of the press by outlining when the press should criticise and how. The legislature and the courts are the judges as to how the journalist is doing his job including the terms he uses. That puts the private press on an equal footing with the highly censored government press for which it was supposed to be an alternative.
Another area the Criminal Code governs is defamation that is defined by Article 613 and caries up to one-year imprisonment or a fine irrespective of the truth of the allegation since what matters is the intent to injure. The provision also punishes a false allegation made negligently with up to one year's imprisonment or a fine. There are interesting exceptions under Article 614.

"A person charged with defamation cannot in general plead in defense that he acted without intent to injure, or that he confined himself to repeating even though not believing them, allegations emanating from another, or that it was a matter of common knowledge, or that he uttered suspicions or conjectures." (Art. 614.1)

We can see the same danger against freedom of opinion and expression in public matters as the one in the Civil Code here. The Criminal Code is even more direct as to the impossibility of proving one acted without 'intent to injure'. As long as the victim feels injured, the defendant cannot prove otherwise. Let alone journalists, even an ordinary person should not repeat what he heard from others or rumours unless he has a proof as to the truth. In addition to the truth or having sufficient ground to believe something is true, he also has to prove:

a) He did not have the intention to injure the honour or reputation of another; or
b) He acted in the public interest or he was actuated by a higher interest or moral aim.

Without going into questioning the necessity of expressing only the truth, it is not clear how someone can prove he has "*a* sufficient ground to believe" something is true. Even though one may prove he acted in the public interest, there is no reason why the law requires a separate proof of intending no injury since the one excludes the other. Then again, we are still in limbo because what constitutes "public interest" let alone "higher interest or moral aim" is far from clear. It seems as if journalists are against the "public interest" and they have to prove otherwise all the time. The Code also insulates public servants from the public and the press in Article 618. When the defamation or calumny is against a public servant in the discharge of his duty, the punishment is cumulative of fines and up to one year's imprisonment for the former and three months for the latter. Article 618(2) provides that this does not free one from being liable on the basis of other provisions relating to injury to the honour of the state, foreign states and interstate institutions.

4. LESSONS TO BE DRAWN

4.1. Reflections

The European Court of Human Rights established the principle of the freedom of the press on a firm basis despite the complexity of issues involved. We have seen that the key to understand Article 10 of the Convention and the case law of the Court is through restrictions under sub – Article two. Still, one should be careful not to overlook important concepts in the first sub – Article. Press freedom involves ideas and information. It should not be considered distinct from freedom of opinion. The Court repeatedly emphasised this point because it protects an essential and large part of expression. Once we acknowledge freedom of opinion as part of press freedom, consequently, we cannot require journalists to provide proof for the truth of their opinion since it is not susceptible to proof and only facts can be proved.

The Court in many instances pointed out not only the right of the press to impart information and ideas but also the right of the public to receive them. The public has such right in matters of public interest, which certainly include political speeches but are not limited to it. The margin of tolerance differs in conjunction with the importance of speech to democratic society. As repeatedly emphasised by the Court, highly critical and even polemical speech against politicians, judges and other public officials is tolerated. It could even be aggressive depending on the level of provocation. In addition, professional independence of journalists is guaranteed since it is not only speech that is protected but also the manner and form in which it is communicated. A crucial reminder of the level of protection is that press freedom does include expressions "that offend, shock or disturb". In addition to that, a certain level of exaggeration and provocation is acceptable.

According to the Court's celebrated and influential formulation, every restriction on freedom of the press must fulfil the three-pronged requirements prescribed by law, legitimate aim and necessary in a democratic society. Prescribed by law does not only mean that there should be a rule of law imposing the restriction but that it also has to be clear and precise as to the conditions where such restrictions are applicable. Usually, restrictions have some grand objectives like national security, public morality, privacy, etc., but there has to be a pressing social need to outweigh journalistic freedom and the public's right to know. Moreover, such legitimate aim also has to be necessary in democratic society. In order to be necessary in democratic society it is not enough to have a legitimate aim but the formality, restriction, condition and penalty must be proportionate to the aim and also effective in protecting such aim.

In light of these principles set out by the European Court of Human Rights, the Ethiopian press law lags far behind.
The requirement of registration for technical purposes would not be problematic if there were no refusal or sanction attached to it. The Court in *Gaweda v. Poland*[38] confirms this because when there is a possibility of refusal and sanction on registration it will be "inappropriate from the standpoint of freedom of the press." However, the press law clearly violates this because it requires licences in addition to registration and sanctions it severely. According to Article 5, any Ethiopian has the right to engage in press activity, thus, there is no need for a licence and even if there is, it should not be linked with any sanction.

The press law imposes heavy sanctions, without considering the ones in the Civil and Criminal Codes. The range goes up to three years of imprisonment coupled with a fine of about 5000€. The reasons could be as trivial as not keeping a record of authors or not depositing two copies with the authorities and apparently serious ones such as failure to insure that the press product does not have any content giving rise to civil or criminal liabilities. The impact of this has been clearly indicated by the following passage from ARTICLE 19:

"...Several of these prohibitions merely repeat prohibitions that are already established by existing laws...It is illegitimate to give journalists a 'double warning' of this sort as it suggests that journalists will be watched more closely than others in society, which is bound to have a chilling effect *on media freedom."* [39][Emphasis added]

Here, "double warning" should be read to mean triple warning since the prohibitions are established in all the three laws examined in section 3. In addition, the above quotation has been taken from a passage examining the press law and claims that prohibitions already existing in other laws should not have been repeated in the press law but this does not mean that those other laws cannot be scrutinised vis-à-vis press freedom or are in conformity with it.

Matters of professional responsibility like mentioning the source of news and pennames are highly penalised. Prior restraint has been addressed as though it does not have any danger. Whenever the prosecutor believes a press might cause "serious damage", he can stop publication at least for 48 hours. The

---

[38] ECHR 14 March 2002, *Gaweda v. Poland*, para. 43.
[39] *Supra* note 34, 21.

European Court of Human Rights succinctly put that "*news is a perishable commodity*" and a little delay can waste it. This wide power of the prosecutor is a serious danger to the press because it does not lay down clearly what constitutes a harm that can outweigh the freedom. Unless there are higher standards and clear conditions to be met, prior restraint is as bad as censorship. Freedom of information is recognised by both the press law and the constitution but its application is undermined by many factors such as absence of clear secrecy laws with circumstances of secrecy and absence of rules defining the manner and condition by which the press acquires information from public organs. In addition, court reporting in a regular proceeding is totally prohibited while the right to public trial is recognised by the constitution.

As the established principle of the European Court of Human Rights shows, the limits of acceptable criticism against public officials are very wide in order for the press to play their role of a public watchdog. There is no distinction of speech in the Civil Code and Criminal Code provisions discussed above. Within the general law of defamation, clear exceptions have to be made for journalists not only to enable them to impart information and ideas on matters of public interest but for the public's right to receive those ideas and information. This kind of exception should also extend to expressions of opinion or value–judgment. Even though the constitution clearly protects freedom of opinion, these laws do not conform to such standard, as they require proof for matters of opinion, which cannot be achieved. These provisions totally insulate public authorities from public scrutiny, making it impossible for the press to play their pivotal role in and for democracy. Moreover, they are expected to forward only "well founded criticisms" with "moderate" words. They need to have "good faith" and avoid "intent to injure" even if such task is very difficult to fulfil. More importantly, it is not for the legislature or courts "*…to substitute their own views for those of the press as to what technique of reporting should be adopted by journalists… Article 10 protects not only the substance of the ideas and information expressed, but also the form in which they are conveyed.*"[40] Nevertheless, the Civil and Criminal Codes are highly intrusive in matters of the professional conduct of journalists.

The press law, the Civil Code and the Criminal Code are not compatible with freedom of the press as recognised by the Ethiopian Constitution and as interpreted by the European Court of Human Rights. These laws have to be revised to embrace and promote freedom of opinion, freedom of the press to impart information and ideas, and freedom of the public to receive information and ideas. The laws regulating the press and press-related activities must conform to the requirements of prescribed by law, legitimate aim and necessary in democratic society. The requirement of prescribed by law should be taken, in this regard, to refer to avoiding vagueness and ambiguity. In relation to this, le-

[40] ECHR 23 September 1994, *Jersild v. Denmark*, para. 31.

gitimate aims should be the only aims of these laws and the latter should set out clear conditions under which the restrictions are applicable. Those restrictions and conditions must also be necessary in democratic society and proportionate to the aim pursued. Proportionality refers to avoiding the "chilling effect" of limitations and penalties. For a democratic society, speech on maters of public interest must be protected whether involving maters of fact or opinion. Procedural laws should be made to conform to this with regard to the requirement of proof as to the truth of speech. Coupled with freedom of association, freedom of press guarantees journalists to organise independently and decide on rules of conduct that apply to their profession. The same is true for the press with regard to determining editorial policy. One of the justifications for freedom of the press in a democracy is to ensure government accountability and transparency. This means that no barrier, except under the three requirements discussed above, can be imposed on journalists while trying to investigate government and its organs or seeking information about them. States have also a corresponding duty to make their organs accessible and provide information to journalists. These are the requirements of freedom of information that laws relating to the press and public organs must promote and respect.

4.2. Conclusion

The laws of Ethiopia concerning the press were made at different times and for different reasons. The Civil Code 1960 still serves without undergoing any change on its part that affects press freedom. The change in political landscape in 1991 brought with it the press law and the private press. Nevertheless, this law, in as far as it gave birth to a free press, became its obstacle later on. After the 1995 Constitution came into force and reaffirmed freedom of expression, many changes in the rules were necessary accordingly. As part of this plan, the 1957 Penal Code was revised in 2004 but the changes were on regulating the press more strictly. Recent efforts of revising the press law also showed such desire of more regulation of the press than before and, consequently, faced stiff resistance from stakeholders such as journalists and civil society. However, it is commendable that the government consulted with the stakeholders, decided to abandon the controversial draft and resorted to preparing a new draft.

This study tried to show the shortcomings of the existing press law and the other laws at the backdrop of the well-established case law of the European Court of Human Rights. The Court has proved itself as a highly valuable source to formulate the detailed principles of freedom of the press. The width and variety of members of the European Convention of Human Rights under the Court's jurisdiction and the cases brought to it is also a fundamental tool to learn and understand how each system failed or succeeded in its attempt to address problems of press freedom. That is why, I believe, this study may make a timely contribution to the ongoing debate in Ethiopia on how any draft press law to come forth should be formulated to promote press freedom. In addition, the study highly emphasised that the problem of press freedom is not going to be solved by revising the press law, which is the only focus of the debate, but also requires revising the other laws such as the Civil Code and Criminal Code.

Many stakeholders such as the government, the private press and civil society believe that the problem of press freedom is political. That refers to the situation where the press considers the government as a relentless enemy trying to choke them while the government perceives the press as agents of the opposition bent on dismantling the constitutional order and without professional competence. If such is the case, then it is a very different problem to be addressed here but it deserves, for certain, the attention of the appropriate professionals and stakeholders concerned. However, even if legal reform may require a political will and whatever the existing problems of the private press, the laws should pave the way and lead it to the extensive freedom it aspires to. On the other hand, since press freedom carries with it duties and responsibilities, journalists should organise themselves and determine their code of conduct. One should not forget, as we have seen, that press freedom is not only the freedom of this or that newspaper but also the freedom of the Ethiopian public.

13. Gender Equality: Understanding Affirmative Action in Ethiopia

Tigist Gossaye Melka[•]

1. INTRODUCTION

Ensuring gender equality has been the focal point of the international community, which has been particularly the case after the adoption of the Convention on the Elimination of All Forms of Discrimination against Women (CEDAW) in 1979. The Convention calls for gender equality in its true form - equality in law and equality in fact. Through such strong appeal to promote gender equality, the CEDAW refers to the elimination of discrimination as one of the tools to end inequality between the sexes. Being the first comprehensive binding international document for the protection of women and the prevention of discrimination against them, the CEDAW defines discrimination along with temporary special measures as exceptions to it.

This article briefly summarises the notion of gender equality, non-discrimination and how they are related to temporary special measures. It then goes on to revise the concept of 'temporary special measures' alternatively known as 'affirmative action' within the Ethiopian context. Starting from the hypothesis that affirmative action is 'the victim of its own success' in Ethiopia, attempts will be made to prove the assertion. Methodology employed to verify the hypothesis will be the analysis of relevant international and national human rights, legal and policy documents. Practical evidence will also be drawn from how affirmative action is carried out in higher education institutions and parliaments in Ethiopia.

Finally, this article forwards possible points of recommendation as the way forward to avail women in Ethiopia of affirmative action in all aspects of their private and public lives.

[•] LLB Addis Ababa University, M.A. in the Theory and Practice of Human Rights (University of Oslo, Norwegian Centre for Human Rights), lecturer at the Mekelle University Faculty of Law and Human Rights Assistant with UNMEE. E-mail: tigistgos@yahoo.com

2. GENDER EQUALITY AND NON-DISCRIMINATION: BRIEF OVERVIEW (INTERNATIONAL LAW PERSPECTIVE)

The major aim of this section is to discuss briefly the concepts of gender equality and non-discrimination. As such, it will not attempt to provide an in-depth analysis of the concept. It rather makes use of the same to highlight the major focus of this article; namely, affirmative action for women. Insofar as the latter is the tool for the realisation of the former, I argue that the two are complementary and coexisting.

- *Gender Equality*

Equality is a core value of the UN system, which all countries share in common. Promoting gender equality, *Goal Three,* is also one of the effective means of achieving the Millennium Development Goals (MDGs) with the indicators being equality in education, work and political participation.[1]

International law affirms that human beings are equal in worth and dignity and deserve equal protection of their rights and fundamental freedoms that are inherent in their nature. Therefore, the principle of equality is implicit in the concept of human rights, as belonging to all human beings and therefore to all equally.[2] It is an instrumental and cross cutting issue in human rights discourse as it occupies a central place in international human rights law, as well as in the constitutional laws of many states.[3]

The issue of equality became a point of contention within the United Nations system since its establishment, calling for the need to specify the particular framework within which equality or inequality has to be perceived. It was a long time ago that the norm of non-discrimination or non-separation on the basis of race became a rule of customary international law.[4] Besides, the UN Charter included it as one of the impermissible grounds for discrimination. Then came into being the International Convention on the Elimination of All Forms of Racial Discrimination (ICERD, 1965) with a growing scale of coverage of rights and freedoms in the exercise of which no one should be discriminated against on the basis of his/her race.

Gender equality *per se* gathered the attention of the international community since the adoption of the UN Charter in 1945. The early recognition of gender (sex?) equality in international human rights law is apparent from the relevant

[1] Progress towards the Millenium development Goals, 1990-2005, UN Department of Economic and Social Affairs, Statistics Division, 1.
[2] L. Henkin, G.L. Neuman, D.F. Orentlicher, D.W. Leebron, *Human Rights* 1025 (New York: Foundation Press, 1999).
[3] Ibid.
[4] Id. 1038.

provisions of the UN Charter. Accordingly, the Charter affirms the faith of the United Nations "in... the equal rights of men and women".[5] Like race, a person's sex or gender is also a ground on the basis of which no discrimination is permitted in international human rights law.

This is also emphasised as one of the purposes of the UN, which include achieving, by Member States, of "*international cooperation in promoting and encouraging respect for human rights and fundamental freedoms for all without distinction as to ...sex*".[6](Omission mine)

In addition, the Universal Declaration of Human Rights and the two international Bills of Rights of 1966 are based on the principles of gender equality. Both the International Covenant on Civil and Political Rights (ICCPR) and the International Covenant on Economic, Social and Cultural Rights (ICESCR) require states, under their common Articles 2 and 3, to ensure the realisation of the respective rights on the basis of equality and without any distinctions on the basis of race, colour, ***sex***[•]... and other grounds.

The CEDAW (1979) came up as a document clarifying what amounts to be gender equality and included the prohibition of gender discrimination.

Later developments within the UN also reaffirmed similar recognition for gender equality. General Comment no. 28 of the Human Rights Committee is worth mentioning in this regard. Referring to the importance of Article 3 of the ICCPR that provides for equality of rights between men and women, the Committee has decided that:

"*Article 3 implies that all human beings should enjoy the rights provided for in the Covenant, on an equal basis and in their totality. The full effect of this provision is impaired whenever any person is denied the full and equal enjoyment of any right. Consequently, States should ensure to men and women equally the enjoyment of all rights provided for in the Covenant.*"[7]

Nevertheless, the scope of the principles and the corresponding state obligations to ensure gender equality need further clarification.

---

[5] UN Charter, preamble, para. 2.

[6] *Ibid*, Art 1(3).

[•] It seems that the reference to equality in this context is in terms of sex and not gender. This also seems to be the pattern followed by some when they identify 'gender' with 'women'. But gender is not just about women. Later developments in international human rights standards and the observations of the relevant bodies within the UN human rights system reveal that it is not only sex, which is a biological relationship between men and women, but also the gender aspect as it is defined as the social, economical, cultural and political roles of men and women in their society, that has direct and profound impact on the rights of women. Mention in this regard can be made of the General comment 28 of the ICCPR and paragraph 8 General Comment 25 of the CEDAW.

[7] CCPR/C/21/Rev.1/Add.10, General Comment No. 28, para. 2.

- Non -Discrimination

In international human rights law, the norm of non-discrimination is inextricably linked with the principle of equality. This can be gathered from various relevant provisions of the major human rights instruments such as the UDHR, ICCPR, ICESCR, ICERD and CEDAW. All of these instruments provide for equality in terms of ensuring the rights they guarantee to all without distinctions on the specified grounds there under. A specific instance worth mentioning in relation to this is what is provided by the Human Rights Committee, under its General Comment No 28 paragraph 4. Hence,

"*Articles 2 and 3* (of the ICCPR) *mandate States Parties to take all steps necessary, including the prohibition of discrimination on the ground of sex, to put an end to discriminatory actions, both in the public and the private sector, which impair the equal enjoyment of rights.*" [8]

What amounts to discrimination and what does not? The ICERD and CEDAW have defined discrimination. Accordingly, Article 1 of the CEDAW defines discrimination as follows:

"*any distinction, exclusion or restriction made on the basis of sex which has the effect or purpose of impairing or nullifying the recognition, enjoyment or exercise by women of human rights and fundamental freedoms in the political, economic, social, cultural, civil or any other field.*"[9]

In short, discrimination or invidious treatment of women by any person, organisation or enterprise has been outlawed by the Convention. This provision is intended to abrogate any existing discrimination against women and charges states with a duty of ensuring equality of everyone, men and women, implying that they are not to be discriminated against in the enjoyment and exercise of their fundamental rights and freedoms.

International law's prohibition of discrimination in the enjoyment of human rights does not apply to special measures. In other words, not all distinction amounts to discrimination. It is only the invidious ones that are to be eliminated. This is apparent from Article 4 of the CEDAW, which has clearly provided that,

" *1. Adoption by States Parties of temporary special measures aimed at accelerating de facto equality between men and women* shall not be considered discrimination *as defined in the present Convention, but shall in no way entail as a consequence the maintenance of unequal or separate standards; these meas-*

[8] *Ibid.* para. 4.
[9] Article 1 of the CEDAW.

ures shall be discontinued when the objectives of equality of opportunity and treatment have been achieved. (Emphasis added)
2. Adoption by States Parties of special measures, including those measures contained in the present Convention, aimed at protecting maternity
shall not be considered discriminatory." (Emphasis added)

The next section will highlight the import of this particular provision in light of the main subject of discussion: affirmative action or temporary special measures.

3. AFFIRMATIVE ACTION: GENERAL OVERVIEW

The concept of affirmative action was first developed in the USA in the mid - 1960s when President L. Johnson introduced it as a policy that would redress racial imbalances that at the time existed in the USA, in spite of constitutional guarantees and laws banning discrimination.[10] There are also references to earlier related court decisions, i.e. the famous Brown V. the Education Board of Topeka Kansas case rendered by the US Supreme Court in 1954 to allow mixed schools for black and whites.[11] Affirmative action also forms substantive part of international human rights law particularly relevant for racial minorities and women.

- *Definition of affirmative action*

Various attempts have been made to define the term affirmative action, also called positive discrimination, temporary special measures, etc. Sociological and legal definitions are provided here. According to the first,

"*Affirmative action is a temporary partial remedy for and continuing discrimination against historically marginalized and disenfranchised groups in any society.*"[12]

According to this definition, affirmative action works to provide marginalized groups with greater equality of opportunity in diverse contexts marked by substantial inequalities and structural forces that impede a fair assessment of their abilities and capabilities. In the US where affirmative action started to be implemented earlier, it was articulated as a "*temporary measure that was neces-*

---

[10] Sisonke Msimang, Affirmative Action in the New South Africa: The Politics of Representation, Law and Equity, http://www.isiswomen.org/wia/wiawcar/affirmative.htm (last visited on 03 April 2008).
[11] Ruth N. Kibiti, *Models of Affirmative action for women* 1 (University of Nairobi: Institute of African Studies, 2002).
[12] Ibid.

sary in order to level the playing ground for all races alike."[13] A similar definition has been adopted in the South African context as well where affirmative action was adopted as "*a policy of creating equal opportunity for the least privileged people in society, blacks and black women, by ensuring access to education, employment and political participation through adopting various progressive legislations to that effect, the major one being the Employment Equity Act (EEA, 1998).*" [14]

- Affirmative action under international human rights law: a follow up concept

The ICERD and the CEDAW oblige State Parties to take special measures for the benefit of disadvantaged racial groups and women in the social, economic, cultural and other fields.

Article 1(4) of the ICERD provides that special measures taken for the sole purpose of securing adequate advancement of certain special and ethnic groups or individuals to ensure such groups or individuals' equal enjoyment or exercise of rights shall not be deemed racial discrimination so long as such measures are temporary.

Looking at the historical inequalities women have suffered through the ages and intending to give both men and women an equal start, the CEDAW puts forward exceptions to its definition of discrimination under Article 1. This is envisaged when the State Parties employ temporary special measures aimed at accelerating *de facto* equality between men and women.[15] The Committee on the CEDAW elaborated what constitutes temporary special measures. It did so as it is convinced that a purely legal or programmatic approach is not sufficient to achieve women's *de facto* equality or 'substantive equality' or equality of result.[16] States are obliged under Article 4 of the Convention to do more than guarantee women identical treatment as men. The Committee underlines that,

"*Biological as well as socially and culturally constructed differences between men and women must be taken into account. Under certain circumstances, unidentical treatment of women and men will be required in order to address such differences.*"[17]

The obligations that states assume under the present article are clearly different from those that are stated under Articles 2 and 24 of the Convention. The major difference lies in their purpose. While the general obligations deal with the

---

[13] Sisonke Msimang, *supra* note 10.
[14] Ibid.
[15] Article 4 of the CEDAW.
[16] General Recommendations No. 25 of the Committee on the Elimination of All Forms of Discrimination Against Women, CEDAW/C/2004/I/WP.1/Rev.1, para. 8.
[17] *Ibid.*

appropriate measures that states should take to ensure the equality of women with men in important aspects of their lives, the temporary special measures are different in the sense that their main goal is to rectify the inequalities women suffered in the past.

They are of temporary nature and are to be discontinued when the *de facto* equality of women with men is achieved and when there is equal representation of women in the economic, social, cultural, political and civil areas. On the other hand, the states' obligations to amend discriminatory laws, to design policies and plan of actions and other administrative measures with a view to promote gender equality should not be construed as affirmative measures that do have remedying effects and that are temporary. They are rather to be in place permanently. In the words of the committee,

"*...the obligation of states parties under the Convention to improve the position of women to one of de facto or substantive equality with men exists irrespective of any proof of past discrimination.*"[18]

Therefore, affirmative action or, as it might alternatively be called, special measures, positive measures or reverse discrimination, should not be construed as the overall obligations of states in this regard. The latter obligation exists all the time and is permanent by nature.

Following along the same line of argument, the Human Rights Committee has also recognised the need to take affirmative measures under its General Comment 18 paragraph 10.[19] Hence, it provides that the principles of equality sometimes require State Parties to take affirmative action in order to diminish or eliminate conditions that cause or help to perpetuate discrimination prohibited by the convention. The scope of applicability of this statement is not only restricted to women but to any section of a population in a given state that is prevented or impaired from enjoying human rights.

It is also clear from the above-mentioned paragraph that such measures have the purpose of correcting such conditions. The action may involve granting for the time being, to the part of the population concerned, certain preferential treatment in specific matters as compared with the rest of the population.[20] Read in light with previous specific documents on rights of women and racial minorities and the areas of lack of participation of these groups of people, this provision equally justifies the need to resort to affirmative action to promote gender equality in the areas of education, employment and political participation.

---

[18] *Ibid.* para. 18.
[19] CCPR General Comment 18, CCPR/37th session10/11/89, para. 10.
[20] *Ibid.*

- Areas of implementation of affirmative action

Though it was historically developed as a concept in the USA, affirmative action is not implemented only in the USA. Following the adoption of the policy in the international human rights plane and other domestic developments, it has worked successfully in many countries around the world particularly in some African countries. Mention in this regard could be made of Uganda, Zambia, Tanzania and South Africa. As will be discussed later in this article, Ethiopia has also started implementing the policy for some time now.

The major focus of affirmative action measures in all the above cases has been on promoting political participation, which is a recent development in Ethiopia compared to the implementation of the measures to promote gender equality in the field of education and employment. The national constitutions of Rwanda and Burundi, for example, now include provisions to reserve seats for women. In 2003, elections in Rwanda saw the greatest proportion of women elected to any parliament in history with 48% of women in parliament.[21] In South Africa and Mozambique, the introduction of quota mechanisms by political parties meant that, in 2004, post-conflict and post-crisis countries ranked among the highest in the world in terms of women's representation (in Eritrea, Mozambique and South Africa women comprise between 22% to 35% of the legislature).[22]

The increase in women's parliamentary representation in Latin America and the Caribbean is also attributable to the introduction of affirmative action measures. Various quotas for women's political participation exist in 17 countries in this region.[23]

Common features of all these different legal systems adopting affirmative action policy is that they all perceive it as a means of creating equitable and fair grounds for the historically marginalized sections of their societies, prominently women.

Now follows a discussion on affirmative measures adopted in the Ethiopian legal system so as to bridge the legacy of gender inequality in the country. Here key observations are made regarding how affirmative action has been construed in the Ethiopian legal system and policy frameworks. This will be done through analysing the various reports the country submitted to the Committee on the Elimination of Discrimination against Women along with the concluding observations and remarks of the Committee.

---

[21] Women in Politics, Inter-Parliamentary Union, http://www.ipu.org/PDF/publications/wmn45-05_en.pdf (last visited on 04 April 2008).

[22] *Ibid.*

[23] *Ibid.*

4. AFFIRMATIVE ACTION IN ETHIOPIA: THE LEGAL BASIS

Ethiopia adopted the policy on 10 October 1981 when it adopted and ratified the CEDAW. The Constitution of the People's Democratic Republic of Ethiopia of 1987 stated under its Article 36 that "*women and men have equal rights*" and that "*the state shall provide women with special support, particularly in education, training and employment so that they may participate in political, economical, social and cultural affairs on equal basis with men.*" Some however argue that despite these lofty words, little affirmative action was taken on behalf of women and that these words did not often coincide with reality.[24]

Then the 1994 Education and Training Policy recognised what resembles affirmative action as one of the government strategies to enhance education and empowerment of women.[25] And later on, the FDRE (Federal Democratic Republic of Ethiopia) Constitution provided for women's entitlement to affirmative measures under its Article 35(3), which reads,

"*The historical legacy of inequality and discrimination suffered by women in Ethiopia taken into account, women, in order to remedy this legacy, are entitled to affirmative measures.*"

This constitutional provision draws on the provisions of the CEDAW. Among the roads to gender equality in Ethiopia, affirmative action seems to be the most followed as will be demonstrated later on.

- Federal Civil Servants Proclamation No. 262/2002[26]

The Federal civil Servants Proclamation Article 13(1) prohibits discrimination among job seekers in filling vacancies because of their sex. It also provides for affirmative action stating that female candidates shall be preferred where they have equal or close scores with other candidates. However, no data is available on the number or percentage of women who have benefited from this opportunity.

- Proclamation on Higher Education no 351/2003[27]

The FDRE proclamation on higher education is also another legal basis that reaffirms and explicitly provides for affirmative action policy. Article 33 is the provision of the proclamation on special support. The higher education institutions being the immediate bearers of the duty to implement the policy and the

[24] CEDAW/C/ETH/1-3, 21 May 1993.

[25] Education and Training Policy of Ethiopia, 1994 sec 3.4.10 cum 3.7.6.

[26] Federal Civil Servants Proclamation, 8th Year No. 8, *Federal Negarit Gazeta*, 3 January 2002.

[27] Higher Education Proclamation, 9th Year No. 72, *Federal Negarit Gazeta*, 3 July 2003.

prime addressees of the proclamation, such a provision would expedite the process of enforcing the policy, making the institutions accountable.

- Other relevant policy documents

'Education and training policy' is the first document that sets forth what resembles 'temporary special measures' or affirmative action. Under its section 3.7.6, the policy provides that special support will be given to women and to regions that were deprived of education opportunities in the preparation, distribution and utilisation of educational supports. Here the focus is not only on women but also on students from *disadvantaged regions* that are beneficiaries of special support.

The FDRE Executive Capacity Building Strategies and Programmes[28] also considered affirmative action as one of the tools to increase the participation of women and students from disadvantaged regions in the country in the field of education. It has not spelled out the specific modalities of implementing it, though. But it asserts that quality should not be compromised in the venture of making higher education accessible equitably. The strategies and programmes document emphasised that the efficiency of higher education should not be measured by the number of students failing every year.[29] Offering special support in this regard for those who need it is considered an essential part of the measures to acquire equitably accessible higher education.

5. AREAS OF IMPLEMENTATION OF AFFIRMATIVE ACTION IN ETHIOPIA

Like most of the countries discussed previously, affirmative measures within the Ethiopian context are also implemented to promote the participation of women in the field of education, employment and political decision-making. This is evident from Article 35(3) of the FDRE Constitution, which outlines the major purpose of such measures as follows;

"*to provide special attention to women so as to enable them to compete and participate on the basis of equality with men in political, social and economic life as well as in public and private institutions*."

- Education

With the exception of the Federal Civil Servants Proclamation No. 262/2002, all the above mentioned legal and policy documents provide for affirmative

[28] FDRE Document on Executive Capacity Building Strategies and Programmes, 2002, 170.
[29] *Ibid.*

action to boost the participation of women in education. This is also a common element in the official reports of Ethiopia to various international bodies. Mention in this regard can be made of Ethiopia's 1st to 3rd combined report and 4th and 5th combined reports submitted to the CEDAW Committee in 1993 and 2002 respectively.♠

In Ethiopia's report on progress made in the implementation of the Beijing Platform for Action "*affirmative action being taken to increase the number of females in teacher training and in higher education*" is considered one of the measures taken to promote girls' education in Ethiopia.[30] The report also asserts that such affirmative measures, among others, have contributed to rapid growth of female participation in education.[31] Such affirmative measures included reduction of the Grade Point Average required for enrolment in universities and the provision of tutorials.[32] The secondary data obtained from the Ministry of Education provide the following figures showing female participation before the implementation of affirmative action policy and afterwards.

Levels	1995/1996	2001/2002	2002/2003	Target set for 2004/2005
Teachers Teaching Institute	36.6%	40.0%	44%	-
Higher education (Universities)	10.7%	11.1%	25.3%	30%

Source: Ministry of Education, 2004

In many higher education institutions, currently the ultimate figure of 30% has been nearly achieved. What this means, however, is that the total number of first-year entrants to universities and colleges has increased. This however, does not imply any sort of increase in the number of girls who have completed higher education. Even if it does, there is no evidence to show that such increase is because of the implementation of affirmative action policy as there has never been data disaggregated by beneficiaries of affirmative action measures. This goes against the commitment of the country to come up with gen-

♠ The 1st to 3rd reports do not clearly contain such phrases on affirmative action as the policy was not yet adopted during the reporting period. But as could be gathered from its concluding remarks on the same reports in 1996 (after such major developments as the adoption of the Education and Training Policy, the FDRE Constitution, took place in the country), the Committee welcomed the affirmative action efforts for women at university level (see CEDAW/C/SR.292, 293 and 299, para. 143). The 4th and 5th combined reports to the CEDAW also include a paragraph on the implementation of affirmative action to increase female participation in education with 30% of the total number of seats in universities set aside for female students (see CEDAW/C/ETH/4-5, 28 October 2002, para.19).

[30] A National Report on Progress made in the Implementation of the Beijing Platform for Action (Beijing +10), Ethiopia, Prime Minister Office/Women's Affairs Sub Sector, March 2004, para.19.

[31] *Ibid.*

[32] CEDAW/C/SR.645, 30th session, 26 January 2004, para.47.

der-specific statistics to monitor the impact of policies and programmes on girls and women.[33]

Finally, it is also worth noting here that affirmative measures in higher education in Ethiopia are synonymous with just setting aside quota (some percentage (so far 30%) for the total number of seats in universities) for female students. But without any indicator to evaluate the impact of other measures that should be in place to further support those who have gained the seats,[♦] it becomes difficult to assess the success or otherwise of the policy in the context of higher education in Ethiopia. Yet, it is a paradox to note that government policy of affirmative action has been reported as a major step toward achieving gender equality.[♣] The CEDAW monitoring Committee also did not make in-depth observations and remarks on the issue in its various concluding remarks addressed to Ethiopia.

- *Employment*

Except that the above-cited Federal Civil Servants Proclamation No. 262/2002 provides for affirmative measures to increase women's employment, one cannot find the impact the policy has registered in light of its purpose. The institutional set of many governmental entities now recognises the establishment of the gender focal points.[34] The sole purpose of these sections is to oversee and monitor whether gender is mainstreamed in the respective organisations. Their actual capacities and success in this regard, however, need further and thorough research.

- *Political participation*

As could be gathered from previous legal documents, it is the FDRE Constitution that entitles women to affirmative action to increase their political participation. When it comes to practice, it is only to ensure access to a higher level of education that affirmative action has been applied for more than a decade now.

---

[33] CEDAW/C/SR.292, 293 and 299, para. 137.

[♦] See CEDAW General Recommendation no.25, para.18, which gives broader meaning to what amounts to 'temporary special measures'.

[♣] All the reports Ethiopia submitted to the CEDAW (1993-2002), Ethiopia's National report on the Implementation of the Beijing Platform for Action (March, 2004) magnify the success of affirmative action policy in the country. The exception in this regard seems to be the recent Report of the Federal Democratic Republic of Ethiopia on the Implementation of the AU solemn Declaration on Gender Equality in Africa (August 2006), where no mention of affirmative action as a measure employed to enhance female participation in higher education is made.

[34] The Ethiopian National Policy on Women, 1993.

Whether affirmative action should be extended to promote women's participation in other aspects of their lives, such as political aspects, was discouraged in the 4th and 5th reports mentioned above.

Accordingly, paragraph 47 of the concluding observation of the CEDAW, where it considered the 4th and 5th reports of Ethiopia, also confirms the absence of a quota system for parliament.[35] Hence, some commented that the government itself is against its own affirmative measure policy when it comes to political participation.[36] The CEDAW did not comment on such a limited application of affirmative action.

The resultant effect of such limited understanding of the scope of affirmative action in Ethiopia has been that the number of seats held by women in the House of Peoples' Representatives (Federal Parliament) after the 2000 election was only 42 out of 544 or 7.7%. This apparently shows the defiance of the concept of equality to its fullest extent: equality in law (*de jure*) and equality in fact - equality of result (*de facto*). As such it compromised the state's obligation of result-ensuring absolute equality (equality in law and equality in fact) in the economic, social and political lives of men and women.

- *Progressive move towards better understanding*

The Ethiopian robust position not to employ affirmative action or quota systems in political participation changed during the 2005 national election. This happened after the adoption of the CEDAW General Recommendation No. 25 that clarified that "*measures taken under art 4(1) by* State Parties *should aim to accelerate the equal participation of women in the political, economical, social, cultural, civil or any other field.*"[37] (Emphasis added) Currently, there are noticeable achievements in the participation of women, particularly in the Federal Parliament as well as in Regional Councils.

What accounts for this significant change is the fact that the ruling party (EPRDF) took an important stride by making 30% of its candidates for the 2005 election (both for the Federal House of Peoples' Representatives and the Regional Councils) women.[38] This is a progressive step toward a better understanding of the scope of affirmative action. However, it leaves much to be de-

[35] *Supra* note 32, para. 47.

[36] S. Pausewang, K.Tronvoll and L. Aalen (eds.), *Ethiopia since the Derg: A decade of democratic pretension and performance* 49 (London: Zed Books, 2002) quoted in Tigist Gossaye Melka, *Gender Equality in Higher Education: the Ethiopian Case Study,* thesis Submitted in partial fulfillment of the requirements for the degree of Master of Arts in the Theory and Practice of Human Rights, Norwegian Centre for Human Rights, Faculty of Law, University of Oslo, Norway, 26 August 2004, 63.

[37] *Supra* note 16, para.18.

[38] Report of the Federal Democratic Republic of Ethiopia on the Implementation of the AU solemn Declaration on Gender Equality in Africa, August, 2006, 9.

sired, as such measure is not taken as a State Party commitment to realise its obligation. It rather represents a political party commitment, which casts doubt on the sustainability of the positive shift in understanding the far- reaching scope of affirmative action measures in Ethiopia. And it is as a State Party to the CEDAW that Ethiopia is expected to adopt such obligation of conduct.•

The following table summarises the percentage of women parliamentarians in Ethiopia after the 2000 and 2005 National Elections.

Year	2000			2005		
	Male	Female	Female percentage	Male	Female	Female Percentage
House of Peoples' Representatives	502	42	7.7	413	117	22
House of the Federation	110	7	5.9	91	21	18.7

Source: House of Peoples' Representatives, 2006

- *Women's Representation in the Executive Branch*

The following table summarises the gender composition in the executive branch of government. As the figures show, women's participation in higher governmental position is meagre with more executive positions created and yet similar or lower numbers of women appointed. This leaves much more to be done to enhance gender parity in this regard as well.

• The Committee on the CEDAW did not consider in depth what amounted to temporary special measures under Art.4(1) of the CEDAW by the time it was reviewing the initial, second, third, fourth and fifth report of Ethiopia over a period of six years (1996-2002). This could be gathered from the Concluding Observations of the Committee on the Elimination of Discrimination Against Women: Ethiopia Initial, second, third, fourth and fifth report (CEDAW/C/ETH/1-3 & 4 -5) (1996-2002). But it has now come up with a clear and detailed clarification of the elements of affirmative action through its General Recommendations No. 25 of the Committee on the Elimination of All Forms of Discrimination Against Women, CEDAW/C/2004/I/WP.1/Rev. This is a crucial step taken internationally that could help in improving the way affirmative action is understood and implemented in Ethiopia.

Year	2000		2005	
Positions	Male	Female	Male	Female
Ministers	16	1	20	2
Deputy Minister/State Min-isters	12	4	30	5
State Ministers			30	5
Ambassadors	16	4	35	3

Source: Federal Civil Service Agency, 2006

6. CONCLUDING REMARKS AND POINTS OF RECOMMENDATION

As much as the incorporation of affirmative action policy in Ethiopia throughout most of its laws and policies on women is commendable, it is a paradox to observe that the policy has been the victim of its own success. In almost all of the instruments and practices shown above, affirmative measures have been mentioned as vague and general. It is a policy, the implementation of which has not been effectively monitored. Likewise, the procedures of its implementation are not clearly laid down. This can be inferred from the absence of any specific law or regulation or of an official guideline spelling out the modes of implementation of the policy. This is particularly true for the application of the policy in higher education institutions.

When it comes to enhancing political participation of women, one could observe that there is lack of ownership of the states' obligations set forth in the relevant international human rights standards such as the CEDAW and the General Recommendations of its monitoring body. The mere commitment of the ruling party and not the desire to fulfil a legal obligation of the State Party as such seems to be the driving force behind the implementation of the policy of affirmative action in Ethiopia. This has created confusion in following up the major achievements gained through the policy as much as making data collection in this regard a formidable task. Therefore, it is possible to conclude that the policy, in the Ethiopian context, has been equated mainly with the superficial increment of the numbers of first year female higher education students in case of university enrolment. This can also be deduced from the successive combined reports of Ethiopia to the Committee on the Elimination of all Forms of Discrimination Against Women (CEDAW).

All this is done, however, in an institutional lacuna, where there is no implementing legislation and no indicators set to evaluate the changes the policy has brought to promote gender equality in the country. From the above observations, it is not difficult to sense that the temporary measure is mistaken for an ultimate goal and an end in itself. This goes outside the intention and meaning attached to affirmative measures in international human rights law as was shown in the above sections.

A weak legal and institutional framework cannot bring about an ever-lasting change in gender bias and harmful practices that target women in Ethiopia. Nor can they change the status quo for the better and create a pattern of societal behaviour that defends the equality of women in its true sense.

Hence, the Ethiopian state needs to build on and realise its already demonstrated political commitment and legal obligation by streamlining the institutional and policy framework within which the affirmative action policy can be effective. This would call for compiling and publishing data disaggregated by beneficiaries of the policy, setting up guidelines and strengthening gender focal points and organisations to successfully monitor its implementation.

14. Development and Maintenance of the Ethiopian Legal Information Website

Getaneh Agegn Alemu•

1. INTRODUCTION

1.1 Legal Information

"Information is the need for every need"
Noah A. Samara

Information plays quite a significant role in every aspect of human life. Noah A. Samara in his keynote speech stated that, "*information is truly the need for every need. It is at the heart of education, health, economy, social relationship…even our notions of legitimacy, fairness and trust, are all based on information.*" [1]

Since the existence of human beings, there has been the existence of information in various forms communicated through various media. By the same token, laws have been in force inscribed on stones, parchment, paper, tapes and nowadays in electronic formats.

Lyytikäinen et al. discussed that the information and communication technologies have opened up new possibilities for access to legal information. The authors described the impact of global information infrastructure as "*Internationalization in general has also led to an increasing need to know more about legal norms and regulations in other countries*".[2]

The digital divide has created disparities at the level of application and utilization of these technological tools in developing countries. Literature shows that this digital gap can be narrowed so developing nations like Ethiopia can reap the benefits of using the tools.

• Lecturer and University Librarian, Mekelle University, Ethiopia.
E-mail: getanehagegn@yahoo.com

[1] Noah A. Samara is an Ethiopian, the founder of Worldspace Corporation; N.A. Samara, *Ethiopia in the Knowledge Age,* Keynote Speech, Addis Ababa.[cited on Nov. 14, 2004] Available from World Wide Web:
(http://www.ethiopiaknowledge.org/Final%20Papers/Keynote%20Address,%20Samara.PDF).

[2] V. Lyytikäinen, P. Tiitinen and A. Salminen, Challenges for European legal information retrieval, in: F. Galindo and G. Quirchmayer (Eds.), *Proceedings of the IFIP 8.5 Working Conference on Advances in Electronic Government* (pp. 121-132) (Zaragoza: Seminario de Informatica y Derecho, Universidad de Zaragoza).[cited on 5 April 2005] Available from World Wide Web: (http://www.cs.jyu.fi/~airi/papers/IFIP-2000.pdf) .

Information and communication technologies have greatly contributed to the creation, organization, storage, preservation and dissemination of legal information. We are witnessing the fact that an enormous amount of legal information is available on the Internet. To mention some, Belgian laws are available on the Internet for free and anyone can have access to them online at www.juridat.be. AUTLII is a large free online database of laws in Australia. Lexis-Nexis and Westlaw are huge databases of American laws. Companies like Lexis-Nexis and Westlaw earn millions by selling legal information for law firms, lawyers and law schools.

Websites have become a common way of publishing legal information for the public in many countries. While very recent attempts have been made by the Ethiopian telecom agency to expand the services, the availability and utilization of the Internet by legal professionals have remained limited.

1.2 Application of Information Technologies to Ethiopian Laws

In Ethiopia, the application of information technologies in the legal domain is in its infancy. The Ethiopian constitution is available on the Internet on different websites. However, no other basic Ethiopian law so far has been accessible on the Internet. As a result, it has been a problem for the public, researchers, professors, law firms and legal professionals to access these basic laws on the Internet and other digital formats.

The non-availability of Ethiopian laws on digital media such as CD-ROMs and the Internet and the absence of the application of electronic document management systems to the laws, have initiated this research on the possibilities of converting hard copy laws to softcopies and hence applying existing document management systems such as the Internet to Ethiopian laws.

2. USERS NEEDS AND REQUIREMENTS ANALYSIS

Users: refers to persons who reside in Ethiopia or abroad and who use or have the interest to use Ethiopian laws.

2.1. Respondents Background (profile)

In order to assess the need to apply Internet technologies to the basic Ethiopian laws questionnaires were distributed by email and in person to 80 respondents out of which 34 filled out and returned the completed form. The reply rate was therefore 42.5%. 85% of the respondents were in the age group between 26 and 40. 38% of the respondents were legal practitioners working in government institutions, 32% were teachers working both in government and private training institutions, 12% were students who are doing their masters degrees in law in European Universities and 18% were from other working areas like project coordinators.

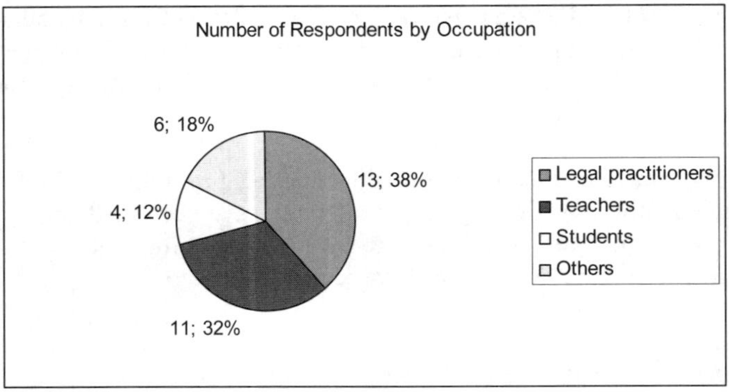

Fig. 2.1. Respondents' Occupation

Responses from many regional and zonal administrative areas of Ethiopia, including practitioners working in the remotest regions of Ethiopia, like Gambella, Somali and Harari were obtained.

From figure 2.1. above one can see that respondents represented the users of legal information. Although it was attempted to reach users outside Ethiopia, most attention went to users residing inside the country and consequently 85% of the respondents resided in Ethiopia.

2.2. Analysis of Respondents' Access to the Basic Ethiopian Laws

From the data analysis, it can be understood that a great number of respondents have access to the basic laws of Ethiopia. All the basic laws (Constitution, Civil Code, Penal Code, Civil Procedure Code, Criminal Procedure Code, Commercial Code and Family Law) have similar rates of consultation by users.

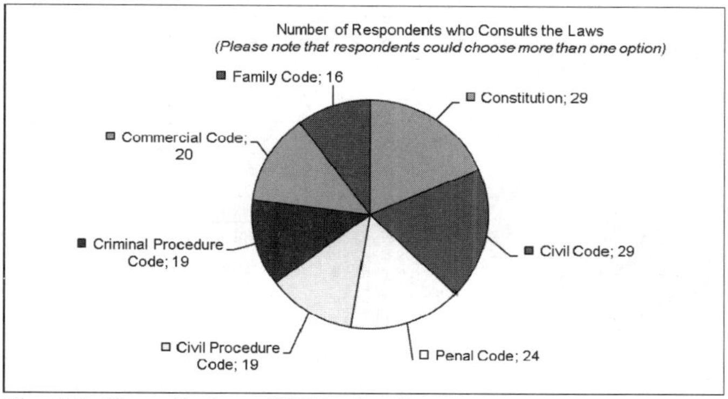

Fig. 2.2. Consultation of Ethiopian Laws

But the format used to access (consult) the laws is solely hard copy (book/paper) formats. One of the reasons for this is the non-availability of the Ethiopian legal information in digital format.

There exists little or no digitised format of the basic laws. This in turn calls for the need to convert the hard copy laws into soft copies.

2.3. Access to the Internet

A generic question was asked if the respondents had access to the Internet. Since most of the respondents had some form of legal qualification and were in different working environments (many in the capital city), they had the orientation and access to the Internet. Out of the 34 respondents, 24 (71%) had access to the Internet. Most of the respondents who resided in Ethiopia use the Internet at their work place (office). Some of them use it at cyber cafés. Only 6% of the respondents had access to the Internet at home.

It was noticed from the responses that most respondents from the regional areas (places outside the capital, Addis Ababa) did not have the skills to use computers or did not have access to computers. It is thus important for the government to give due emphasis to avail people of personal computers and provide the necessary computing skills training for the regional offices. The telecom agency should also improve access to the Internet for legal professionals. Currently, Ethiopia has only 30,000 Internet lines for a total population of 71 million.

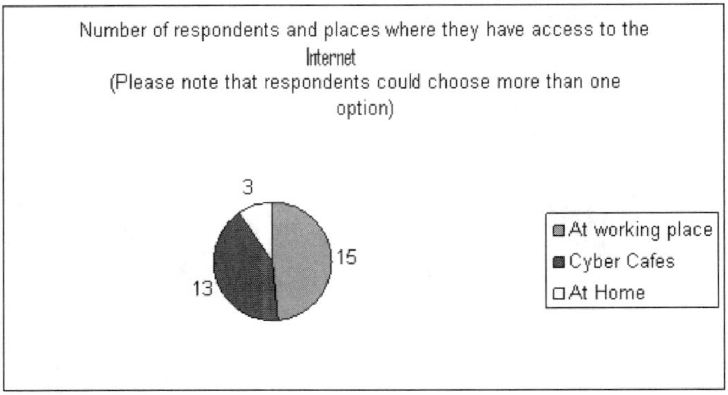

Fig.2.3. Internet Access

Respondents were asked which search engine(s) they use for general Internet use.

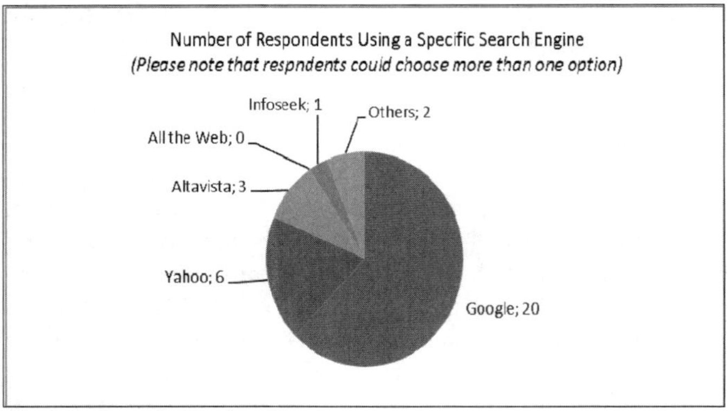

Fig.2.4. Search Engine Use

From the above chart, it can be deduced that most users use google to search for information on the Internet.

From 24 respondents who had access to the Internet, 14 of them said they had problems with search engines. As shown in figure 2.5., most of the respondents who use search engines received too many search hits in their search.

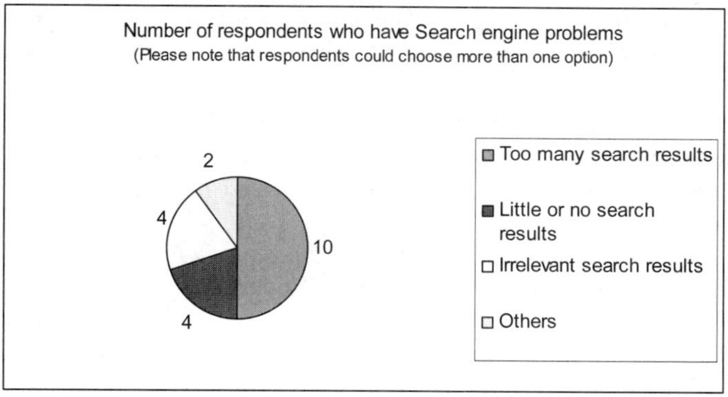

Fig.2.5. Search Engine Problems

The respondents indicated that when using the Internet for legal and related information retrieval, they consult and use the following websites: UN website, EU website, Lexis-Nexis, Westlaw, Soul beat Africa, WIPO, www.juridat.be, www.law.Ugent.be, HRW, Amnesty International and IBA legal brief Africa. They visit these websites in order to retrieve information on Ethiopian legal information (legislation, articles, court decisions, etc). Based on the list we received from the respondents, we visited the web sites mentioned but we found little or no legal information about Ethiopia. Besides, almost all the respondents said that there is not enough content (legal information) about Ethiopia. One responded by saying "*I do not get Ethiopian legal information except sometimes news articles about a proclamation or a court decision.*"

The respondents also mentioned that systematised and categorised digital Ethiopian laws (legislation, amendments, court decisions, legal publications, etc) should be available on the Internet and other media (CD-ROM). This shows that there is not enough content pertaining to Ethiopian legal information. As a result, it is necessary to make digital content available and publish Ethiopian legal material on these and related websites.

2.4. Importance of Soft Copy Laws

Respondents listed the importance of converting hard copy laws into digital formats and hence publishing on the Internet and on CD-ROMs as follows:

- *computerised information can be easily organised and accessed;*
- *it simplifies research;*
- *users need not carry the hard copy laws when they travel (e.g. Ethiopian students who study and research abroad);*

- *easy access to Ethiopian laws, updated laws can be used and complete coverage of all the available laws can be ensured;*
- *to keep abreast with the repeal of laws, amendments;*
- *one can easily find specific relevant provisions of the laws;*
- *the laws will be more accessible especially for foreign experts and those interested in Ethiopian laws (e.g. those interested in investing in the country);*
- *access of students and practitioners in Ethiopia to the laws will also be improved since hard copies are not so plentiful here.*

One respondent described the significance of having the laws in an organised digital format as follows,

> "*I remember an assignment given to me by a senior judge while I was working as a law clerk to the Ethiopian Supreme Court. He asked me simply to search for a proclamation on a certain matter. After tireless searching for one week, I told him that I could not find one. When I use now (in Belgium) a highly developed legal database and I find the information within a split second, it is the difference between the Stone Age and digital world.... I hope the future Ethiopian law clerks will not have the same problem.*"

As one can easily understand, these lawyers indeed have problems with the availability of computerised legal information. They all understand the potential significances of the digital versions. After determining the requirements of the respondents, an Ethiopian Legal Information Web portal was designed, developed and implemented. The following section shows how the site has been developed and maintained.

3. DEVELOPING AND PUBLISHING OF ETHIOPIAN LAWS ON THE INTERNET

3.1. Website Development

The hard copy laws have been converted to digital format using an optical character recognition (OCR) scanner. Each chapter of the basic law again is converted from text format to an Internet format. The website is developed with HTML and with the Dreamweaver application package. A consistent navigation scheme is designed for the basic Ethiopian laws namely the Constitution, Civil Code, Civil Procedure Code, Criminal Procedure Code, Commercial Code, and Family Law. The Penal Code is not included in the website since the conversion to digital format has not yet been completed. Eight buttons were chosen to access the contents. Having a home page (an index page) with introductory information, the buttons are arranged horizontally and vertically. Each basic law also has its own main page. The pages are designed in frames so that the navigation buttons stay intact on each page.

3.2. Website Publishing

The Ethiopian Legal Information Website is published online at: http://www.law.ugent.be/pub/nwr/elw/index.html

Fig.3.1. *Screen dump of the home page of the Ethiopian Legal Website*

The website has its present layout after thorough comments from legal professionals both in Ethiopia and in Belgium. Existing Ethiopian technological infrastructure was assessed and the navigation scheme and the layout of the contents were modified accordingly.

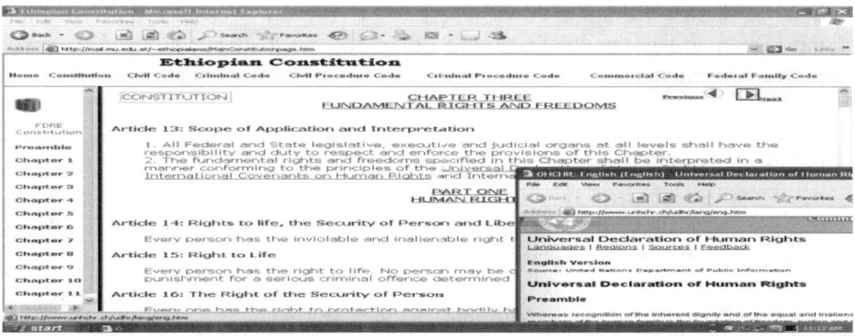

Fig.3.2. *Screen dump of the web page for the Ethiopian Constitution with hyperlinks to other sites*

3. 3. Comments from Users on the Website

After the publication of the site, users were asked for comments. Some of the comments were immediately considered. The navigation buttons, background colours, etc. were modified. Besides, a disclaimer was included based on a suggestion from a lawyer.

Since the website has only federal laws, some users suggested that the regional laws should also be converted to soft copy and included in the website. Another user also suggested that a search interface should be added to the website.

While further work is required to embed a thesaurus-based searching facility, currently a free online search engine (http://www.freefind.com) is included in the home page of this website. With this search facility, users can search using any words which they think are available in the documents thus the engine finds documents related to the given term.

4. CONCLUSIONS AND RECOMMENDATIONS

Based on a literature review and the user needs analysis the following conclusions were drawn and recommendations were forwarded to introduce, adapt and effectively utilise information technologies for Ethiopian laws.

4.1. Conclusions

Electronic information services like the Internet have transformed the legal activities of many countries. It is found that very little or nothing has been done to digitise Ethiopian laws. There exist very few websites that try to tap the Ethiopian legal content and when they do, it is a short commentary or review of an existing law.

Ethiopian legal professionals are in dire need of having Ethiopian legal information on the Internet and in other digital formats. The Ethiopian Telecommunications Corporation is the sole provider of Internet services and currently there are only 30,000 Internet lines. This explains why it has been difficult for legal professionals to have access to the Internet.

Most of the respondents agreed that changes are needed to facilitate legal information access in electronic format. Ethiopian legal scholars who currently study and research abroad pointed out that the digital format of the laws should be available as they have been facing challenges with hard copies.

The website we developed was welcomed by users as a good start for publishing Ethiopian legal information. Comments were provided and included to fine-tune the appearances of the pages.

To sum up, ICT has a paramount significance in transforming the Ethiopian legal system. Strategic planning and action are critically essential to introduce, implement and efficiently utilise these enabling technologies. Proper adoption and implementation of EDMS and Internet technologies with relevant content will advance the Ethiopian legal system.

4.2. Recommendations

Based on the reviewed literature and data analysed from the questionnaires, the following recommendations were forwarded:

- The Ethiopian Ministry of Justice and the courts should draft policies and strategies to digitise the laws (past and present, federal and regional), create web portals for the public for free-to-access basic laws, cases, new legal proclamations, amendments, etc. The Ethiopian telecom agency should provide fast Internet access for the legal professions, courts and law schools.
- Since content is essential to make it readily available for society at large and legal professionals in particular, authorities and responsible bodies of courts, legal research institutes and others should put their effort into providing documents and information to website managers, database administrators and electronic document managers. For this to happen, collaboration and content/knowledge sharing among the legal professionals and law firms is vital.
- Training in the use of the Internet and legal online information systems should be offered.
- Hardware and browsing software should be made available to regional and zonal legal institutions and to district courts.
- At national and regional levels, Legal Information Systems should be developed to effectively systematise the legal documents by creating databases of court proceedings (cases), proclamations, legal notices, basic human rights documents and related legal information. These Legal Information Systems should be staffed with professionals both from the computing (information science/computer science) and the legal domain.
- Future research on the application of web technologies, challenges and opportunities should be conducted.